Women in Tang China

Women in Tang China

Bret Hinsch

唐

ROWMAN & LITTLEFIELD
Lanham • Boulder • New York • London

Published by Rowman & Littlefield
An imprint of The Rowman & Littlefield Publishing Group, Inc.
4501 Forbes Boulevard, Suite 200, Lanham, Maryland 20706
www.rowman.com

6 Tinworth Street, London SE11 5AL, United Kingdom

British Library Cataloguing in Publication Information Available

Library of Congress Cataloging-in-Publication Data

Names: Hinsch, Bret, author.
Title: Women in Tang China / Bret Hinsch.
Description: Lanham : Rowman & Littlefield, [2020] | Includes bibliographical
   references and index. | Summary: "This important book provides the first
   comprehensive survey of women in China during the Sui and Tang dynasties from
   the sixth through tenth centuries CE. Bret Hinsch provides rich insight into female
   life in the medieval era, ranging from political power, wealth, and work to family,
   religious roles, and virtues. He explores women's lived experiences but also delves
   into the subjective side of their emotional life and the ideals they pursued. Deeply
   researched, the book draws on a wide range of sources, including standard histories,
   poetry, prose literature, and epigraphic sources such as epitaphs, commemorative
   religious inscriptions, and Dunhuang documents. Building on the best Western and
   Japanese scholarship, Hinsch also draws heavily on Chinese scholarship, most of
   which is unknown outside China. As the first study in English about women in the
   medieval era, this groundbreaking work will open a new window into Chinese history
   for Western readers"— Provided by publisher.
Identifiers: LCCN 2019038810 (print) | LCCN 2019038811 (ebook) | ISBN
   9781538134894 (cloth) | ISBN 9781538159033 (pbk) | ISBN 9781538134900 (epub)
Subjects: LCSH: Women—China—History—To 1500. | Women—China—Social life
   and customs. | Women—China—Social conditions. | Women—History—Middle
   Ages, 500–1500. | China—History—Tang dynasty, 618–907.
Classification: LCC HQ1147.C6 H57 2020 (print) | LCC HQ1147.C6 (ebook) | DDC
   305.40951/0902—dc23
LC record available at https://lccn.loc.gov/2019038810
LC ebook record available at https://lccn.loc.gov/2019038811

these gorgeous young creatures
who knows what they'll come to?

the clouds float north
the clouds float south.

—Yu Xuanji, "Three Beautiful Sisters, Orphaned Young"

Contents

Introduction

The Chinese tend to envision their nation's past as a long succession of dynasties, each colored by emotionally loaded stereotypes. In the popular imagination, the Tang dynasty stands out from other epochs as a special period of history. Movies and novels depict the Tang as a time when China faced outward and confidently engaged with the wider world, initiating a glorious age of cultural effervescence. In contrast, historians take a far more nuanced view of this complex period.[1] Art and literature indeed flourished. And Chinese felt far more at ease with foreign goods and ideas than in most eras. However, the nation also suffered long bouts of traumatizing warfare and endured disorienting social convulsions that ended in the destruction of an entire way of life. Naitō Konan, doyen of the Kyoto School of historiography, argued that the decline and fall of the Tang dynasty marked a major rupture in the course of Chinese history. In this conservative medieval society, an aristocratic elite exercised hereditary privilege to dominate those beneath them. But during the subsequent Song dynasty, merit became far more important than ever before, fostering social mobility and economic growth in what Naitō described as the birth of early modern China.

The Sui and Tang dynasties also stand out for having put an end to centuries of national partition. After the fall of the Eastern Han in the early third century, authorities failed to establish a stable system of government. China's immense size has always posed a challenge to those governing it. Holding together the world's largest state was never easy, and dynasties regularly failed and collapsed. After the fall of Han, even though everyone agreed that China should be united, no one could hold the nation together. Pastoral peoples took advantage of institutional failures to overrun the north, dividing China for more than three centuries. The long era of disunion brought ceaseless war, chaos, and suffering. This tumult caused society to regress in

1

many respects, and China became poorer and very unequal. So when the Sui dynasty finally managed to reunite north and south after such a long spell of division, people rejoiced that their national nightmare had finally come to an end.[2]

Yang Jian, the first emperor of a reunified China, had served as regent overseeing a child ruler of the Northern Zhou dynasty. Not content with ruling through a puppet, Yang used the authority of his daughter, the empress dowager, to usurp the throne. He declared himself Emperor Wen (r. 581–604) of the new Sui dynasty. Centuries of bitter experience had taught northerners the futility of fighting southern rivals. Nevertheless, this ambitious monarch launched a massive invasion of the south. Against all odds, he managed to get his army across the broad Yangzi River. Then in 589 he conquered the capital of the rival Chen dynasty and reunited the nation.

Wen's success in ending the long age of division earned him a place beside the greatest rulers in Chinese history. Yet his successor Emperor Yang (r. 604–618) squandered this glorious legacy. Yang alienated key nomadic allies, initiated ruinously expensive engineering projects, and fought inconclusive wars against distant kingdoms. Even as he presided over a string of catastrophes and oppressed the populace, this incompetent ruler flaunted his ruinously expensive sybaritic lifestyle, earning the hatred and contempt of his subjects.

The unbearable burdens of conscription, high taxes, and corvée labor eventually goaded desperate peasants into rebellion. General Li Yuan, fearful of being made a scapegoat for military setbacks, led an army mutiny. Soon Li annihilated the detested Sui and declared himself Emperor Gaozu (618–626), initiating a new dynasty that he called Tang.[3] Subsequent emperors stabilized the state, established a capable administration, and managed to hold off outlying nomadic hordes. Even so, national unity often remained little more than a polite fiction. Although Chinese today usually imagine Tang China as a tightly incorporated state, in fact it cohered very loosely.[4] The central government did not directly manage all of the nation's territory but only ruled over a central core. To hold the country together, emperors had to constantly nurture ties with warlords and semi-independent governors who controlled peripheral regions, and they cooperated with the central government to varying degrees. Beyond the nation's official borders, some adjacent peoples threatened hostility, while others assisted their giant neighbor and sometimes even expressed deference.

The greatest crisis of the early Tang stands out as one of the most unusual episodes in Chinese history. In 683, a callow youth ascended the throne. Following custom, his mother, the ambitious Empress Wu Zetian, became regent and took control of the government. Then she unexpectedly cast aside tradition by abolishing the Tang and declaring herself ruler of a new dynasty called Zhou. Wu Zetian was the only woman in Chinese history to have assumed the title of emperor (*huangdi*). Although imperial historians denounced her as an illegitimate usurper and excoriated her actions, in fact she ruled capably. This formidable woman weakened in old age, however, and eventually could no longer continue to dominate the government. A palace coup unseated the female emperor in 705, and she died a few months later. Several other women played important roles in affairs of state immediately thereafter, most notably Empress Wei (d. 710) and Princess Taiping (d. 713), marking this brief period as a high point of female power.

A far greater crisis occurred decades later. During the long reign of Emperor Xuanzong (r. 713–756), the Tang reached a zenith of prosperity, stability, and cultural vibrancy. However, Xuanzong made the mistake of blindly trusting the duplicitous General An Lushan, who tricked the credulous ruler into granting him immense powers. In 755 the general rose up in rebellion and tried to bring down the Tang. Although An Lushan failed to overthrow the dynasty, the resulting chaos wrought immense destruction. Savvy gentry families used the upheaval to their advantage and rose in status, while some old families declined. The population decreased markedly during this cruel civil war. Peasants abandoned prime land, large areas suffered impoverishment, and the economy regressed. As the emperors lost control of key regions, they increasingly relied on foreign allies to stay in power.[5] Accumulated catastrophes fostered a conservative cultural atmosphere of caution and restraint.[6]

Although the Tang emperors managed to put down the rebellion and reestablish their authority, the realm remained weak and fragile. In response, hereditary military governors became increasingly autonomous. Some reigned as sovereign rulers in all but name, keeping tax revenues for themselves and maintaining private armies. These regional strongmen continued to display fealty to the Tang emperors in order to stave off widespread chaos, thus keeping the dynasty formally alive. Even so, the imperial system steadily decayed and some areas fell into anarchy. Emperor Xianzong (r. 805–820) managed to subdue most of the military governors and reassert imperial authority for a time, initiating a final burst of dynastic glory. Yet his mediocre successors failed to capitalize on these achievements, and the Tang continued to weaken. Finally, after decades of rebellions and army mutinies, the dynasty formally came to an end in 907.

Historians often refer to the long period between Han and Song as the medieval era. At this time, society was not only extremely unequal but also offered little social mobility. During the chaotic period of disunion prior to the Sui, people belonged to castes, and both law and custom strictly prohibited the people of different strata from intermarrying. Even after reunification, a hereditary elite continued to dominate society.[7] Although most of these families lacked noble titles, they nevertheless enjoyed supremacy and privilege, so historians classify them as an aristocracy. Powerful aristocratic clans emerged during the second century and maintained an elevated position for seven hundred years. By the beginning of the Tang, they had already enjoyed prominence for four centuries.[8] In this aristocratic society, power, genealogy, and wealth remained closely intertwined.

A very small group constituted the uppermost elite. Four great families in Shandong stood at the peak of society. Below them were the major families of Guanzhong, who had previously intermarried with pastoral invaders. Next came wealthy gentry whose prominence did not extend beyond their immediate region. Although different types of aristocrats enjoyed varying degrees of prestige, all exerted immense power over those below them. One woman from an important family even enjoyed whipping those under her control.[9]

The Tang emperors came from a Guanzhong military family of mixed Chinese-nomad extraction. Because they did not trace their ancestry back to the highest reaches of society, the grand aristocracy condescended to the dynasty's rulers. Imperial titles did not impress the arrogant Shandong nobility, which saw genealogy as the foundation of status. They dismissed the imperial clan as semi-barbaric parvenus. In turn, the emperors felt threatened by supercilious aristocrats. To limit the powers of the nobility who despised them, the monarchs came to rely on educated men from the minor gentry as officials. This new class of officeholders felt grateful for their expanded opportunities and sided with the throne to oppose the pretensions of the high nobility.[10] As emperors sought to increase their authority, they deliberately pitted ambitious literati against the old aristocracy.

Over the course of the Tang, the uppermost elite steadily gravitated to the preeminent cities of Luoyang and Chang'an. Powerful aristocrats settled in the capital region, as proximity to the court made it easier for them to monopolize the upper echelons of government. These wealthy and cultured families also enjoyed the sophisticated urban lifestyle in China's cultural center. But by congregating in such a compact area, the aristocracy made themselves highly vulnerable. When the Tang dynasty collapsed, rebel troops massacred the inhabitants of these two cities, specifically targeting the wealthy and powerful.[11] The nobles who escaped death often found themselves destitute. Because of this targeted massacre of the elite, the aristocracy that had lorded over China for centuries suddenly disappeared.

The fall of the Tang dynasty may have been violent and terrifying, but it ultimately brought some positive consequences as well. Historians often single out the An Lushan uprising of 755 as the starting point of the momentous

Figure I.1 A Woman with an Elaborate Hairstyle (Cleveland Museum of Art)

Tang-Song transition, which lasted until the mid-thirteenth century.[12] After the massacre of the old elite, new men filled the vacuum and reorganized society along novel lines, giving rise to the energetic society of the Song dynasty. During this protracted process, a new political system, economy, and social structure gradually emerged. As warfare depopulated the north, many people fled south in search of refuge, shifting the center of gravity of China's population. The rich paddy lands of the south had far greater productive capacity than dry northern soil, so grain production increased dramatically, making China increasingly populous and affluent. Between the eighth and twelfth centuries the population doubled, cities flourished, and commercial activity soared, transforming almost every aspect of life. In the long run, the terrible collapse of the Tang made it possible for China to eventually develop a far more dynamic, prosperous, and refined society.

This book explores the major roles that high medieval women embodied, the problems they faced, and the opportunities they enjoyed. In neither the Tang nor in any other era did women comprise a unitary group. Gender may have been fundamental to individual identity, but many other factors conditioned a woman's life as well. Social stratum, profession, region, kinship, education, and religion all circumscribed potential and offered prospects, making the life of each individual somewhat different. Understanding these key features, and how various women reacted to them, highlights the diversity of female experiences. Rather than simplistically describing the status of medieval women as either high or low, it is far more fruitful to examine how they overcame barriers and acted resourcefully to create the best possible life using the opportunities at hand.

In every society, records of men's activities far exceed those for women. Fortunately, during the Tang writings about women became far more numerous, diverse, and informative than before.[13] When examined together, the material from various media provides extensive and nuanced information and varied points of view. By putting this jumble of sundry sources together and organizing them coherently, an intelligible history of the era's women takes shape.

The standard histories of Sui and Tang provide biographies of empresses, imperial consorts, princesses, consort kinsmen, and moral paragons.[14] This era also stands out as the golden age of Chinese poetry, and more than fifty thousand works from the Tang have come down to the present. Women wrote numerous poems, and men discussed female matters from their own perspectives. Prose fiction reached a high degree of sophistication as well, allowing authors to craft complex narratives that showcased a wide array of female types. Among 1,361 female characters in major works of Tang fiction, 46 percent are commoners, 31 percent are supernatural beings, 17 percent palace ladies, and 6 percent entertainers.[15] These narratives may be fictional, but they nevertheless provide valuable insights into the possible actions, feelings, and motivations of different social types and suggest how society regarded women of different backgrounds.

Posthumous eulogies engraved on stone had become common, providing a rich trove of material about individual women and their families. Of the six thousand or so surviving epitaphs from the Sui and Tang, around 1,500 are dedicated exclusively to a deceased woman.[16] Many other inscriptions describe a married couple, and sometimes a man's epitaph mentions his wife. These commemorations are much longer and more detailed than earlier epitaphs and often convey details about family background and personal life. Although most inscriptions describe elite women, 6 percent came from modest circumstances, providing invaluable insights into ordinary female life.

When speaking about the Tang in general terms, historians often describe it as an "open" era during which women enjoyed an unusually high level of freedom compared to other dynasties.[17] Yet in fact medieval society both favored and limited female agency, and women faced complex and fluctuating conditions. Due to complexity of contemporary trends, the sources can seem inconsistent.[18] Some emphasize the power and privilege of women at the top of society, while others take a negative tone. While painters depicted female subjects as cheerful, lively, and confident, writers often described them as moody and anxious.[19] Moreover, certain types of female autonomy markedly decreased over time. The reunification of China empowered state authorities who were intent on imposing Confucian patriarchy on society.[20] And as the aristocratic system decayed, the rise of new literati families threatened the hereditary prestige of aristocratic ladies.[21]

The lavish lifestyle of elite Tang women stands out as another characteristic of the age. Noble families had huge landholdings that provided them with immense wealth. They felt no compunction about flaunting their affluence and engaged in conspicuous consumption to publicly affirm their high station. In particular, female aristocrats reveled in extravagant luxury.[22] Ladies in wealthy households had few duties to claim their time, so they amused themselves with leisure pursuits such as board games, music, and poetry. Due to the influence of steppe culture, some enjoyed physical pastimes such as horseback riding, archery, and hunting.[23] Women even played a kind of ball game akin to soccer called *cuju*.[24] The calendar included numerous festivals, allowing them to enliven their daily routine with seasonal entertainments.[25] Noblewomen also traveled for fun. They visited scenic spots to banquet among beautiful natural surroundings and accompanied the ruler on his peregrinations.[26]

Steppe culture exerted immense influence on popular customs. As in previous centuries, the upper strata of Tang society intermarried with the nomadic elite. As a result, they assimilated many pastoral practices and ideas, giving them new perspectives on a wide range of matters. While historians tend to stress changes and transformations, many aspects of Tang life showed considerable continuity with the recent past. Such was the case with the influence of pastoral customs, which shaped many aspects of Chinese society, including views toward women. Because nomadic peoples lacked Confucian ethics and the classical rites, when Chinese looked at the world from a pastoral point of view, they felt emboldened to challenge restrictive ethical rules, including those that restricted female autonomy. For example, whereas Confucianism promoted the idea that women should not remarry, pastoralists traditionally practiced levirate, forcing a widow to marry a kinsman of her deceased husband. As steppe influence infiltrated all levels of society, even some Tang imperial clansmen practiced levirate.[27] In consequence, some Chinese questioned the need for widows to remain chaste and even encouraged them to remarry.

Steppe women often enjoyed considerable autonomy and authority, and their behavior sometimes inspired Chinese counterparts.[28] Whereas Chinese moralists encouraged women to modestly seclude themselves in inner recesses of the home, nomadic women could not possibly confine themselves to a small yurt. Instead they worked outdoors alongside men, riding horses, herding livestock, and hunting, fostering self-reliance and confidence. Steppe women had a say in important public matters as well. Because nomads used marriage ties to bind together various lineages, women often served as mediators between the kin groups of their fathers and husbands, giving them an important place in tribal politics. They aided their fathers, advised their husbands, and guided their sons.

As before, this era's texts usually do not depict women as unique individuals. Instead writers conventionally described a woman as embodying one of the three key female kinship roles: daughter, wife, and mother. Although society also expected men to conform to standard social positions, these categories did not comprise the totality of male identity.[29] A man could have other achievements and identities beyond the circle of kinship. For most women, however, the three roles of daughter, wife, and mother usually summed up everything that those around her considered significant about her life.

Literature shows the importance that society placed on these three fundamental kinship roles. Among a group of 622 fictional female characters, wives comprise 41 percent of the total, mothers 20 percent, and daughters 8 percent.[30] Only 13 percent of these women lack overt attachment to a man or family. Each of the kinship roles in a woman's life came with demanding norms, so she knew how people expected her to behave at each stage of her life. As a daughter, she was to honor her parents. A good wife obeyed her husband and cultivated a harmonious relationship with in-laws. And the dutiful mother would nurture and educate her children to give them a good start in life. Women experienced these three roles in succession, so when taken together they conveyed the idealized female life course.[31] Rituals such as the hair pinning ceremony that marked adulthood, and the subsequent wedding rites, publicly announced the transitions between kinship identities.

Because people closely associated the model life trajectory with gender, they had extremely different expectations for men and women. While the exemplary man concentrated on education and an official career, his female counterpart remained at home. Even if a woman had received an extensive education or held greater ambitions, her family expected her to devote herself to domestic duties that contributed to the family's collective success.

Nevertheless, reducing female experience to just three kinship roles cannot possibly encompass the complexity of real life. A woman usually inhabited multiple roles at once. After marrying and bearing children, she might simultaneously be daughter, wife, and mother. Occupying multiple kinship positions at the same time could cause problems. Sometimes two roles came with contrary expectations, giving rise to moral dilemmas.[32] For example, if a woman's husband and father came into conflict, she would have to choose between being a faithful wife or obedient daughter.

Although historians conventionally divide Chinese history according to dynasties, this political periodization scheme does not capture the shifting contours of women's lives. The Tang in particular passed through several phases, each exhibiting distinct political, social, and economic factors that affected women's circumstances. In the early Tang, traditional rites and ethics initially had little effect on women. With the onset of chaos in the mid-eighth century, however, thinkers revived restrictive ancient ideas about female behavior, and the atmosphere became increasingly conservative.[33] These ideas continued to gain ground in the latter part of the dynasty, so women had less freedom to move about and socialize outside the home. Moreover, people increasingly disparaged the remarriage of widows. Faced with shrinking boundaries, female personalities altered, and women became more reserved and cautious.[34]

In spite of these many caveats regarding sources, causation, agency, and periodization, Sui and Tang women can be understood far better than those of earlier eras. Some women stood out for their achievements. Powerful figures at court, bold poets, and talented calligraphers helped shape their society.

But women faced many challenges as well, as seen in the hardships faced by impoverished widows, lonely merchant wives, and degraded courtesans. It is impossible to simplistically sum up the lives of Tang women as high or low, good or bad, free or constrained. Women experienced all of these qualities, and many more as well. When viewed together, their lives take on the form of a living mosaic that people today find captivating, moving, and deeply meaningful.

Chapter 1

Marriage

Tang writers often referred to lofty sentiments when discussing marriage. Some emphasized the shared commitment of spouses to venerate the husband's ancestors, a duty so important that it made marriage a foundation of human relations.[1] Other moralists stressed the importance of using righteousness (*yi*) to regulate the interactions of wife and husband, lest their relationship devolve into licentiousness. Tang law embraced this key Confucian virtue and employed it to recast marriage and the family along manifestly ethical lines. And those who preferred to conceptualize the world in religious terms used even grander language. Some compared marriage to Daoist transcendence of the mundane world, claiming that a bond of such intimacy gives people a foretaste of mystical union with divinity.[2]

Since antiquity, the bond between spouses had grown steadily closer so that by the medieval era many couples exhibited deep emotional attachment. A wife might write a poem to praise a husband's success, lament his failure, or express dismay at forced separation.[3] One man who committed suicide strangled his wife, concubine, and children first.[4] Because they constituted a single unit, he thought it fitting to include them in his own self-destruction. However, not every husband and wife conceived of themselves as one half of a couple. Epitaphs reveal that spouses maintained varying degrees of intimacy.[5] Some spouses shared a single epitaph, emphasizing a common identity. But the epitaphs for other joint burials describe only the husband and ignore the wife. This omission highlighted male privilege and displayed a sense of aloofness between spouses.

Marriages varied considerably. Many men treated their wives with respect and valued their opinions and advice.[6] Some educated couples even became literary companions, regularly exchanging poetry to share their thoughts and feelings. Nevertheless, the patriarchal gender hierarchy always kept woman

11

and man apart to some extent.[7] Medieval law officially placed the wife in an inferior and subservient position to her husband and obliged her to obey him. Husbands mourned less for wives than wives did for husbands, and children were supposed to mourn fathers more elaborately than mothers.[8] The *Tang Code* (*Tang lü*) even set down heavier penalties for a wife who beat or killed her husband than for a man who abused his spouse.[9] Officials enforced this code unevenly, with some regions of the realm more law abiding than others. Nevertheless, these legal provisions reveal that government ministers wanted to make patriarchal primacy a fundamental principle of law and administration.

Most people did not choose their spouse, as parents usually arranged their children's marriages. In doing so, above all they sought to benefit the family as a whole and not necessarily the couple involved. Spouses often did not even meet before the wedding, and of course they did not necessarily exhibit any affection for one another. Spouses may have lived together, but this did not always make them feel close. In fact, many people showed little interest in a spouse that had been foisted upon them. The poems of Li Bai and Du Fu refer to their wives with uncharacteristically unemotional language. Instead of love or intimacy, they often depicted their wives as an unavoidable burden.[10]

People of the time pondered the ambiguities and inconsistencies that plagued the inequitable institution of marriage. A poem by the Daoist nun and courtesan Li Ye (d. 784) sums up these contradictions.

> Furthest and nearest are east and west;
> deepest and most shallow
> are pure clear valley streams.
> Highest and brightest are the sun and moon;
> closest and most distant are husband and wife.

The basic rules for marriage, in both law and custom, grew out of the dictates of classical ritual.[11] A wife assumed a social rank comparable to her husband while a widow tracked her son's status.[12] In previous centuries, custom had regulated most aspects of marriage. During the Tang, however, jurists placed this institution firmly under the purview of the law. The *Tang Code* differed significantly from earlier jurisprudence. Ministers increasingly sought to resolve social conflicts by imposing Confucian ethics and ritual on every rung of society, so they integrated these values into the law. They believed that a Confucianized legal code could teach the common people their moral obligations and thus elevate the general tone of society. As a result of this project, regulating marriage with the law increasingly subjected it to the ethical principles set down in Confucianism and the rites.[13] This

Confucianization of marriage had a major impact on women, increasingly limiting their autonomy and making them subservient to male kin.

The moralized law code prohibited certain kinds of people from marrying, including close relatives, people of the same surname, and those belonging to different generations. A man could only have one wife, and he could not elevate a concubine to wifely status. The law prohibited a widow or widower from remarrying during the mourning period for a deceased spouse. The government also barred local administrators from forcing women under their jurisdiction to marry them, thereby preventing a tyrannous official from abusing his authority to gain a better marriage partner.[14] On paper, these regulations and procedures seem clear-cut. In practice, however, the actual circumstances of marriage varied considerably. For example, although spouses were supposed to live with the husband's family, matrilocal residence was not uncommon.[15] Expedience often took precedence over abstract ideals.

The size of households increased in this era, particularly among the elite, thereby affecting women's position in the family. Historians have had trouble calculating the average family size for the Tang, as family and household did not necessarily include the same people.[16] Overall, medieval Chinese families seem to have been larger than those of the early imperial era, when the small nuclear family was standard. Because Tang authorities wanted to repopulate the realm, they encouraged people to marry and bear numerous children.[17] Many Tang households were clearly much larger than those of the Han dynasty, when most families had four or five members.[18]

Tang aristocrats normally maintained a large household that included concubines and multiple generations of extended relatives. Household registers show that prosperous families tended to have more members than average. These elite families not only had more members but were also organized in a more complex structure that included a wider range of kin. Among the aristocracy, adult brothers often continued to live together after the deaths of their parents. This sort of collateral family could have more than ten members.[19] Although Confucian teachings encouraged brothers to live together, coresidence had practical benefits as well. Pooling economic resources benefitted all of the members of a large family by giving them potential access to more resources. And their sons could study together and possibly obtain a superior education. Nevertheless, because people often died relatively young, complex families tended to be fragile. They often broke down into smaller units upon the death of a central member.

Although inscriptional information deals only with the elite, popular literature gives impressions of the sizes of families among various social strata. In general, families of more modest means tended to be smaller. A study of families mentioned in the narrative collection *Extensive Records of the Taiping Era* (*Taiping guangji*), completed in the year 978, describes the highest-ranking families as having 2.8 children on average, with commoners having 1.4 children and merchants only 0.7 children.[20] Even many commoners lived in large and complex households. A tax register of 747 shows the average family had 6.3 members, and a quarter had nine people or more.[21] The general condition of society also affected family size. In times of peace, families tended to contract, whereas relatives sought collective security by drawing together and forming larger groupings during periods of chaos.[22]

Ever since nomadic peoples invaded and occupied north China in the third century, steppe cultures had exerted a direct influence on Chinese marriage customs.[23] Many nomads practiced sororal polygyny (marrying two or more sisters) and levirate (a widow marrying her deceased husband's kinsman). Chinese had accepted these two customs in antiquity, then subsequently abandoned them.[24] Since then, ritual norms strictly forbade these arrangements, condemning them as incestuous and licentious. Nevertheless, cultural mixing made many Chinese receptive to unorthodox steppe customs, so marital arrangements sometimes violated the rites.

Medieval marriage practices were highly unstable, and over the course of this tumultuous period, they changed in many respects.[25] Generally speaking, the rites steadily gained authority and exerted more influence over married life. Shifting practical concerns also shaped marriage practices. During the early Tang, people usually arranged marriages according to family status, but by the end of the dynasty they often prioritized political advantage. Early Tang authorities encouraged remarriage, but officials later in the dynasty discouraged the practice.

Marriage reflected the steep inequality and status consciousness of Tang society. As before, the law upheld the prevailing social framework by prohibiting marriage between people of extremely different standing.[26] A vast gap separated the aristocracy from commoners, and commoners stood far above debased slaves and entertainers. As before, officials looked down on merchants, looking askance at their mercenary and footloose way of life. The state thus classified merchants as a lowly group and tried to prevent them from marrying too high.[27]

A wife shared her husband's status, so marriage determined a woman's general social position.[28] Because custom barred women from most public activities, a good marriage usually represented the greatest distinction that they could hope to achieve.[29] Nevertheless, marrying too high could have drawbacks. If a wife came from a lower background than her husband, she would have to endure a depressed status within his household.[30] For that reason, it made sense for a woman to marry someone of similar background. In contrast to the elite, people of humble standing had relatively little to gain

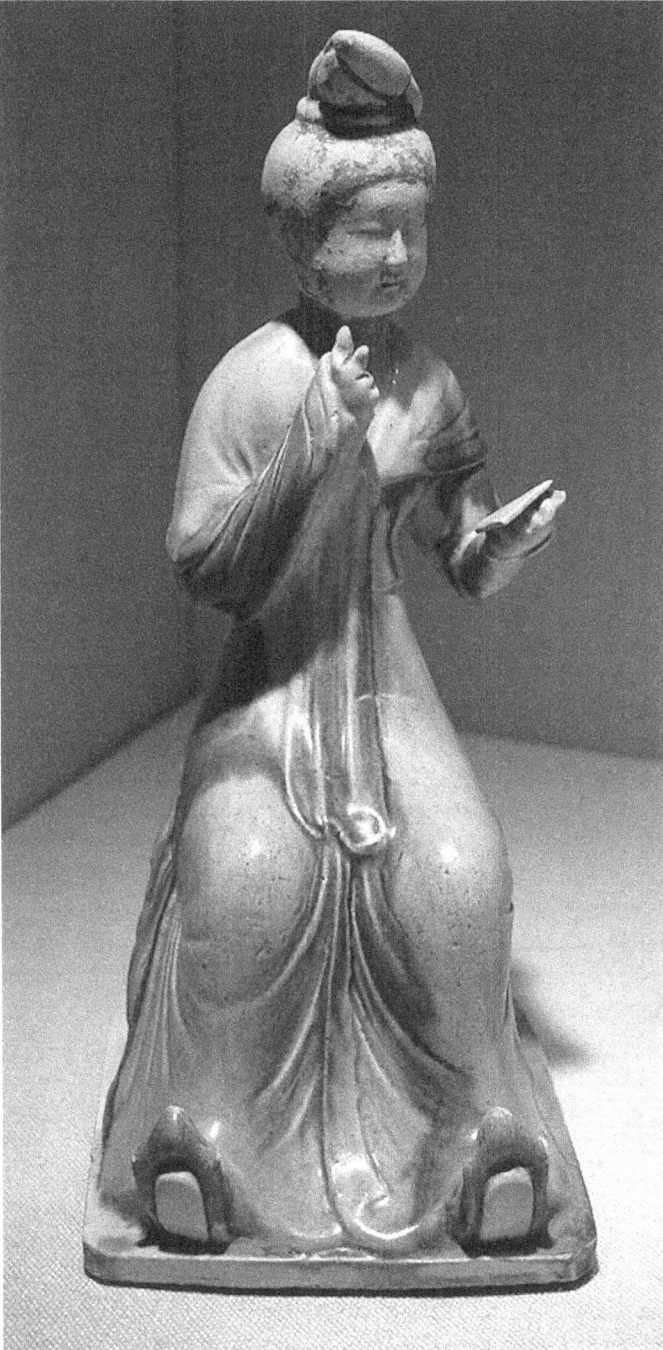

Figure 1.1 Woman with a Mirror (Sailko)

or lose from marriage, so they faced few restrictions. Documents from Dun-huang show that commoners married a wide range of partners. Some wed close relatives, while others ended up marrying someone from a different ethnic group.[31]

Unlike commoners, the aristocracy selected their in-laws very carefully. To preserve their unique status, those at the top of society practiced class endogamy. By intermarrying within a small group of similarly prominent families, they closed off their privileged caste and prevented outsiders from rising to their own level. And when a noble family made a good match for a child, they publicly demonstrated that the aristocracy accepted their family as peers. The elite strategy of repeated intermarriage succeeded, allowing the medieval aristocracy to remain ascendant for centuries. As a result of this marriage pattern, aristocrats felt proud of a wife who boasted exalted ances-try, whereas marrying down brought disgrace.[32] Someone could humiliate a defeated enemy by forcing him at swordpoint to take a wife from a much lower background.[33] Because aristocrats married primarily for status, parents required their children to wed whomever they chose. Many noble families educated their daughters in Confucian teachings that stressed obedience to parental authority to ensure that they would meekly accept an arranged mar-riage, regardless of their own feelings on the matter.

The Tang elite did not constitute a unitary block. Noble families enjoyed varying degrees of prestige, ranging from local prominence to national fame and power. Given this diversity among the upper ranks of society, not only did aristocratic families seek to intermarry, but they also hoped to wed peers with the same level of prestige. Class endogamy used women as the inter-mediaries who tied together powerful families. The so-called five great sur-names of Shandong enjoyed preeminent status, and they frequently married with one another to reinforce their unique standing.[34] Over the course of the Tang, marriage became even more important to their fortunes. The exami-nation system and economic shifts brought new blood into the elite, so the five surnames increasingly relied on marriage connections to maintain their primacy. The Cui married with the other four great surnames 62 percent of the time, the Lu did so 73 percent of the time, and the Deng 65 percent.[35] The emperors detested the pretentions of these ancient families and twice banned them from intermarrying, but these prohibitions soon lapsed and the five great surnames continued to wed within their constricted circle.

Despite the importance of marrying a spouse from a similarly exalted fam-ily, sometimes even the greatest families accepted an in-law from a lower background. The famed Cui family from Boling married a counterpart from one of the great surnames 52 percent of the time. Otherwise, however, their spouses came from the lower elite.[36] The small number of available marriage partners among the great surnames made these matches inevitable. Moreover, occasionally binding themselves to a lesser aristocratic family, who often wielded more power and wealth than the uppermost elite, could provide tangible advantages.

The marriage strategy of the great surnames affected Tang culture. These families had a reputation for expertise in the classics, history, and ritual. They flaunted this cultural sophistication to demand respect from society at large. They also displayed a devotion to filial piety and other Confucian principles, inculcating these virtues in their daughters to mold them into exemplars of wifely and maternal virtue. Due to this training, when women from the great surnames married with the lower nobility, they transmitted the values of the highest aristocracy downward and helped spread them throughout the entire elite.[37] This process gave these women an important role in the development of Tang culture. By elevating the cultural level of their husband's families, the daughters of the five surnames helped Confucianize the lower aristocracy and elevated the overall tenor of cultural life.

Below the handful of top families, the lower elite also arranged marriage ties for optimal advantage. Some constructed a binary bond with counterparts of comparable status. Others participated in a "marriage clique" (*yinlian*) of families that regularly intermarried. By periodically renewing these affinal connections, clique members forged extremely strong bonds that allowed them to act in concert, augmenting their reach and influence.[38] Two particularly prominent marriage cliques stand out. A group based around Luoyang used their collective prestige to obtain high civil offices. And a clique of military families intermarried with the imperial clan and dominated the army. In addition, regional marriage groupings integrated the leading families of certain geographic areas. For example, the Wei of Guanzhong forged marriage connections with other powerful families in that region and also married with the imperial line.[39] This strategy served them well, as they produced seventeen prime ministers and two empresses for the Tang. After the An Lushan Rebellion, the mutual support network of families involved in marriage cliques served as a buffer against chaos, so elite families intermarried with a small peer group at even higher rates.[40]

Given the density of ties within a marriage clique, participants often ended up marrying relatives. Although cross-cousin marriage was not a goal of this marriage strategy, it often occurred as a by-product of endogamy. From a global perspective, cross-cousin marriage is not uncommon, as many peoples throughout the world consider it desirable to wed kin.[41] And during the medieval era, Chinese incest restrictions relaxed. The Xianbei and other northern peoples residing in north China did not prohibit marriage between close kin, and southern society held a similarly lenient attitude, so it became common for people to marry their relations. The elite had long married cousins, and during the Tang this sort of arrangement remained common.[42] However, Tang cross-cousin marriage differed somewhat from the practice in later eras. Subsequently, a man would most often marry his mother's sister's daughter. But during the Tang, marriage between cousins took several forms. A man might marry his mother's sister's daughter (matrilateral parallel cousin), his mother's brother's daughter (matrilateral cross-cousin), or his father's sister's daughter (patrilineal cousin).[43]

The chaos of the late Tang transformed China's social structure. People responded to mounting anarchy in different ways. Some of the great families closed ranks and married within a close circle even more intensively.[44] For them, intermarriage with prestigious peers confirmed their social primacy and built strong bonds with useful affines. Overall, though, class endogamy declined. The wealth and power of newly prominent families made them irresistible marriage partners, so the old families married down more frequently. Building bridges with successful parvenus brought useful connections and a welcome infusion of wealth. As the allure of lineage waned, elite families increasingly stressed practical considerations. Some members of the aristocracy even deigned to marry with wealthy merchant families.[45]

Because the exchange of women bound elite families together, the relationship between a wife and her natal family could affect the fortunes of her husband and children. In theory, a wife was a member of her husband's family. This custom had ancient origins. According to classical ritual, a person could not sacrifice to someone else's ancestors. So when a woman venerated her husband's ancestors, she accepted them as her own forebears and joined his family.[46] The Tang instituted increasingly elaborate rituals to mark a bride's first sacrifice to her husband's ancestors, deliberately lending this ceremony even greater significance as a way to bring her closer to her husband's kin. Moralists also exhorted wives to extend the scope of their filial sentiments beyond their parents to include parents-in-law, thus further integrating them into the families of their husbands.[47]

Yet even though ritual and law recognized the wife as a member of her husband's family, actual circumstances could be ambiguous. Blood and emotion continued to tie a wife to her own kin. In practice, a married woman retained membership in the family of her birth. She could even earn praise for faithfully serving blood relatives.[48] Given these conflicting loyalties, a wife occupied a position in the kinship network somewhere in between the families of her husband and father.[49]

Families encouraged wives to keep in touch with their blood kin. High-ranking natal kin conferred considerable prestige, so after marriage a wife could be expected to maintain ties with the family of her birth. Women from lower backgrounds remained close to their natal kin as well. At the very least, a wife visited her blood kin on special occasions, and they might even meet daily if they lived nearby. The legal system also shows that a married woman and her family could maintain an intense bond. Divorce documents recovered from Dunhuang have a parent's signature affixed, implying that a wife required parental consent to dissolve her marriage. And a married woman could inherit property from her parents if she lacked brothers. The large size of many Tang families made it easier for women to return home if necessary, as households with many members could readily support an additional resident. As a result, widows and divorcees often moved back to live with their parents.[50] Married women also participated in funerals for natal kin and mourned for them.[51] Some even helped conduct their parents' funerals.[52] And a wife who had not borne children might herself be buried in the cemetery of her natal family. People justified this arrangement with the metaphysical idea that the deceased woman shared a common "life force" (*qi*) with her siblings and thus belonged near them in death.[53]

The epitaph of a Madame Cui (d. 831) documents the close links that one married woman maintained with her natal kin.[54] Both she and her husband belonged to prestigious families that had intermarried for centuries. After the wedding, Madame Cui not only remained involved in the affairs of her blood relatives but also depended on them financially. Although her husband came from an important family, he had been born into a collateral branch and not the main line. Due to his marginal status, he could only attain a minor official post that yielded modest income. Because Madame Cui's husband could not provide for her properly, her family provided her with additional support. They also made sure that her offspring found good marriage partners. This inscription drives home the fact that the Tang elite saw marriage as a union of families, not individuals. In light of this attitude, it seemed sensible for a wife to maintain close links with her own kin.

Husbands did not resent close attachment between wives and their natal families. To the contrary, they often encouraged their wives to maintain strong ties with blood kin. Successive reforms to the administrative system motivated men to become closer to their affines. With the rising importance of the civil service examination system and increasing professionalization of the bureaucracy, elite men increasingly depended on maternal relatives and in-laws, particularly their maternal uncles, for patronage.[55] Aristocrats in the capital region who dominated top government posts put great stress on affinal relations, as their in-laws helped them advance their careers.[56] With patronage essential for success, affines strove to strengthen mutual bonds. During important life events, they displayed and reaffirmed these ties. Affinal kin mourned for one another and sometimes helped arrange the funerals of in-laws.[57] They also frequently interacted informally. Some educated men exchanged poetry with their in-laws on a regular basis.[58] These sorts of shared cultural activities provided an excuse for them to meet and socialize. By maintaining close ties in this way, they ensured that they would support one another's careers.

∘━━╾─╼━━∘

The average age of couples at the time of marriage varied over the course of the Sui and Tang. Family background and particular circumstances affected when a person would wed. The government also tried to influence the marriage age.[59] Soon after the founding of the Tang, in 627 Emperor Taizong issued an edict decreeing that his subjects ought to wed at the ages specified by classical ritual, with men marrying at age twenty and women at fifteen. A subsequent edict of 734 reduced these ages to fifteen for men and thirteen for women. Lowering the ideal marriage age likely had a pragmatic objective. Centuries of war had left many areas deserted, particularly in the north, so early marriage would help repopulate those regions more quickly. Also, if the number of people increased, tax revenues would rise in tandem. Increasing the population therefore became a major policy objective during the early Tang.[60] However, people paid little attention to government pronouncements regarding family matters, so these decrees seem to have had no tangible impact.

Almost a fifth of epitaphs for Tang women record the age when they married. Social status influenced the age of brides. A sample of twenty epitaphs of princesses shows that their age at the time of marriage varied widely, from three to twenty-eight.[61] Half wed between the ages of fifteen and twenty. However, eight of these women married quite late by aristocratic standards, delaying marriage until their twenties. Many princesses were likely in no hurry to abandon the opulent precincts of the palace for a more modest and less interesting lifestyle in the provinces. Moreover, because the emperors arranged the marriages of princesses for political gain, they may have held some of their daughters in reserve to marry off when the need arose.

Most funerary epitaphs document the lives of the lower aristocracy. According to these inscriptions, grooms customarily wed younger brides. While elite men usually married between the ages of fifteen and twenty, women commonly wed soon after puberty, from thirteen to fifteen.[62] It is misleading to calculate an average marriage age for the entire dynasty because this number rose over time. One study concluded that women married at an average age of 15.91 in the early Tang, 16.4 in the mid-Tang, and 17.4 in the dynasty's final phase.[63] Another analysis sees the marriage age for women increasing more modestly from 15.3 to 15.6 and that for men rising from 23 to 27 over the same time frame.[64] An analysis of a particular family's marriage patterns confirms the general trend of rising marriage age. The average age of marriage for men of the Wang family of Taiyuan rose 3.4 years over the length of the Tang.[65] Increasing chaos and impoverishment seem to have accounted for delayed marriages. During the late Tang, warfare and political turmoil took a heavy toll on the elite, sometimes forcing them to postpone marriage plans. Also, the declining fortunes of numerous prominent families made it harder for them to find a suitable match or amass a sufficient betrothal gift or dowry, so they ended up marrying late.

Women at the bottom of the social scale faced very different conditions, and they rarely wed as young as their social superiors. Most married at age sixteen or later. Documents preserved at Turpan, which record the circumstances of ordinary people along the frontier, give high average marriage ages for women.[66] Only 26.5 percent married as teenagers, while 55.9 percent wed in their twenties. Dunhuang documents show similarly high ages for brides.[67] According to these records, 32.79 percent married in their teens and 52.45 percent in their twenties. Many women had trouble marrying at all. A sample of sixteen Dunhuang families included forty-three unmarried adult women.[68]

Poets lamented the difficulties that poor women faced in getting married, helping to account for the trend toward late marriage or failure to wed. Two factors contributed to the extremely high age of marriage in the far west. Due to incessant warfare in these borderlands, many men died young, skewing the sex ratio. A sample of ninety Turpan households consisted of 208 women but only 158 men.[69] Because of this gender mismatch, many women had trouble finding a marriageable man, elevating marriage ages. Moreover, the rising cost of a dowry also pushed the ages of brides upward, as families needed more time to accumulate an appropriate sum.[70]

Tang marriage law ostensibly stressed Confucian principles and ancient ritual norms. In fact, however, the process was highly legalistic. By putting marriage firmly under the purview of the law, the Tang set an important precedent followed by later dynasties.[71] The law gave parents the power to arrange their children's marriages, and the couple involved did not have to consent to the union. Nevertheless, most young women looked forward to becoming wives and mothers, and they readily accepted matches settled by their elders. For the average woman, the worst possibility was not entering into marriage with an unloved stranger but failing to marry at all. The courtesan Xue Tao lamented her inability to leave the entertainment world for married life.[72]

> Days of zephyrs and blossoms
> are coming to an end;
> and still my wedding day would seem

indefinitely postponed.
Yet to meet a man
with whom I have one heart,
in vain I bind the tie
that shows we'd never part.

Marriages did not have to be registered with government authorities. However, the law required the two families to come to a formal agreement and exchange betrothal gifts to legitimize the union. Representatives of each family negotiated the particulars and set them down in a written marriage record (*hunshu*). Although families still employed a putative matchmaker in conformity with ancient ritual, it seems that parents usually handled these important negotiations themselves. Although the law recognized the validity of oral marriage agreements, written contracts were common, and the Dunhuang trove has yielded examples.[73] The wording of these documents implies that the groom's parents proposed marriage and the family of the bride accepted. Most importantly, the marriage contract specified the betrothal gifts. Other routine information included the identities of the bride and groom, the family heads and any other relevant people involved, as well as the ages of the couple and the date of marriage. When the groom's family delivered the marriage document to the bride's home, they often brought along the betrothal gifts.

Once the two families formally agreed to a marriage, failure to honor the pledge constituted breach of contract, and judicial authorities might become involved in the ensuing dispute.[74] Because most spouses did not choose one another, and did not even necessarily meet prior to the wedding, sometimes parents misrepresented their child's qualities to prospective in-laws. A bride or groom might be sickly, or older or younger than supposed, or else a bride could unexpectedly be designated a concubine instead of wife. In these sorts of situations, a family might try to nullify the engagement when the truth emerged. However, once the betrothal gifts had been accepted, breaking an engagement would likely give rise to mutual recriminations and lawsuits.

Tang wedding customs combined ancient rites and traditions with more recent innovations. The principal rituals took place in the bride's home.[75] During these elaborate ceremonies the bride remained fairly passive while others carried out the main activities. A proper wedding featured feasting, music, and dance. Some families blessed the new couple with Buddhist charms. In addition to the dowry that the bride brought into the marriage, the groom's family would also present her with additional trousseau items during the wedding. They might even read out a poem boasting of the extravagance of her dowry.

In this era, influence from northern steppe peoples caused many Chinese to depart from native traditions.[76] As in nomadic societies, families often erected a tent to serve as a temporary venue for the festivities. The groom rode a horse around the bride's carriage three times. Some pastoral peoples considered it acceptable to kidnap a woman and force her into marriage to avoid paying brideprice. In an echo of this custom, Chinese families sealed the exit to make a show of preventing the bride from escaping. Before the bride arrived in the groom's home, she exited the carriage and entered her new abode on horseback.

Most marriages lasted until one spouse died. As before, people considered it proper to bury a wife alongside her husband.[77] Although Tang authorities encouraged joint spousal burial by claiming that the practice dated back to antiquity, in fact classical writings are ambiguous on this matter. Burying spouses together emphasized the importance of the conjugal bond. However, some people interpreted this custom as symbolizing female submission, with "wife following husband" even in death.[78]

Although it was conventional to inter spouses together, complications often arose. Couples rarely died at the same time, so even if they ended up buried together, their bodies were usually placed in the tomb at different times. Also, not everyone died at home. If a man passed away in a distant place, his wife had to attempt to transport his body home for burial, a difficult and expensive process that did not always succeed. Sometimes people remarried after the death of a spouse, confounding burial arrangements. If a woman remarried, she would be buried with her new husband. But if a man remarried, his survivors faced a quandary: Should they bury him with his first or second wife? If both wives predeceased their husband, people considered it appropriate for him to be buried with the first spouse. However, in some cases a man was interred with the second spouse. People lauded a second wife who allowed her husband to be buried with his first spouse as exceptionally virtuous.

Joint burial may have been the norm, but spouses still often ended up entombed singly.[79] In fact, even though writings on the subject emphasize the orthodoxy of burying wife and husband together, archaeologists have unearthed more single tombs than joint spousal burials. Practical considerations often led to spouses being buried separately. They rarely died at the same time, and if the survivor moved somewhere else, the couple would probably end up buried apart. Moreover, Buddhism encouraged the separate internment of spouses.[80] Some pious women preferred to be cremated and have their ashes placed in a pagoda near the remains of a famous monk. And occasionally a woman's blood kin would transport her body home for burial. People clearly had considerable leeway in deciding how they, their deceased spouse, and their blood kin ought to be buried. Pragmatism and personal wishes often prevailed over ritual norms in deciding how to handle a funeral.

Given the importance of marriage to social identity, families often conducted a wedding for two people who died before having a chance to marry, a custom that stretched back to antiquity.[81] As with ordinary marriage, elaborate negotiations between two families culminated in a ceremony that united two recently deceased individuals. Afterward the families would inter the newlyweds together in a joint grave so that the couple could spend eternity together. Although government authorities discouraged this practice, regarding it as somewhat unseemly, society at large regarded posthumous marriage as respectable, and it was extremely common. Epitaphs, literature, and the standard histories all document this practice in detail. The utility of marriage ties helps account for its popularity. A child's untimely death deprived the family of an opportunity to forge a marriage alliance with useful in-laws, so they conducted a posthumous wedding to achieve the same goal. The rise of Buddhism also resulted in a reinterpretation of death rites. Dead people who ascended to a Buddhist paradise would require a spouse in the afterlife, providing a religious justification for posthumous marriage. Nevertheless, during the late Tang posthumous marriage went into decline, perhaps because Confucians regarded it as outside the classical rites and hence unorthodox.

⊂═══╬═══⊃

As marriage increasingly came under the jurisdiction of the law, divorce procedures became more formal and systematic as well.[82] Like marriage, divorce had traditionally been carried out according to custom rather than law. However, the *Tang Code* included detailed laws regarding divorce, bringing the dissolution of marriage under the law and standardizing the requisite measures. Jurists based divorce law on classical ritual, in line with the general Confucianization of legal principles during the Tang. Thus while many divorce measures in the *Tang Code* remained identical with traditional practices, they became legal requirements rather than customary expectations.

There were several types of divorce, depending on how the process was initiated. As couples did not marry out of love or compatibility, an unhappy marriage usually did not end in separation. People regarded marriage primarily as an economic and social arrangement, so they usually terminated it for pragmatic reasons, such as infertility. A husband could readily divorce his wife, but in theory he had to observe certain restrictions. Tang law integrated the ancient ritual requirement that a husband had to cite one of seven reasons to justify divorce: a wife's disobedience to his parents, barrenness, licentiousness, jealousy, illness, loquaciousness, or theft. However, even if one of these rationales validated divorce, he still could not divorce her in three circumstances: she had no family to return to, she had mourned his parents for three years, or the couple had married while poor and subsequently become rich. In earlier times, violating these ritual principles carried no penalty. But when the ritual norms of divorce became codified as law, a man who contravened them might be subject to punishment. Nevertheless, while officials intended these restrictions to safeguard the interests of wives, the guidelines were so vague and subjective that a husband could easily find an excuse to cast off an unwanted spouse.

If both parties agreed to a separation, they could initiate a consensual divorce.[83] The law allowed couples to agree to divorce for any reason, including incompatibility. Sometimes spouses had practical motives for separation. Noble couples sometimes split up due to politics because their families joined different factions, or one partner's relatives suffered disgrace or punishment.[84] When a couple declared their intention to divorce by mutual consent, an official could demand that they seek arbitration. If attempts at reconciliation failed and both spouses still wanted to separate, they could negotiate a breakup.

Sometimes a government functionary would compel a couple to divorce, a practice that had been a standard bureaucratic procedure for centuries. If spouses had married illegally, an official could dissolve their union, with or without their consent, according to a process called righteous separation (*yijue*).[85] Local magistrates also had the power to annul prohibited forms of marriage such as incest and bigamy.[86] More frequently, an official invoked this measure in response to domestic violence. If a wife suffered physical abuse from her husband or in-laws, or if she had perpetrated violence against her husband, an official could void the marriage in order to protect the vulnerable spouse.

Significantly, with the exception of righteous separation, the law did not allow a woman to divorce an unwilling spouse. A wife trapped in an unbearable marriage could only try to convince her husband to accept consensual divorce. Unless a man beat his wife, she could not divorce him without his consent. If a wife left her husband without first obtaining a divorce, according to the law she had absconded.[87] As her marriage remained valid, she could not legally wed someone else or even become another man's concubine. However, even if wives had been able to initiate divorce, in all likelihood few would have dared abandon married life. Poets lamented the fate of divorced women, portraying them as destitute objects of pity.[88]

Eleven documents recovered from Dunhuang spell out specific divorce procedures.[89] Nine served as model templates used to draw up divorce papers while the two others are actual cases. According to these texts, divorce commonly took place without official oversight. The families of the two spouses met and negotiated the details themselves. Even so, they had to follow set procedures. Dunhuang divorce documents have a standard format consisting of three parts. First the text describes the ideal marriage, using concepts from Buddhism, classical rites, and literature. Some even state that each marriage is predestined or the result of karma. While texts occasionally describe marriage as a union of two families, most depict it as a bond between individuals. These documents refer to two basic principles believed to underpin marriage. In accordance with ancient writings, righteousness (*yi*) could lend marriage a moral foundation. Yet these documents also stress the importance of sentiment (*qing*) to a successful conjugal relationship. Ideally, love and other deep emotions ought to bind spouses together.

The divorce document then goes on to describe the couple's circumstances, justifying the separation by highlighting how much their actual relationship departs from conjugal ideals. Sometimes a text cites a specific reason for divorce. It might even invoke supernatural forces such as the will of heaven or divine intervention. Some documents fault the wife for the breakup, but most apportion blame on both spouses. Incompatibility is the most common reason given for divorce.

Finally the document specifies what will happen after the marriage is dissolved. Most importantly, it spells out the division of property and custody of children. The *Tang Code* declared that a wife could take her dowry with her when she divorced, but she had no claim on any of her husband's property. Drawing up a formal divorce paper dissolved the marriage in the eyes of the law, thus freeing both parties to enter a new union. It seems that everyone expected divorcees to try to find new spouses. Some documents even state that a husband should not feel regretful if he subsequently hears that his former wife has remarried. Finally, divorce documents end with an unexpectedly gracious farewell section in which the spouses wish one another future happiness and success.

Besides marrying a wife, a man could also bring concubines into the household. The practice of concubinage varied considerably. Some women came into a home for a limited time, while other relationships were stable and produced children. Men tended to marry later than women, so they sometimes took a concubine prior to marriage. Besides the desire for sexual release, some unmarried men took a concubine to bear children and start a family. Men sometimes found concubinage so convenient that they never bothered to formally marry.[90] The custom of concubinage depressed the status of wives by bringing rival women into a household.[91] Nevertheless, people always considered a man's wife far superior to his concubine.

A concubine had an ambiguous place within the home. Even though she occupied a far lower position than a wife, people nevertheless considered her a kind of family member. Chinese traditionally conceived of family in extremely broad terms. Concubines, wet nurses, nannies, and even servants and slaves were akin to family members, albeit very marginal and low in rank. However, when people with extremely dissimilar backgrounds and conflicting interests resided in the same household, friction could easily result. Although men found concubinage expedient, it could also give rise to domestic discord.

During the early Tang, prosperity, commercialization, and urbanization made concubines more numerous and visible than before, so the problems raised by their presence in the home became more pressing.[92] Previously, informal custom had loosely regulated concubinage. But because officials sought to systematically control family matters, the *Tang Code* included provisions regarding concubinage. Most importantly, the law strictly distinguished between the status of wife and concubine.[93] A man purchased a concubine, usually from her family, so she had a position in the household somewhat above that of bondservant. From a legal perspective, a concubine's children were not her own offspring. They were to regard their father's official wife as their mother. Although concubines no doubt found this legal fiction painful, it benefitted their children. Because the law considered them the wife's offspring, they enjoyed a respectable social status and the same inheritance rights as their father's other children.[94]

A man had the right to take a concubine if he could afford the expense, and the law forbade his wife from expressing jealousy. However, poetry and epitaphs show that a man's relationship with a concubine could sometimes become deeply affectionate, inevitably provoking ill feelings from an insecure wife.[95] However much law and ethics sought to restrain jealousy, the fundamental inequity of a system that demanded strict chastity from women but allowed men to bring sex partners into the home inevitably challenged domestic harmony.

The burial arrangements for concubines illustrate their conflicted status.[96] A concubine was usually buried apart from her master, even if they had been unusually close. Of thirty-two concubines who had the unusual honor of being commemorated with an epitaph, 78 percent received individual burial. The location of a concubine's tomb reflected her standing in the family. If she had lived with a man for a long time and born his children, she might be buried near his tomb. Because her offspring oversaw the funeral arrangements, they would want to bury her in a respectable location. Nevertheless, even a concubine who bore children might be interred five hundred paces from her master's tomb to symbolize her marginal status. Many concubines ended up buried singly, sometimes in a remote place far from other graves, deliberately signifying their alienation from the core family.

In addition to traditional concubinage, a new form of the practice emerged during the Tang. Previously a concubine lived in her master's house together with his wife and family. In this era, however, some men kept a concubine in a separate residence. People distinguished nonresident concubines (*biezhaifu*) from their live-in counterparts.[97] This pragmatic arrangement would have decreased tension in the home and also shielded a concubine from a wife's jealous wrath. However, in 715 the government tried to outlaw nonresident concubinage. The rationale for this ban remains unclear, as does its effectiveness. At this time the state also prohibited lavish funerals and certain luxury goods, so this prohibition may have been part of a larger sumptuary campaign. Because it cost considerably more to maintain a woman in a separate home, people considered nonresident concubines a sign of wealth. Some men may even have kept a nonresident concubine as a form of conspicuous consumption. So as men conceived of new ways to circumvent the restrictions of monogamous marriage, the state reacted by promulgating new regulations. The increasing popularity of concubinage, and government attempts to limit it, highlights the enduring contradiction between the official promotion of stable marriage and men's desire for sexual autonomy.

Chapter 2

Mothers

Even though custom discouraged women from participating in matters outside the home, they still controlled many vital activities within the household. Because most women lived out their lives within the constricted realm of family, their three main social roles were all determined by kinship: daughter, wife, and mother. Of the three, motherhood provided women with the most opportunities to raise their status within the family and even gain respect from society at large. A mother had authority over the children who would determine the family's future, giving her considerable power in the home.[1] She had a say in major decisions regarding her offspring and oversaw their upbringing and early education. The extraordinary power of mothers within the domestic sphere affected the overall status of women. Exclusion from formal public institutions does not necessarily make women powerless. Instead it can shift female power into the intimate family realm. In a society organized around the family, the authority of mothers within the household gave them considerable influence. They made important decisions concerning those closest to them, controlled key resources, and exercised authority over the next generation. The prestige associated with motherhood helped put women on a stronger footing in their interactions with men.

In every society, the particular dynamics of family interactions shape gendered identities.[2] In China, mothers traditionally demanded obedience and affection from their children and gained respect from others for successfully fulfilling their maternal duties. Steppe peoples also treated their mothers with great respect, so the influence of nomadic cultures further bolstered maternal authority.[3] Accordingly, Tang women could use the role of mother to empower themselves as figures of domestic authority. The narratives of family life portrayed mothers as virtuous and dependable. Women embraced these stereotypes, socializing those around them to pay them the respect due to their maternal status.

In historic China as elsewhere, the size and structure of the family had a major influence on a particular woman's maternal role. In larger kin groups, a mother has to compete for influence with numerous in-laws and senior men, thereby lessening their authority.[4] So as the number of adult men in a household increases, women tend to have less influence over matters of common concern. Moreover, a woman's power in the home tends to increase as she bears more children, particularly sons. Although the government encouraged people to have large families, women did not need to be convinced to bear children. They often implored fertility deities for divine aid, and physicians dispensed medicines intended to stimulate pregnancy.

The average women recorded in Sui epitaphs bore 3.61 children.[5] Similarly, according to one analysis of Tang epitaphs, the average family had 3.58 children.[6] Other studies concluded that the average woman had between 3.3 and 4.77 children.[7] A group of fourteen mid-Tang women mentioned in Dunhuang documents had an average of 3.5 children each.[8] The popularity of concubinage lowered the overall fertility of wives in elite families, so they had fewer children than counterparts in premodern Europe and subsequent Chinese dynasties. Combining the children of both wives and concubines, it becomes clear that elite men had more children than those recorded in the epitaphs of deceased wives. The population seems to have had a highly skewed sex ratio, with an estimated 117.21 boys per hundred girls. Many children died young. In one group of epitaphs, 20 percent of the inscriptions record the death of a child.

Tang views toward childbirth affected the status of mothers. An aura of danger enveloped delivery, making motherhood an emotionally charged experience. People believed that this extraordinary liminal event could bring women closer to the supernatural. The standard histories follow earlier conventions in relating stories of strange events alleged to have occurred during pregnancy or delivery. Historians even noted the birth of triplets, considering this a portentous omen.[9] Sometimes a strange birth could foretell greatness. The mother of Emperor Wen of Sui gave birth to him in a Buddhist temple. As the baby emerged, purple vapors filled the room. A nun who witnessed this miracle declared that a child born with such auspicious signs would surely be extraordinary.[10] On another occasion, when a child emerged from the womb, black vapors poured out as well. The servants mistook the baby for a huge snake and fled in terror. However, he grew up to be an important personage, so in retrospect his weird birth also portended future success.[11]

As before, people considered childbirth extremely dangerous. They knew that the delivery might bring joy or sadness. Either a new member would join the family or mother and child could die. Tang records mention many cases of women succumbing to complications from pregnancy or delivery.[12] Physicians tried to ameliorate the dangers associated with childbirth and used many methods to ease the process. Medical texts described every aspect of birth in detail, from the optimal place of delivery to the best physical position.[13] Certain medicines supposedly made the fetus more slippery, allowing for a speedy delivery with minimum discomfort and danger. A keen awareness of the dangers attending childbirth, together with its supernatural associations, cloaked motherhood in a veil of intimidating mystery. Most children recognized the troubles that their mothers had endured and rewarded them with genuine gratitude. Poetry shows that mothers and sons in particular could develop highly charged emotional bonds. So in addition to duty and propriety, sentiment bound them together as well.[14]

A mother exercised tangible power over her children. She retained a degree of authority over her children even after they reached maturity. A mother had a say in the marriage, divorce, and remarriage of her offspring.[15] Upon widowhood, a mother gained even more authority. A widowed mother usually acted as de facto family head and managed her husband's estate on behalf of her sons until they reached adulthood. The law forbade children from dividing up household property while either parent remained alive, and it seems that people observed this rule. Household registers do not show any examples of children dividing up a deceased father's land while their mother was still alive.[16] In theory, children were not even supposed to distribute family property while still in mourning for a deceased parent.

A mother also had responsibility for a child's early education. Most importantly, society expected her to inculcate basic moral virtues in her offspring and socialize them to thrive in their expected place in life. In addition, women in elite households taught their children the rudiments of reading and writing, starting them off on their studies. As the civil service examinations became an avenue to success, maternal instruction grew in importance. Even successful men welcomed career advice from their mothers.[17]

Because people put so much emphasis on the importance of maternal instruction, they praised the mothers of virtuous and successful men. Writers portrayed good mothers as nurturing, advising, directing, and encouraging their sons, allowing them to claim credit for their children's achievements.[18] Although patriarchal convention banned women from participating in public life, they could nevertheless savor vicarious success by sharing credit for a son's achievements. Many commemorative epitaphs praise an outstanding mother who raised and educated her children in an exemplary manner.

The biographies of famous men often attributed their achievements to good upbringing. The mother of Ouyang Tong (d. 691) instructed him in

Figure 2.1 A Plump Beauty (Sailko)

the art of calligraphy and encouraged him to practice diligently. As a result, his handwriting eventually rivaled that of his father, the famous calligrapher Ouyang Xun. The story of Zhao Wumeng shows maternal guidance as even more influential. When young, Zhao enjoyed hunting instead of serious pursuits.[19] One day he proudly presented his mother with some wild game. But instead of thanking him for the gift, she broke out in tears, complaining that he wasted his time hunting and ignored his studies. She declared that she had given up hope and refused to eat the food he had given her. Moved by his mother's protests, Zhao began to devote himself to learning. In the end he passed the imperial examinations and became a high official and respected author. According to this story, Zhao Wumeng could only succeed because of his mother.

With motherhood so highly esteemed, some people strove to extend it to encompass analogous social roles. Tang law describes a person as having "three fathers and eight mothers," thus granting parental status to the main authority figures who guided or nurtured a child.[20] Some stepmothers also enthusiastically embraced the role of surrogate mother. Traditionally stepmothers and stepsons had awkward or even acrimonious relations. Tang authorities fostered domestic harmony by elevating the stepmother to a status akin to birth mother. During the Tang, both law and ritual treated the stepmother as equal to biological mothers in almost every way.[21] For example, when a stepmother died, her stepson would conduct the funeral.[22] The intensification of this relationship heightened expectations for both sides. Society expected stepchildren to obey stepmothers and stepmothers to demonstrate genuine love to all of their husband's children.

Elevating motherhood to an almost sacred state imbued it with an ideological dimension. Some people fetishized mothers and used this idealized image to advance their political and social goals. Most importantly, officials associated service to parents with loyalty to the state. Promoting filial piety thus became an important political goal, particularly in the late Tang when officials promoted the importance of loyalty as a way to strengthen allegiance to the tottering dynasty. The *Tang Code* classed a lack of filial piety as one of the "ten abominations" constituting the most serious crimes, thereby making it a primary legal duty.[23] Emperors even bolstered their power by claiming a maternal role over their subjects. By claiming to be both father and mother of the people, rulers paradoxically transformed motherhood into a political tool for male aggrandizement.[24]

Filial piety (*xiao*) determined family hierarchy according to age rather than gender, putting the older generation above their juniors. Just as older brothers and sisters had authority over their younger siblings, children had to venerate and obey both parents. "Being good to one's father and mother is filial piety."[25] Although the father theoretically came first, children tended to feel closer to their mothers and usually showed them more enthusiastic devotion. This central moral dictate placed mothers in a position far superior to their sons, empowering women within the family and earning respect from society and the state.

Not everyone lived up to the demanding standards of filial virtue. Sons did not always treat their mothers well. These negligent offspring made attentive sons seem even more virtuous in comparison.[26] Biographies of important ministers and moral paragons frequently stress their exceptional devotion to their mothers to illustrate their good character.[27] For example, one man who felt compelled to commit suicide decided to remain alive just so that he could continue to care for his mother.[28] Nor did the elite monopolize this virtue. People of all classes and backgrounds lavished their mothers with love, attention, and deference. Even the poor and marginal could gain a modicum of honor by being a good son, so men frequently showed off this virtue to bolster their reputations.[29]

Although filial piety placed women and men beneath their elders, subservience could nevertheless bring benefits. A daughter who fulfilled her obligations to her parents in an exemplary manner might gain respect as a moral icon. Writers lauded filial acts, and readers enjoyed these tales of exemplary behavior. Stories about filial women describe them caring for a sickly older relative, protecting a vulnerable family member, seeking vengeance for an elder who had been wronged, or overcoming difficult circumstances to conduct a proper funeral for a dead parent.[30] Most of these stories describe women who had not yet married, as exemplary filiality constituted the prime way for young women to express a commitment to virtue. Some women even became Buddhist nuns to generate karmic merit that could benefit their parents. Filial piety presented the astute woman with a powerful weapon that she could deploy to her advantage, regardless of whether she presented herself to the world as venerated mother or self-sacrificing daughter.

The ongoing revival of the rites bolstered the academic importance of filial piety.[31] Tang scholars studied the *Classic of Filial Piety* (*Xiaojing*) and wrote new commentaries to this revered work.[32] They elevated *Records of Ritual* (*Liji*) to a canonical status, putting it on the same level as more ancient classics. And they discussed the application of rites to particular family matters in great detail. Nor was the growing interest in the classical rites limited to rarified intellectual circles. Documents from Dunhuang include popular works on ritual aimed at a wide audience, showing that these concepts had gained currency among ordinary people, even on the outer margins of the Chinese oikoumene. As more people took interest in ethical orthodoxy, any family that ignored basic ritual principles risked becoming a laughingstock. Most fundamentally, works on the rites demanded that individuals adhere to virtues appropriate to their particular social roles. Sons ought to be filial, wives obedient, husbands righteous, and so on. The rites emphasized filial piety in particular, as Confucius and Mencius had declared it the fountainhead of all virtue.[33]

Given the increasing veneration of filial piety, some rulers used it as a pragmatic ideology.[34] Emperor Wen, founder of the Sui dynasty, had received a Buddhist education and showed little interest in Confucianism or learned pursuits in general. Yet in spite of his anti-intellectualism, even he praised the *Classic of Filial Piety*.[35] Emperors promoted filiality to stake a claim to moral legitimacy and thereby attract support. And heirs to the throne studied this classic to instill core values that would prepare them to carry out a ruler's duties in an exemplary manner.[36]

The state sought to organize society according to filial principles. Devoted children could receive official commendations and honors such as official rank, the erection of a commemorative stele, and permission to use the character *xiao* (filial) in their posthumous name. Ordinary people proved extremely receptive to filial teachings. In rural China, age had always been associated with social status. By placing this traditional social priority within an ethical framework, the government valorized the status quo and reinforced order.[37] Because filial piety inculcated deference to superiors, obedience to the prevailing social hierarchy served the interests of the authorities.

Buddhism also promoted filial piety, sometimes presenting it as a spiritual practice.[38] A Chinese translation of the *jātaka* story of Sāmaka (Shanzi) describes an Indian man who treated his parents exceptionally well and enjoyed good fortune as a result. This narrative presented filiality within the moralistic Buddhist cosmology based on karmic reward and punishment.[39] The synthetic nature of Tang Buddhism, which encompassed native Chinese teachings as well as orthodox Indian doctrines, encouraged Buddhists to embrace filial piety as a spiritual priority. The apocryphal *Sutra on Parental Benevolence* (*Fo shuo fumu enzhong jing*) fused Buddhist and Confucian ideas about filial piety and expressed the resulting synthesis in a colloquial style that rendered it accessible to a popular audience.[40] This text put particular stress on the dangers of childbirth and difficulties of motherhood. The author reasoned that because mothers sacrifice so much, children owe them respect and obedience.

During the Tang, Confucian scholars extended filial piety beyond parents to include a woman's parents-in-law. In contrast, Buddhism contracted the scope of this virtue. To Buddhists, filial devotion should be directed to parents, and they put particular stress on the relationship between mothers and sons.[41] Apologists stressed that a son should feel beholden to his mother for all that she has done for him. At the same time, they reminded men that even a kindly mother could still commit sins and end up in hell. They used this disturbing idea to encourage men to engage in Buddhist practice and direct their accumulated merit to save their mothers from torment in the afterlife. Stories about the virtuous sons Uttara and Mulian described heroic men who saved their sinful mothers from perdition by pursuing Buddhist practice.[42]

During the Tang, filial piety became thoroughly integrated into the law. The criminalization of unfilial behavior was not new. Officials in earlier eras had often sought to unify law and ritual, using one to reinforce the other. The Northern Qi dynasty legal code had made unfilial behavior illegal, setting an important precedent.[43] The *Tang Code* elaborated on this principle and applied it to a wide range of actions. Incorporating filial piety into the law had mixed effects on women. State authorities required daughters to obey their parents, wives to defer to husbands, and daughters-in-law to serve parents-in-law. In consequence, female position in the family rose in some respects and fell in others, and a woman's relationships with those around her depended on her particular kinship roles.

The *Tang Code* punished eight types of unfilial behavior: cursing parents, dividing up family property while a parent remained alive, disobeying a father's teachings, not caring for parents, failing to properly mourn a parent, marrying while still in mourning for a parent, falsely stating that a parent had died, and reconciling with someone who had killed one's parent.[44] Because the law mandated filiality, mothers could sue offspring to compel obedience. As a result, mothers and sons sometimes ended up in acrimonious lawsuits.[45] In general, however, children willingly submitted to their parents' commands.

With filial virtue so celebrated, some children went to extreme lengths to demonstrate fervent devotion to their mothers. For example, they might fetishize the act of feeding mothers.[46] Because the loving mother nursed and fed her children, filial children reversed the roles and showed reciprocal affection by feeding elderly parents. This practice emerged during the Han dynasty but became much more common in the medieval era. Sometimes feeding consisted of basic sustenance delivered in the face of difficulty. In other cases, a devoted child would present a parent with a favorite food or rare delicacy. In a typical story, a six-year-old boy found himself caring for his sick mother.[47] She was so weak that she did not drink anything for six days, so he also abstained from liquids to share her suffering. Eventually he was able to get her to drink something, thereby saving her life—and his own as well.

Some people displayed exceptional filial virtue by punctiliously mourning deceased parents. Biographies of female paragons often mention them conducting mourning in an exemplary manner.[48] Adhering to the onerous classical mourning regulations required significant sacrifices. Even so, the law required children to observe these rules to the letter. While few people carried out full mourning, they nevertheless saw it as a goal that ought to be fulfilled if possible. Mourning customs regarding women underwent a major revision in this era.[49] Prior to the reign of Empress Wu, the children of a woman who predeceased her husband only mourned her for one year. Wu increased this term to three years, aligning the mourning periods for father and mother.[50] Although Emperor Xuanzong discontinued the practice, arguing that children should not consider the mother as important as the father, in 732 the government reinstated the three-year mourning period and thereafter it remained the official norm.

The government strove to ensure that officials would correctly mourn their parents, thereby maintaining a high moral tone among administrators. According to the law, an official had to vacate his post during the three years of mourning.[51] Those who failed to observe proper mourning could find themselves demoted upon reentry into the bureaucracy.[52] Superiors offered condolences on the death of a subordinate's mother, with the expectation that he would immediately resign.[53] As in the early medieval era, some men took this responsibility one step further and quit their post merely because their mother was old so that they could care for her in the final stage of life.[54]

Children sometimes went to extraordinary lengths to conduct proper mourning to display their virtue to the world. One filial paragon traveled thousands of *li* just to carry out his parents' funerals.[55] Another model son took great care to ensure that his mother had a proper tomb.[56] Sometimes a child honored a mother's memory by devoting himself to his studies after mourning had ended, becoming extremely learned and respected in consequence.[57] Although the earliest stories of filial children focused on sons, some Tang biographies of exemplary women praise them for fastidiously managing a parent's funeral or mourning for a deceased parent.[58]

Ritual experts debated the rules of mourning, and the resulting conflict of opinions opened the way for extreme behavior.[59] Self-destruction was the most radical way to express grief. One story told of a son and his mother who were crossing a river when a sudden storm capsized their vessel. Although the woman quickly perished, her devoted son nevertheless jumped into the river and embraced his mother's corpse until he also drowned.[60] Instead of criticizing this needless suicide, readers lauded him for sacrificing himself for the sake of a lofty moral principle.

Self-destructive behavior was not limited to mourning the death of a parent. Sometimes children demonstrated their devotion to a living mother by mutilating themselves. Chinese medicine provided one impetus for this practice. Physicians classified human flesh as a kind of medicinal ingredient with powerful healing properties.[61] Of course this material could not be purchased. The only way to acquire it on behalf of a sick parent was for children to cut off a piece of their own flesh. Buddhists also had a long tradition of using self-mutilation and suicide to show their contempt for the polluted physical form.[62] And some Indian tales about filial children feature mutilation and cannibalism. The translation and dissemination of these sorts of Buddhist ideas helped push the Chinese understanding of filial virtue to extremes.[63] Even so, the revered *Classic of Filial Piety* strictly prohibited a child from self-mutilation. This text reasoned that because people receive their body as a precious gift from their parents, deliberately injuring it would seem ungrateful and even insulting.[64] Some people cited this classical injunction to criticize self-harm in the name of filial piety. The ebb and flow of various views of filial obedience pushed devoted children in different directions. Even as destructive expressions of filiality gained attention, moderate voices condemned extreme measures, making the relation between mother and child a highly contested ethical topic.

Chapter 3

Government

As in previous eras, during the Tang dynasty proximity to the emperor presented women with the best opportunities to gain distinction, wealth, and power. A graded system of honorific titles reflected these perquisites. Titled ladies could sometimes visit the palace, attend an audience with the ruler, and participate in certain palace events and rituals. Women outside the palace could receive six degrees of honorific designations.[1] A woman usually received one of these titles according to the position of her husband or son, so when the rank of a key male family member changed, the government would adjust her title in tandem.[2] Occasionally a woman earned a title in her own right as a reward for an outstanding achievement. In one instance, a courageous woman received a title for rallying women and children to defend the walls of a city besieged by Khitan troops.[3]

The empress stood above all other titled ladies. Since the advent of the imperial system, rulers had usually named a primary consort as empress. However, during the early medieval era, nomadic invaders who traditionally lacked queens ruled northern China, and they showed little interest in this Chinese custom. Moreover, they feared that an empress and kinsmen might seize control of the government, a problem that plagued the Han dynasty. As a result, some early medieval rulers declined to name an empress, while others selected a spouse from a lowly background, sometimes even a slave.

In contrast, Sui and Tang rulers revived Han dynasty customs regarding the institution of empress.[4] In doing so, they restored the empress to a position of respect. Having elevated the position of empress, it seemed inappropriate for a ruler to wed a woman of debased status, so most Tang monarchs wed a woman from a respectable family with a distinguished record of government service.[5] In addition, the Tang ruling house scrupulously observed the "six rites" of the classical marriage ceremony set down in the ancient ritual canon, which endowed the emperor's wife with legitimacy and prestige.[6] Moreover, they buried Tang empresses in subsidiary tombs near the emperor to emphasize their close bond.

Elaborate ritual and symbolism regulated every aspect of an empress's life, thereby endowing her with great dignity. The empress participated in an array of court rituals and ensconced herself within an environment of flamboyant luxury.[7] Every item that she used, from seals to carriages, had to be of the finest quality. Palace officials classified each item according to grade and carefully defined when it ought to be used.[8] For example, court ceremony categorized the clothing of a Sui empress into five grades, each to be worn on a particular kind of occasion.[9] Empresses also used rare and prestigious goods to materialize their lofty identity. Unique objects provided a tangible framework that presented the empress not as a person but as a formidable institution. A changing display of luxury goods, carefully calibrated to every occasion, gave the empress a public identity appropriate to her station, imbued her actions with significance, and reproduced the institution of empress down through the generations.[10]

In addition to the empress, a Tang emperor also had numerous minor consorts.[11] The number of women in the palace varied considerably in each era. An emperor tended to accumulate concubines and favorites over time, so the longer his reign, the more women resided in the palace. During the prosperous reign of Emperor Xuanzong (r. 713–756), the palace seems to have had the highest number of female residents. *New Tang Records* (*Xin Tangshu*) claims that at that time the palace housed forty thousand women and three thousand eunuchs.[12] At first glance this number seems highly exaggerated, but contemporary poems also mention thousands of palace ladies, so Xuanzong clearly surrounded himself with an enormous number of women.

Minor palace women came from a wide range of circumstances.[13] Officials chose the daughters of ordinary people to serve in the palace according to appearance or talent. The wives and daughters of convicts were also sometimes condemned to serve in the palace as menials. Foreign rulers provided beautiful women as tribute and gifts. And princesses and consort kin sent skilled female entertainers to the palace as gifts. Because women came into the palace in different ways, the emperor's concubines and minor consorts had extremely varied backgrounds. Some came from lowly families while others had been born into the nobility. Many officials considered it an honor to have a daughter taken into the palace.

Given the enormous number of palace women, authorities had to organize them into a clear hierarchy to enforce order and reduce discord. During the early medieval dynasties, officials had come up with a detailed system of palace ranks. The Sui and Tang further elaborated this system, classifying palace women into twenty-seven grades.[14] They treated ladies of the highest grade as secondary consorts while the rest had a status akin to concubines. A palace woman's rank determined every aspect of her life: the quality of her clothing, carriage, and even the material used to make the seal that she used on official documents.[15] A resident of the palace did not necessarily hold a particular rank permanently.[16] Many emperors fathered numerous children, usually born by women other than the empress, and they favored certain companions. If a concubine attained imperial favor or bore the heir apparent, she would be promoted, perhaps even becoming empress. Rulers also handed out gifts to palace ladies on an ad hoc basis.[17] Alternatively, a woman could suffer demotion to punish malfeasance.

The enormous Tang palace required a large and sophisticated bureaucracy to function. Previous dynasties had established a complex organization scheme that the Sui and Tang kept in place. As before, many officials managing palace affairs were female. Even some imperial concubines participated in palace administration. As a result, some ladies had two different titles, as concubine and palace official, each positioning her within a different hierarchy. Moreover, the "female scribes" (*nüshi*) of the palace also had specific titles. Epitaphs of Sui palace women reveal seventeen official titles, and the Tang had a comparable system.[18] Female bureaucrats managed many routine matters and helped keep the enormous palace running smoothly. Specialized female officials oversaw rituals, music, clothing and ornaments, record keeping, guests, food, carriages, lamps, gardens, medicines, and so on.[19] The active participation of many imperial concubines in such detailed administrative work attests to their education and competence.

Although palace women lived in opulent environs, poetry portrays their lives as insecure and often unhappy. An emperor surrounded himself with thousands of women, so few of them had much contact with him. Most were relegated to the outer margins of palace life. With so many women vying for the attentions of one man, rivalry was intense. A concubine who captured the ruler's gaze would instantly find herself at the center of palace life. But if the emperor shifted his attention to someone else, a favorite could suddenly be discarded and forgotten. Poets depict palace ladies terrified of losing the ruler's favor.[20] A poem by Xu Hui (627–650), a talented consort of Emperor Taizong, sums up the grief felt by a former favorite.[21]

> You used to love my Cypress Rafter Terrace,
> But now you dote upon her Bright Yang Palace.
> I know my place, take leave of your palanquin,
> Hold in my feelings, weep for a cast-off fan.
> There was a time my dances, songs, brought honor.
> These letters and poems of long ago? Despised!
> It's true, I think—your favor collapsed like waves.
> Hard to offer water that's been spilled.

In spite of the luxurious surroundings, palace life was infamously boring and claustrophobic. Numerous poets, usually male, took on a female voice to complain about confinement in the palace.[22] These emotional poems contrast the petty boredom and melancholy of palace residents with their magnificent backdrop.[23] In particular, palace women detested their isolation. One poem describes how a group of ladies crowded around a man who had come into the palace to sweep a courtyard.[24] They excitedly questioned him, desperate to find out what was going on in the outside world. Nor were these grievances mere poetic conceit. It seems that many palace women did indeed object to their confinement. Once Emperor Zhongzong allowed thousands of palace women to celebrate the lunar New Year by traveling to the mansion of a high official to view the lanterns hung in his garden. When released from the palace for this special occasion, many of them absconded.[25]

Most palace women did not spend their entire life in the palace, as large numbers of surplus women were periodically expelled.[26] Most dramatically, whenever an emperor died, the palace experienced a major turnover. Incest taboos prohibited the new ruler from intimate contact with his predecessor's concubines, so they had to leave. Concubines also departed when they became old. Only a few women remained in the palace their entire lives, mostly talented entertainers. Women who left the palace usually returned to their families, who might help them find a husband.[27] Others became Buddhist and Daoist nuns.

If a woman died while serving in the palace, her remains were interred in a special cemetery.[28] Due to ongoing urban development around the capital, the location of these burial grounds shifted over the course of the dynasty. Imperial consorts received elaborate funerals, but an ordinary concubine was laid to rest without much ceremony.[29] Only a simple plaque marked her grave. This simple memorial often did not even record her name, only the date of death.[30] If a woman died after leaving the palace, her family gave her a more elaborate burial. The tomb of a woman from an elite family sometimes had a stone slab engraved with a commemorative epitaph.

A consort who bore the emperor a child handed over the baby to servants to be nursed and raised.[31] Some emperors had numerous offspring, requiring the presence of many wet nurses and nannies. In this respect, the palace followed aristocratic custom. Wealthy people had long considered child care a tedious menial duty, so the Tang elite followed Han dynasty precedent in handing over their infants to be raised by servants.[32] A wealthy household would bring in a poor lactating mother to nurse a new baby. Slaves owned by Buddhist and Daoist temples also sometimes worked as nursemaids. A wet nurse might continue to care for a child after weaning, becoming a nanny, and children often developed very close relationships with these caregivers.

Government-owned slaves usually nursed the emperor's children. A slave woman who cared for a prince or empress might rise in status when her charge came of age. If she had nursed the future emperor, she could even find herself catapulted from the bottom rungs of society to the uppermost elite. Han dynasty moralists had lamented the unseemly elevation of such lowly women to the upper ranks of society, but the Tang court accepted this custom without complaint.[33] Palace wet nurses routinely received titles and enjoyed wealth, honor, and tangible opportunities. While alive, the emperor's nursemaid could receive wealth and title. And after she died, she might be honored with an elaborate funeral and an engraved epitaph. However, unlike the Han, the family members of these women rarely served in office. Rewards went solely to the women themselves, not their kinsmen. Some nursemaids became implicated in plots and scandals that involved their former charges. However, given the hostility of literati toward people of base background and the historiographic tradition of molding portrayals of particular individuals according to the scholar's moral judgments, historical accounts tend to exaggerate their misconduct.[34]

There were more than two hundred princesses over the course of the Tang, and they resided in the palace until they married. These women did not enjoy equal status, as the palace bureaucracy classified them into ranks according to birth order and their relation to the reigning emperor. Because the title and status of a princess depended on her place in the imperial kinship system, unlike most women, her rank remained fairly stable throughout life and did not change in tandem with that of her husband or son.[35] People called a princess by her title, not her given name. Her title often included the name of a region, making it sound like she presided over a fief. However, this archaic appellation merely imitated ancient aristocratic titles, and she did not actually rule that place.[36]

Princesses rarely influenced politics, so the standard histories include few substantial biographies.[37] Nevertheless, as princesses were exempt from observing many standard rites and customs, they enjoyed unique privileges.[38] Upon marriage, a princess left the palace but did not move into her husband's home. Instead the government constructed a mansion nearby. Her dowry included an array of luxury goods and, most importantly, lifelong income consisting of the tax payments collected from a special administrative district (*shishifeng*) composed of hundreds of households.[39] A princess came into marriage with an entourage of officials to manage her finances and other matters. The economic independence of princesses, together with their high birth, emboldened them, and they could be proud and domineering. Princesses usually married important men, so their sons had extremely exalted parentage and often served in high office.[40] When a princess died, she had the right to burial in the imperial cemetery, but most ended up interred near their husbands.[41]

Princesses usually played only a symbolic role in politics. Most importantly, they represented the imperial line in marriage. Allying two powerful groups through marriage was a time-tested strategy that dated back to antiquity, and the Tang emperors carefully arranged the marriages of princesses to bind useful in-laws to the throne. Given the weakness of the Tang central government, rulers often had to depend on in-laws for support. Emperors usually blocked their sons from acquiring political power so as to prevent them from threatening orderly succession. Because princes could not provide the throne with tangible support, rulers relied heavily on their in-laws.[42] The husband of a princess often received a noble title and promotion to higher office, thereby making him a more valuable ally for the ruler.[43] When a man married a princess, all of his close male kin could suddenly find themselves elevated to great prominence. However, empowering in-laws posed risks. Sometimes men who married princesses used their heightened power to oppose imperial interests. More often, though, kinship solidarity successfully bound together the emperors and their in-laws, and they cooperated to uphold the interests of the ruling house.[44]

The politics of princess marriage changed over the course of the dynasty.[45] In the early Tang, many princesses married the kinsmen of empresses, making these marriages endogamous.[46] A small number of families, some ethnic Han and others of nomadic extraction, repeatedly intermarried with the imperial line to perpetuate their special status.[47] Because the loftiest aristocrats looked down on the Tang ruling house as barbarized upstarts, the emperors bolstered the status of their marriage partners so that they could rival the prestige of the greatest families. In the dynasty's latter phase, princesses usually married men from families that had produced meritorious officials. As the dynasty decayed, princess marriage became an increasingly important political tool. Princesses either married men from consort families or wed warlords in unstable border regions to bind them to the central government.[48]

The Sui and Tang also sent out princesses to wed foreign chieftains and thus build alliances. This era marks the highpoint of marriage diplomacy, and thirty Sui and Tang princesses married foreign rulers.[49] Nomads considered the practice so common that some Sogdians even named their daughters using the Chinese word for princess.[50] Uighur rulers sent troops to help put down the An Lushan Rebellion and thereafter helped the Tang emperors maintain order. To maintain this useful tie, the Tang emperors sent out three princesses to marry Uighur qaghans, creating an especially intense bond between the Chinese and Uighur ruling lines. After the fall of the Tang, this practice fell into abeyance until the Manchus revived it during the Qing dynasty.

The Tang ruling line had nomadic ancestry and observed some steppe customs, facilitating intermarriage with foreign tribesmen. The resulting alliances often proved beneficial to China, as marriage bonds with surrounding peoples could help pacify unruly tribes, stabilize the frontier, and provide allies in times of crisis.[51] For example, the marriage of three princesses to Uighur rulers helped stabilize this crucial relationship.[52] Uighur troops even provided support to Tang forces and quelled domestic rebellions.

Despite the utility of marriages to foreign leaders, Chinese considered these relationships somewhat embarrassing and referred to them as "marrying down."[53] Sometimes the emperor granted a distant female relative the title of princess so that he could wed a faux princess to a foreign khan and reserve his daughters for more respectable Chinese husbands.[54] Because Chinese disliked these arrangements, emperors usually resorted to them in times of national weakness, marrying off princesses to gain useful foreign allies when they felt exposed. A confident emperor would usually refuse to marry his daughter to a foreigner. However, when an emperor refused a foreigner's offer of marriage, the insulted khan might consider it a sign of hostility and act accordingly.[55]

Nomadic peoples normally chose competent adults to lead them, so the ruler's spouse and her kinsmen usually had little influence in their new homeland. Because steppe chieftains did not feel threatened by affines, they traditionally sought out powerful in-laws, making them amenable to marriage with China's ruling family.[56] Nevertheless, occasionally a Chinese princess who married a foreign ruler could attain a position of influence among her husband's people, as illustrated by the case of Princess Qianjin (d. 593), who married Ishbara, a Turkic qaghan.[57] Qianjin was the daughter of a Northern Zhou dynasty emperor. She came from a culturally mixed background, with both Tuoba and ethnic Chinese ancestry. Her nomadic roots helped her to thrive in her new home, where she became deeply involved in politics. After the fall of the Northern Zhou, Emperor Wen of Sui suspected her of encouraging the Western Türks to overthrow him. When her husband sent Emperor Wen a message requesting a marriage alliance to bind him to China's new ruling line, the emperor replied that he would only consent to a match if the khan got rid of his troublesome wife. Princess Qianjin had no link to the current dynasty, making her useless to the qaghan, so he killed her to curry favor with China's new ruling family.

Female political power reached an apogee in the early Tang, making it a key era in the history of Chinese women. Aggressive female intervention in state affairs provoked strong reactions from important men, with ramifications that reverberated for centuries. Tang women tended to exercise power differently than their predecessors. During the Eastern Han dynasty, a time when the mothers and wives of emperors repeatedly gained control over the state, empresses dowager usually cooperated with kinsmen to dominate the government. Their fathers, uncles, and brothers generally took the lead, and they used the dowager's authority to legitimize their actions. Given the kinship structure of the Tang ruling clan, ambitious women could potentially have employed a similar strategy. As during the Eastern Han, Tang emperors had extremely close bonds with their mothers' kinsmen, and maternal uncles in particular.[58] Nevertheless, consort kin did not play a very important role in government during the Tang. Powerful women usually acted on their own instead of serving as surrogates for male kin.[59]

A concatenation of factors allowed women to gain so much influence over government in this era. The ideas and customs of steppe peoples had permeated Chinese consciousness for centuries. The wives and mothers of nomadic rulers sometimes had a say in important decisions, so pastoral influence helped condition the Tang court to defer to strong women.[60] Historians also point to the weakness of classical rites at that time. The limited influence of these restrictive rules opened up more space for female action.[61] Metaphysics also strengthened the position of important women. Tang ideology compared the emperor to heaven and his mother to earth, giving the empress dowager a high place not only in the palace but within the entire cosmos as well.[62] Writers further legitimized powerful women by documenting female authority in other nations, such as Lady Qiaoguo's rule over a kingdom in what is now Guangdong.[63] Moreover, thinkers sometimes compared the positions of consort and minister. Earlier writers had often likened these two social roles, as they had analogous relationships with the ruler in some respects. Equating palace women and government officials implicitly sanctioned female authority.[64]

The nature of Tang imperial marriage also fostered female power.[65] In earlier centuries, rulers had often taken consorts from lowly backgrounds to prevent interference from powerful consort kin. In contrast, Tang empresses usually came from important noble families. High birth endowed them with an air of prestige that strengthened their position at court. These privileged ladies had also received a comprehensive education in their youth, so they could read complicated documents and understand the rarified language of politics. At the same time, as the officialdom became more meritocratic, it became possible for men from lower-status families to assume high positions.

In an age obsessed with genealogy, a haughty empress with a grand aristocratic upbringing could browbeat a minister from far more humble origins.

Furthermore, the Tang did not practice primogeniture. Although all of the emperors descended from the dynasty's founder, they had various relationships with their immediate predecessors. Some were a brother or younger son of the previous ruler, so their accession had not been preordained. Ambiguous succession practices allowed empresses dowager to assume a leading role in politics at critical moments, making them powerful figures at court. Of course, not all women who entered the political arena saw their plans succeed. Princess Yongtai (684–701) suffered execution for criticizing a favored courtier of Empress Wu.[66] But emperors often aided and protected ambitious mothers, wives, and sisters. When a military commander accused Empress Liu (d. 693) of trying to overthrow Emperor Ruizong, the ruler sentenced him to death for his temerity.[67]

Unusual events at the onset of this era also bolstered female power. The Sui dynasty may have been short lived, but it pioneered institutions and practices appropriate for the newly reunified state, setting many standards that the Tang continued to uphold. Significantly, Emperor Wen, founder of the Sui, married an unusually capable and willful woman.[68] The father of his wife, Empress Wenxian (544–602), had been a prominent general under the previous dynasty. Although their marriage had been arranged for practical reasons, the couple came from similar backgrounds, had much in common, wed at a young age, and fell deeply in love. Wen trusted his wife and she helped him govern the newly united realm. Whenever the emperor held court, she waited nearby. Wenxian received ongoing reports on the proceedings from a eunuch messenger, who also relayed her opinions on the matters under discussion to her husband.

Although Emperor Wen genuinely loved his wife, she was unusually insecure and felt threatened by potential rivals. When the emperor took concubines, as was customary, Wenxian reacted with rage. She felt so strongly about the matter that she came to hate the institution of concubinage in general. Empress Wenxian's severe jealousy altered the course of the Sui. Her son Yang Yong, the heir apparent, had a concubine who had born him four sons. Another son, Yang Guang, knew how much his mother loathed concubinage and realized that he could harness her wrath to bring down his brother. Guang slandered the crown prince, knowing that the empress disliked him because he favored his concubines. As expected, she supported these false charges. Emperor Wen accordingly deposed Yong as heir and replaced him with Guang, who eventually succeeded to the throne as Emperor Yang.

Sui precedents sparked the ambitions of palace women and accustomed men to accept the involvement of women in politics. Palace ladies maintained a high profile in the early decades of the Tang. Emperor Taizong, the dynasty's second ruler, had an extremely close relationship with his wife Empress Zhangsun (601–636) and gave her a say in important matters.[69] Zhangsun came from a military Xianbei family that had been deeply involved in the tumultuous politics leading up to the reunification of China. The emperor married Zhangsun to guarantee her family's support. As a girl, Zhangsun received an extensive Confucian education that she put to good use as empress. She cultivated a reputation for ethical probity, earning respect for her prudence and modesty. The empress counseled her husband on important matters, and sometimes Taizong heeded her advice. Most dramatically, she successfully pleaded for leniency after her elder brother had been accused of treason, thereby saving him from execution. Taizong's concubine Worthy Consort Xu also tendered useful advice, notably urging him to abandon his invasion of the Goguryeo kingdom of Korea and reduce expenditures on palace luxuries.[70] The judicious advice and mild demeanor of these two women in the early years of the dynasty conditioned the court to accept a high degree of female influence on matters of state.

◦━━◆━━◦

The woman who dominated the succeeding era, Empress Wu Zetian (Wu Zhao, 624–705), stands out as one of the most extraordinary, unusual, controversial, and influential figures in Chinese history.[71] She temporarily supplanted the Tang with a short-lived new dynasty and ruled in her own name as the only female emperor in Chinese history, thereby earning the wrath of generations of male historians. Yet she also implemented innovative policies, some of which endured beyond her reign. The shocking sight of a woman emperor seated on the throne had a lasting impact, influencing Chinese views of womanhood down to the present.

Wu Zetian's family had close ties to the first ruler of the Tang, so they enjoyed wealth and prominence under the dynasty. Trusted by the ruling line as loyal allies, her kinsmen served in high positions. Wu received an extensive education in her youth, as was customary in aristocratic families at the time. Unusually, however, instead of concentrating on the study of poetry and domestic ethics, she undertook a stereotypically masculine curriculum of serious works aimed at ambitious men. As Wu gained power, this practical knowledge proved invaluable. She displayed easy conversance with history, religion, and political ideology, and used this knowledge to her advantage.

At age fourteen Wu Zetian left home for the palace to become a concubine of Emperor Taizong. Although she seems to have had sexual relations with him, they never became close. Instead she had a passionate affair with

Figure 3.1 Illustration of Empress Wu Zetian, published in 1690

Taizong's son, the future Emperor Gaozong. Even though incest taboos strictly prohibited a man from sexual contact with his father's concubine, the smitten Gaozong ignored this injunction. After Taizong's death, Wu Zetian adhered to convention and entered a monastery, becoming a Buddhist nun. However, she saw monastic life as a temporary interlude and plotted her return to the palace. A poem shows her determination to maintain her lover's attentions.[72]

> Watching red turn to green, my thoughts entangled and scattered,
> I am disheveled and torn from my longing for you, my lord.
> If you fail to believe that of late I have constantly shed tears,
> Open the chest and look for the skirt of pomegranate-red.

She did not have to wait long. Soon the new emperor recalled Wu to the palace as a high-ranking concubine. Intelligent, merciless, and ambitious, she easily dominated the weak and sickly ruler. She gathered together a faction of powerful supporters, dethroned the empress, and married Gaozong.[73]

The capable Empress Wu often handled routine administrative matters on her incapable husband's behalf, gradually coming to dominate the government. However, she did not rely on competence alone to secure her ambitions. Wu ruthlessly persecuted anyone who dared to challenge her. Gaozong belatedly realized her cunning and considered replacing her with a more benign empress. Ultimately, however, he lacked the will to defy her.[74] As Wu's powers increased, she brooked no opposition. She even murdered two of her sons, a daughter, and grandchildren.[75] People today might find it unfathomable that a mother would murder her children for political gain, but the Tang had a tradition of filicide, so she acted within the moral framework of the time.[76]

After Gaozong died in 683, a son of Empress Wu ascended the throne as Emperor Zhongzong. However, Wu quickly discovered that she could not bend him to her will, so after just six weeks she deposed him and sent him into exile. Another son replaced him as Emperor Ruizong. This time, Wu confined the titular monarch to the inner palace and acted as de facto ruler. In 690 she finally felt confident enough to depose Ruizong and abolish the Tang dynasty. In its place she initiated a new dynasty called Zhou. Wu Zetian then took the unprecedented step of calling herself emperor (*huangdi*), the only woman in Chinese history ever to hold that title.

In addition to disquiet at the unprecedented sight of a female emperor, many powerful figures opposed her usurpation of the throne and abolition of the Tang, so an air of illegitimacy hung over the court. At first Wu unleashed a reign of terror to cow her opponents. But she did not maintain her position through violence alone. Wu Zetian also strove to carry out her duties in an exemplary manner and proved to be an attentive and capable ruler. Because the high aristocracy opposed her, she promoted talented men from lesser backgrounds who would feel indebted for their unexpected advancement. The sudden influx of competent administrators into government spurred rapid social and political change, an unintended side effect of her machinations.[77] Some people preferred a competent and charismatic female leader to the traditional system dominated by reactionary aristocrats, so Wu gained support from those who yearned for good government.[78]

To overcome her patent illegitimacy, Empress Wu put enormous stress on ideology. Sometimes she employed traditional tools of legitimation, often taking them to unusual lengths.[79] For example, she declared nineteen different reign eras and chose the name of each to publicize her achievements and divine blessings.[80] And to harness the cult of motherhood, she portrayed herself as an ideal mother—even though she had murdered two sons.[81] Her comprehensive legitimation campaign allowed her to wield supreme power within a patriarchal system. Ambitious women of later eras looked back to her example to learn how to bolster their own strength.

Wu promoted religion while directing it to ideological ends. Genuinely pious, she understood the political utility of religion in an age of fervent faith. To garner support, Wu associated herself with figures from various religious traditions.[82] She likened herself to the primordial Dao, the ancient goddess Nü Wa (Nü Gua), and the Queen Mother of the West (Xiwangmu).[83] She also publicized mystical omens to claim supernatural support for her reign.[84] And Empress Wu generously patronized Buddhist art, architecture, and scholarship, cultivating the image of a *chakravartin* (*zhuanlun wang*)— the ideal benevolent Buddhist monarch.[85] She ordered the printing of so many sutras that publishers had to improve printing technology in order to handle the unprecedented demand.[86] Subsequent empresses often copied the ways that Wu Zetian deployed religion to counter Confucian restraints on women.[87]

Initially Wu projected an image of strength. Faced with firm opposition and endless intrigues, she handled matters deftly and knew when to delegate tasks to skilled officials. However, her health declined with age and she increasingly relied on a handful of key advisers, allowing them to accrue power. Given the blatant illegitimacy of her reign, Empress Wu had ruled largely by strength of personality. As she repeatedly suffered long bouts of illness and withdrew into the recesses of the palace, her air of invincibility evaporated and adversaries plotted to depose her. In 705 a cabal restored her son Zhongzong as emperor, revived the Tang dynasty, and demoted Wu back to the rank of empress dowager. She died later that year. Instead of receiving an emperor's burial, her family interred her alongside her spouse Emperor

Gaozong, portraying her not as a formidable monarch but merely as the wife of an orthodox male ruler.[88]

∘━━◆━━∘

The death of Wu Zetian did not mark an end to female power at court.[89] The participation of women in politics had become the norm, and so the trend continued for a time. During the second reign of Emperor Zhongzong, his wife Empress Wei (d. 710), her daughter the Princess Anle (685–710), and Empress Wu's daughter Princess Taiping (d. 713) all surrounded themselves with cliques of powerful officials and participated in affairs of state. After the death of Zhongzong in 710, these factions battled for supremacy, resulting in the deaths of Empress Wei and Princess Anle. Later, when Emperor Xuanzong ascended the throne, Princess Taiping feared for her life and tried to poison him. When this scheme failed, she committed suicide. Her death marked an end to this era of extraordinary female power.

Historians regard the subsequent decades as the highpoint of the Tang, marked by prosperity, cultural effervescence, and confident cosmopolitanism. However, the An Lushan Rebellion of 755 brought this golden age to an abrupt end. Significantly, many people considered a woman partly culpable for the catastrophic uprising, making her one of the most infamous figures in Chinese history. Yang Yuhuan (719–756) came from an important family and was initially betrothed to marry the eighteenth son of Emperor Xuanzong.[90] After she caught the emperor's eye, however, he called off the marriage and she entered a Daoist nunnery. After spending a short time there for the sake of propriety, she then entered the palace as an imperial concubine. Yang is known to history by her title *guifei* ("precious consort").

Yang Guifei seems to have been unusually close to the emperor, and Xuanzong adored her beauty and playfulness. As was customary, the ruler promoted the kinsmen of his favored consort, and he gave her cousin Yang Guozhong a sensitive military post. Fictionalized accounts later blamed the general for much of the ensuing chaos. In fact, Xuanzong himself bore prime responsibility. The emperor made the fatal mistake of empowering the duplicitous military governor An Lushan. Yang Guifei simply followed his lead, engaging An Lushan with lighthearted banter and silly games whenever he visited the palace.

When An Lushan rebelled, the emperor ignominiously fled the capital in terror. His troops sought a scapegoat for this debacle and ended up blaming General Yang Guozhong for their predicament. A mob of soldiers killed the general along with his family and followers. The unruly soldiers then demanded that Emperor Xuanzong have Yang Guifei killed as well. Faced

Figure 3.2 Qing Dynasty Painting of Yang Guifei (Cleveland Museum of Art)

with no alternative, the feeble ruler ordered his beloved consort to be stran-gled.[91] After the rebellion had been crushed and Xuanzong returned to the capital, he lamented the unjust execution of his beloved concubine and had her portrait installed in the palace as a memorial.

Unjustly or not, generations of writers held Yang Guifei partly responsible for the disastrous uprising that almost destroyed the dynasty and brought ter-rible hardship to millions. Although the rebellion had complex causes, writ-ers found that blaming a beautiful woman for the catastrophe made a better story. Under ordinary circumstances Yang Guifei would have been a minor figure, forgotten soon after her death. However, a popular poem written by Bai Juyi (772–846) exaggerated her importance and misrepresented her actions. Later authors followed Bai's lead and wrote numerous fictionalized accounts of her life, and the story of Yang Guifei became increasingly exag-gerated over time.[92] For example, the early ninth-century writer Chen Hong relates her death in realistic terms, then veers off into fantasy to describe how Emperor Xuanzong used Daoist magic to search heaven and hell for her spirit. Tang authors often blithely mixed fact and fantasy to make their works more appealing, and over time the story of Yang Guifei took on mythic proportions. The prejudices of popular fiction spilled over into serious writ-ing as well. Historians exaggerated Yang Guifei's importance and gave her an oversized share of blame for the catastrophe of the An Lushan Rebellion, with her alleged misdeeds steadily increasing.[93] Due to centuries of mischar-acterization, this inconsequential figure ended up taking much of the blame for one of the major catastrophes in Chinese history.

Mounting fury toward Yang Guifei's alleged culpability for the greatest disaster of the Tang sparked a backlash against female influence in govern-ment. This critique widened to condemn Wu Zetian and other powerful ladies of the early Tang as well. Thereafter, no women wielded much political influence for the remainder of the dynasty.[94] Most of the remaining emper-ors did not even dare to formally name an empress. While rulers still chose wives and consorts from families of the officialdom, their partners no longer came from the highest backgrounds. In a society obsessed with genealogy, choosing consorts from modest families effectively limited their influence. Officials at court also kept palace ladies in check by enforcing classical rites that restrained female behavior.[95]

These preventive measures succeeded.[96] Whereas the official histories provide extensive biographies for the early Tang empresses, those from the latter part of the dynasty have short and uninformative entries. Of course, this backlash did not bring an end to female power. During the anarchy of the Five Dynasties era that followed the collapse of Tang, the wives and consorts of resurgent steppe peoples once again influenced powerful men, in line with their native customs.[97] Nevertheless, in the wake of Wu Zetian and Yang Gui-fei, the place of women in the Chinese palace would never be the same. The reaction against female power that began in the mid-eighth century marks a major turning point in the history of China's political institutions. Henceforth, men took a far more critical view of female participation in politics. Song dynasty empresses faced burdensome restrictions, and officials condemned any sign of authority or ambition.[98] Faced with hostility and mistrust, the empresses of subsequent eras tempered their goals. Rather than seeking to wield power outright, they usually sought only to gain approbation by dis-playing virtue and sagacity.

Representations of powerful women changed as well.[99] Male authors demonized the powerful women of the early Tang, seeing them as proof of the danger of female aspirations. This revisionist movement began in litera-ture. Authors wrote alternative biographies of Yang Guifei based on salacious gossip, deliberately blackening her name to titillate readers.[100] The authors of history and fiction also lambasted Wu Zetian for calling herself emperor and usurping the dynasty. Depictions of this controversial female figure evolved over time in conformity with larger literary and cultural trends.[101] During the Tang, literary and historical images of Empress Wu remained roughly con-gruent. But writers of the Song and Yuan dynasties took a far more critical attitude toward Wu Zetian and the Tang in general. They used nationalistic language to criticize her as culturally alien and unorthodox. Ming dynasty writers of sensational novels turned Wu Zetian into a cartoonish erotic char-acter. Overall, Ming fiction portrays her as foolish, incompetent, and sexually depraved. During the Qing dynasty, the quality of writing about Empress Wu rose somewhat. Nevertheless, many writers continued to demonize her, portraying her reign as an unmitigated catastrophe that brought misery to her subjects.

Aside from fictionalized representations of particular women, Tang writ-ers also began to issue blanket warnings against female power. They wrote frequently and forcefully about the dangers posed by ambitious women.[102] Critics often simply declared women a menace to good government. *Old Tang Records* (*Jiu Tangshu*) prefaces the section on empresses' biographies with a long admonition concerning the corrosive influence of palace wom-en.[103] Artists expressed similar views in visual form. Portraits of emperors tended to depict good rulers surrounded by men, while evil ones have female attendants.[104]

Historians often framed their criticism of women within the mandate of heaven ideology. As elaborated by Sima Qian (d. 86 BCE), this historical model contends that a dynasty's first ruler and his consort always display exemplary virtue. Over time, as monarchs become lax and immoral, the tenor of government inevitably declines. Eventually a foolish ruler in concert with a dissolute female accomplice bring down the dynasty. This moralistic vision of the rise and fall of dynasties affected interpretations of the early Tang. Historians praised Empress Dou, wife of the first Tang emperor, for her mild virtues.[105] In contrast, they blamed Yang Guifei for causing the Tang to temporarily lose the mandate of heaven, thereby giving rise to the An Lushan Rebellion.[106]

Thinkers also used the elaborate cosmology underlying portent theory to justify excluding women from governance.[107] Han dynasty scholars had declared that female influence can give rise to natural disasters such as floods, droughts, locusts, earthquakes, plagues, sandstorms, and hail. According to their cosmological theories, an excess of the feminine yin element in the palace will disrupt the balance of the entire cosmos and bring widespread disaster. In sum, they believed that female power directly threatens the natural order. These ideas had a major impact on later dynasties, including the Tang. To stave off catastrophe, Tang officials sometimes demanded that rulers expel excess women from the palace.[108] This sort of misogynistic discourse kept a check on female ambition. Henceforth, palace women rarely had much power. Moreover, ideological constructs intended to restrain the women around the emperor affected popular ideas about womanhood in general, shaping gender relations for centuries to come.

Chapter 4

Wealth

After the restoration of national unity under the Sui, China's economy not only recovered but became more prosperous than ever before. Nevertheless, society remained highly unequal, and the outlook for people of different backgrounds varied immensely. A woman's economic potential dictated many of the basic circumstances of her life. Although Western feminists stress the importance of gender for understanding the past, historians in China tend to put greater emphasis on social class, as it bounded the range of possibilities available to both sexes. A woman was never just a woman. She was also a member of a certain social stratum. A princess, merchant wife, and prostitute may have shared a common gender, but they had very different standards of living. To appreciate the life experiences of different types of medieval women, it is essential to understand the economic positions of each.

Generally speaking, laws and customs regarding property evolve to maintain the prevailing economic and social structure.[1] However, instead of reflecting real behavior, these rules often promote aspirational ideals. The actual practices regarding the ownership and inheritance of property tend to emerge as a compromise between society's objectives and the pragmatic circumstances of real life.[2] The Tang inheritance system regulated three matters: kinship rank, noble title, and property.[3] Kinship ranks and titles followed patrilineal descent, with priority given to the wife's eldest son. Male noble titles often included income from the fiscal unit called a "food benefice" (*shiyi*). Usually the eldest son inherited the benefice along with his father's title. If a man had no sons, his widow would not inherit the title, but she would receive income from the food benefice for the rest of her life.[4]

Tangible assets had far more complex inheritance regulations. Scholars still debate the ideology that shaped historic Chinese property rights. Some believe that all household members owned family property in common, while others hold that key assets belonged to individuals and passed down the male line.[5] Moreover, people also held somewhat contradictory attitudes toward the relation between women and family property. While they considered daughters to be family members, they did not see females as true progeny for the purposes of reckoning the line of descent.[6] Given the priorities of this patrilineal kinship system, it was considered proper, and even imperative, to curtail the inheritance rights of daughters.

According to both law and tradition, an elder (*jiazhang*), usually the oldest male in the household, headed the family and exercised immense power over the control and disposal of collective assets.[7] The elder had many other responsibilities as well: protecting the family, educating children, conducting rituals, and making key decisions. This institution gave husbands immense power over their wives and daughters. When the family elder was away from home, in theory the eldest son would temporarily assume his powers. The law prohibited children from usurping the rights of the family head. As long as one of the parents remained alive, it was illegal for sons and grandsons to divide up family property and set up separate households, as this would violate the dictates of filial piety.

Family heads were usually male.[8] If a family consisted of only a mother and one or more sons, the eldest boy officially served as head of the family, not his mother. Only if there were no surviving men could a woman head the family, and even then she would probably not be called an elder. Even though the elder supposedly controlled collective wealth, actual circumstances tended toward pragmatism. Although a young boy might nominally serve as family head, he would not be not capable of carrying out his duties, so his mother exercised stewardship. Because the law guaranteed a mother's authority over her sons, sometimes a woman would file a lawsuit to force a refractory offspring to obey her, particularly if she were a widow.[9]

In spite of the principle that only a man could manage family matters, documents recovered from Turpan in far west China use the term "big woman" (or "great woman," *danü*) to identify an adult woman who headed up a household. Transmitted historical accounts lack this expression, but these contemporary documents confirm that a woman could in fact lead a household.[10] A "big woman" was an adult woman who managed the resources of a household that lacked male members. Even in a family without men, a woman could not officially serve as a family elder. However, a big woman had a similar status and powers. Due to chaotic conditions on the frontier, Turpan had a large number of broken families, so big women were not uncommon there. A wife could also temporarily serve as a big woman when her husband was away performing military service or corvée duty.

While adult men usually managed the family's land, they sometimes allowed women to oversee movable property.[11] A wife might have responsibility for money and valuables kept locked in chests. Because she handled routine purchases, she needed petty cash to pay for daily household expenses. However, she could not freely dispose of these assets. The family elder had ultimate authority over this wealth.

During a wedding, two families exchanged a significant amount of property. When family elders agreed on the terms of the engagement, the groom's side presented betrothal gifts to the bride's parents, as dictated by the ancient rites. The payment of bridewealth had great ritual significance, as it distinguished wife from concubine. The relative status of the two families influenced the value of the betrothal gift. As during the earlier era of division, an obsession with genealogy drove the elite to marry with the highest possible counterparts.[12] Elite families sought to ally themselves with in-laws who displayed prestigious cultural capital or seemed destined for success, and some were willing to pay out a large betrothal gift to ensure a prestigious match. Lesser families imitated their example, and so-called financial marriages were commonplace.[13] The greatest families usually demanded enormous betrothal gifts for the privilege of marrying one of their daughters.[14]

Lavish bridewealth caused problems. Some people compared marrying off a daughter to selling merchandise, and critics condemned this overtly mercenary attitude as unseemly.[15] Moreover, the cost of marriage presented the parents of sons with a considerable burden. And men of humble means sometimes lacked money for a decent betrothal gift, so they could not afford to marry. The government periodically tried to limit the value of betrothal gifts, but these efforts failed. To help remedy the situation, an edict of 627 ordered local governments to provide a basic betrothal gift for unmarried men aged twenty or older to allow the poor to wed.[16]

Although men normally controlled a family's collective wealth, women could still own private assets. When a daughter left home to wed, she received a trousseau and, if the family's financial situation permitted, a dowry. While the betrothal gift went to the bride's parents, a wife owned her dowry. This custom guaranteed a woman's right to own property. Anthropologists debate the significance of dowry. While some regard it as a form of female inheritance, others see it as an excuse for disinheriting women.[17] During the Tang, the value of dowry varied enormously, depending on the means and inclinations of the bride's family and the respective social standing of the bride and groom.[18] Poor women received only a pittance, as this was all that their family could afford. In contrast, some wealthy people dowered their daughters generously and sent them away with money, carriages, and slaves.

Although bridewealth still outweighed dowry, the value of dowry was increasing. Both Tang law and documents from Dunhuang show that a woman's dowry was often half the value of the betrothal gifts presented during her brothers' weddings.[19] In later eras people calculated the value of dowry as a proportion of the amount to be inherited by her brothers, but during the Tang it was still linked to the betrothal gift.[20] So even though dowries increased in value during the Tang, they remained smaller than those in subsequent eras. The growing importance of dowry may have caused the age of marriage to rise, as the families of some brides needed time to accumulate a proper dowry. Some poor women found it difficult to marry at all.[21]

Although custom held that family members owned major assets in common, dowry presented a notable exception. The law specified that dowry belonged to the wife and protected her ownership of these private assets.[22] A woman who used her dowry to help support her husband or family stood out as exceptionally virtuous, as neither law nor custom required her to use her own wealth to support others.[23] Nevertheless, the deeply rooted idea that husband and wife constitute a single social unit challenged the financial independence of wives, and husbands sometimes had a say in the use of dowries.[24] A revealing vignette shows that some husbands considered it proper for a man to control his wife's dowry. One poor man in need of cash wanted to sell the clothes that his wife had brought as her trousseau, but she refused. When he eventually rose to become a prosperous official, he resented her selfishness and divorced her.[25]

Female property rights depended on a woman's particular relationship with her family, so they varied over the course of her life. Overall, women had restricted inheritance rights compared to men.[26] Kinship principles required that property be transmitted down the male line of descent. Because a woman left her father's family, she did not receive an equal share of inheritance, as this would disperse family wealth to outsiders.[27] According to the *Tang Code*, upon a father's death, his sons divided the family property equally. However, an unmarried daughter received a share equal to half that paid out for her brothers' betrothal gifts as her future dowry. Another way of calculating this amount held that an unmarried daughter should receive a one-third share and sons a two-thirds share of the estate. People assumed that women severed financial ties with their natal family upon marriage, so married women normally did not inherit from their parents.

In imperial China, families used two main methods for apportioning collective property. After the death of both parents, their children divided up the family assets. Unless there were unmarried sisters in the household, brothers apportioned the estate among themselves. If a family lacked male heirs, authorities declared it "extinct" (*hujue*). In such a case, daughters or more distant agnatic relatives would inherit the estate.[28] In the early Tang, unmarried daughters would inherit all the assets of an extinct household. If all daughters had married, however, their father's relatives would divide up the estate.[29] A fiscal reform of 780 had an unintended impact on female inheritance rights.[30] Prior to that date, only men paid taxes, so it was in the interest of the state to limit property holdings to men. But after this reform, women could also be taxed. This change made the government much amenable to allowing women to inherit property. Accordingly, an edict of 836 proclaimed that if the only surviving heirs of an extinct household were married daughters, they should inherit some of the natal property, thereby increasing female inheritance rights. The actual situation might not have been simple, however, as some large households included several married men.[31] Daughters without brothers might not inherit family property in this sort of complex household. The girl's uncles would likely inherit most of the property and unmarried daughters would receive a portion of the estate for their dowry.

When a man died, his sons divided up most of the family property and set aside sufficient funds for the dowries of any unmarried daughters. A widow with sons inherited nothing. But given the age of marriage and life expectancy for men, a widow's sons were often still minors when their father died. Unless the deceased man's parents were still alive, his widow would have to manage the estate until her sons came of age. And even if adult sons gained control of family property upon the death of their father, they could not divide up the estate immediately. Tang law forbade the division of a property among sons if either parent remained alive.[32] So as long as the widow lived, her sons could not split up the family estate among themselves. They had to manage it collectively until her death.

If a couple had no sons, the widow gained control of her deceased husband's estate.[33] However, unlike ordinary inheritance, her control of this property was conditional. She assumed the role of custodian of her deceased husband's estate, not its owner. She could not liquidate major assets, and it would revert to her husband's kinsmen after her death. If she remarried, she could not take this property with her into her new union. Instead her husband's male relations would divide it among themselves upon her remarriage.

A "big woman" had considerable authority over family assets, comparable to that of a family elder.[34] Sometimes she had to pay tax on behalf of the household. Women also sometimes acted as guarantors for men taking out loans, and they promised to repay the debt in case of default. This arrangement implies that if a man took out a loan and died or became incapacitated, the female guarantor would take control of the family's property. Documents also show that women could enter into contracts involving family assets, including the rental and sale of land. However, the women with the most control over household assets often faced dire financial circumstances. They usually presided over broken households. Because the family lacked a productive adult man, a woman had no choice but to assume responsibility. Although many records describe women taking out loans, none record a woman lending money to others. And numerous documents record women borrowing money or pawning goods on behalf of their households, attesting to their poverty.

Medieval women did various kinds of work. By the High Tang, although the economy had recovered from the widespread destitution that plagued the previous age of disunion, the commercial economy remained relatively small compared to later eras, providing few opportunities for women to work outside the home. Most tasks were associated with one sex or the other, although women sometimes performed stereotypical male jobs. Most importantly, people expected women to take care of household matters—cooking, cleaning, and other necessary domestic chores. Men considered marriage a necessity because they needed a wife to keep their house in order. In one case, a man married soon after his mother died simply because he needed a woman to do housework.[35]

At the apex of society, a small number of women did no work. Instead they devoted themselves to consumption. Women of means spent freely, and their purchases had immense impact on the economy, driving production and supporting specialized jobs.[36] Poetry details the luxurious lifestyle of elite women, particularly in the capital. Chang'an was the largest and wealthiest city in the world at the time, making it synonymous with extravagance. Poets conventionally associated luxury goods with women, as they were the most active consumers of clothing, ornaments, and cosmetics. Trade with Central Asia and other distant regions provided a steady supply of foreign goods, and wealthy women eagerly purchased exotic foods, spices, fragrances, garments, and musical instruments. While elite men often devoted themselves to practical matters, their female counterparts filled their days with entertainments, religious events, outings, feasts, games, and other pleasurable pastimes. Their opulent lifestyle made them far more active consumers than ordinary people, who could afford to purchase only bare necessities.

Although popular accounts depict the Tang as an age of prosperity and extravagance, in fact most people lived not far above the subsistence level. As a result, poets made poverty a major literary topos. In particular, they lamented the plight of poor women.[37] The female characters in these poems had fallen into destitution because they lacked economic support from a man. Poets detailed the plight of destitute widows, abandoned wives, and women married to soldiers and other absent men. According to these depictions, a solitary woman suffered terribly, and she had to work very hard just to survive. A ninth-century poem by Zhang Yaotiao cries out at the plight of a woman living in a society impoverished by incessant warfare.[38]

> Yesterday, I sold
>   a blouse, a skirt.
> Today, another blouse,
>   another skirt.
> All my blouses, all
>   my skirts, are sold.
> Ashamed, I steal
>   a glance at my dowry chest.
> With things to sell,
>   I still held off
>   these griefs.
> Now, in nothing
>   flat, my heart's
>   come round to pain

The women in these poems blame the unfairness and corruption of their society for their predicaments.

Some poems describe the plight of poor women unable to marry. Literary critics traditionally held that impoverished literati composed these works to express frustration with their own downward mobility. Documents from Dunhuang and Turpan show that some women did in fact remain unmarried. Families with daughters expected potential grooms to present them with a betrothal gift, making it difficult for people at the bottom of society to wed. And the obsession with genealogy made it harder for women to marry someone from a different background. As a result, some women found themselves locked out of marriage. Because the family constituted society's fundamental unit of production, women who were unable to marry found themselves relegated to the economic margins.

The relation of women to the land underwent a fundamental change at this time. Centuries earlier, amid the war and confusion that followed the collapse of the Eastern Han, peasants had abandoned a great deal of fertile farmland. To encourage the cultivation of deserted fields, successive governments instituted the equal field (*juntian*) system that allocated land to both men and women for them to till.[39] This institution brought women into the heart of agricultural production, and poetry describes them doing every sort of farm work.[40]

The Sui modified the equal field system, centering it on families rather than individuals.[41] As China's economy recovered, however, the government no longer considered female participation in agriculture a necessity. Moreover, due to population growth, in many places there may not have been enough land to distribute to both sexes. Under the new land system, the male head of household took responsibility for tax payments and corvée labor, strengthening the patriarchal family at the expense of female economic autonomy. Unmarried women no longer received land allocations. In light of the reduced productive capacity of women, the government exempted them from direct taxation, although women still produced the cloth that their families used to make tax payments. The Tang maintained a similar arrangement. Men received almost all allocated land.[42] Widows and unmarried daughters were the only women eligible for land allotments. However, these women received smaller fields than men, and they could only obtain them after all eligible men had received land.

Since antiquity, people considered textile production to be normative female labor. Tang literature describes women spinning, weaving, sewing clothes, and making cloth shoes.[43] Thinkers had long valorized these activities by declaring this sort of work to be a way for women to actualize their virtue and make it visible. Inspired by Zhou and Han dynasty stories of rulers' wives who did textile work simply to prove their commitment to virtue, even medieval empresses sometimes made cloth.[44] Yet in spite of these lofty associations, Tang poets writing about ordinary women usually did not romanticize textile work. They described peasant women working very hard all day, keeping house, laboring in the fields, and raising silkworms. Then in the evenings, they wove by lamplight in spite of their exhaustion. These poets wanted the reader to empathize with rural women who toiled from morning to night.

Cloth was a valuable commodity that could readily be sold or bartered, so a woman could potentially earn a living by making textiles. A typical biography of a chaste widow describes her supporting herself and two sons by spinning thread.[45] The money she earned not only allowed her to raise her children but also paid for the funerals of her husbands and other relatives. The emphasis on funeral expenses evokes the ancient associations of cloth making with morality. The author praised this widow's industriousness because she directed her work toward good ends. Ideally, a woman did not make money in pursuit of profit, but only to raise her sons and uphold the ritual order. The intimate familiarity of women with the mechanics of textile production could have practical benefits. A Madame Liu invented a new technique for dyeing and printing cloth using wooden blocks.[46] An educated woman from a good family, she made cloth due to its associations with female integrity. As she became involved in this task, she applied her creativity to move textile technology forward.

Although women traditionally confined themselves to domestic labor, economic growth gradually gave rise to a more complex economy, providing some women with opportunities to work outside the home. Merchant households developed a lifestyle centered on commerce, and wives sometimes participated in the family business. In earlier eras, writers rarely mentioned merchant women. During the Tang, however, the wives of merchants became extremely visible and poets described their unique lifestyle in detail.[47] Poetry about merchant wives grew out of early medieval boudoir poetry that described a lonely woman separated from her distant lover. Most merchants traveled exten-

Figure 4.1 Buddhist Donors

sively to conduct business. Some of these women traveled together with their husbands, but most remained at home, so a couple could be separated for long intervals. Poetry describes the merchant wife managing the household as best she can during her husband's frequent absences. She struggles to cope with practical matters and suffers from intense loneliness and jealousy. The unhappy women in these poems often seek consolation in music, poetry, and religion.

Ambitious women took advantage of whatever opportunities they had at hand. Although rural women had few chances to work outside the home, city dwellers had better prospects. Women usually worked in service industries as matchmakers, fortune-tellers, shamans, and maids. And women living near small rivers earned money by ferrying people across the water on rafts and simple boats.[48] When women engaged in commerce, they usually had little capital and could not travel far to procure items to sell, so most did small-scale peddling.[49] Those with more means could open a shop, buying goods wholesale and selling them retail. Some women sold items that they had produced, such as vegetables, flowers, and tea. They also made garments and brewed alcohol for sale. Women often sold food and beverages, and the most successful might open a restaurant. Sogdian women opened bars where they performed Central Asian music and dance, and poets portray these establishments as festive places.[50] The beauty and exotic culture of these women left a lasting impression on their patrons, affecting Chinese aesthetics.

Women served as the primary healers and caregivers in their families, taking care of sick children and parents-in-law. In consequence, they learned how to concoct medicines and undertake other treatments. Women acquired medical knowledge informally via family lore, practical experience, and discussions with their peers. The most skilled healers offered medical services to others in exchange for payment.[51] Also, shamans performed ceremonies to cure the sick. And Buddhist nuns engaged in healing, although the government outlawed this practice in the seventh century. Female physicians used a variety of treatments. Some practiced shamanistic healing, using prayers and charms to relieve illness. Others used more orthodox remedies, such as herbal medicine and massage. Most frequently, female healers specialized in gynecological and fertility problems and served as midwives. Yet in spite of women's practical experience with medical treatments, male physicians belittled the skill of female competitors.[52] Men looked down on female healers as untrained and potentially dangerous. In addition, people commonly considered the female body inherently polluted due to periodic menstrual discharge, and male physicians worried that this pollution would render the medicines decocted by women ineffective or even injurious.

During the Tang, female entertainers become increasingly numerous and visible. As before, many entertainers offered sexual services, so the distinction between performer and prostitute was often ambiguous. In earlier eras, skilled entertainers had been slaves and servants of the wealthy, and they gave private performances in palaces and mansions. But by the Tang, increasing prosperity and the commoditization of labor made it common for entertainers to work in bars, restaurants, and brothels.[53] Most performers were female. Although they held a lowly place in society, widespread economic hardship nevertheless ensured that a steady stream of attractive young women would take this path in life. They sang, danced, and even performed acrobatics for paying audiences.

Customers distinguished various grades of female entertainers and sex workers.[54] Ordinary prostitutes with no special skills were called *chang*. In contrast, *ji* had received training in music, dance, and poetry, so they could provide men with amusement and companionship.[55] There were several types of *ji*.[56] Court entertainers sang and danced for the ruler, high officials, and palace ladies.[57] They usually performed on a stage and remained separated from their audience. Other official entertainers performed for government ministers and soldiers. Government functionaries provided these women with food and clothing and managed their training and performances. And as before, wealthy men kept entertainers on their staff, a form of conspicuous consumption that people interpreted as a sign of wealth and status.[58] Private household entertainers residing in a wealthy household held a lowly status somewhere between concubine and servant.

Men had contradictory attitudes toward prostitutes and entertainers. Literature shows that a man might treat an enemy's wife as a courtesan to disgrace her husband.[59] But society had very different expectations for wives and entertainers, so even though men valued the honor of their wives, they did not mind fraternizing with lowly entertainers. When the famed Li Bai declared himself a recluse and sought to distance himself from the mundane world, he even brought along a prostitute for company.[60] Li knew that others would consider his behavior contradictory—withdrawing from society to show his moral superiority while sharing his reclusion with a woman who embodied sensuality. Yet he considered himself so spiritually disciplined that he could achieve the moral benefits of reclusion even while indulging in carnal pleasures.

The most accomplished performers underwent intensive training that allowed them to become highly skilled courtesans. Although a courtesan sometimes had sex with a client, these women primarily served as entertainers and companions. In Chang'an, many women worked in a red-light district called the Northern Quarters (Beili), where unmarried madams managed numerous entertainment establishments.[61] The finest courtesan houses were spacious and attractive buildings that had large rooms for banquets and performances, as well as smaller areas for women to entertain customers individually or in small groups. Most of the female residents had been sold to a madam in childhood, and they led difficult lives.[62] Aspiring courtesans followed a comprehensive training regimen, and those who did not live up to the expected standard would be brutally beaten. When a woman finally became proficient in music and dance, she began to entertain clients and might also be expected to have sex with them. Yet in spite of the tawdry environment, clients adored these women and praised them as paragons of beauty, elegance, and talent.

Courtesans became increasingly visible through the course of the dynasty. In the early Tang, men wrote relatively few poems about entertainers. These women became prominent in men's poetry starting in the middle of the dynasty.[63] The ways that poets portrayed entertainers changed considerably over time.[64] Initially poets described these women from a distance, usually after seeing them sing or dance at a banquet. Audience members had no chance to become acquainted with the performers, so early Tang poems focused on their appearance.

After the An Lushan Rebellion, many men sought to escape from the terrible problems of their shattered society and turned to amusements in search of distraction and consolation. Poets portrayed entertainers as not just gorgeous but almost divine.[65] This religious imagery shows that men immersed themselves in the world of entertainers to transcend unpleasant reality. As the two sides drew closer, elite men and female performers sometimes developed an emotional bond, and poetry began to focus on how men felt toward these women. Literary portrayals of courtesans changed yet again during the late Tang, when a *fin de siècle* atmosphere evoked a sense of widespread hopelessness. In reaction, many elite men cast off ambition and devoted themselves to music, drink, and carnal pleasures. Poetry reflected their decadent mood, and writing about courtesans became much more sexually explicit.[66]

The popular "Tale of Li Wa" exemplifies the erotic portrayal of female entertainers at the end of the dynasty.[67] This story describes how a cynical courtesan named Li Wa and her madam trick a naïve student into falling in love and squandering all of his money on sensual pastimes. After convincing him to spend all of his money on her, Li Wa callously abandons him. Reduced to penury, he falls to the bottom of society and works as a professional mourner just to survive. When his father discovers this shameful behavior, he disowns his wayward son, furiously beats him, and leaves him for dead. The injured young man is then reduced to begging. Unexpectedly, however, he then earns the courtesan's true love. Afterward he studies hard and manages to pass the civil service examination, obtaining an official position and regaining his father's respect. Although the courtesan Li Wa eventually expresses sincere love, overall

Figure 4.2 Musicians

the narrative portrays her very negatively. This tale depicts the courtesan as sensual, shrewd, unsentimental, and amoral.

While men writing about female entertainers usually focused on the women themselves, in fact one of the main goals of courtesan culture was to create a congenial setting where men could come together and build useful friendships. Bai Juyi addressed a poem to a friend in which he recalled the happy times they shared together in the company of female entertainers. In this poem, Bai does not express any feelings toward the women who had been present at these gatherings. With the passage of time, they no longer seem meaningful. He remembers them only for bringing him closer to a valued friend who shared the entertainments. The poem ends with the two men staying up all night reminiscing. "We talk until first morning light, in happiness, then in tears—those looking on laugh at us, but we two grieve for one another."[68] Men may have enjoyed the time they spent with amusing women, but in the end their relationships with other men remained paramount.

Because courtesans interacted with the cultural elite, they had an impact on the development of literature and aesthetics. Men appreciated the poetry of courtesans for its directness, which contrasted with the oblique politesse favored by erudite male authors.[69] For example, the famed courtesan Zhao Luanluan wrote an explicit tribute to the female nipple.[70]

> A whiff of powder, damp with sweat,
>   rare jade tuning-pegs;
> Aroused by spring, they glisten, gleam,
>   sleek as silkfloss-rains.
> When, fresh from the bath, her sweet-scent man
>   teases with a touch,
> Those magical buds feel shivery wet—
>   those dusky-purple grapes!

This sort of poem could not be more different from the cautious verses produced by self-important men. But instead of dismissing courtesan poetry as crude, men enjoyed the accessibility, emotionalism, and playfulness. The poems of courtesans presented a refreshing alternative to the serious literature of the masculine mainstream, and male critics sometimes praised these women for their talent. By fostering unlikely interactions of people from different ends of the social spectrum, courtesan culture allowed women from lowly backgrounds to affect the development of literature in the Tang dynasty, the golden age of Chinese poetry.

Chapter 5

Religion

In the second century, as the Han dynasty faltered, fundamental secular institutions fell into disarray. In response, many people turned to religion in search of meaning, solace, and practical support. War, chaos, and impoverishment marred the subsequent centuries of the early medieval era, yet it also stands out as a time of fervent faith. Disillusioned by the mundane world, many people devoted themselves to religious pursuits, seeking wisdom and transcendence. During the Sui and Tang eras, religion remained a powerful force in many people's lives. Women were particularly enthusiastic.

This trend favored the interests of women, as they could achieve significant roles in the religious sphere. History has few hard and fast rules, but one pattern stands out. Generally speaking, the more formalized and systematic an organization became, the most likely that men would dominate it. Many religious practices were casual and open to all participants, so ambitious women often directed their talents toward spiritual pursuits. With men monopolizing important secular roles, religion allowed women autonomy and creative space. Given the importance of religion to women's lives, these beliefs and practices had a major impact on female behavior and ideas about womanhood.

The freewheeling realm of popular religion appealed strongly to women, particularly those at the lower levels of society, as it welcomed their participation. Myths constituted the basis for many popular beliefs. Some ancient myths about female figures continued to attract believers during the Tang, affecting views about the fundamental nature of the feminine.[1] The ancient creator goddess Nü Wa (Nü Gua) had a prominent place in medieval poetry and prose. Writers transformed her from a distant religious figure into an engaging literary image. Making Nü Wa's story into polished literature gave

71

her cult even wider appeal.[2] The ancient moon goddess Chang E also became extremely popular.[3] According to tradition, Chang E stole the elixir of immortality from her husband and suffered exile to the moon as punishment. During the Tang, she often featured in art and literature. For example, numerous bronze and silver Tang mirrors have an image of Chang E on the backside. People seem to have considered metal mirrors evocative of the moon goddess, as both were yin, feminine, passive, and cold.

The pious worshipped many other goddesses as well. Some of these deities had ancient roots. Virtually every body of water in China had a local goddess associated with it, and many aquatic cults had a long history.[4] Other goddesses had become the focus of devotion more recently. Purple Maiden (Zi Gu), a goddess associated with toilets and sericulture, only emerged in the early medieval era.[5] Other deities had foreign origins. The goddess Doumu emerged as the Chinese equivalent of the Indian deity Marīci, a tempest demon. People worshipped her to implore for prosperity, good health, painless childbirth, fertility, and safety for children.[6] Some deities had a regional following. Pious worshippers in Shanxi enthusiastically venerated the Sage Mother (*Shengmu*) and constructed numerous temples in her honor.[7] As ideas about the Sage Mother developed, she assimilated aspects of other female deities, so she ended up with many identities, dimensions, and manifestations. Worshippers venerated her as a powerful maternal goddess who also had a hand in flood control.

Women continued to serve as shamans, a religious role that dates back to the beginnings of civilization.[8] During the Tang, women still conducted rituals in sacred mulberry groves, one of the earliest recorded religious practices.[9] Female shamans venerated a wide range of nature deities, such as the gods of mountains and rivers, thereby keeping alive an ancient substrate of Chinese religion. Because women worshipped nature deities so enthusiastically, many of these gods took on a female identity.[10] Attitudes toward shamanism hardened over the centuries, and the elite increasingly associated it with unorthodox beliefs and licentiousness. Nevertheless, the Sui government kept some shamans on the government payroll.[11] Although shamans lacked formal standing under the Tang, officials sometimes ordered them to conduct ceremonies to bless the realm.[12] More commonly, shamanesses practiced magic and conducted sacrifices that appealed to the sensibilities of ordinary people. They employed a variety of props in these rites, ranging from winnowing baskets to menstrual fluid. Because so many shamans were women, some rites focused on female concerns such as fertility, contraception, safe pregnancy and delivery, lactation, and the protection of children.[13] Female diviners also used a variety of techniques to foretell the future.[14] Although most shamanistic practices were beneficent, some were intended to harm enemies. Both sexes employed black magic, curses, and demon worship. This sort of heterodox lore passed down within families along the maternal line.[15]

⚬══╪══⚬

Religious Daoism reached a pinnacle of popularity and influence at this time. The political situation favored Daoism, as Tang emperors showed far less enthusiasm for Buddhism than their predecessors. In the mid-ninth century the government aggressively persecuted Buddhism, sending the religion into decline.[16] In contrast, many of the dynasty's rulers, Xuanzong in particular, enthusiastically patronized Daoism. Political expediency helps explain the turn toward Daoism among the ruling elite. The Tang imperial clan, embarrassed by their modest origins, fabricated a lineage that connected them to the mysterious ancient sage Laozi. This alleged hereditary connection allowed the emperors to unite the imperial clan's ancestor worship with state religion by patronizing Daoism. As a result, the government gave Daoist clerics official precedence over their Buddhist counterparts.[17] Although not all rulers preferred Daoism, the government tended to favor Daoism over Buddhism, affecting the relative influence of these two faiths during the Tang.

The official precedence of Daoism had a clear impact on ideas about gender. Descriptions of female deities in Daoist scriptures influenced views of ideal womanhood. Because the Dao operates as a generative force that creates all things, it seemed akin to a metaphysical mother. Female imagery has a prominent place in religious Daoism, as believers emphasized cultivation of the yin element as a corrective for the general dominance of yang.[18] Daoism thus offered women spiritual sustenance and welcomed their active participation.

Daoism absorbed many aspects of popular religion, including goddess worship, making it even more appealing to female believers. The moon goddess Chang E became integrated into the Daoist pantheon. Believers respected Chang E for her ability to decoct elixirs of immortality.[19] The Mysterious Woman of the Nine Heavens (Jiutian Xuannü) underwent similar appropriation. Originally she was a Han dynasty goddess of war, sex, and immortality, but medieval Daoists modified her attributes to suit their own ends.[20] In her new incarnation, the Mysterious Woman became a link in the transmission of sacred wisdom from the highest Daoist deities down to the first human adept, the Yellow Thearch (Huang Di).

The Queen Mother of the West (Xiwangmu), another deity with ancient roots, became the most important Daoist goddess of the time. Daoists reinterpreted her powers and personality to make her a focal point of their devotion.[21] They believed that a large number of Jade Maidens (Yu Nü) waited on the

Figure 5.1 Female Daoist Immortal Riding a Bird (Cleveland Museum of Art)

Queen Mother.[22] These beautiful attendants served peaches of immortality at feasts, entertained her guests with music and dances, and conveyed messages and sacred texts down to humanity. Jade Maidens served as role models for courtesans and performers, while female and male adepts emulated the Queen Mother herself. Xiwangmu exemplifies the complex interrelations between divine and mundane aspects of femininity. The Queen Mother did not represent ordinary womanhood. Instead she embodied alluring alternatives to quotidian existence, thereby legitimizing female creativity and independence.

Daoists believed that a person who devoutly performed spiritual exercises could transcend their innate humanity and become an immortal with godlike powers. Both sexes could attain this perfected status, and many popular stories described female immortals.[23] During the Han dynasty, believers envisioned immortals as lofty and remote and assumed that they had little contact with the earthly realm. But secularized Tang narratives made immortals seem far more human, and they frequently interacted with ordinary people. The female immortals in these stories resemble stereotypical mortal women in many respects, exhibiting both strong desires and frailties. Many authors described emotional or sexual encounters between a female immortal and mortal man, using these interactions to explore the personalities and feelings of the characters involved.

Humans may have envied female immortals, yet Tang writers often depicted them as lonely. In many stories, an immortal descends to the mortal realm in search of excitement, as meeting ordinary humans allowed her a respite from splendid isolation in the heavens. However, when immortals participated in the mundane realm, they had to confront unfamiliar codes of conduct. Conventional ethics restrained mortal women in fundamental ways, and immortals were unaccustomed to these sorts of restrictions. As a result, literature often described them behaving in ways that ran contrary to propriety. The immortal's deviant conduct would shock her human lover, often a student. But instead of recoiling, he would revel in the novelty of female authenticity. Furthermore, a man could receive tangible benefits from a liaison with an immortal. She could grant him longevity, high status, and immense wealth. Male readers surely felt unsettled by the idea of a powerful woman serving as a man's patron. For this reason, authors made sure to depict female immortals as psychologically vulnerable, thus projecting standard views of femininity onto the supernatural.[24] The emotional frailty of female immortals made them seem approachable, so they could serve as fantasy material for men in spite of their superior powers.

Women turned to Daoism for different reasons, depending on their situation and temperament.[25] Some grew up in pious families and imbibed the tenets of the religion in their youth. Others married a Daoist husband and adopted their spouse's beliefs. According to epitaphs, sometimes two spouses felt equally committed to their shared religion. The government also encouraged Daoist practice, so when Buddhism came under persecution, Daoism represented a safe alternative for those inclined toward spirituality. As a result, believers often fused the two religions together, adding Buddhist elements to their Daoist practice.

Women frequently turned to Daoism to overcome particular challenges. Many became active in the religion after the death of a spouse. Their faith provided solace and also served as the foundation of an independent social identity. The poor and lowly saw clerical life as a path toward upward mobility. Sometimes sickly women practiced Daoism in the hope that spiritual practices and alchemy might cure them. Daoist teachings also held out the prospect of longevity and even immortality.

Daoist beliefs also addressed women's psychological needs. Most importantly, the ideal of "free and easy wandering" offered a liberating alternative to restrictive social conventions. Expansive Daoist notions presented an alluring alternative to Confucianism, the classical rites, and a lay world dominated by patriarchal ideas and institutions.[26] Women wrote Daoist-inspired poetry criticizing attachment to ordinary matters and reminding readers of the transitory nature of life. The profound metaphysics of Daoism provided them with considerable material for rumination.

An acceptance of worldliness and sensuality also made the Daoist path far less demanding than Buddhism, which was very austere in comparison. Aristocratic ladies could lead a devout Daoist lifestyle while continuing to indulge in luxuries. Clerics were allowed to wear beautiful clothes, live in grand surroundings, and even engage in romantic liaisons. This atmosphere of openness attracted widows, courtesans, and prostitutes to the faith. Even so, most believers took the religion very seriously, upheld spiritual discipline, and distanced themselves from the lay world to some degree. Epitaphs of Daoist laywomen emphasize their sincere piety and boast of their religious accomplishments.[27]

Daoism offered women a wide variety of opportunities for religious cultivation. Most believers remained in the mundane world while conducting sacred practices.[28] They could study, memorize, and chant Daoist scriptures. Devotees meditated, worshipped deities, and conducted rituals. Many practiced breath control techniques and regulated their diet, forgoing grain or eating only wild foods. Literary accounts of Daoist women stress the importance of proper dietary regimen to spiritual advancement. Those with sufficient funds could engage in alchemy, compounding and ingesting the materials believed to foster longevity and imbue the practitioner with superhuman powers. Exotic alchemical materials were costly, however, so usually only the wealthy could afford to pursue this path.

The most serious believers might delve into esoteric mysteries. Female devotees put themselves in trances and imagined visualizations that allowed them to travel on ecstatic mental journeys through the cosmos. Men could also go into a trance and then ingest plasmas of the sun and moon delivered from the mouth of a Jade Maiden.[29] She would then become his spiritual wife and visit him whenever he fell into a trance. Although this sort of practice was mostly associated with men, some women undertook comparable spiritual exercises.

Although men and women mostly engaged in similar Daoist practices, there was one major difference. For men, renunciation of wealth and worldly power constituted the greatest possible sacrifice they could make for the sake of religion. But because women usually lacked these advantages, their disavowal of mundane life took other forms. Instead of emphasizing external bonds, they often manipulated their bodies to express religious commitment.[30] Chinese thinkers traditionally regarded the body as the site of both thought and action, so pious women often emphasized physical regimens as the path to transcendence.

Some Daoist texts discuss sexual techniques.[31] However, the religion never emphasized these practices, and believers approached them with caution. Even so, a willing woman could pair with a male believer and engage in specific sex acts to achieve spiritual and physical transformations. She could undertake this sort of religious practice on her own initiative, under the supervision of a master, or as part of a group of lay believers.

Daoists believed that intense spiritual refinement could ultimately bring about a miraculous metamorphosis, with the successful adept gaining magical powers.[32] She might be able to walk through water without getting wet, feel no cold in winter, sit in a fire without being burned, move large objects with her mind, make things change size, and so on. Most importantly, the perfected Daoist did not die. At the end of her life, she rose up to assume a place in one of the heavenly realms. The degree of a woman's spiritual attainment determined how far she would ascend. The most accomplished could enter the heavens while still alive, perhaps rising into the air before an astonished crowd. Lesser female saints appeared to die and leave a body behind to be buried when in fact their spirits ascended to the heavens. The lowest form of transformation consisted of a woman who appeared to die but in fact traveled to a spiritual realm, where she lived in a holy grotto and served as an official in the Daoist bureaucracy. She would remain there until the end of the current phase of the world cycle, at which time she would finally take her place in the heavens.

The most committed believer could join the clergy and become a Daoist nun or priestess (*nüguan, nüshi*).[33] Every kind of woman entered the clergy, from prostitutes to princesses. As with lay practitioners, women became nuns for a variety of reasons, from sincere piety to the pursuit of material advantage. Daoist nuns often left home to live in a hermitage or monastery. But unlike Buddhists, who were supposed to sever family ties, Daoists did not forbid participation in mundane activities. Some nuns cut ties with their families, while others resided in a monastery but maintained close links with the lay world.[34] Women who had born children before they took vows might even periodically return home to look after them. Daoist nuns could not marry. However, a woman's vows did not have to be permanent, and she could readily reenter lay life and wed.

Many Daoist nuns remained at home and pursued spiritual practice in a domestic setting. In fact, there are more epitaphs for these sorts of nuns than for those who resided in temples. Nuns had various motives for remaining at home. Parents might not give their permission for a daughter to leave, in which case she had no choice but to stay with her family after taking holy vows. A woman with a weak constitution would not want to leave the safety and comforts of home. Moreover, even the most pious women often had trouble finding a monastery that would accept them. Given the finite financial resources of these institutions, they could only support a limited number of residents.

Men and women underwent similar procedures to join the clergy. Before a woman entered a Daoist convent, she had to obtain the consent of a parent or another responsible family member, as in Buddhism. At first, she would either establish her own individual hermitage or go to live with a female teacher. She dedicated this initial period of practice to purifying her body and mind. An aspiring nun would avoid contact with laypeople and try to attain the right mental state to pursue further cultivation. When she felt ready, she might enter a larger Daoist institution to receive extensive training. When she felt sufficiently prepared, she took formal vows. Male and female clerics wore similar attire, although women had a different headdress. Men and women had comparable systems of ranks that were theoretically equal, and a woman could advance to the highest levels of her order. Only senior nuns had the authority to perform the most important religious rites.

Although Daoism offered valuable opportunities to women, they still faced more restrictions than men. Some temples had clerics of both sexes, organized into similar ranks. However, women participated in fewer ceremonies than men, had limited powers over institutional matters, and rarely wrote religious works. In spite of these constraints, some of the most talented women distinguished themselves and gained respect. The influential Shanqing school of Daoism, which reached its apex under the Tang, considered Wei Huacun (251–334) to be their matriarch.[35] This sect was especially welcoming to female adherents, and they played key roles in its activities.

Daoist nuns had a special link to the palace, as harem women often became nuns. Imperial consorts often entered a nunnery when they became old or when a new emperor expelled them from the palace. Some princesses became nuns, and their unusual lifestyle attracted the attention of poets.[36] Of the 210 known Tang princesses, although none became Buddhist nuns, at least seventeen took Daoist vows. Most remained clerics for the rest of their lives, but a few reentered the lay world after a period of religious service. Princesses joined the clergy at various times in their lives, ranging from childhood to middle age.

Princesses ostensibly became nuns to seek spiritual advancement or to invoke blessings for a parent or grandparent. However, it seems that practical factors, not piety, usually motivated an emperor's daughter to enter a Daoist convent. Few seem to have had a genuine spiritual vocation. In particular, princesses seem to have joined the clergy as a way to evade marriage. As the Tang declined and emperors scrambled to find useful allies, they increasingly married their daughters to warlords and foreign leaders. A princess who took vows could avoid being exiled to a remote frontier region. Not coincidentally, most princess nuns came from the later part of the dynasty, when many were being married off to foreign allies. Other princesses many have seen the clerical life as a way to liberate themselves from the constraints that accompanied their position. High rank brought many privileges but also came with many restrictions. Life in a Daoist nunnery freed princesses from tedious rules that governed their lives. And some palace women may have become clerics to escape court politics. Convents served as refuges for those involved in failed factions and plots.

Princesses and other palace ladies who became nuns lived in special convents in the capital region.[37] Some princesses even converted their mansions into luxurious Daoist monasteries. These elite nunneries were renowned for their splendor. Artworks and lavish ornamentation emulated the heavenly abode of the immortals. And large gardens not only evoked the Daoist ideal of naturalism but also frequently incorporated Daoist mythology and metaphysical principles.

When a princess became a Daoist nun, her retainers also took vows so that they could continue to serve her. Some of these women had previously been palace singers and dancers, and the entry of these talented female performers into prestigious nunneries piqued the curiosity of poets. Poems about beautiful and talented nuns changed public perception of Daoism, making the religion seem extremely alluring, cultured, and sensual.[38]

Daoist nuns had an unusual relationship with men. Male admirers sometimes referred to them as immortals, and these women also used this term to describe themselves. Adopting a transcendent identity sanctioned a woman's interactions with men and bolstered her confidence. Moreover, clerics were exempt from many of the usual restrictions on female behavior. For example, when a pious woman took vows, she received a certificate that allowed her to travel freely so that she could visit academic and cultural centers to meet learned men. Some nuns became very cosmopolitan and gained a wide circle of male acquaintances.

Nuns from aristocratic families had also been educated in poetry, music, calligraphy, and other refined pursuits, and they excelled in cultured pursuits.[39] High-ranking nuns had an extensive knowledge of the Daoist scriptures, indicating a high level of learning. Hu Yin (fl. 848) wrote a book on Daoist longevity techniques and another on general medical theory, thereby influencing teachings on Daoist internal alchemy as well as general medical theory.[40] Elite nuns could meet with educated men to discuss intellectual and literary topics and enjoy entertainment together, engaging as equals.[41] The most talented women exchanged poetry with men and publicly circulated their verses for the enjoyment of male readers.[42] Some nunneries gained notice for hosting cultured salons attended by both sexes, where nuns sometimes dazzled male companions with their erudition and talent.

Female Daoist and Buddhist clerics differed in one highly visible respect. In spite of the high literacy rate of Buddhist nuns, they rarely wrote poetry. Their religion discouraged strong emotions of the type that writers expressed in verse. Moreover, Buddhist women probably felt uneasy using a mode of female expression so closely associated with courtesans.[43] In contrast, some Daoist nuns gained fame for their literary achievements.[44] Although the Tang stands out as the golden age of Chinese poetry, few women publicly circulated their works, as they usually hesitated to expose themselves to public view.[45] But because Daoist nuns had cast off secular conventions, they felt comfortable writing poetry for a wide readership. The style and content of their poetry shows impressive self-confidence. In many respects the writings of Daoist women resemble those of contemporary courtesans.[46] Both Daoist nuns and courtesans felt unrestrained by ordinary social expectations, so they sometimes displayed similarly strong personalities and wrote candidly about intense feelings.

Li Ye (also called Li Jilan, d. 784) exemplifies the passionate Daoist woman.[47] Whereas poets had traditionally portrayed the female subject as fragile, helpless, and pathetically dependent on a man's attentions, Li presented a diametrically opposed vision of womanhood. She positioned herself as strong and energetic. Her literary persona did not pursue a man to make herself feel whole but simply out of independent desire. These feelings resembled the autonomous emotions expressed by men. Song dynasty critics assessed her forthright poetry from a moralistic Neo-Confucian viewpoint and classified her as a courtesan, an implicit condemnation of her self-assured persona.

Li Ye exchanged poems with a range of talented men intrigued by her talent and unorthodox views. Her correspondents included literati, hermits, artists, monks, officials, and even the emperor. Some of Li Ye's poetry expresses conventional Daoist sentiments of otherworldly withdrawal.[48]

> Don't get attached
> to fame that won't last;
> better to trim
> bureaucrat's whims.
> A century's like a day and a night;
> things of the past are now gone from sight.

In other cases, she cleverly combined religious imagery with feelings of longing.[49]

> Off in the floating clouds,
> my heart is far away,
> how do I know you might
> never come back some day?
> The clouds of my heart

> have gathered between
> being and nothingness;
> why in the world does the crazy wind
> kick up such a fuss,
> raging at the mountains south
> and the mountains north?

Some poems express longing for a refined male companion. Li did not seek someone wealthy or handsome but rather a cultured man of letters who could engage her in intelligent conversation.[50]

> Far rivers float your immortal boat,
> cold stars go with the envoy carriage.
> When you pass the Dalei shore,
> send just a few lines—please remember.

When compared with the polite and predictable poems of Ban Zhao (45–ca. 116) or the miserable boudoir laments of the Liang dynasty, Li Ye's works still come across as fresh, confident, and exciting. These self-assured expressions of female desire may have shocked many male readers, but women found them inspirational. Subsequent writers took Li Ye's works as a template for the self-assured female literary voice.

In spite of periodic persecution, Buddhism remained a major force in Chinese society throughout the Sui and Tang and affected gender norms in complex and contradictory ways. The contents of the vast Buddhist canon vary widely in substance, popularity, and orthodoxy. Some texts portray women in an extremely negative light, describing them as morally weak, licentious, hateful, foolish, jealous, and a potential source of disaster for men.[51] However, other aspects of this complex belief system empowered women. In particular, the religion's egalitarian spirit awakened many women's desires and gave them confidence.

In spite of the uneasy relations between the officialdom and Buddhist clergy, many residents of the palace practiced the religion and patronized its activities. Links between Buddhism and the state dated back to the founding of the Sui. Emperor Wen, the dynasty's first monarch, had received a comprehensive Buddhist education, and his enthusiastic promotion of the faith affected religious life in his newly reunited nation.[52] As always, powerful women used Buddhism to legitimize their authority and lend them prestige.[53] In addition, exclusive nunneries had extremely intimate connections with the court and provided useful resources for palace ladies.[54]

Syncretic court Buddhism combined conventional beliefs with Daoism and other elements. The monk Fazang gained prominence at the court of Empress Wu Zetian largely because of his concurrent mastery of Buddhist and Daoist practices. Although Fazang distinguished himself as an accomplished philosopher of the profound Huayan School of Buddhist metaphysics and convinced Empress Wu to promote this challenging philosophy, he gained Wu's attention largely because he could perform Daoist rituals and spells to induce longevity, invoke rain, and curse her enemies.[55]

The epitaph of Princess Dazhang, twelfth daughter of Emperor Gaozu and younger sister of Emperor Taizong, describes the spiritual life of a sincerely devout woman who practiced Buddhism within the palace.[56] While young, Dazhang learned how to play Buddhist songs on a stringed instrument, and it seems that she absorbed her religion's fundamental beliefs from memorizing pious lyrics. Dazhang grew up to be an enthusiastic Buddhist laywoman. She attended large-scale religious ceremonies held in the palace and also practiced the faith on her own.

In a continuation of earlier practices, empresses and other important women publicly expressed their religious devotion through extravagant patronage. During the Sui, women as well as men converted some of their mansions into Buddhist temples and also paid for the renovation of existing religious sites, thereby establishing religious sponsorship as a standard feature of court life in the reunited nation.[57] Empresses and imperial relatives commissioned sacred statuary at the Longmen shrines and elsewhere, usually as a way to generate merit on behalf of a deceased family member.[58] Wu Zetian stands out as the most active imperial patron of the era. During her reign, religious images became extremely large and elaborate. She financed the creation of numerous eleven-faced statues of the bodhisattva Guanyin.[59] Wu also sponsored a series of large-scale projects at Longmen, adding impressively decorated grottoes to that site.[60] And she constructed a large temple complex in Luoyang that combined native religious architecture with foreign styles.[61] A tall pagoda at the temple housed a Buddhist image and astronomical instruments. Wu also introduced the custom of relic worship into China, distributing holy objects and encouraging believers to venerate them.[62] Other palace ladies carried out similar works of patronage, albeit on a much smaller scale. The beliefs of Princess Jinxian (689–732) exemplified the blithe fusion of Buddhism and Daoism that characterized Tang religious life.[63] Although she became a Daoist nun, she also helped finance an enormous project to engrave Buddhist sutras onto stone slabs at Yunju temple.

High-profile patronage by the ruling elite inspired women outside the palace to undertake similar acts, with the scale of support varying according to their financial means. Sometimes a pious couple would commission a Buddhist image together. A general and his wife, herself the daughter of a general, dedicated an image and inscription at the Tianlongshan grottoes in 706.[64] A more ambitious couple financed a series of figures in a grotto and added their own images as well.[65] Sometimes a woman paid for an image on her own. Nuns were particularly enthusiastic sponsors of sacred sculpture.[66] These women usually had modest resources, so they would pay to have a small image carved in a marginal location within a grotto. Interestingly, the inscriptions accompanying these images indicate that some nuns dedicated the merit that they generated to all womankind.

Most believers practiced their religion while remaining in the secular world. Laywomen of every social level sought solace in Buddhism. This faith helped them address feelings of loneliness and emptiness, encouraged them to sacrifice their own interests for the sake of their families, and strengthened their commitment to moral values. People believed that Buddhist ethics made women into good mothers who could imbue their children with a clear moral compass.[67]

Most prominently, members of the uppermost elite favored Buddhism. Although the great aristocratic families of the northeast had a reputation for devotion to Confucianism and classical studies, many were also devout Buddhists. Because they put such stress on secular ethical propriety, their religious beliefs often fused Buddhism and Confucianism.[68] Aristocratic devotees presented secular virtues, such as filial piety, as Buddhist duties central to their religious practice. And because Confucianism stressed motherhood, they emphasized maternal love and devotion as a key Buddhist ideal as well.

Buddhism attracted believers from every rung of society. Epitaphs show that women from the lower reaches of the aristocracy frequently practiced the religion. About 10 percent of women's epitaphs identify the deceased as a lay Buddhist.[69] Much farther down the social ladder, poor laywomen mentioned in Dunhuang documents often have names with Buddhist connotations.[70] The popularity of Buddhist names among women from humble backgrounds shows that the religion had even penetrated deep into the lives of women from very modest families.

Women turned to Buddhism for various reasons.[71] Some grew up in pious households and became believers in childhood. Others saw religious practice as a way to help those close to them. They often devoted the merit generated by their spiritual exercises to parents or family. Buddhism also offered practical benefits. Spells and charms promised to cure disease and induce fertility. And the prospect of rebirth in paradise assuaged fear of death. For that reason, many women became enthusiastic believers in the wake of a major life event, such as a major illness or the funeral of a parent.[72] Displaying piety could also raise a woman's status by gaining the respect of those around her.

Figure 5.2 Guanyin (Sailko)

And in a society regulated by restrictive secular rites, Buddhism enlarged the space for female self-expression.

At the grassroots level, popular Buddhism stressed bodhisattva worship.[73] Believers worshipped the statues of these religious figures as they would folk deities. For example, during the Tang many women treated the bodhisattva Guanyin as a fertility goddess. They believed that due to her compassion, she would allow sufficiently devout women to bear sons. The association of Guanyin with fertility helps account for the explosive growth of this cult during the Tang. Women also worshipped many other buddhas and bodhisattvas in the manner of folk deities, imploring them for practical benefits. Besides Guanyin, Dizang (Kṣitigarbha) and the Medicine Buddha (Yaoshifo) also attracted fervent devotions. The assumption that pious women could access divine aid empowered even women of lowly station.

These sorts of popular practices affected mainstream Buddhist teachings.[74] Originally Indian Buddhism directed spiritual practice toward obtaining a state of nirvana. But Chinese had far less interest in this abstract goal. Instead virtually all believers sought rebirth in a paradise ruled by a buddha or bodhisattva. Many women repeatedly chanted a buddha's name in the belief that they would enter the Pure Land upon death. By turning the focus of Buddhist belief and practice toward their own priorities, female devotees helped to shift Chinese concepts of karma and rebirth away from ancient Indian teachings.

Aside from worship at temples and shrines, many women also attended sermons and lectures on religious topics.[75] Popular teachers spoke in simple and entertaining ways that could inspire unschooled audiences. Women from ordinary families showed great interest in these lectures, which allowed even the illiterate to learn about the faith. Sermons served as an important form of popular education, giving women from humble backgrounds a precious opportunity to learn about abstract ideas.

Most female religious practice took place in a domestic environment.[76] A pious woman might take a Buddhist name. She could burn incense and pray to images of holy figures at home. And she might chant or copy sutras. She could also give food or money to clerics or religious institutions. Believers also often became vegetarian and sometimes undertook additional fasts and austerities as well. A particularly dedicated laywoman could take special bodhisattva vows and declare herself an *upāsikā* (*youpoyi*)—an attendant of the Buddha.[77] Although an *upāsikā* remained in the mundane world, she promised to observe certain austerities such as not using cosmetics, eating after noon, or riding in a vehicle. She was expected to live a relatively spartan life, maintain a serious demeanor, deal with others compassionately, and devote her spare time to religious practice. Some pregnant laywomen became extremely devout as a prelude to childbirth. They temporarily intensified their religious activities in the belief that this would benefit the fetus.[78] A pregnant woman might undertake periodic fasting, gaze at auspicious symbols, and copy sutras.

Burial practices also attested to the influence of Buddhism on personal identity.[79] Ritual propriety taught that spouses ought to be buried together due to the importance of the conjugal bond. However, some Buddhist women wanted to be buried separately from their spouses. Widows most often desired separate burial, but even some women who predeceased their spouses wanted to be buried apart. Compared to Confucianism, Buddhism places relatively little importance on marriage. As a result, devout women often preferred cremation to conventional burial. Instead of being placed in a joint tomb with a husband, their ashes would be interred in a pagoda on the grounds of a temple, often near the remains of a famous monk.

Laywomen did not have to engage in religious practice alone. Groups of likeminded believers frequently came together to provide mutual encouragement, support, and cooperation.[80] Collaborating as a group allowed believers to organize their worship systematically, thereby raising the collective level of enthusiasm and piety. Documents from Dunhuang show that religious confraternities were very common during the Tang. Most groups included only men, although women sometimes participated in primarily male groups. In addition, a minority of coalitions consisted only of women. These groups conducted religious ceremonies and ate vegetarian meals together. Members channeled some domestic financial resources to the group. Even if each woman made only a small contribution, by pooling their funds they could commission a religious image or pay to have a sutra copied.

Although female coalitions usually came together for religious reasons, the group could pursue other goals as well. By reaching outside the family and constructing a wide network of friends and contacts, women could enjoy socializing with a broad circle of acquaintances outside the home. In addition, confraternities provided practical benefits as well. Building ties with a group of likeminded people helped women cope with their family's shortcomings and provided additional security in a society where many people teetered on the edge of subsistence. Members helped each other in time of need, caring for the sick or those who had suffered temporary setbacks. Cultivating a larger circle of acquaintances made it easier to find suitable marriage partners for the younger generation. Also, women from humble backgrounds might have a chance to build ties with people of higher social station. Most importantly, when a member died, her coalition could help organize the funeral and provide her family with food and temporary financial aid.

The most dedicated Buddhists could join the clergy. As with lay believers, various factors motivated women to join a religious order. Many nuns were sincerely dedicated to their vocation. And devout Buddhists believed that a cleric brought blessings to all of her kin. Nevertheless, it was not uncommon for a woman to take the tonsure for pragmatic reasons. Some saw a nunnery as a refuge against war, chaos, or poverty. Women who became nuns in middle age usually did so after the death of a husband or divorce, suggesting that they saw monasticism as preferable to remarriage.[81] For the poor, convent life might offer upward mobility. The most famous nuns could win respect and even fame, so an ambitious woman might view religion as a career path that could allow her to employ her talents. Educated and well-connected nuns could even gain political clout. Some became confidants of important figures at court and in the palace.

Women had practical financial reasons to become nuns as well.[82] Under the Tang equal field system, Buddhist and Daoist male clerics received thirty *mu* of farmland, while the nuns of these two religions received twenty *mu* each. Income from this land gave a nun economic independence. Moreover, nuns were exempt from taxation. Many temples owned large tracts of land and received regular donations from the faithful, allowing them to provide nuns with food, lodging, and other basic support. The economic benefits of joining the clergy help account for the large number of monastics during the medieval era. The Tang government looked on the growing number of tax-free clerics and temples with alarm. Removing so many people from the productive economy affected government revenue. The threat that Buddhist monasticism posed to fiscal integrity probably accounts for the persecutions that began in this era, which initiated the religion's gradual decline in China.

The government had different policies toward Buddhism in each era of the Tang, so the number of nuns fluctuated over the course of the dynasty. Officials considered monasteries an extension of the state, as these organizations promoted the spiritual wellbeing of the populace and invoked blessings to protect the nation from harm. When Buddhism first gained prominence in China, the government registered clerics and established a religious bureaucracy that granted official rank to the heads of important temples, thus bringing monks and nuns into the state apparatus.[83] Likewise, the Tang bureaucracy compiled official lists of Buddhist and Daoist clerics.[84] Surviving epitaphs of nuns date mostly to the early Tang, suggesting that their numbers fell overall during the dynasty's chaotic latter half.[85] Documents from Turpan in the west show that the number of nuns steadily increased from 171 to 693 between the years 788 and 895, then dropped back to 450 nuns by the year 936.[86] At most, there were probably around 50,000 nuns residing in temples across China at any given time. Many nuns took the tonsure at a very young age, often before puberty and sometimes in infancy. For example, the nun Fale entered a temple at three years of age and lived to be seventy-four.[87] Forty epitaphs of nuns report that these women died at an average age of 64.7. This is much higher than the lifespans given in epitaphs for lay women (52.1) and even for men (60.6).[88]

Not all Buddhist nuns resided in a religious community.[89] Although "registered" (*guaji*) nuns were considered regular clerics, they did not live in a temple. After a registered nun took her vows, she continued to live with her family. In addition, some believers became "private" (*sidu*) nuns. These women also remained at home but were not registered with the government. The state often imposed limits on the number of clerics in order to maintain a healthy tax base, and they did not recognize the clerical status of nuns over this quota. Although it was officially illegal to become a private nun, this practice was not uncommon, and the number of licensed nuns surged in the late Tang.

According to the monastic code, a nun was expected to cut ties with her family and devote her full attention to spiritual affairs.[90] In Dunhuang, it was customary for a novice to formally bid farewell to her mother (her father is not mentioned), thanking her for nursing and raising her.[91] The government tried to foster an otherworldly ethos among the clergy to discourage them from meddling in politics. As a result, the law did not recognize Buddhist clerics as members of the family of their birth. If a nun's kinsman committed a crime so serious that his family members shared the punishment, she was exempted from the collective penalty.[92]

Although monastic rules demanded that nuns sever their ties with the mundane world, in fact many of them remained in close contact with their families.[93] The epitaphs of many nuns provide detailed information about their family background, suggesting that they had retained membership in their family. Some nuns even put great emphasis on their family ties. To a degree, the hierarchy of the Buddhist sangha replicated that of the secular world. Because clerics born into important families attained higher ranks, a nun from a politically influential family might even take over leadership of a nunnery under imperial patronage, so it behooved her to accentuate her prestigious family background.[94]

Even for nuns from ordinary families, filial obligations continued to bind them to their families. Hagiography and inscribed commemorations often celebrated the Confucian virtues of nuns, filial piety in particular.[95] Sometimes a nun would direct her religious practice toward gaining merit for her parents, thereby using her religious role to prove herself a dutiful daughter. In addition, many nuns actively participated in family life, particularly when important matters arose.[96] Sometimes they conducted Buddhist rites together with their family members. Nuns cared for parents in need. They also felt responsible for looking after younger siblings when their parents died.[97] Most commonly, clergy participated in the funerals of parents.[98] Some nuns received a secular burial in their family cemetery rather than being cremated and having their ashes interred in a pagoda, as was expected. After a nun's death, her family might commission a commemorative epitaph. For example, the nieces of a nun named Jinggan paid for a posthumous inscription, implicitly attesting to the close links between the nun and her kin.[99]

The lifestyles and activities of nuns varied considerably according to situation and temperament.[100] Like their male counterparts, nuns usually practiced moderate asceticism, devoting their days to worship, prayer, and meditation. They studied and chanted sutras and might receive advanced instruction in the most challenging teachings. According to popular literature, the most accomplished female religious figures could even perform miracles.[101] Because women had fewer resources at their disposal than men, they were more likely to practice in groups.[102]

Some male-dominated sects were more welcoming to women than others. Compared to later eras, religious organization was still relatively lax during the Tang, allowing women more opportunities to distinguish themselves than in later eras. Most notably, "Chan women" (*chanpo*) participated in mainstream Chan (Zen) activities.[103] Chan put particular stress on Buddha nature (*foxing*), the belief that each being has potential for achieving enlightenment regardless of sex, making this sect particularly welcoming to women. Also, Chan had only recently emerged, so it still had flexible ideas and institutions. Women were attracted to this welcoming new style of religious practice, which allowed them to engage with male counterparts more freely. Compendia of Chan wisdom preserve statements made by women, showing that male writers took their ideas seriously. Chan writings also describe how a woman would sometimes pretend to seduce a senior monk as a way to test his commitment.

Nuns also established female-friendly institutions and practices outside of patriarchal organizations.[104] For example, an inscription commemorating the nun Puxiang (d. 643) asserts that even though she achieved enlightenment, she did not inform others of her attainment. The men who controlled mainstream Buddhist institutions would probably not have taken a woman's claim to enlightenment seriously. In consequence, women like Puxiang conducted their religious practice outside of male-dominated institutions. Nuns took part in many of the same spiritual activities as pious laywomen, but within a structured environment conducive to religious practice. In general, the religious activities of nuns resembled those of monks, and the two groups routinely interacted.[105] Male monasteries housed religious texts of interest to nuns and also hosted the most accomplished teachers, so they attracted female students. Sometimes a nun would even live in a male religious community for a time to study. Groups of male and female clerics helped one another and traded holy

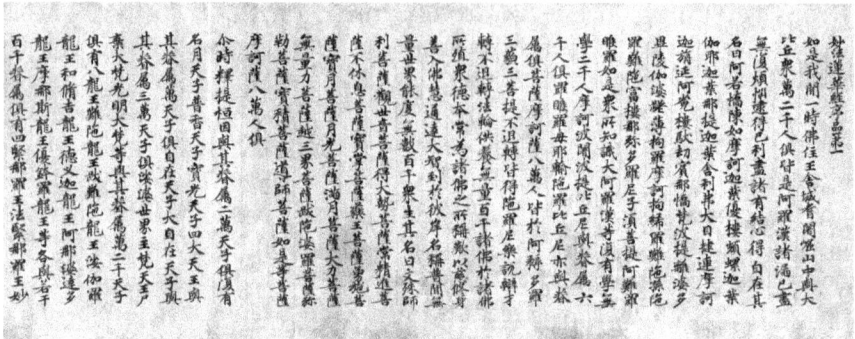

Figure 5.3 The Lotus Sutra

objects and alms. Also, monks and nuns sometimes held religious activities in tandem.

In a few respects, nuns developed distinctive religious ideas that differed from those of male believers. Women were particularly enthusiastic about the *Lotus Sutra* (*Lianhua jing*), and they were instrumental in disseminating this influential text.[106] Nuns often studied and recited this sutra, so it had a particularly strong influence on their beliefs. Several aspects of this sutra differ from other major Buddhist scriptures. Although the *Lotus Sutra* exhorts believers to refrain from killing living things, the text also strongly advocates self-sacrifice as a key spiritual practice. Accordingly, a believer might immolate herself to cast off the material body and offer herself to the Buddha. These extreme teachings help account for occasional examples of fanaticism and suicide among medieval nuns. The sutra also includes the mythical story of the eight-year-old daughter of a dragon who became a buddha. This narrative legitimized the idea that, like men, a devoted woman could achieve enlightenment and achieve buddhahood.

Believers worked very hard to propagate their religion.[107] Some nuns preached Buddhist doctrine to lay society. Women usually taught in temples. Some preached in a formal style, while others employed a colloquial manner comparable to secular storytelling as a way to attract new believers and bolster enthusiasm. Educating laypeople about Buddhism gave nuns a chance to assume the honored role of teacher while interacting with society at large. It was very rare for a woman to gain esteem for speaking to the general public. However, whereas the gaze of strangers would usually threaten a woman's reputation, clerics were exempted from ordinary standards of behavior. Due to the special status of nuns, a prominent public profile could even win praise. The success of so many medieval nuns illustrates how these resourceful women creatively employed religion to expand female autonomy, employ their talents, and win respect.

Chapter 6

Learning

A woman's place in society usually determined what she learned and how she could use her talents. For those working at home in a rural village, literate learning had little practical value. Their education consisted of training in practical skills, such as cooking and childcare, that could help them succeed as wives and mothers. However, even the illiterate could acquire useful knowledge. For example, some women employed mystical techniques to seek insights into important events. Tang dynasty stories often describe a woman's dreams, with the assumption that these images could be meaningful and portentous. Readers believed that dreams might allow a woman to acquire knowledge and wisdom far beyond her personal experience.[1]

Most often, women obtained information orally, usually by chatting with neighbors and kin. Although men dismissed these conversations as empty gossip, most women had few opportunities to travel and meet new people, so they relied heavily on oral discourse to learn about the world.[2] So-called gossip allowed women to hear about things and events beyond their immediate horizons. Moreover, because gossip emerged from the community, it could serve as a unifying social force. Gossip enforced group cohesion and common behavioral norms. Membership in a group of gossipy women empowered participants by allowing them to shape the community's mainstream opinions. Gossip also acted as a tool of social control. Any woman whose behavior strayed too far from convention would become the subject of public discussions. The resulting embarrassment would likely shame her into conforming to social expectations.

Beyond oral knowledge, some women managed to obtain a literate education. Book learning was not limited to the elite. Even some prostitutes, courtesans, and slave women wrote poetry, proving that they could read and write difficult texts. Women usually only pursued a literate education if they thought that it might be useful. Aristocratic women often found education extremely worthwhile. They could spend some of their copious leisure time reading and then discuss what they had read with the women and men around them. But for those who toiled hard each day on the edge of subsistence, mastering the ancient classics and proper literary style would have seemed like a waste of time.

The usefulness of education for women varied not just by social class but also according to the content of lessons, which changed significantly over the course of the dynasty.[3] In the early Tang, the upper aristocracy dominated the education system, and their priorities determined what women studied. At that time, female education not only conveyed information but also sought to cultivate talent. Aristocratic ladies received broad tuition that included training in artistic skills such as poetry, music, and calligraphy. They also frequently studied the teachings of Buddhism or Daoism as well. As the dynasty progressed, however, the priorities of families further down the social scale had an increasing impact on the content of women's education. People from the lower elite had a more restrictive vision of female learning, so the scope of education narrowed. By the mid-Tang, female students often focused on texts that conveyed Confucian ethics and the rites. The turn away from talent toward virtue elevated the overall moral tenor of female education. This shift change made it easier for advocates of female learning to justify educating women, as this sort of curriculum was intended to prepare women to become virtuous wives and mothers.[4]

Political changes also affected education. The rise of the examination system meant that any man who sought a post in the civil service had to have considerable learning, and a mastery of the classical canon in particular. In response to escalating criteria for employment, the officialdom became increasingly learned. Families that produced officials took pride in owning many books and nurturing a cultured atmosphere at home. Women benefitted from the growing stress on high culture among the elite. An ambitious man wanted an educated wife who would fit into a refined environment, so families had to educate their daughters so that they could marry well.

The growing stress on education among the elite altered the relationship between mothers and sons. Aristocratic families expected mothers to oversee the early education of their sons, starting them on the path to a successful career.[5] This effort was not entirely altruistic, as helping a son to succeed could elevate his mother's standing in society. A woman's social position followed that of the man closest to her, so a son's success or failure ultimately affected his mother as well. As long as a woman's husband was alive, his rank determined her social standing. But after his death, his widow's status depended on that of her most outstanding offspring. If a son passed the imperial exams and ascended the bureaucratic hierarchy, his mother's position rose in tandem.[6] For this reason, it was useful for women from elite families to educate themselves so that they could transmit this learning to their sons, thus potentially raising their own position. This idea that female education could raise a woman's rank gradually spread downward through society, spurring women far removed from examination culture to pursue learning.

Society at large lauded maternal instruction. People showed great respect toward the mother who successfully taught her children. And women whose sons excelled in the civil service became icons of motherhood. High-ranking men often attributed their success to lessons that they absorbed from diligent mothers. As a result, stories about dedicated maternal teachers proliferated.[7] In particular, writers lauded widows who educated their sons in the face of difficulty and held up these women as role models.[8]

During the Tang, men's education increasingly shifted toward a standard curriculum designed to prepare them for the civil service examinations. But because women could not participate in these exams, they lacked a consistent curriculum.[9] There were no schools for girls, so they studied at home. Like their male counterparts, female students copied model texts as a way to learn reading and writing and also to become familiar with the contents of canonical works. Usually a girl's mother served as her teacher. Sometimes a family would hire a female teacher (*mushi*) to come into the home and teach a girl specialized subjects.

A girl's curriculum depended on her mother's educational background and her own interests. In addition to learning how to write poetry, which people considered a necessity for refined ladies, some women also became proficient in history, the ancient classics, and Buddhist learning.[10] Confucian pedagogy stressed ethics, so textbooks for women stressed female virtues such as maternal dedication, wifely righteousness, and the general submission of women to men. Young women were also expected to master the rites pertaining to orthodox female behavior. Students often studied classic Han dynasty texts by Liu Xiang (77–6 BCE) and Ban Zhao (45–ca. 116), as well as more recent works on female ethics and family values.[11] In addition to textual learning, families also expected girls to master spinning and weaving, as these skills were traditionally associated with domestic virtue. Many women also learned how to play a musical instrument.

The palace had an organized system of female education, as the rulers wanted their daughters, wives, and consorts to have a solid grasp of ethical teachings. Some women residing in the palace became known for their learning and talent. Palace ladies often showed an interest in poetry, calligraphy, and painting, and the standard Tang histories record the literary accomplishments of about a quarter of the empresses from that era.[12] Sometimes they displayed their achievements publicly by composing and reciting poems at banquets to provide cultured entertainment for the assembled guests.

Some palace women attained a reputation for exceptional learning or talent. Empress Zhangsun (601–636), wife of Emperor Taizong and mother of Gaozong, stands out as the most accomplished imperial consort of the early Tang.[13] She authored a book titled *Rules for Women* (*Nüze*) that outlined Confucian principles of female virtue. Due to her high educational level, Zhangsun was able to discuss policy with her husband, so she had an impact on matters of state. The formidable Empress Wu also circulated an extensive corpus of writings, mostly political and social works describing normative rules of behavior.[14] Although most of these texts were ghostwritten by erudite scholars in state employ, some came from her own hand. The fact that all these works were disseminated in her name shows that the public believed that a woman could potentially compose extremely difficult texts on serious topics.

Xu Hui (627–650) attracted renown for a different kind of writing. A favored concubine of Emperor Taizong, she originally gained attention as a child prodigy.[15] By the age of four she could recite the *Analects* (*Lunyu*) and *Classic of Poetry* (*Shijing*). By age eight she eagerly devoured all kinds of literature, and her father encouraged her voracious reading. When the emperor heard of her exceptional erudition, he took her into the harem as a concubine and she became one of his favorites. Xu distinguished herself as a significant poet, and critics hold her works in high regard. Similarly, the talented Shangguan Waner (664–710) stood out as a leading light in the highly cultured court of Emperor Zhongzong.[16] The vitality of her well-crafted verses, together with her prominence in the cultural life of the capital, attracted the notice of other writers.

The education of palace ladies became a higher priority in the later phase of the dynasty. As in society at large, at that time the focus of learning shifted from the arts to ethics. In reaction to the unusual power of palace women early in the dynasty, Emperor Xuanzong wanted women to study restrictive Confucian values intended to make them meek and submissive.[17] Many imperial consorts had received a solid education at home. They could continue their studies in the harem, under the professional teachers who staffed the palace school.[18] An outstanding teacher oversaw the education system for palace ladies. Beneath him were five experts on the classics as well as three specialists in history, philosophy, and literature. Others taught calligraphy, Daoism, law, poetry chanting, music, arithmetic, and the board game *weiqi* (*go*). In addition to these professional teachers, female officials working in the palace also sometimes taught various subjects. Moreover, educated concubines served as tutors to other palace ladies. And sometimes a learned female companion provided an empress with private tuition and intellectual companionship.[19] In addition to formal textual education, female residents of the palace had other ways to learn as well. Didactic paintings illustrated female virtue, and women with a low level of education could use these props to study basic ethical principles.[20] Given this elaborate educational infrastructure, it comes as no surprise that some empresses and consorts stood out as highly learned.[21]

Princesses also received a full education before they left the palace as brides.[22] Besides studying model texts they also learned practical matters, such as court ritual and deportment. The emperors' daughters received formal lessons in these skills and also imitated the behavior of those around them. Some princesses became highly educated and displayed proficiency in difficult subjects, including history, the rites, and philosophy. Because the emperors regarded education as a way to moderate and restrain their daughters' behavior, palace teachers went to great lengths to inculcate restrictive Confucian virtues. After receiving such an extensive education, these women were well qualified to educate their own children. Tang princesses married into important families, and many of their sons went on to serve as high officials. Having an educated mother gave these men a useful head start in preparing for official service.

<hr />

In spite of the difficulty of mastering imperial China's written language, which differed significantly from colloquial speech, literate women wrote sophisticated works in both prose and verse. For example, Buddhist nuns commissioned dedicatory inscriptions at religious sites, and some of these texts note that the female donor composed the text herself.[23] Although these sorts of inscriptions employed highly stylized language, some nuns had mastered elevated diction. Most often, however, women wrote letters. Although writing a letter might not sound difficult, in fact it was not easy to compose utilitarian writings correctly. People expected epistolary texts to follow set patterns, and there were many rules and conventions. For example, a writer had to use different grades of formality and address when writing to different types of relatives. Proper style was especially important when discussing funeral arrangements. Family members of each degree of kinship mourned the deceased differently, and these complex gradations could be confusing. A woman who wanted to write letters correctly had to master many complex rules. Only if she adhered to the standard format could she be certain that her letter would be understood and appreciated.

Due to the difficulty of writing letters correctly, women often relied on reference books of model epistles. The earliest collection of women's letters dates to the early medieval era. By the Tang, these stylebooks had become an established format.[24] Tang bibliographies list the names of reference works consisting of letters appropriate for female writers. Unfortunately, these works have not transmitted down to the present.[25] However, some letters intended as guides for women have been preserved at Dunhuang. These model letters were addressed to members of a woman's natal family (parents, grandparents, and siblings), husbands, and in-laws. Model letters usually dealt with important life events such as a marriage or funeral, which required a strictly prescribed format. Women relied on epistolary stylebooks to learn the proper tone and language for a particular type of letter and how to address each kind of correspondent.

The rising level of female education produced a large number of female readers. To provide uplifting reading material for women, Tang authors composed works that taught female ethics. Of these, six have survived down to the present.[26] Two books by female authors gained a wide readership and had a major impact on ideas about gender. A woman named Madame Zheng wrote an influential book called *Classic of Filial Piety for Women* (*Nü xiaojing*).[27] Almost nothing is known about the author. She seems to have come from an elite background and wrote this book in the early or mid-eighth century.[28] The text initially had a limited circulation and does not appear in Tang bibliographies. When printing became common during the Song dynasty, however, publishers produced many copies and disseminated them widely, finally making this book readily available. As a result of this delayed distribution, although *Classic of Filial Piety for Women* had a limited impact during the Tang, its influence on subsequent generations was considerable.

Because a female author intended this book for a female readership, it constituted one of the most important statements about womanhood since the Han dynasty. To lend her ideas moral authority, Madame Zheng imitates the brief but revered *Classic of Filial Piety* (*Xiaojing*), perhaps the most widely read Confucian text at the time. Ten of the eighteen chapters correspond to similar themes in the original classic, and often copy the exact wording of the guiding text. In addition to this canonical work on filial piety, the author cites other influences as well. Most importantly, she refers to the two major Han dynasty texts about women: Liu Xiang's *Biographies of Women* (*Lienü zhuan*) and Ban Zhao's *Admonitions for Women* (*Nüjie*). Zheng takes ideas and themes from these classic works and inserts them into a new framework to make them relevant to her own time.

As indicated by the title, Zheng sees filial piety as the most fundamental virtue, for women as well as for men. Because it is the most basic moral principle, it can serve as the starting point for discussing the general nature of ideal womanhood.[29] Previous writings about filial piety had usually been aimed at men, so women had little guidance on how to correctly practice this virtue. The author makes filiality more relevant to women by explaining in detail how they should carry out this moral imperative in a manner appropriate to their sex.

Given the title of this book, the reader would expect the author to urge women to be meek and reclusive. And indeed, Madame Zheng warns women not to seek profit or follow their desires. But she also encourages them to cultivate their talents, as she assumes that a clever and resourceful woman will be more capable of fulfilling her family duties. Although a wife ranks below her husband, she nevertheless provides him with indispensable support and is largely responsible for the proper functioning of the household. To carry out her demanding duties correctly, a woman must be strong and capable. Overall, this book's tone seems somewhat contradictory. Zheng demands that women place themselves below men. Yet she also elevates women by portraying the roles of wife and mother as vital to a family's success.

Another Tang dynasty book written by a woman, *Analects for Women* (*Nü lunyu*), had an even greater and more immediate impact.[30] Song Ruoxin (d. ca. 820) allegedly wrote this book, and her sister Song Ruozhao (761–828) is said to have annotated it, although the authorship remains contested.[31] This was the only Tang work to be included in the "Four Books for Women" (*nü sishu*) canonized as the standard textbooks of female education during the later part of the Ming dynasty. Thereafter these four texts constituted the foundation of orthodox female education in Korea and Japan as well as China, so *Analects for Women* had an immense impact on ideas about gender throughout the region.[32]

The Song sisters were born into a family that had produced a long line of scholars. Their father considered their obtuse brother unteachable, so he gave his daughters an extensive education instead. Due to their unusual erudition, the Emperor Dezong took the two sisters into the palace to serve as teachers and to work in the inner palace bureaucracy. These talented women gained the emperor's notice, and some imperial scholars even believe that he made them imperial concubines.

The twelve chapters of this short book show the influence of more than twenty previous works, mostly those affiliated with the Confucian canon.[33] This strongly Confucian content conforms to the intellectual trends of the time.[34] By the late Tang, many educated people had become disillusioned with Daoism and Buddhism as political ideologies. They blamed China's growing chaos on the prominence of religious schools of thought, which they deemed inadequate to address the nation's current challenges. In reaction,

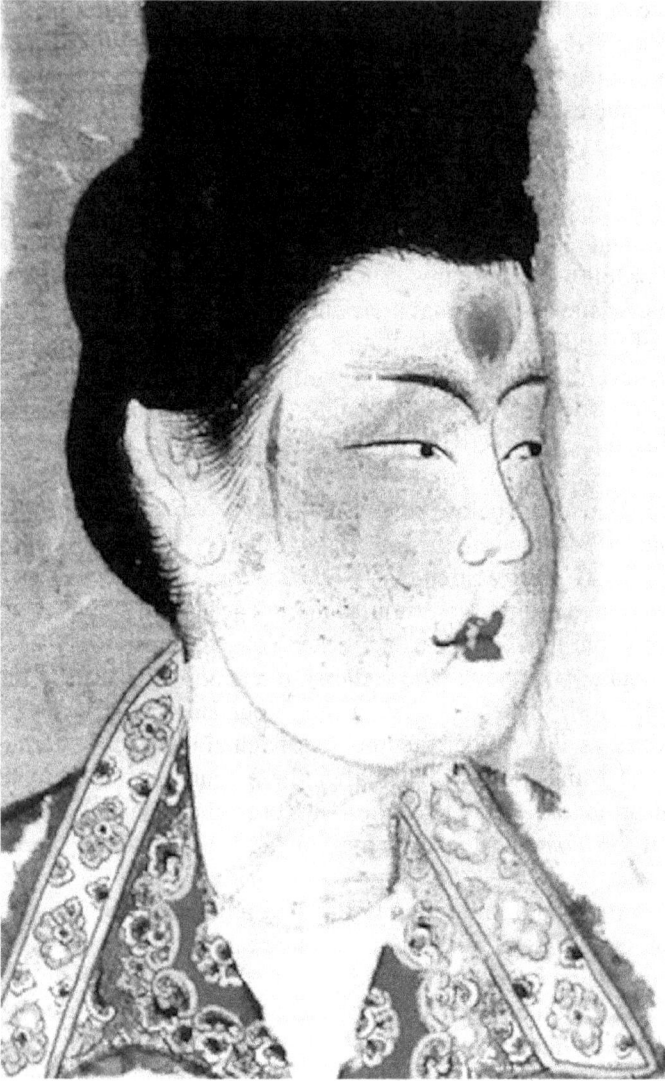

Figure 6.1 Wealthy Women Applied Copious Amounts of Cosmetics

revisionists strove to revive Confucianism, assuming that this ideology could stabilize the state and society. Moreover, as imperial power declined in the north, the great families of the northeast stepped in to fill the resulting vacuum. These families had traditionally put enormous stress on the rites and classical ethics, so their political ascent helped drive the Confucianization of late Tang culture.

Like *Classic of Filial Piety for Women, Analects for Women* took the name of an ancient classic and sought to apply similar ethical principles to female circumstances. However, the general style and tone differs substantially from the alleged model. Whereas the original Confucian *Analects* consists of loosely connected sayings attributed to the sage, each chapter of *Analects for Women* explores a specific issue in a coherent and comprehensive manner. The author writes in a colloquial rhyming style reminiscent of oral literature and popular Buddhist devotional works and often employs a sarcastic tone.

Critics have struggled to understand the use of such debased style in a Confucian textbook on ethics.[35] Perhaps the author spent time in the lower reaches of society and absorbed popular taste in literature. Or maybe she deliberately wrote in a colloquial manner to make the text accessible to a larger audience. Even an illiterate woman would find it easy to memorize and recite these rhymes. The contents of the work also differ from more theoretical discussions of gender. Although the work is ostensibly Confucian, it focuses on practice rather than theory, making it readily applicable to realistic situations encountered in daily life. Given the unrefined style and practical contents, the author clearly aimed the book at a mass audience rather than the cultured elite. As a result, despite the popularity of this important ethical text, critics decried its vulgarity.

The emphasis on ritual propriety in a popular work attests to the Confucianization of the lower rungs of society in the late Tang. Although Confucianism had been an elite school of thought for most of the dynasty, over time it increasingly permeated society at large. By writing in a way that would appeal to ordinary women, the author hoped to spread Confucian values to a wide readership. *Analects for Women* may not have been the first textbook intended for female students, but it marked the beginning of efforts to popularize Confucian-style female education.

The author probably named *Analects for Women* after the book most closely associated with Confucius to lend it prestige. Yet in fact the author borrowed most heavily from the famed *Admonitions for Women (Nüjie)* by the Han dynasty author Ban Zhao.[36] The text is even framed as being presented in the voice of Ban Zhao herself, giving it greater authority by connecting it to China's most famed female intellectual. *Analects for Women* emphasizes many of the same themes as this prototype but casts them in an informal and accessible style. Nevertheless, in some ways this book departs significantly from Ban's orthodox vision of virtuous womanhood. Most importantly, *Analects for Women* puts far fewer restrictions on women, making female rectitude more easily attainable. Although the author admonishes readers to adhere to the path of virtue, in fact this book mostly promotes practical values, such as industriousness. Other moral imperatives, such as obedience to senior kin, often apply to men as well as women.

Because *Analects for Women* borrows so heavily from Ban Zhao, it emphasizes duty, sacrifice, and harmony. A woman should put her family's interests before her own. She should be chaste and avoid mingling with men. A virtuous woman should treat her parents with filial regard before marriage and humbly revere her parents-in-law after she weds. A wife should make her husband the focal point for her life. And as a mother, the good woman must raise her children correctly. Most importantly, she must educate her sons in the classics and teach her daughters the rites. If a woman is widowed, she should decline remarriage and remain chaste if possible.

This book contains a few surprises. Although *Analects for Women* repeats earlier rhetoric about how women should restrain themselves lest they neglect their duties or cause trouble, overall it offers a more positive vision of the ideal woman than earlier texts on female ethics. Nowhere does the author valorize weakness. And even though late imperial works on female virtue tend to downplay women's intellectual capacity, this text portrays wisdom and talent as female assets. The author encourages women to use good judgment and cultivate their abilities. *Analects for Women* also offers a fresh perspective on sex and marriage. Whereas the purity of brides had usually been taken for granted, the author of this work explicitly emphasizes the need for unmarried women to safeguard their virginity. And in describing marriage, the author goes beyond moral duties such as righteousness to celebrate the emotional bond between spouses as important for maintaining conjugal harmony and fidelity.

⚬━━◆━━⚬

The Tang stands out as the golden age of poetry, which Chinese traditionally regarded as the loftiest type of literature. Although most poets were male, educated women wrote verse as well. Biographies and epitaphs of women frequently mention their poetic attainments. And a Dunhuang fragment of the collected works of female poets shows that several women sometimes circulated their writings together.[37] Women even wrote on walls while traveling to share their poetry with the public, a common practice at the time.[38] The massive anthology *Complete Tang Poems* (*Quan Tang shi*) includes a significant number of works by women. There are more than six hundred poems written in a wide range of styles and genres by more than one hundred women of different backgrounds, ranging from members of the imperial clan to courtesans. Even so, women's poems constitute a mere 1.34 percent of the entire collection.[39]

Educated readers believed that poetry not only expresses a person's ideas and sentiments but also displays the writer's inner character. Poems transmitted personal thoughts and memories to others and possibly preserved them for posterity. This exposure made female writers uneasy; they felt embarrassed revealing their inner feelings in public. Women writing for a large audience usually tried to maintain a sense of propriety by censoring themselves and refusing to reveal strong and intimate emotions. Nevertheless, many works still deal with extremely private feelings such as love and sadness.[40]

Unfortunately, readers today find much of this poetry difficult to understand. In conformity with the literary conventions of the time, female poets often expressed themselves very obliquely. For example, they evoked images of material objects that had feminine associations, such as textiles and mirrors, to express abstract notions. They also frequently alluded to historical figures and tropes from past poems to demonstrate erudition and convey their ideas in a sophisticated manner. Once modern readers understand these techniques, however, they can use these firsthand sources to explore how women viewed their own lives.

Although a great deal of Tang women's poetry employed standard styles and predictable content, creative women experimented with bold new modes of expression. In earlier centuries, most poetry about women had been written by men. Male poets sometimes found it interesting to take on a feminine voice and write from a woman's point of view. The sophistication of this ventriloquistic style peaked in the Liang and Qi dynasties of the sixth century. Of course, men writing as women expressed stereotypical male views of womanhood, portraying the female subject as extremely passive and dependent. The fictional woman of the male imagination required a man's attentions to be happy or even psychologically whole.

When large numbers of women began writing poetry, they often looked to these ventriloquisitic poems for guidance. A few Tang women also wrote in a faux feminine style, expressing gender stereotypes in deliberately delicate and pretty language.[41] However, some female poets cast aside men's ideas about proper female expression to appropriate the voice and themes of men's poetry. Women who wrote like men deliberately transgressed gender stereotypes. Instead of writing in the alleged feminine voice created by men, they shocked their readers by unexpectedly expressing anger, sarcasm, and an independent spirit.[42]

The masculine voice in women's poetry did not emerge suddenly. This technique evolved over the course of the Tang, steadily increasing in refinement and daring. The language of the most highly developed masculine-style poems by women cannot be readily distinguished from that of men. Women who wrote this way used spare diction and avoided ornamental flourishes, expressing their thoughts and aspirations in a straightforward manner. Appropriating the masculine voice not only let women compete with male poets but also opened up a far wider range of topics, allowing them to address the most pressing public issues of the day.[43] Previously, female poets had usually written about their private emotions and life in the inner quarters. By adopting manly diction, the scope of women's poetry expanded to include matters of public concern, such as warfare, chaos, and the struggles of life in a collapsing state.

The Daoist nun Yu Xuanji (844–ca. 868) stands out as perhaps the most sophisticated and daring female poet of the Tang.[44] Like some of her peers, she used stereotypical masculine-style language to write in a straightforward manner. However, instead of simply mimicking male poetry, she used the language traditionally associated with men to address themes that resonated with women.[45] This educated woman was not content to write poetry for a small circle of acquaintances. Instead she abandoned decorum and daringly put her unorthodox ideas and feelings on public display.[46] Having positioned herself outside the domestic sphere, Yu observed society from an unusual independent perspective that led her to ask difficult questions and make demands on those around her. Her poetry reflects an extremely insightful and critical worldview.

> It's easy to find a priceless treasure,
> Much harder to get a man with a heart!
> On my pillow, secretly flow my tears;
> Amidst the flowers, silently my guts are sliced.

In this remarkable poem, Yu takes on the hackneyed situation of a woman yearning for a man and gives it a shocking twist. As the poem's subject miserably contemplates an absent beloved, she does not passively accept her fate, as was customary. Instead she seethes with anger and resentment and ends up startling the reader with violent imagery.

Yu Xuanji had a short and tumultuous life.[47] She was passionate, sensitive, and beautiful. When young, Yu was taken into a cultured family as a concubine. There she received extensive literary training. Eventually Yu entered a Daoist convent, where she documented her tumultuous life with poetry. Her works describe both affairs with talented gentlemen and erotic feelings for women. Ultimately, however, Yu's strong passions ultimately proved to be her undoing. One day she became so enraged at her maid that she beat the woman to death. The authorities arrested her and she was eventually executed for murder. This shocking scandal may have cut short her life, but it also guaranteed her posthumous fame. While alive, Yu did not participate in elite literary circles and remained a hidden talent. But readers were drawn to the strange story of a nun executed for homicide, sparking curiosity about her life and poetry, and so she became a major literary figure after her death.

Some other talented Daoist nuns also became known for their poetry. Li Ye (d. 784) also lived a turbulent life.[48] She received an extensive literary education as a child and eventually became a courtesan, attracting renown for her beauty and talent. Li participated in major literary circles and made friends with important male poets who praised her writing. As her poetry gained fame, Emperor Daizong invited her to court. However, she disliked the tedious formality of palace life and soon returned home. Li Ye had the misfortune of living in a chaotic time. When a rebel army captured the capital and tried to usurp the dynasty, their would-be emperor forced Li to write poems denigrating the Tang ruling house. After Tang forces defeated this pretender, she was executed for treason.

Xue Tao (768–ca. 831) stands out as the most famous courtesan poet of the Tang.[49] Although she was born into the family of a minor official, after her father died her family descended into poverty. Out of necessity, Xue became a courtesan. In her youth she had received an extensive education centered on poetic composition, and she put her literary training to good use in her performances. In addition to composing creative poetry, Xue also made an unusual contribution to Chinese cultural history.[50] Originally sheets of writing paper had been fairly large. Xue Tao considered these big sheets unwieldy, so she wrote her poems on smaller pages. This sensible practice caught on and it soon became common for poets to write on small sheets of paper, which they named after Xue Tao to commemorate her invention.

Palace ladies also sometimes gained fame for their poetry. Their proximity to the ruler allowed talented women to gain the attention of influential courtiers and become well known. Empress Wu Zetian was a talented poet, and she wrote about a wide range of subjects.[51] Her poems cover a wide range of topics, including politics, religion, and the natural world. Xu Hui (627–650), a favored concubine of Emperor Taizong, also gained a reputation for exceptional verses.[52] She came from a literary family, and in her youth her father exposed her to ancient poetry as well as the Confucian classics. When she entered the palace, Xu made good use of the extensive imperial library and expert teachers to perfect her technique. Although her contemporaries regarded Xu as a significant poet, she was forgotten soon after her death. Even though she likely wrote a large volume of poetry, only five examples survive.

The interaction between talented men and women stands out as an important feature of Tang literary culture. Women did not always write in isolation or limit themselves to female literary readership. A few talented women engaged with men as cultured equals. Both sides seem to have found these exchanges stimulating and refreshing. The adoption of the masculine voice made it easier for women to interact with male peers. By writing in a stereotypical masculine style, female poets could engage male counterparts in ways that men immediately understood and appreciated. Writers of both sexes would sometimes compose poems on a common topic, usually one of the standard themes of men's poetry. As a result of these literary exchanges, female poets ended up writing about stock male themes that earlier generations of women had previously avoided, such as war and politics.[53] Men interacted with talented women in various ways. Sometimes a couple developed a romantic relationship, while in other cases, a common love of literature served as the basis of a cultured friendship.

Men sometimes addressed a respected female poet as a peer, downplaying gender difference. When the respected teacher Li She met a woman named Song Tai, the concubine of one of Li's old friends, he wrote two poems for her in which he reminisced about the banquets he had attended at his friend's home.[54] The two felt a common bond because of their shared intimacy with the same man, even though each had a very different relationship with him. Exchanging poems with men about shared experiences helped push women toward employing the masculine voice. Because Xue Tao exchanged poetry with male writers, her poems often employ a stereotypical masculine style.[55] Her works do not show any trace of resistance or critique. Instead she simply embraced the literary mainstream in order to gain acceptance by male cultural figures.

When men and women came together for cultural activities, they did not interact as complete equals. Prevailing masculine privilege gave male poets an air of authority, and talented women deferred to them. In one poem to a high official, Xue Tao cautiously places herself in a subservient position by taking on the role of student.[56]

> Brush and inkstone ready at hand
> poetry books surround my chair;
> you have been so attentive to me,
> I could be your protégée.

These unequal relationships did not always go smoothly. Yu Xuanji felt immensely frustrated because her sex barred her from participating in the imperial exams and having an official career. Once she accompanied a group of men who had just passed the civil service examinations on an excursion to a Buddhist temple to inscribe their names on a commemorative plaque. She resented their success and wrote a poem to vent her jealousy and anger.[57]

> Cloudy peaks fill the eyes,
> far from the lightness of spring;
> silver spools of calligraphy
> take shape beneath my hand.
> Too bad my silken women's dress
> obscures my poetry;
> looking up, I uselessly
> envy the names on the list I see.

No matter how much talent a woman possessed, she still faced frustrating limits. A female writer might win admiration for her skill and creativity, yet she remained excluded from the most central realms of male-dominated society.

Chapter 7

Virtue

The Tang stands out as an important time of transition in ethical standards. Ever since the Eastern Han dynasty, the authority of Confucianism had been on the wane. The declining appeal of this stringent school of ethics allowed novel visions of the ideal woman to emerge. However, chaos marred the era of intellectual dominance by Daoism and Buddhism, causing many thinkers and officials to feel disillusioned. They realized that religious and metaphysical teachings were often ill suited to address practical matters, and many concluded that the popularity of otherworldly ideas had brought disorder. The An Lushan Rebellion of 755 shocked many people into reassessing Confucianism. Many officials came to believe that robust Confucian ideals could strengthen the state and mend their fractured society.[1] As a result, Confucianism's advocates engaged intensively with politics and society. Scholars turned away from bookish exegesis to stress socially transformative ethics, such as loyalty to superiors and the maintenance of orderly hierarchies.

The nascent Confucian revival affected views toward women. Writers put renewed emphasis on women's virtue while downplaying talent, beauty, and domestic labor. They underscored the ancient idea that female malfeasance invites chaos and perhaps even dynastic collapse.[2] Rulers and officials sought to restrain the behavior of palace ladies to avoid the rise of another Wu Zetian or Yang Guifei. However, as Confucian thinkers sought to address women's matters, they faced a major problem. The classical canon has little to say about female virtue, and terse statements on the subject sometimes conflicted. So even though the patriarchal organization of society forced women to confront moral dilemmas more often than men, classical Confucian guidelines for female behavior were neither clear nor coherent.[3]

Confucianism stresses intellectual and moral cultivation as necessary prerequisites for comprehending ethical imperatives. In consequence, as this way of thought regained influence, people put increasing stress on female education. However, in line with Confucian priorities, the goal of education shifted away from nurturing talent and instead stressed the inculcation of virtue. Writers promulgated innovative new textbooks aimed at women that addressed moral issues in detail. This ethical program seems to have had some success, and stringent Confucian moral concepts reverberated through the larger society. By the ninth century, more people followed classical norms to ensure the orthodoxy of family arrangements, and marriage practices showed increased Confucian influence.[4]

Some families enthusiastically embraced these demanding ethics. The great Shandong families adhered to strict ritual regulations as a way to distinguish themselves from the hoi polloi, and both epitaphs and poetry show that their women often sought to practice Confucian virtues such as filiality and ritual orthodoxy.[5] Nevertheless, in this era the Confucian revival had only just begun, and most of the elite still showed little interest in classical injunctions about virtue. Because the Tang ruling house and many aristocratic families had intermarried with the Xianbei and other pastoral peoples for centuries, their hybrid culture had little regard for Confucian orthodoxy. Members of the Tang imperial clan even ignored incest taboos and intermarried freely with relatives.[6]

Literature suggests that women held a range of positions toward Confucian ethics.[7] The female protagonists in some fictional works acknowledge these principles, occasionally with enthusiasm, and authors depict them citing Confucian ideas to justify their behavior. In other cases, however, fictional characters ignored or challenged these regulations. In extreme cases, they actively rebelled, choosing to exercise individual autonomy rather than conform to ancient moral ideals. Popular stories even described women expressing erotic desire and engaging in extramarital trysts.

Confucianism was not the only wellspring of ethical thought in this era. Many women continued to turn to Buddhism for guidance, often in response to personal crisis or loneliness.[8] Confucianism and Buddhism differ in many ways, so these two schools of thought sometimes promoted contradictory priorities. Whereas Confucianism focuses on society, Buddhism emphasizes the individual's inner life. The impact of Buddhism on Chinese ethics cut across social ranks. While the uppermost elite increasingly asserted their fealty to the rites and classics, they often respected Buddhist teachings as well. The sinicization of Buddhism made it easier for the aristocracy to embrace the religion's ethical program. Over the centuries, Buddhism had assimilated many secular ideas about virtue, including Confucian teachings, and presented them to believers as sacred obligations. For example, sinicized Buddhism reinterpreted some Chinese ritual norms as tools to extinguish selfishness and cultivate compassion. Monks and nuns taught women to fulfill conventional family roles, diligently carry out maternal responsibilities, and embrace filial piety.

Both religious and secular ethics framed women's lives within a domestic context. Unlike men, women ideally had little to do with people outside their circle of kin, so their ethical responsibilities consisted mostly of correctly fulfilling family roles. The *New Tang History* (*Xin Tangshu*) prefaces a section of women's biographies by noting that each of the major female kinship roles carries ethical imperatives.[9] Daughters must be filial, wives should maintain their integrity, and mothers ought to be righteous and kind. Emphasizing family as the context of female ethics carried other implications as well. Inscribed eulogies often associated virtue with lofty ancestry, attributing exemplary behavior to high social background.[10] This viewpoint portrayed female virtue as heritable, an assumption that would fade in later eras.

The Tang dynasty saw the compilation of some important works devoted to female virtue. Based largely on classical ideas, these texts usually taught moderation and flexibility. Didactic biographies also described female virtue, but framed them within concrete situations expressed through narrative. The collection of the Han dynasty biographer Liu Xiang remained most influential, and epigones circulated similar works. For example, Lu Shinan (558–638) compiled a book called *Biographies of Women* (*Lienü zhuan*). Although praised at the time, the text has not been transmitted down to the present.[11] Given the title, it appears to have been an imitation of Liu Xiang's canonical collection. Due to the derivative nature of this genre, collections of women's biographies tended to maintain Han dynasty ideas about female virtue and did not necessarily reflect contemporary attitudes.

In addition to independent compilations of the lives of virtuous women, the standard histories also include biographies of female figures chosen to represent key virtues.[12] In an age of ethnic intermixing, native virtues became markers of Chinese identity, which helps explain why scholars emphasized them in their writings.[13] *Records of Sui* (*Suishu*), compiled by imperial command and completed in the year 636, incorporates ethical ideals that were common among the elite at the time. Widow chastity, filial piety, and maternal instruction constitute particularly important themes.[14] However, the emphasis on ritual propriety marks a disjunction from female biography in previous standard histories.[15] Only 15 percent of the women in this collection stand out as talented or wise, with the remainder gaining recognition for their adherence to stringent moral standards.

The two Tang dynasty histories, written about a century apart, present greater interpretive difficulties. Song dynasty historians assembled and edited the sections on female moral biography. Because these texts were compiled after the Tang, the authors might have projected anachronistic values onto this material.[16] Severe Neo-Confucian gender values may have influenced how Song scholars portrayed Tang ideas about female virtue, such as the assumption that righteousness requires women to submit to men.[17] Whatever the reason, these two histories highlight women whose actions exemplify important moral themes, including chastity, filial piety, righteousness, and loyalty. As with *Records of Sui*, the biographical sections of these two works depart from early medieval antecedents in downplaying the significance of female wisdom.

The two Tang standard histories also reveal new ethical priorities. Some narratives describe the behavior of daughters who went to great lengths to express filial devotion. These stories mostly focus on women who performed funeral rites for their parents in a painstaking fashion or undertook unusually arduous mourning. The ideal wives in these biographies show their dedication to the conjugal bond by maintaining chastity at all costs, even if this required them to resort to self-mutilation or suicide. Chastity receives more emphasis in these works than in the previous standard histories or in Liu Xiang's prototype. In particular, the Tang histories describe widows who suffer threats or assaults, and they can often only maintain their chastity by mutilating themselves or committing suicide. The subjects of these biographies mostly come from important families that were more likely to adhere to the most stringent ethical standards, including uncompromising chastity.

While the two Tang histories express new moral concerns, they also maintain certain traditional ideals. One biography describes how a model woman beat her father's murderer to death with a brick. Another vengeful woman killed a man who had injured her father, then cut out his heart and liver and used them to conduct a sacrifice on her father's tomb.[18] Although righteous vengeance was not uncommon in the Eastern Han, some medieval authorities looked askance at this sort of violence. Nevertheless, the two Tang standard histories sanction female vengeance as a laudable expression of righteousness. Other genres featured similar vengeance stories. Authors of fiction wrote stories about female "knights errant" (*nüxia*). The strong women in these tales employ their wit and physical strength to redress wrongs and bring a modicum of justice to the world.[19] Poems, biographies, official histories, and other prose narratives all celebrated female avengers. However, writers found it difficult to reconcile the violence of these vindictive women with the gentle stereotypes of conventional femininity. While the behavior of female avengers sometimes earned praise, it also elicited concern. During the Tang, old and new ideas about female virtue intermingled. The resulting contrasts and contradictions ultimately transformed gender ethics.

As people increasingly emphasized the importance of female virtue, the government redirected the official commendation system (*jingbiao*) to encourage women to adhere to high ethical standards. This system dated back to the Han dynasty.[20] At that time, an emperor would occasionally respond to a report sent up from the provinces and publicly commend a moral paragon who embodied a key virtue such as filial piety, loyalty, or chastity. Women sometimes received this sort of honor, which came with various possible rewards—a memorial arch or stele, honorific title, or valuables. In addition to the national commendation system managed by the central government, some local officials also honored virtuous women in their districts on an ad hoc basis.

The Tang revived the commendation system and made it more systematic and comprehensive than before. As part of Empress Wu Zetian's project to legitimize her controversial reign, she cultivated an image of rectitude by rewarding filial piety and righteousness.[21] Subsequent rulers issued commendations to promote politically useful values such as filial piety and loyalty. Toward the end of the dynasty, officials enthusiastically promoted this institution. In their view, the decline of ethical standards had led to a breakdown in discipline, fomenting anarchy and rebellion. They dispensed commendations to promote Confucian virtues among the populace in the hope that fostering individual morality would somehow stabilize the realm.

As officials standardized and enlarged the commendation system, they promulgated detailed bureaucratic procedures to make it more reliable.[22] Some recipients received tangible prizes, mostly exemptions from taxes and corvée duty. This practice drew some criticism, as removing productive people from the fiscal system reduced government revenues. To reduce the burden borne by the state, many honorees received only symbolic awards such as commemorative monuments or titles. Over time, the types of virtue singled out for recognition gradually shifted. It was often no longer sufficient to display virtue in a conventional manner. Instead commendations increasingly rewarded people who undertook extreme measures in the name of virtue, such as living in a crude hut next to a parent's grave during the entire three-year mourning period. Widow chastity also became increasingly worthy of commendation, presaging the future direction of state patronage of virtue. In the late imperial era, this system mostly commemorated widows who declined remarriage.[23]

○══✦══○

During the Tang, novel ideas about the nature of marriage informed discussions of conjugal ethics. Most importantly, many poems and stories portrayed marriage as determined by heaven (*tian*) or fate (*ming*).[24] According to this belief, no matter how much someone wanted to marry a particular person, if heaven did not resolve to bring the marriage about, it could not take place.

The reverse also held true. Even if two families were sworn enemies, their children would definitely wed if heaven fated it. The central place of religion in medieval society helps account for the rise of this supernatural view of marriage.[25] Centuries of influence from Buddhism and Daoism had made prevailing ideas and values much more otherworldly, and people had become accustomed to viewing their own lives through the prism of religion. Buddhist teachings emphasize the importance of karma in determining the course of a person's life. As this attitude entered popular culture, people reimagined karma as the machinations of heaven. According to this viewpoint, heaven's will determines major life events, including marriage. The custom of arranged marriage further bolstered people's sense of resignation in the face of fate. Because family elders chose their children's spouses, many people had little say in their choice of partner. Under these circumstances, bride and groom could come to feel that mysterious divine forces had predetermined their marriage.[26]

This belief that marriages have divine inspiration affected how people viewed the institution. Most importantly, society increasingly emphasized the importance of wifely fidelity and widow chastity.[27] If heaven had fated two people to marry, how could they possibly divorce? And how could a widow marry someone other than her original spouse, who had been selected by heaven? According to this line of reasoning, because marriage has a supernatural foundation, it ought to be permanent. In light of these increasingly stringent views, some widows declined remarriage in the belief that they should remain faithful to a heavenly fated spouse until the end of their lives. The rising importance of chastity represents one of the key trends in Tang moral life. In later eras, the rhetoric of chastity would steadily intensify to take on the fervor of a religious cult.

More generally, as a result of the intensification of marital ethics, separation of the sexes became increasingly visible. The classical rites enjoined women to seclude themselves within the inner quarters of the home and avoid contact with unrelated men. Isolation made it easier for them to reserve their bodies for their husbands alone.[28] As before, domestic architecture strictly separated the male and female realms in accordance with propriety. In large houses and palaces, the two areas came together at a place called the central gate (*zhongmen*) or main hall threshold (*tangyu*).[29] Whether or not a man could pass through this gate and enter the women's realm depended on his age, status, and relationship with the master of the house. In some households, monks could enter the woman's quarters freely, as could close male relatives. Most men, however, were strictly forbidden from crossing into the female areas of the home.

The physical threats that women might face fueled concerns about female sexual integrity. Bandits and foreign invaders often killed the men that they captured but carried off women as booty, along with valuables such as gold, cloth, and useful animals.[30] Even in peaceful times, rogue officials could be extremely vicious, abducting women from their families to ravish them. The state did not necessarily demand lifelong fidelity either. Medieval governments sometimes forced women to marry soldiers, a practice that continued into the Sui.[31] And if a married man had an affair with an unmarried woman, Tang law did not even consider it adultery (*tongjian*).[32]

Nevertheless, compared to later eras, Tang women still had considerable freedom to go outside the home and mingle with men. For example, one poem describes women watching men play polo.[33] Casual interaction of this sort presented opportunities to flirt and arrange trysts. In the popular imagination, this independence gave rise to opportunities for them to engage in voluntary sexual encounters. Historical writings duly describe many instances of adultery and extramarital affairs.[34] And documents from Dunhuang record children being born out of wedlock.[35]

Parents worried about the problems that could arise from sexual license. If an unmarried daughter ruined her reputation or became pregnant, she decreased her value on the marriage market and deprived them of a valuable betrothal gift. The perennial popularity of the old story of Qiu Hu, a shameless lothario who embarrassed himself by accidently propositioning his own wife, thinking that she was a stranger, reflected this anxiety. Popular literature preserved at Dunhuang shows that people continued to retell this instructive tale, as it resonated with their own concerns about the difficulties of protecting women from unruly men.[36]

Views toward sex altered significantly at this time.[37] Previously, Daoism had exerted the most visible influence on how people understood sexuality. Han dynasty texts on sexual technique, for example, employed Daoist terminology to describe intercourse. Some Tang authors maintained a Daoist point of view and continued to use this sort of jargon when discussing sexual acts. However, the rise of esoteric Vajrayāna Buddhism introduced radically different ways of thinking about sex and the body. While ancient Buddhists had seen celibacy as a precondition for serious religious practice, practitioners of tantra believed that certain sex acts could be harnessed to attain wisdom and spiritual awakening. This compelling notion spurred people to rethink their views of sexuality and helps account for the rising popularity of erotic literature.

Although a society might tolerate premarital or extramarital sexual behavior, people do not regard it as positive, as informal liaisons rarely benefit the family.[38] The Tang marriage system made the consequences of premarital sex even more undesirable. The marriage of a daughter brought her parents financial gain, as they collected a generous betrothal gift. And aristocratic families used the marriages of their daughters to ally themselves with useful in-laws. Given the advantages of arranged marriage, the loss of a young woman's virginity could represent a significant setback for her entire family. If an unmarried woman gained a reputation for lax sexual morals, finding a good marriage would become very difficult. Potential in-laws would think twice before handing out a large betrothal gift for a sexually incontinent bride.[39] And if an unmarried woman became pregnant, she might end up having to marry the father of her child, even if he came from a much lower background. Given the dangers of allowing women to become sexually active before marriage, it made sense for families to stress bridal virginity. Although these concerns affected the aristocracy the most, ordinary families began to display similar attitudes. People often emulated those of a higher station, taking on the same behaviors and values as a way to stake a claim to prestige. As a result, even humble families whose marital alliances had little use might still stress virginity and chastity to raise their social ranking.[40]

Demanding that women safeguard their bodies increased male power in the family, as it provided a rationale for men to seclude women and control their bodies. Moreover, as virginity increased in social importance, this quality took on important secondary meanings as well. People did not just justify virginity as a practical measure that benefited the family but also valorized it as a lofty virtue. Female chastity rose in importance to become a prime moral trait analogous to male loyalty.[41] The desire for virginal brides led to an increased emphasis on all forms of female sexual integrity, including wifely fidelity and widow chastity.

As in many other societies, female chastity became a component in the masculine honor of male kin.[42] Someone could disgrace an entire family by compromising their daughter's virginity. For example, after killing an enemy, one man forced his victim's daughter to become his concubine, thus humiliating his foe's family.[43] Across the social spectrum, women's sexual integrity became associated with family honor. In particular, it became an important component of the public image of her male family members.

Views toward chastity evolved considerably during this period. With the advent of the Sui dynasty, chastity very suddenly became a topic of major concern at the top of society. The violent jealousy of Empress Wenxian, the formidable wife of Emperor Wen, affected views of marital fidelity.[44] Even though concubinage had been common since antiquity, Wenxian brought the morality of this practice into question. She helped depose the heir apparent because of his close relationship with a concubine and shunned officials whose concubines became pregnant. Not coincidentally, the standard history of the dynasty gives unusual emphasis to chastity. Didactic biographies of women in *Records of Sui* abridge female virtue down to two key moral obligations: widow chastity and fidelity.[45] Epitaphs from the dynasty also put great stress on chastity. These commemorations include forty-six chaste widows and one woman who declined to marry at all.[46]

During the early Tang, chastity was not a key moral priority. Many short stories show women divorcing, remarrying, and pursuing love outside of marriage.[47] And even though Confucian revivalists encouraged female fidelity, they did not view chastity as one of the most important ethical issues. At the time, Confucian moralists did not demand that widows avoid remarriage. They merely saw lifelong chastity as a virtuous option that widows should consider.[48] But gradually, the rising emphasis on the rites elicited a more stringent view of marital ethics. Although the aristocracy put greatest stress on these regulations, these ideas had a steadily increasing influence throughout society. During the late Tang, edicts sought to restrict remarriage, and popular literature portrayed chastity as an important female virtue.[49]

The Confucian revival spurred an intensification of chastity rhetoric. But by valorizing chastity, people came to demand immense sacrifices from widows. Everyone knew that it was extremely difficult for a woman to live without the support of an adult man. With the exception of nuns, who lived within a supportive community of peers, a woman without a husband seemed pitiful. Even if a man only went away from home temporarily, poetry still describes the wife he left behind as lonely and miserable. Poems sent to absent husbands express anxiety for their health and safety, as women feared that their spouses might never return. Some wives suspected that an absent man had found a new woman, and jealousy combined with uncertainty compounded their unhappiness.[50] Intense concern over separation highlighted the importance of a supportive man to a woman's well-being. If a man abandoned or divorced his wife, her life might be very difficult. Poetry depicts unattached women as powerless victims haunted by the specter of destitution.[51]

Widowhood had an equally grim image. A poem warns the wife to enjoy her present life, as the death of her husband will bring an end to her happiness and security.[52]

Flower-gazing yesterday—
    flowers bright with bloom.
Flower-gazing at dawn today—
    flowers soon to fall.
Best drain it dry, this joy, this pleasure,
    underneath the flowers;
Don't wait for those springtime winds
    to gust them all away.[53]

If a widow's in-laws did not want her, and her own family would not take her back, she would have to work very hard just to survive. Able-bodied widows could make a modest living by spinning and weaving. However, this sort of life was very hard and uncertain. When a widow became too old to work or fell ill, she would have no way to survive. Given the fragility of the widow's existence, a husband's death could quickly turn his spouse into a pathetic beggar.[53]

A widow's age at the time of her husband's death helped determine her opportunities. Poems lamented the fate of elderly women who were unmarriageable due to advanced age. In contrast, a young widow had the option of finding a new spouse.[54] Women usually entered their first marriage in their mid- to late teens, and they were at least a few years younger than their husbands. If a man's previous spouse had died and she was his second wife, the age gap would likely be even larger. Also, many officials delayed marriage until they had established a successful career, which did not occur until they were in their forties. In the meantime, they would often take a concubine who could begin to bear children immediately. When such a man finally married, the age gap between him and his wife would likely be very large. The customary difference in ages made it likely that a wife would outlive her husband, so many women's lives ended in widowhood.

Estimates of the average age of death of elite women, as recorded in epitaphs, range from 42.1 to 64.2.[55] A study of Sui epitaphs concluded that elite men and women had approximately the same life span, dying at an average age of 62.2 years. And a particularly detailed study of 1,844 Tang epitaphs that mention a woman's age of death puts the average at 56.84.[56] The typical age at death shifted considerably over the course of the dynasty. Women died younger as society became more chaotic.[57] Whereas the average age at death was 62.92 in the early part of the dynasty (618–712), by the middle Tang (713–805) it had decreased to 55.63, and female life expectancy fell to 49.67 in the late Tang (806–904). In the mid-seventh century, the life spans of men and women were roughly equal, but by the mid-ninth century, men lived 15.41 years longer than women on average. Overall, the husbands of most widows (51 percent) died within the first fifteen years of marriage.[58] Epitaphs of Tang widows show that 24.5 percent lost their husbands when they were between the ages of 40 and 49, and 26.3 percent when they were 50 to 59 years old.[59] Another study of inscriptions shows the average age of widowhood as 50.7. On average, the widows mentioned in epitaphs continued to live for 19.13 years after the death of their husbands.[60]

These figures show that widows fell into two main types, each faced with different possibilities. Older women had few good options, but young widows could easily remarry and get a fresh start in life, particularly if they lacked children. Regardless of whether a widow remarried or not, her primary duty was to give her husband a proper funeral and burial.[61] Given the cost and complexity of these arrangements, widows immediately found themselves saddled with a huge burden. If a widow had an adult son, he would take charge of the obsequies. However, if her children were young or if her adult sons lived in a distant place, this arduous responsibility fell to the widow. If her husband had died while away from home on business, moving his body home could be particularly difficult and expensive, and epitaphs describe these logistical nightmares.

Next, a widow had the responsibility of raising her children to maturity.[62] If she came from an elite background, she was expected to educate them to qualify for a civil service career. Epitaphs show that a widow's children were often very young when her husband died, so caring for them until adulthood and seeing to their education could entail a lengthy obligation. Widows often had to do much of the teaching themselves, and epitaphs praise mothers able to explain the classical canon to their children. When a widow's sons reached adulthood, if they came from an elite background she would have to help them build relationships with well-connected men and embark on an official career.

A woman's social background also influenced the conditions of widowhood. Although a widow did not inherit property from her husband, if he lacked an adult son she would have to manage the estate on her children's behalf until they reached maturity, or for the rest of her life if she were childless.[63] From a financial perspective, the widow held a status akin to head of household, holding veto power over the sale, mortgage, and use of family property. The equal field system also allocated land to widows to help them survive.

Over the course of the Tang, a growing number of thinkers came to believe that a widow ought to try to remain chaste if possible.[64] They thought that any widow with sufficient resources should seclude herself in the home, renounce remarriage, and assume the mantle of a paragon of chastity. According to the *Tang Code*, when a man died, his parents assumed power over his children. Because children belonged to the husband's ancestral line, if a widow remarried she would often have to leave them behind with their paternal kin.[65] In theory, a widow was expected to remain in her deceased husband's home and carry out her filial obligation to serve his parents. Many chaste widows remained in the home of their deceased husbands, particularly if they had children. Some elders might welcome the presence of an attentive daughter-in-law to care for them in old age. And they might discourage her from remarrying so as to keep her dowry in their household.[66]

However, living with a deceased husband's kin was not always easy, and widows often had fraught relations with their in-laws. People did not necessarily want a son's widow to continue residing with them.[67] It was often in their interests to force a widow to leave so that they would not have to support her and to reclaim control of family property. They might bully or physically abuse her so that she would remarry or return home. When life with hostile in-laws became unbearable, a chaste widow would usually leave her conjugal home and live out the remainder of her life among blood kin.

Most importantly, a widow had to decide whether or not to remarry. Taking a new spouse never posed a problem for men. Due to the custom of concubinage, society did not expect a husband to remain absolutely faithful to his spouse, even if some wives felt otherwise. In contrast, widows faced difficult and equivocal choices. People increasingly praised widows who declined remarriage, yet everyone knew that such a life might entail terrible privation. Not only were most widows poor, but life outside of marriage, society's most fundamental institution, could also be lonely, inconvenient, and even dangerous. One chaste widow had recurring dreams that a man wanted to marry her, revealing the inner struggle that she faced in resisting remarriage.[68]

Did widows usually remarry or remain chaste? Historians have struggled to reconcile the contradictory and incomplete data regarding the rate of widow remarriage. Some hold that Tang widows remarried frequently, while others see second marriages as fairly rare.[69] At the apex of society, princesses frequently entered a second union.[70] Out of 130 known princesses, twenty-seven married twice and three of them wed three times. Overall, 23 percent of Tang dynasty princesses remarried. Significantly, the rate of princess remarriage changed significantly over time. Princesses took a second spouse most frequently in the early part of the dynasty. After the An Lushan Rebellion in the mid-eighth century, attitudes hardened and Emperor Xuanzong prohibited princesses with children from remarrying.[71] In the ninth century, during the chaotic waning years of the dynasty, princess remarriage ceased.[72] However, these uniquely privileged women cannot be taken to represent mainstream practices. In particular, because the Tang imperial line had intermarried repeatedly with foreign peoples and assimilated nomadic culture to a considerable degree, they may have had a distinct perspective on this matter.[73]

Epitaphs provide mixed clues as to the frequency of widow remarriage. Among thousands of inscriptions, only about fifteen mention a widow remarrying.[74] However, the strange paucity of remarriage among these otherwise informative texts might not accurately reflect the actual behavior of the women they describe. People did not intend commemorative epitaphs to be complete and objective biographies. Family members, usually children, commissioned a funerary inscription to praise the deceased, so they would likely omit any embarrassing details. Whereas a gentry family would have been proud to record that their mother had been a chaste widow, they might not mention awkward facts such as remarriage.

Widows who remarried were often young and lacked children. Offspring could support an unmarried woman in old age, making it easier for her to decline remarriage. A widow also had to consider other aspects of her situation. Did her kinsmen want her to remain chaste? Could she bear to live alone for the rest of her life? Would she possibly face the threat of rape or harassment? If she tried to remarry, would she be able to attract a suitable spouse? And how would her new husband's family treat a remarried widow?

Men did not consider a widow the best possible marriage partner, so a woman who remarried might well end up with a new husband older or poorer than her first. She would also assume a lower position in his family.[75] And she might have to deal with children from her new husband's first marriage. Tang ritual regulations required children to mourn the same way for both mother and stepmother. As mourning relations were carefully calibrated to express the closeness of family bonds, in theory a second wife had the same status as the first. Nevertheless, stepmothers often had tense relations with their husbands' children from a previous marriage. A widow who remarried might have to deal with hostile stepchildren who regarded her as an unwelcome interloper.[76]

After a man's death, if his wife chose not to seek a new husband, she assumed the identity of a chaste widow as her prime social role. People held various views of this practice, and several factors affected an individual's particular attitudes. In this multicultural state, nomadic customs often affected family life.[77] Steppe marriage differed considerably from native Chinese practices. Not only did pastoralists allow widow remarriage, but they sometimes even required it. Among northern nomadic peoples, when a man died the community often expected his widow to enter a levirate marriage with his brother or another kinsman. Because men had to exchange expensive betrothal gifts for a bride, families were loath to allow widows to leave. If a widow married an outsider, the bridewealth paid out by her first husband's family would seem wasted. Levirate allowed them to retain their investment. This custom might also have been a compassionate measure, as a widow unmoored from the kinship network could face sudden impoverishment. Although levirate was usually considered a nomadic custom, Dunhuang documents record this sort of marriage among ethnic Han. Even members of the Tang aristocracy sometimes practiced levirate.

In contrast, Confucianism inspired people to denigrate remarriage. If a widow or her family embraced Confucian teachings, she would be less amenable to taking a second husband. A divorced woman named Madame Pei had read Liu Xiang's *Biographies of Women* and concluded that because none of the role models in the collection had remarried, taking a second husband would be unethical. As she put it, "There is no rite of remarriage."[78] The starkly different moral priorities of Confucianism and pastoral culture pulled widows in opposite directions. The relative importance that a particular woman placed on each ethical system affected how she regarded chastity and remarriage.

Women remarried for various reasons.[79] Epitaphs usually cite economic necessity as the decisive factor. And if a woman had been divorced or abandoned, she would probably feel no reason to remain loyal to a man who did not want her. In other cases, a widow's kin forced her to remarry. The law prohibited the forced remarriage of women—except by parents or grandparents. So the Tang code gave parents and grandparents the power to decide whether or not a widow should enter a second marriage.[80]

Sometimes natal kin arranged for a woman to remarry out of concern for her welfare. However, they often decided the question of remarriage based on common family interests, not the wellbeing or desires of the woman in question. If a woman's family married her off, they would not have to support her. Moreover, they could collect another round of betrothal gifts, gaining a financial windfall. Given these incentives, a widow's relatives sometimes pushed her into remarriage. One woman's biography even records that her maternal uncle forced her to take a new husband.[81]

But families had to consider more than just financial gain. The nobility often discouraged their women from remarrying as a way to publicly display their probity, thereby earning respect for all of a family's members. It seems that some people even considered it unseemly for a woman from an exalted background to remarry. In 596 Emperor Wen prohibited the remarriage of not just the wives of high officials but even their concubines.[82]

The poem "Song of the Widow" (*Jiefu yin*) by Zhang Ji (767–830) praises the chaste widow, holding her up as a virtuous female archetype.[83] However, writers usually described chastity instead of lauding it. This dispassionate rhetoric implies that many people took a neutral attitude toward the practice, seeing it as neither necessary nor undesirable.[84] Opinions about remarriage seem to have hardened over time, with assessments becoming more stringent in the latter half of the Tang. Most records of divorce and remarriage date to the first half of the eighth century, when the dynasty reached its zenith.[85] Both divorce and remarriage seem to have become less frequent in the subsequent era of long decline. In the late Tang, various texts document rising regard for widow chastity among the elite and common people alike.[86] Overall, however, attitudes remained moderate. People saw the decision to remarry or remain chaste as a quandary, and a widow's decision depended on her particular circumstances and inclinations.

Shifting government policies also affected the desirability of remarriage. Although Emperor Wen of Sui sent down an unusual edict prohibiting remarriage among the officialdom, he seems to have been motivated by practical concerns.[87] With the realm in chaos, the justice system had broken down in many places, and the monarch wanted to prevent widows from being sold as wives or concubines by the families of their deceased husbands. Even so, this regulation seems to have been unpopular and was soon repealed. The Sui also faced the problem of soldiers absconding from the army. To tie soldiers to their posts, in 617 Emperor Yang ordered that marriages be arranged between soldiers and local women.[88] The army distributed widows, adulteresses, and female clerics to soldiers as wives. All in all, the Sui took a transactional position toward remarriage, adjusting their policies according to the priorities of the moment.

Over the centuries of internecine warfare that preceded reunification, the population had declined precipitously in many areas. In response, Tang authorities took action to encourage childbearing. And because the ruling house had roots in nomadic culture, they initially felt unmoved by chastity rhetoric. Emperor Taizong encouraged widows and widowers to remarry.[89] If a widow did not have a family to help her arrange a new marriage, local officials were to take the initiative and locate relatives or rich patrons who could provide a suitable betrothal gift. Magistrates even sometimes made immediate remarriage a precondition for divorce as a way of keeping people in wedlock.[90] Even so, the state did not coerce widows over the age of sixty and those with children to remarry.

Fiscal goals also had an impact on official attitudes toward remarriage and chastity.[91] After the founding of the Tang, the population quickly recovered, adding many people to the tax roles. When the state faced less financial pressure, officials no longer aggressively encouraged marriage. Moreover, after the tax reform of 780, widows could easily own property and be taxed, so the government did not have to force a woman into marriage in order to tax her. Not only did changing financial conditions affect attitudes among the officialdom, but they also affected the prospects of widows. A woman had to consider these fluctuating financial realities when pondering her future course in life.

When a woman remarried, her family eventually faced the question of how to bury a second wife.[92] Because epitaphs rarely mentioned remarriage, it is difficult to assess how these women were laid to rest. People generally believed that a wife should be interred next to her husband, as this had been the norm for centuries.[93] But people held various views on which husband a woman should accompany in death. Some people believed that she should be interred with her second spouse. In other cases, remarried women were buried individually or else in the cemetery of their natal family, thereby circumventing this awkward problem. Epitaphs suggest that if a remarried woman had sons, she would usually be buried with the father of her children. If she had children by two husbands, the children of each spouse might quarrel over her burial. Overall, remarried women mentioned in epitaphs were usually buried singly, attesting to their ambiguous position in the kinship system.

Many chaste widows turned to religion—not just for solace but also to construct an acceptable social identity. Religious doctrine justified chastity and helped women endure a life outside of marriage.[94] Epitaphs show that some widows became devout Daoists and a far larger number turned to Buddhism. Of 235 epitaphs that mention that a deceased woman believed in Buddhism, 137 were widows, constituting 58 percent of the total. The clear link between widowhood and faith implies that the loss of a husband provided a strong impetus for intensifying religious practice.[95] Pious widows sometimes stopped using cosmetics and attractive clothing. Instead they cultivated an image of austerity, devoting themselves to prayer and chanting sutras. Those with sufficient resources would sometimes commission holy images or sutra copying.

Widows turned to Buddhism for various reasons. Some elevated widowhood into a state of moral purity by intertwining it with devout religious practice, depicting the rejection of remarriage as a sacred sacrifice. Religion also provided widows with psychological support. Pious women could use their faith to cope with solitude and hardship. Teachings about karma and rebirth provided hope that their sacrifices would eventually be rewarded in the next life. And Buddhism taught that practitioners should try to extinguish carnality and desire. This sort of passionless state would surely help a widow accept a life outside of marriage. Religion also provided devout women with an air of otherworldliness that helped legitimize their withdrawal from mundane affairs. The solace of religious teachings helped poor women cope with material deprivation. Yet even widows from wealthy backgrounds, including the famed Shandong families, sometimes turned to Buddhism. Some rejected burial beside their husbands, in contravention of the Confucian rites, choosing instead to have an individual Buddhist funeral.

The most devoted widows became clerics. Some entered Daoist temples. Of thirteen epitaphs for Tang Daoist nuns, four had entered a temple after the death of their husbands.[96] Other inscriptions record devout widows who practiced Daoism at home. Most widowed clergy, however, were Buddhist. Teachings against carnality helped justify chastity.[97] Nuns who took their vows in middle age usually did so after the death of a husband. Becoming a Buddhist nun provided a widow with a convenient way to maintain her chastity in a safe and supportive environment. In extreme cases, a woman who wanted to avoid marriage altogether could become a nun while young, or else remain at home and devote herself to religious practice, declaring her intention not to wed. These sorts of cases took the ideal of chastity to an extreme, seeing it not as loyalty to a deceased husband but as a state of virginal purity to be maintained throughout life.

Although the Tang saw some fusion of widow chastity with spirituality, most women remained in the mundane world after a husband's death.[98] Many remarried, either willingly or at the behest of family. A wife who decided against remarriage after her husband's demise assumed the role of chaste widow, a social category that came with expectations regarding her proper mindset and behavior. However, if she decided not to marry again, she would have had to navigate a world ill disposed to unattached women. A widow had to construct a social identity other than the standard role of wife. She had to find a way to sustain herself financially. And she also had to be prepared to withstand threats to her physical safety, as a woman without male protection faced the threat of sexual violence. Confronted with these difficulties, many widows returned home to their natal families, where they could receive security and support.[99]

A young widow could expect to live for decades, so she would require considerable financial support. A widow determined to forgo remarriage might want to return to the home of her birth. But many families would find it hard to maintain an extra member for so many years, particularly toward the end of the dynasty when impoverishment became widespread. An epitaph sums up this problem: "It is said that, at the capital, it is difficult to feed oneself; one cannot in the end support widows and young ones."[100] One family addressed this quandary by moving from the capital to the provinces, where expenses were lower. With these savings, they could use their limited resources to support more people, including a chaste widow and her children. The sources show that various kinsmen might potentially step in to help support a widow, including grown children, uncles, and in-laws.[101] Because people considered it costly to support a widow, usually only the gentry could afford to do so. Women from ordinary families had no choice but to remarry. As a result of this disparity, a family's support of a chaste widow became a status symbol indicative of wealth.[102]

Some stories about widowhood include accounts of self-mutilation and even suicide.[103] A link between chastity and violence dates back to the Western Han, when Liu Xiang wrote approvingly of women willing to sacrifice their lives to maintain their virtue. But this sort of extreme discourse stood at the margins of Liu's moral program. In the medieval era, however, violence gradually became a more prominent theme in chastity narratives. Most Tang biographies of female exemplars describe women from prominent backgrounds. These families treasured their collective honor, so their wives and daughters would rather die than be violated. During this era, violence, mutilation, and death became important themes in didactic biographies of women.[104]

The two Tang official histories have far more cases of female self-mutilation than earlier biographical collections.[105] The eighty-four biographies of women in all previous official histories describe only four instances of mutilation. In contrast, out of fifty-three Tang biographies, there are twelve cases of mutilation and an additional eight instances of women who cut off their hair to symbolize casting off physical beauty to preserve chastity. These stories describe how widows sometimes responded to forced remarriage or sexual assault by mutilating their features to become sexually undesirable. In one story, a chaste widow cuts off her ear to avoid remarriage.[106] She declares, "The husband is in heaven. Can he be betrayed?" This woman had read Liu Xiang's *Biographies of Women* (*Lienü zhuan*) and considered herself to be emulating ancient female icons of chastity.

Women who disfigured themselves or committed suicide did not act solely on their own behalf. Chastity rhetoric portrayed them as emblems of collective honor. Some women undertook these sorts of extreme actions to safeguard the reputation of their entire family. Writers expanded the rubric of chastity even further by making the female body a symbol of nationhood. Patriotic accounts portrayed the sacrifices of female martyrs, who killed themselves to maintain physical purity, as representing Chinese determination to resist foreign incursions at any cost.[107] In an age of increasing national weakness, some people found these powerful images emotionally compelling. The innovative ways that writers employed female martyrs to represent larger ideas of collective honor and determination help account for the increasing popularity of violent chastity stories as Tang society descended into chaos.

Chapter 8

Love

While didactic writings portrayed women as static moral archetypes, poetry and short stories often emphasized their inner emotional lives. Literature thus often provides more complex and nuanced views of women than the orthodox sources, which tend to be highly ideological and one dimensional. Writers of fiction attracted attention by creating compelling characters who exhibited intense passions and incompatible feelings. Many stories and poems struck a chord with readers because they illuminated common urges rarely addressed in allegedly factual writings. At the beginning of the Tang, restrictive Confucian ethics and the classical rites had limited impact, so people had considerable psychological space to explore the range of human emotion.[1] Instead of conforming to decorous roles, which demanded considerable self-restraint, some people acted on their desires and sought loving relationships. However, authentic desires often conflicted with propriety, and writers explored these contradictions. Tang literature probed the dimensions of passion by detailing the complications, frustrations, and varied consequences of love.

The literary imagination found rich material in both the exciting beginning of romance and its disappointing conclusion. The poet Xue Tao mused about the nature of affection.[2]

> I wonder when love's
> longings
> stir us most—
>
> when flowers bloom,
> or when flowers fall?

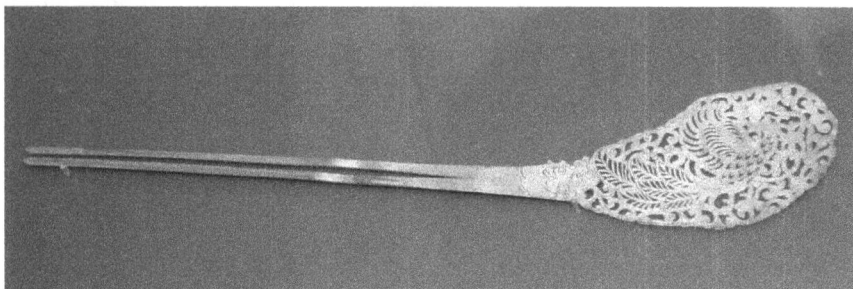

Figure 8.1 Silver Gilt Hairpin

The literature of earlier eras had also expressed strong feelings, and female writers of the Tang often adhered to conventions set down in Southern Dynasties boudoir poetry of the early sixth century. Liang dynasty poets in particular crafted emotionally charged depictions of beautiful women tormented by the absence of lovers who never reappear. The lovelorn woman depicted in these poems depends completely on a man. She must be together with him in order to be happy or even psychologically complete. Only when her lover is present can she feel whole. When he leaves, her life becomes meaningless, and she wastes her empty days pining for a man who never returns.

As the Tang dynasty decayed, the atmosphere increasingly resembled the *fin de siècle* mood that had shrouded the Southern Dynasties. Consumed by a similar sense of alienation and despair, poets such as the idiosyncratic Li He (ca. 790–ca. 816) looked back to that era for inspiration.[3] Tang poets wrote boudoir poetry in imitation of early medieval prototypes, but they imbued the genre with new dynamism.[4] Because tastes in literature had changed over the centuries, Tang poets often transposed old themes into vibrant new styles and genres. For example, the sad woman yearning for an absent lover became an important theme in newly popular *ci* lyric poetry and song lyrics. Writers working in those genres often borrowed from the natural world to express the contrast between a woman's outer beauty and inner turmoil.[5]

Whereas men had created early medieval poems about female longing, during the Tang women explored this theme as well. They often enlivened this stock theme by imbuing their characters with more authentic emotions.[6]

> Drunken she bemoans her fate
> from morning until night;
> longing for another,
> whom can she tell of her plight?

To make their poems more dramatic, female authors approached the theme of love in novel ways. Whereas Liang dynasty writers had eroticized women's yearnings in order to titillate male readers, Tang female poets softened this image. The lovelorn woman of the male imagination was pathetic and help-less, but women created more natural and moderate female characters.[7] They often drew on their own experiences for inspiration, thereby making their works seem more realistic. In doing so, they replaced bathetic melodrama with self-conscious introspection, making love poetry far more profound.

As female poets sought to give depth to amorous passion, they integrated it into larger philosophical frameworks. A poem by the Daoist nun Li Ye exemplifies this contemplative view toward romantic feelings.[8]

> Deep is the ocean of human life
> but the ocean has a shore;
> twice as deep is my longing for you,
> and longing is ever more.
> Lute in hand, I go upstairs,
> but there is no one here;
> moonlight fills the empty room,
> shining from way out there.
> Plucking my lute, I play a tune,
> Song of Pining for You;
> a string snaps as it rends my heart,
> breaking it in two.

As before, the female character feels the sadness of separation from a loved one. But instead of wallowing in the frenzy of despair, her predicament leads her to contemplate the fundamental nature of existence. To conjure up deep reflection, the poet imbues a natural object with human emotion. Literary critics call this sort of trope an affective image. In Li Ye's poem, the moon evokes separation, so moonlight shining on an empty room highlights the abandoned woman's melancholy.[9] When she tries to play a song to vent her despair, the broken instrument symbolizes her inner state.

As female poets explored the hackneyed theme of the lovesick woman, they portrayed them with greater depth and subtlety. In doing so, they showed this stock character in a different light. For example, the forsaken woman might represent the courtier alienated from the ruler in the manner of the ancient *Songs of Chu (Chu ci)*.[10] Female poets also took a different attitude toward the male beloved. He was no longer a flawless paragon to be worshipped from a distance. Instead the heartbroken woman regarded her lover as a multifac-eted human being with both positive and negative aspects. The courtesan Yu Xuanji sent her beloved a poem warning him not to waste his time or succumb to dissipating pleasures.[11] Love did not blind her to his dark side.

Tang poetry was not always bleak, and authors also dealt with requited love. Literati frequently exchanged poems with courtesans, and these women

sometimes reciprocated, resulting in a cultured exchange of romantic sentiments. Previously, the woman in love had been a pathetic figure, ruined by
her unrequited passions. But in a major shift, the capacity for strong romantic
sentiments came to be regarded as a potentially positive trait.[12] This new point
of view grew out of early medieval Daoist thought. Fifth-century writers had
used the term *fengliu* to describe an unrestrained demeanor embodying Daoist
unconventionality. During the ninth century, writers redefined this term by
associating it with romance. In doing so, they elevated the lover's passion by
reinterpreting it as an expression of natural Daoist authenticity. Seeing love
as a potentially constructive emotion made people more willing to openly display their affection. For instance, epitaphs for beloved concubines sometimes
stressed how strongly their masters loved them. Such an open declaration of
intense love, virtually unimaginable during the Han dynasty, shows that this
feeling had acquired far more positive connotations than before.

Romance constitutes an important theme in the oeuvre of the famed Bai
Juyi (772–846). He did not marry until the unusually late age of thirty-six.[13]
It seems that Bai delayed marriage because he had fallen deeply in love with
someone of unsuitably low status, probably a courtesan. As Tang law forbade intermarriage between people of such widely different backgrounds, he
seems to have delayed wedding a spouse who would probably have resented
his preexisting romantic relationship with another woman. This frustrating
dilemma made him think deeply about his passions, thereby inspiring time-
less love poetry.

Women also occasionally wrote about their attractions in a forthright manner. Some poems show a woman pursuing a hesitant man.[14] Portraying women
in the unfamiliar role of sexual aggressor implicitly interrogated conventional
gender roles and legitimized the emotional autonomy of female characters.
However, not all such encounters went smoothly. In fact, as women eagerly
searched for true love, they often ended up feeling disappointed. Finding a
steadfast partner was not an easy task.[15]

> it's easier to find
> rare, unparalleled treasure
>
> than it is to have and hold
> one reliable lover
>
> at night, against out pillows,
> we weep our secret tears
>
> by day, among the flowers,
> we hide our breaking hearts

The most daring female poets publicly explored female passions in unprecedented ways. The idiosyncratic Yu Xuanji wrote a long poem with erotic lesbian content and sent it to three sisters.[16] Although this unusual work had minimal impact on other writers, Yu's candor attests to the open and inquisitive spirit of an age when people felt intense curiosity about the various forms of love.

Although the Tang is most renowned for poetry, prose underwent considerable development as well. Authors of fiction wrote about a far greater range of topics than poets. The short story also became much more sophisticated at this time, and readers responded with enthusiasm. Advances in technique made stories more detailed and supple, and writers provided deeper insights into their characters' personalities. Moreover, Tang readers enjoyed stories about strange and unorthodox happenings, so writers had considerable freedom to discuss unusual topics that they found intriguing. As a result of this stylistic transformation, writers often depicted women with frankness, giving rise to varied representations. Tang prose provides unprecedented perspectives on women's matters, discussing extramarital sex, adultery, divorce, and remarriage.[17] The contents of these stories supplement, and frequently contradict, orthodox genres such as didactic biography and commemorative epitaphs.

As in Western romantic literature, the fundamental tension in many Tang love stories arises from a conflict between individual desire and social norms. People often felt torn between acting on personal feelings (*qing*) or following ritual rules (*li*).[18] In Western literature, the lover usually overcomes these sorts of barriers. But in Chinese love stories, society often proves stronger than the individual. In the end, the Chinese protagonist has no alternative but to conform to expectations.[19]

Whereas Western writers often critique society for imposing unrealistic or hypocritical standards of conduct, Chinese authors blame the individual who dares to upset the status quo by challenging prevailing mores. Tang writers did not celebrate disruptive expressions of autonomy. To the contrary, a happy ending consists of the protagonist capitulating to intense social pressure. A couple might spend one night of bliss together, but at dawn they realize that they must part.[20] Intense passion can only be temporary, as it runs up against social rules that must ultimately be obeyed.[21] Given these insurmountable restrictions, female characters often ended up confronting circumstances beyond their control.[22] The resulting sense of helplessness evoked pathetic sadness. This sort of conclusion may have been realistic, but writers and readers found it unsatisfying. To ameliorate the situation, many stories evoke a beautiful air of gentle melancholy. Writers made the unhappy ending more acceptable by aestheticizing it.

The decades from the An Lushan Rebellion of 755 to the early ninth century saw the golden age of the Chinese love story. War and upheaval loosened the hold of ethical propriety, and writers used the resulting sense of psychological liberation to explore varied emotions. In particular, they turned their attentions toward love, eroticism, and matters involving women. Under the prevailing atmosphere of skepticism, they wrote about romance creatively and in unprecedented detail. As time went on, however, literature took on a darker tone. Late Tang stories often portray women as a threat to men. Intense female emotions might lead a man toward self-destruction.[23]

Writers used different kinds of material to craft love stories. Some reworked traditional plots to suit new styles. Creative authors realized that ancient myths such as the cowherd and weaver girl could be put into a prose format and made into an interesting romantic short story.[24] They also looked back to history in search of captivating plots. Whereas historians described many fascinating people, they rarely gave much insight into the inner lives of past figures. Writers of fiction took material from historical works and infused it with psychological depth. For example, they could evoke a sense of drama by highlighting contradictions, such as a conflict between passion and duty or official rank and true love. Many popular tales speculated on the emotional lives of emperors and imperial consorts, particularly figures from earlier Tang history.[25] A gallery of strong personalities and political intrigues provided ample plot material. A number of stories described the love between Emperor Tang Xuanzong and the alluring Yang Guifei. However, this was an atypical tale, as it demonized the female character and blamed her for catastrophe. Most Tang stories describe historical beauties as benign.[26]

Tang fiction included many narratives about strange occurrences. Although today's readers find many of these stories ridiculously implausible, Tang audiences did not always seek realism or believability. Instead they might spin a far-fetched plot in order to astonish the reader.[27] Many unusual stories involved women, as violating gender norms seemed surprising. Although the contents of shock fiction varied, writers employed stock plots. The "adventure formula" often involved female characters.[28] In this type of story, a male protagonist encounters a mysterious female stranger. After interacting in some way, the pair part. Later the protagonist discovers that the enigmatic woman is actually an animal, ghost, deity, or even an object that had temporarily assumed human form. In some of the most popular stories, a man encounters a beautiful "woman" who is eventually revealed to be an animal, such as a fox, tiger, snake, or gibbon.[29] The reader immediately senses that the mysterious woman has a terrible secret, and uncertainty about her true identity creates suspense. Sometimes the protagonist even marries the disguised animal and they live together for a time before he finally discovers that his wife is not human.[30] These sorts of stories gave female identity a complex new dimension by making women seem sly, mysterious, and unknowable and implied that a woman might not be what she claims to be.

Readers also enjoyed romantic stories about female ghosts. These narratives were very popular during the Tang, and writers in later periods often wrote new versions of these tales, giving this genre enormous influence on Chinese ideas about love and relationships. The prominence of women in this genre reflected the conflicted views of men toward the opposite sex.[31] Men desired women yet also feared the commitments accompanying marriage. Moreover, Confucianism took a dim view toward erotic desire, as such a strong emotion might lead people to violate the rites and ethical norms.

Tang ghost stories exploited these tensions. At first, the male protagonist feels attracted to an alluring ghost. But when he later discovers her disturbing identity, he looks back upon this encounter with horror. Romantic ghost stories followed several stock plots.[32] Sometimes a man fell in love with a ghost and they had a positive relationship. Some male characters even married ghosts. But other men who became intimate with ghosts suffered negative consequences, such as sickness or even death. Finally, some stories featured the resurrection of a dead woman due to the intensity of a man's sincere love. Overall, these narratives depict women as temptresses whose dangerous sexuality threatens innocent men.[33] Beyond this common thread, each stock plot portrayed supernatural relationships somewhat differently. A satisfying encounter between human and ghost and the revival of a dead woman both attested to the power of love. But stories about men falling ill and dying due to their relationship with a harmful ghost reminded the reader that taboo relationships are fundamentally destructive and should be avoided.

Similarly, readers also enjoyed stories about female immortals (*xiannü*) descending from the heavens to seduce a mortal man.[34] Daoism taught that people who excel in spiritual and physical regimens of cultivation might become immortals who wield supernatural powers and reside in an otherworldly paradise. Occasionally these creatures descend to the human realm to interact with people and present them with gifts. Significantly, whereas early descriptions of immortals usually imagined them as male, in Tang literature they are often female. These stories depict immortals as akin to angels who treat men with affection and benevolence. Sometimes an immortal helps a man achieve wealth or worldly success. Or she might seduce him and whisk him away to her supernatural abode. As time went on, writers increasingly emphasized the erotic implications of these relationships, portraying female immortals as highly sexualized creatures.

Narratives about these alluring female beings served as fantasy material for male readers. Although Tang social constraints were weaker than those of later eras, the norms of propriety nevertheless restricted male sexual and emotional autonomy. Also, many men found it difficult to cultivate a satisfying emotional relationship with a woman. Because family elders arranged most marriages, spouses did not necessarily love one another. A man could purchase a concubine or visit a courtesan or prostitute, but a relationship based on financial exchange would not necessarily be fulfilling. In contrast with real women, however, the female immortal showers a lucky man with unconditional love. She is never jealous, angry, or demanding. Men enjoyed these fantasies about passionate romantic relationships that lacked expectations and complications.

Because the immortals in these tales sought sexual and romantic fulfillment outside of marriage, they behaved in ways that would shame a mortal woman. These stories show that men secretly yearned for the sort of woman whom they would normally criticize. Erotic fantasies about female immortals thus highlight the inequities of Tang society. Rites, laws, and ethics did not just restrict women. Men also felt frustrated and oppressed, as many of them lacked a way to build a satisfying relationship with a member of the opposite sex.

Other stories, such as the famous "Tale of Li Wa," took a very different stance toward the transgression of normative gender roles. This story served as the template for the "scholar and beauty" (*caizi jiaren*) genre that became wildly popular in the late imperial era.[35] Although the young protagonist in this tale suffers deceit, physical abuse, abandonment, and destitution, he eventually pulls himself together and passes the civil service examination, thereby restoring his honor. His father forgives him and he resumes a respectable place in society. Yet despite the happy ending, this story nevertheless portrays ardent love in a negative light. A young man's naïve infatuation with a cynical beauty almost destroys him. This tale served as an implicit warning to those who might be tempted to reject conventional relationships and search for love outside of norms and institutions.

The equally famous story of Yingying similarly highlights the dangers of unrestrained love. In this case, however, the author shows destructive passion from the perspective of a female character.[36] When a wealthy student named Zhang notices the beautiful Yingying, the daughter of a poor widow, she responds to his unexpected advances and they initiate a sexual relationship. Her mother discovers the situation but cannot think of a solution to the predicament, so she tells her daughter to handle this unseemly matter on her own. When Zhang eventually leaves for the capital to take the annual civil service examination, Yingying fears that he will abandon her and never return, so she sends him a fervent confession spelling out her feelings. On reading it, Zhang realizes that this relationship can only bring him trouble, so he decides to cut her off. Zhang then passes the examinations, assumes an official position, and puts this romantic encounter behind him. In contrast, Yingying feels horribly betrayed and wallows in misery for the rest of her life. This story warns the reader that even though some women might find free love appealing, it will ultimately bring them nothing but suffering. Relationships between the sexes should take place within the moral framework of the rites.

Early medieval literature had typically portrayed lovers as unmarried. But Tang writers promoted the idea that a married couple can also experience romance.[37] Couples began to conceive of the ideal marriage as a strong and important emotional bond that ought to be harmonious, intimate, and sentimental.[38] It seems that people felt increasingly comfortable cultivating an emotionally rich relationship with their spouses. Poetry, short stories, epitaphs, and Dunhuang documents all describe affectionate marriages. Many poems depict separated spouses expressing their undying love for one another.[39] And lyric *ci* poetry preserved at Dunhuang describes conjugal love from the female perspective.[40] In these verses, couples openly express their love for one another. Significantly, Tang poets often associated loving relationships with married life. True love leads up to a wedding or develops within a successful marriage. As love and marriage intertwined, passionless conjugal life began to seem like a disappointing failure. Poems expressed the resentment of a wife trapped in a loveless match.

Women routinely sent letters and poems to husbands away from home on business or at war, often expressing dissatisfaction with the separation.[41] A poem by Yu Xuanji describes the lovelorn wife yearning for a distant husband.[42]

> pining for her husband
> she spins to make brocade
>
> he's stationed beyond the Great Wall,
> under the open sky
>
> wild geese, fly there fast
> fish, go through the waters
>
> they need your comings and goings
> to carry precious letters.

Poems written to an absent husband followed ancient prototypes that dated back to the Zhou dynasty *Classic of Poetry* (*Shijing*). But in those poems, a woman's longing for an absent spouse may not have been entirely romantic. A wife relied on her husband economically, and the abandoned woman faced dim prospects. Expressing loyalty and intense feelings helped wives maintain this vital relationship while the couple was apart. Tang poets revived this ancient genre but imbued it with more authentic and urgent emotion, thereby giving an impression of genuine affection.

Increasingly sophisticated prose literature offered readers new perspectives on marital relationships. Some anomaly tales and writings in other genres depicted marriage in romantic terms.[43] Short stories described women who marry for love. These characters have a say in choosing their spouse, in direct violation of the marriage rites.[44] Comparable tales described a female immortal choosing a mortal spouse, implicitly legitimizing connubial love by placing it within a supernatural framework.

Burial customs also exhibit increasing intimacy between spouses. For centuries it had been customary for wife and husband to be buried side by side. In this era, people went even further, interring husband and wife in a common tomb. Placing their bodies so close together underscored the significance of the marriage bond to their social identity. Among a body of 2,579 epitaphs for married men, 58.79 percent stated that they had been buried together with their wives.[45] Whereas the epitaphs of deceased women had traditionally been written by their offspring, over the course of the Tang it became increasingly common for men to outlive their wives, and so husbands frequently composed their wives' epitaphs. Husband and children had different perspectives toward the deceased. Whereas a woman's children saw her primarily as a mother and praised her maternal virtues, a husband would often commend her for having exhibited model wifely qualities and fostering marital harmony. Some epitaphs even take an emotional tenor and describe the relationship between spouses in affectionate terms.[46]

As expectations regarding marriage rose, people whose conjugal relations did not meet such high standards could feel severely disappointed. Li Bai (701–762) wrote a poem describing the unhappy wife of a merchant who is often away on business.[47] Because they must spend so much time apart, the affection she feels for her husband makes her miserable. But even for happy couples, intimacy had limits. Although spouses became closer, gender stereotypes and ethical norms still continued to maintain a degree of separation. A poem by Li Ye depicts marriage as a frustratingly contradictory institution.[48]

> Nearest and yet farthest: east and west.
> Deepest and yet shallowest: clear and flowing (water).
> Highest and yet brightest: sun and moon.
> Most intimate and yet most distant: husband and wife.

Spouses had complicated feelings about marriage. Although people felt increasingly comfortable expressing love for a spouse, mainstream opinion still regarded an openly demonstrative marital relationship as somewhat vulgar. Since ancient times, Confucian thinkers had described marriage as an extremely serious institution founded to regularize gender relations, honor the ancestors, and maintain the family line. Using marriage as a vehicle for romance trivialized it. So even as love rose in the popular consciousness, the traditional view of marriage remained influential. As before, some elite men turned to courtesans for romance so that they could maintain a proper air of formal decorum with their wives.[49]

Writers of fiction explored the emotional challenges that people faced as they tried to build intimate relationships. Dragon Girl (Longnü), originally a character in Buddhist works, became secularized into a mortal woman at this time. Narratives about this figure question whether or not marriage should be grounded in love.[50] Although Dragon Girl married a man chosen by her family, she had high expectations for conjugal life. Unfortunately, her marriage ended in failure. Afterward her father tried to force her to remarry an unwanted spouse. Instead she demanded to wed a man of her own choosing in the hope that she could find true love. Traditionally the female characters in Tang fiction feel attracted to men who exhibit virtue and learning, while men are enticed by a woman's physical beauty. Dragon Girl conforms to this traditional stereotype and is determined to marry a man of integrity. She refuses to be a man's toy or a sacrificial object. To the contrary, she envisions marriage as a partnership between equals and demands a spouse worthy of her love and respect.

As expectations regarding marriage rose, wives became disappointed and jealous more easily. During the early medieval era, jealousy had already emerged as an important topic of discussion.[51] Women had long chafed at the gross inequity of the Chinese marriage system, which demanded absolute fidelity from wives but allowed husbands to take concubines and visit prostitutes.[52] The intensifying rhetoric surrounding female chastity made marriage seem even more unjust. When women began to expect their spouses to love them, they regarded male faithlessness as completely unacceptable and sometimes responded with fury.

The era commenced with an unusual episode of intense jealousy at the apex of society. Empress Wenxian, the vengeful wife of Emperor Wen of Sui, sought to alter the standard model of imperial marriage.[53] Whereas previous emperors had numerous concubines, sometimes numbering in the thousands, Wenxian scorned this custom. Instead she held the unusual opinion that an emperor should stay faithful to his spouse. Her unconventional views on marriage continued to attract comment centuries later. The erudite Qing dynasty scholar Zhao Yi (1727–1814) declared Wenxian the most jealous empress of all time.[54] And the historian Arthur Wright called Emperor Wen "the most henpecked emperor in Chinese history."[55]

Figure 8.2 Women Wore Many Types of Hats and Head Ornaments (Cleveland Museum of Art)

This extraordinary imperial marriage set the tone for the following era. Particularly during the early Tang, many accounts describe jealous wives terrorizing weak-willed husbands.[56] Sometimes their passions even led to violence. Once a jealous wife killed two of her husband's serving women, whom she suspected of catching his eye, and buried their bodies in the snow.[57] And as prose stories flourished and poetry reached an apex, literature explored jealousy in unprecedented detail.[58] Authors conventionally portrayed the jealous woman as a hideous shrew driven mad by wild emotions.[59] The mild-mannered husband cowers in terror before her insane fury. When a feast goes on too long, one husband suspects that his wife will be jealous, so he does not dare return home. Another story describes a man who regretfully gives up an illegitimate son for adoption instead of facing his wife's wrath by bringing the boy home.[60]

Tang literature is replete with jealous shrews and browbeaten husbands. Readers seem to have enjoyed these stories because they defied ordinary expectations. Men were supposed to be domineering and women obedient, so the inversion of accepted gender roles drew the attention of readers. And the growing expectation that marriage should be based on love also made men feel guilty about their extramarital liaisons, hence less willing to challenge a wife who complained about them. Moreover, writers usually set shrew stories in the upper reaches of society. Women from a privileged background had education and wealth, making them more likely to vent their ire.

Stories of female jealousy expose the contradictions that riddled the Tang marriage system.[61] Wives had to remain absolutely faithful to a man who could enjoy dalliances with other women, and some women found the blatant inequity of this arrangement unendurable. But even though jealous wives were victims of patriarchal injustice, the vengeance they could inflict on a husband usually had limits, so they most often victimized other women. In shrew stories, the jealous woman often abuses or murders female rivals: concubines, slaves, and prostitutes.

Ironically, violent jealousy was closely related to love. The suspicious wife felt fully committed to her marriage and demanded the same fidelity from her spouse. But as she tried to preserve the marriage, she did so by violating conventional marital ethics. Tolerance for infidelity was a wifely virtue, and jealousy constituted grounds for divorce. The jealous woman violated this injunction to maintain the integrity of her marriage, even if her husband ended up hating her for it. The expansive atmosphere of the Tang allowed women considerable freedom to express their true feelings. Men were shocked when their wives used this opportunity to vent terrifying emotions.

Conclusion

Whenever historians study the lives of women in a particular period of Chinese history, they inevitably feel tempted to make blanket generalizations and declare female status as high or low, their lives as free or repressed, and the era in question as lenient or restrictive. However, when confronted with the large body of available facts, many ambiguous or even contradictory, these sorts of broad statements seem facile. The Sui and Tang dynasties lasted for more than three centuries. Not only did the overarching circumstances conditioning women's lives shift over the course of this long period, but the experiences of each individual also differed according to her family background, region, and particular situation. To complicate matters even further, this era also encompassed a dramatic turning point. The catastrophic An Lushan Rebellion shattered medieval society, affecting the opportunities that women enjoyed and throwing up new barriers to their well-being.

In some respects, the society of the high middle ages stands out as exceptional. Yet when viewed from the vantage point of the entire flow of Chinese history, it seems intimately connected with what came before and after. Although the Sui and Tang saw many innovations, these usually did not come as a sudden disjunction. The changes and creations of this period were often iterations of earlier trends, and these conventions often continued to condition women's lives in later eras. In other words, particular aspects of Tang gender history can be understood as phases of lengthy processes whose large timeframe far exceeded the bounds of any single dynasty.

Many historians classify the Sui and Tang dynasties as part of China's medieval era. They distinguish this epoch from both the unified early imperial culture of the Han dynasty and also the more economically developed society that arose during the Song. In many respects this period has much in common with the early medieval era, a period of disunion. When the Eastern Han dynasty disintegrated in the second century, power devolved to China's many regions. As a result, the most creative thinkers lost faith in Confucianism, which had become closely linked to the Han state. When that dynasty finally failed after four centuries of rule, people looked to religion and metaphysics for wisdom and solace. The conquest of north China by nomadic invaders further degraded the influence of native traditions, causing medieval society to diverge from the confident unified polity of the early Han.

Historians often classify the period of disunity following the fall of Han as China's early Middle Ages. The Sui and Tang remained medieval in many respects, as the earlier and later medieval periods shared some fundamental characteristics. Most obviously, the economy remained relatively undeveloped, and the amount of wealth stood far below that of subsequent eras. During the Song dynasty, the commercial economy blossomed, making China the most prosperous society the world had ever seen. However, that explosion of prosperity had yet to come. The Tang remained a conservative agricultural society. The aristocratic elite spurned merchants and did not actively promote commerce. As a result, women as well as men had to navigate a relatively poor society that offered few opportunities beyond farming.

During the long medieval era, society was dominated by a nobility who based their preeminence primarily on genealogy. Aristocrats from the greatest families looked down on many rulers as parvenus, challenging their authority and spurning their claims to legitimacy. Men often gained high office due to exalted ancestry rather than ability, so the bureaucracy was staffed with middling talents. The dominance of the nobility, coupled with feeble administration, kept the central government weak and fragile.

This weak administrative system affected society in various ways. Compared to the late imperial era, when the state took an active role in promoting particular visions of womanhood, the Tang government remained fairly passive and did little to manage matters regarding women. A comprehensive code of law may have instituted an array of new regulations, but the government still rarely intervened in family life. Administrative passivity left some women unprotected from exploitation and abuse. Yet weak regulation also allowed creative expression. During the long period between Han and Song, numerous women expressed bold opinions.

As in the earlier phase of the medieval era, the Sui and Tang remained heavily influenced by steppe peoples. Chinese culture fused together native and pastoral elements, which affected views of kinship and gender. Nomads who settled in China often maintained traditional practices, such as expensive bridewealth and levirate. And they lacked many fundamental Chinese concepts, including Confucianism, the rites, concubinage, and surname exogamy. The confrontation between pastoral and native ideals implicitly challenged classical Chinese norms, forcing people of each era to question their ideas about marriage, family, and female ethics.

Even without pastoral influence, the impact of classical concepts had declined considerably. Whereas the intellectual elites of Han and Song looked to ancient teachings for guidance, during the medieval era relatively few thinkers devoted themselves to the Confucian canon. Although some Tang scholars had begun to revive Confucianism and the classical rites, these ideas still had little effect on the average person. The relative vigor of Confucian rhetoric in each era had a major impact on women's lives, as this body of thought sought to restrict female behavior and impose a stringent gender hierarchy upon society. When Confucianism was weak, restrictive values such as female chastity received less attention as well. However, Confucianism began to rise in influence during this period. The beginnings of the Confucian revival saw a rise in chastity rhetoric, a trend that would become increasingly important in centuries to come.

Religion also remained extremely important during the Tang. In addition to shaping people's views of the supernatural, faith also had a major impact on many worldly matters, including ideas about gender. Daoism, Buddhism, and popular religions provided people of all social strata with comprehensive repositories of ideas and values. They used these concepts to understand their existence and decide how they ought to live their lives. These beliefs were not static. Changing teachings affected the ways that society viewed and treated women. Religion also provided women with varied opportunities. In both the Six Dynasties and Tang, elite women elevated their standing through patronage of religion. And for women of ordinary means, their active participation in an array of religious activities helped give their lives structure and meaning.

Some key aspects of family life also remained similar to earlier practices. Writings from the Six Dynasties frequently depict confident and outspoken women. During the Sui and Tang, family life maintained a similar atmosphere. Some women asserted themselves within the domestic realm, displaying great confidence in dealing with those around them. However, assertive behavior sometimes became extreme, eliciting concern. At this time, the shrew became a common character in literature. Moreover, women were weakly integrated into their husbands' families. Even after a wife married, she often still maintained close links with natal kin, and her standing among her husband's relations remained somewhat marginal. People had just begun to embrace the idea that the reach of filial piety extends beyond a woman's blood relations to include her husband's parents as well. Overall, women had yet to be accepted as full members of their husbands' families, relegating them to the margins of the patrilineal kinship system.

The representation of women during the Sui and Tang often maintained prior language, images, and tone. As before, men wrote almost all poems and stories about women. Literary taste changed slowly, and many tropes remained common for centuries. For example, decadent Liang dynasty boudoir poetry continued to inform authors writing about women. In Liang poems, an unhappy lady ensconced in gorgeous surroundings wallows in misery, obsessed with an absent lover. Her beloved never reappears, and presumably never will, so her wretched state has no resolution. This style of poetry portrayed women as hysterical and psychologically dependent on men. Although Tang poetry became far more sophisticated and profound than before, writers maintained many of these previous images of womanhood and reproduced them in ways that readers would accept as normative depictions of gendered behavior.

The commonalities between the Tang and earlier medieval societies were clearly numerous and fundamental. And yet this was also a transitional time that would eventually give way to the Song, a far more prosperous and dynamic age during which women faced very different conditions. Already many aspects of Tang society had begun to show signs of change. Compared to earlier eras, the economy began to grow more rapidly, gradually increasing overall prosperity and fueling urbanization. These fundamental changes threw up the conditions for a very different kind of society in which women were to play different roles. The government changed as well. Administration began to become more meritocratic. The talented and highly educated minor gentry who took up office were more amenable to Confucian ideas. The Confucianization of Tang law shows an intellectual shift among the powerful that would intensify in centuries to come. And rhetoric about restrictive female virtue, such as widow chastity, became increasingly common. At the same time, however, more women expressed themselves in poetry that has been preserved, presaging the explosion of women's literature in later periods.

Religion changed as well. Whereas early medieval rulers had an almost uniformly enthusiastic attitude toward religion, the Tang undertook several campaigns to reduce the wealth and influence of Buddhism. These episodes of persecution mark the beginning of Buddhism's decline in China. Although many people remained fervent believers, the wealth, power, and intellectual vitality of Buddhism began to deteriorate, and the religion never recovered its former prestige. As a result, religious depictions of ideal womanhood decreased in relevance, to be supplanted by secular ideas.

In spite of these numerous connections between the earlier and later phases of the medieval era, it would be unfair to dismiss the Tang as merely a transitional phase between what occurred before and after. In certain respects, the Tang also displayed a distinctive spirit that altered how people thought about gender issues. Most visibly, over the course of this tumultuous period the literary and artistic conventions used to represent women changed dramatically. Standard ideas about ideal womanhood often emerged through a complex interplay between literature and painting, both created mostly by men. In constructing these images, they drew on a rich tradition of thought and culture and also looked to the behavior of contemporary women.

During the medieval era, people increasingly associated gender difference with the body. For example, medical theory became increasingly gendered, highlighting the differences between female and male bodies.[1] But beyond physical distinctions, people believed that men and women enact their gender by engaging in stereotypical behaviors. As Tang writers and artists pondered the nature of the feminine, they created many stock female types that remained popular for the remainder of imperial history.[2] Supernatural beings, palace ladies, courtesans, and other standard characters each received considerable attention. Creative minds fleshed out the main female types to craft a gallery of standard images. Although these idealized figures were not necessarily realistic, they nevertheless affected real lives. Women measured their own appearance and conduct against these ideals, as did those around them. By embracing, manipulating, or resisting these models, women could communicate their individual identity to society at large.[3]

The development of art exemplifies how the Tang generated new and extremely different ideas about how women should look and act.[4] Severe Confucian decorum had restrained Han dynasty artists, so they showed little interest in something as frivolous as female beauty. For example, Han tomb figurines of servants appear plain and highly restrained in order to emphasize their dignified humility. In contrast, early medieval artists often depicted female figures in a highly aestheticized manner, thus presenting fresh perspectives on ideal womanhood. Tang dynasty tomb figures and funerary wall paintings depict even humble female servants as beautiful. Even as they perform quotidian activities, these figures smile and exhibit a relaxed demeanor, implicitly expressing a vision of femininity that seemed both highly aesthetic and yet also very casual.

Han dynasty art usually depicted women with bland features in static poses. Instead of looking like dynamic individuals, they serve as inert representations of a particular social role or moral archetype. In contrast, medieval painters emphasized the beautiful side of the feminine, thereby bringing the genre of beautiful women (*shinü*) to maturity.[5] These women not only have pretty features but also wear gorgeous clothing and appear in luxurious surroundings. Their confident and easygoing demeanor makes them seem even more alluring. Tang paintings often depict women enjoying themselves— chasing butterflies, spending time with a pet, playing a board game, tossing a ball, or happily laughing. Artists aestheticized playfulness and made it an expression of female beauty. They also used their art to depict a female subject's inner spirit (*shen*).[6] A relaxed and spontaneous depiction revealed far more insights into a woman's character than the stiff portrayals of earlier eras.

Over time, the ways that artists painted women steadily shifted. Female figures gradually became far more diverse and emotional than before. And during the late seventh and early eight centuries, the mixing of native and pastoral elements further altered the depiction of women. Artists began to portray them wearing foreign clothing, riding on horseback, and engaged in sports and other physical activities. High Tang art of the mid-eighth century shows women with unique or even eccentric characteristics. At this time, the aestheticization of women reached a height, and artists often painted them wearing elaborate costumes intended to underscore their beauty. Finally, amid the chaos of the Late Tang, the ideal woman became less lively but even more elegant than before. People knew that China was disintegrating, and they sought escapism from the harsh realities of daily life. As a result, painters turned their attentions away from society to focus on the natural world. They often represented idealized women in landscape settings, thereby juxtaposing female beauty with that of nature.

Authors of prose fiction realized that readers appreciated the highly aestheticized female images pioneered in the visual arts, so they altered conventional literary descriptions of women to emphasize their beauty. For example, when Tang authors wrote about sinister female fox spirits, they not only described these creatures in far greater detail than ever before but also put far more emphasis on their seductive beauty.[7] Similarly, while earlier works had often described concubines and courtesans as attractive, Tang authors extended the rubric of female beauty to encompass wives as well.[8] Ancient descriptions of wives had deliberately downplayed appearance and instead highlighted their character, as people considered female beauty and conjugal virtue somewhat incongruous. The Tang aestheticization of wives grew out of the general redefinition of beauty. Instead of viewing attractiveness in purely physical terms, as had often been the case in the Six Dynasties, Tang writers revived the Han dynasty idea that virtue makes a woman appealing. By extending beauty to encompass both the moral and the physical, they could extend this attribute to wives.

In spite of the influence of painting and sculpture, the elite considered literary texts more orthodox than the visual arts, so artists sought to translate written descriptions of female beauty into visual form. In particular, the canonical *Classic of Poetry* (*Shijing*) informed the works of Tang painters, who adopted the gendered "gaze" employed in this collection.[9] These ancient poems never describe a woman observing another woman. In ancient poetry, the "gaze" is implicitly male. Tang artists embraced this literary convention and depicted women in situations, costumes, and poses designed to appeal to men.

Early medieval palace poetry, such as the boudoir poems of the sixth-century collection *New Songs from a Jade Terrace* (*Yutai xinyong*), also influenced Tang ideas about how women ought to look.[10] This genre employed elaborate codes to depict female appearance, using symbols and postures to convey ideas about ideal womanhood. For example, poets alluded to certain plants in order to evoke aspects of femininity. Even the choice of setting conveyed encoded information, as stock characters appeared in particular settings. When the poet described a beautiful woman in her boudoir, the reader immediately assumed that she was lovelorn, bored, and unhappy. Most importantly, the women in palace poetry seem highly unrealistic. Early medieval poets presented the reader with romanticized stereotypes, not actual people. This literary practice influenced the art of later periods. Tang viewers expected to encounter highly aestheticized female stereotypes, not realistic individuals.

Aside from literature, other aspects of culture furthered the aestheticization of women as well. The flourishing art of dance, which reached new heights in the medieval period, affected artistic views of ideal femininity. Poets describing professional dancers portray them as not only skillful but beautiful as well.[11] However, the dancers in these poems seem neither strong nor assertive. Slim and delicate, they have been reduced to pretty playthings to be enjoyed by wealthy men. Although poets often depict professional dancers as unhappy with their degraded lives, these women nevertheless represent ideal feminine grace. These stereotypes influenced popular views of womanhood, and ordinary women sometimes adopted a diminutive pose. Tang women sometimes called themselves by the pronoun *er*, which previously referred to a baby or young child. Taking on a juvenile identity made them seem innocent and cute.[12] In doing so, they embraced immaturity and weakness as traits of the beautiful woman.

Invasion and cultural exchange also brought new and transformative images of femininity to China. Largely as a result of ethnic mixing, Tang art shows a far greater range in female appearance than before. At this time, Chinese were in regular contact with hundreds of foreign countries, peoples, and regions. Artists and craftsmen replicated this cultural diversity by portraying foreign women from the western regions.[13] Among the figurines depicting Central Asians unearthed from Sui and Tang tombs, only about 3 percent are female. However, images of foreign women have also been found on other media as well, including coins, sculpture, metalwork, and painting. The relative absence of Central Asian women from funerary art suggests that Chinese associated them with sensuality and even licentiousness, making them

inappropriate for a serious mortuary context. Poets often described alluring Central Asian women performing music and dance in bars to entertain
enthusiastic male patrons. Images of sensual foreign womanhood challenged
conventional female aesthetics. The exoticism of these lively women made
them far more intriguing than demure native dancers. This taste for foreign
beauty had a lasting impact, as Central Asian beauties acted as important
transmitters of foreign culture into the Chinese heartland. Because men found
Central Asian women so fascinating, they became more accepting of the culture they represented, and they adopted foreign clothing, food, music, dance,
and customs.

Dunhuang wall paintings reveal the convergence of various visions of
beauty.[14] These depictions went through several phases. Women in early
Tang paintings appear gentle, and artists rendered them in a florid style. High
Tang art shows much more Indian influence. As in subcontinental depictions
of women, the waist is often sensuously curved.[15] Figures also begin to look
more three dimensional, and the painter puts more emphasis on their elaborate ornaments. Then artists reacted to the depressing chaos of the late Tang
by creating a world of extravagant luxury that viewers could use as escapist
fantasy material. And in the subsequent Five Dynasties era (907–960), artists
infantilized women, making the slender adolescent a new feminine ideal.[16]

Women of every era associated beauty with youth. Poems describe them
lamenting the passage of time that steadily eroded their looks.[17]

> the sound of the water-clock's close by—
> just outside your chamber
> and night by night, next to the lamp,
> your hair is turning white.

Aside from youth, a woman also had to have a particular body type to
be considered attractive. However, the ideal female physique changed over
time. Whatever the standards of the day, women strove to live up to these
criteria when possible, as exhibiting conventional beauty garnered praise.
Women also manipulated aspects of their appearance to materialize their
taste and social position.[18] However, the standards of appearance repeatedly
shifted through the course of the dynasty. In earlier eras, slender women
were considered beautiful, and during the early Tang a thin body remained
ideal.[19] Poets praised small waists, and painters showcased willowy beauties.
Over time, however, fuller figures gained appreciation. Foreign influence
emanating from India, Central Asia, and particularly from nomads to the
north affected views toward the ideal female body. Women from pastoral
societies often worked hard, hunted, and rode horses, so they tended to have
a sturdy physique. Chinese women sometimes imitated the steppe lifestyle

and enjoyed outdoor activities. As a result, people came to appreciate larger frames. The beautiful Empress Wu Zetian had a square forehead and broad chin, and observers associated her thick features with good health and vigor.

For a brief time in the early eighth century, people even admired chubby women.[20] That era marks the highpoint of the dynasty, and heavy beauties physically embodied the era's spirit of prosperity and confidence. Poets compared beautiful women to the peony, a huge flower that readily suggested an ample female build. The infamous imperial concubine Yang Guifei exemplified this physical type. Poets described her round face and full figure as extremely attractive. Artists sometimes took the appreciation of large women to an extreme. The stoutest female figures have bloated faces and a neck ringed with fat. Nevertheless, observers always distinguished between pleasantly plump and corpulent. Even a heavy woman was expected to have delicate bones and fine features and to move with fluid grace.

After the An Lushan Rebellion of the mid-eighth century, tastes changed once again. People in a chaotic society had little time for extravagance. Moreover, many influential people took refuge in the south, where pastoral culture had the least impact and ideas about beauty remained traditional. Thin bodies once again became the ideal, and both poets and artists celebrated beautiful dancers with slender waists. Even so, compared to the lithe, frail, and even anemic-looking women of Ming and Qing dynasty art, the women in late Tang painting still look quite sturdy.[21]

Tang records include the earliest accounts of foot binding.[22] This practice did not gain currency suddenly. It began as a marginal custom and advanced gradually over centuries, eventually becoming widespread. Changes in home furnishings in this era made foot binding feasible. Previously people sat on mats on the floor, so a woman with bound feet would have had difficulty standing up. But during the tenth century, tables and chairs became common furnishings. Although women from good families did not yet bind their feet, Central Asian dancers with dainty feet appeared on stage. Writers began to consider small feet an emblem of beauty, encouraging the subsequent rise of foot binding.

The Tang love of opulence together with the increasing beautification of women's lives caused clothing, hairstyles, ornaments, and cosmetics to become extremely elaborate and diverse.[23] Poetry and the visual arts focused on these external adornments, taking them as an essential component of female beauty.[24] Some women delighted in flaunting a luxurious appearance. The courtesan Xue Tao wrote a poem describing her happy excitement when she tried on new clothes.[25]

A wardrobe was far more than simple ornament. Clothes can serve as a metaphor for the person, allowing the wearer to silently communicate with

Figure C.1 Elaborate Hairstyle and Cosmetics

those around her. Because fashion constitutes a system, even minor changes in one element can be extremely meaningful.[26] Consequently, new types of attire sometimes expressed deep changes in female identity.[27] Wealthy women sported an expensive wardrobe to signal their high rank. An exclusive style of dress served as an important status symbol, distinguishing them from ordinary women while expressing their place in the female hierarchy of the palace. The most obvious attribute of privileged women's clothing was its inconvenience. A woman attired in a deliberately fussy manner could not possibly work. The impracticality of elegant clothing thus conveyed leisure, a trait that marked a woman's membership in the elite.

Given the importance of clothing as a social marker, even sober historians described the clothing worn by empresses and other palace ladies in great detail. The clothing of a Sui empress consisted of twelve grades, each matched to a particular activity or level of formality.[28] Palace ladies of each rank wore different types of clothing to signal their particular rank in the harem.[29] Tang empresses and imperial consorts had a similar sartorial system.[30] As clothing became increasingly associated with social position, elite women either emulated the clothing of their peers or else tried to raise themselves even higher by outdoing their competitors.[31] Eventually elements of dress originating in the upper classes "trickled down" as people in lower social positions adopted them.[32]

In the early Tang, fashions were fairly demure. A woman would even wear a hat with a scarf when traveling so that she could pull down the fabric to shield her face from the embarrassing male gaze. After the mid-seventh century, however, society no longer expected women to hide their faces in public.[33] To the contrary, clothing became increasingly sensual and even erotic. One aspect of Tang clothing seems shocking even to contemporary Chinese sensibilities. While the main function of clothing is concealment, it can also reveal and even highlight certain parts of the body.[34] Chinese women in other eras usually wore loose-fitting clothes that enveloped all of the body except for the hands and head. In contrast, medieval attire sometimes deliberately emphasized the breasts and even revealed décolletage.[35] No other artifact attests to the famed cultural openness of the Tang as clearly as these garments, which people in other periods would have regarded as blatantly obscene.

As the Tang dynasty decayed, rising chaos made people newly sensitive to the passage of time.[36] Instead of understanding the world through eternal verities, they increasingly felt their lives to be in rapid flux. Sartorial change reflected these disorienting shifts. In the twilight of the dynasty, increased sensitivity toward temporality gave rise to a new lexicon for discussing fashion. Aspects of women's clothing changed with increasing rapidity, mirroring changes in society at large.

At this time, some people became fascinated with androgyny and cross-dressing.[37] In earlier centuries, both men and women had worn loose robes. In contrast, clothing for both sexes became less voluminous during the Tang, fitting more closely to the body. Moreover, during the long occupation of China by the Xianbei and other pastoral peoples in the early medieval era, some Chinese men adopted nomadic dress. They wore trousers, boots, and tunics or robes with narrow sleeves. During the fifth century, Xianbei women living in China initially wore similar clothing. However, they gradually abandoned their traditional dress and adopted styles from China and Central Asia. By the Sui dynasty, women in China did not wear steppe clothing. However, in the early Tang, some ethnic Chinese women began to dress in male pastoral fashions. A figurine of a woman on horseback dating to 643 is the earliest known example of a Tang woman dressed in male clothing. In the latter half of the seventh century, artists often depicted women wearing clothing associated with male nomads from the northern and western regions, such as the proto-Turkic Türük (Tujue) people.[38]

Classical ritual required men and women to wear distinctive gendered clothing, so women's embrace of male clothing violated traditional cultural norms. Elite women rarely engaged in cross-dressing. Instead artists usually depict low-status women, such as servants, wearing the clothes of male nomads. Close-fitting pants and tunics were far more practical than traditional robes, making them appropriate attire for working women. Some poems even describe women donning men's clothes to go into battle.[39] Although these poems seem to have been based on imagination rather than observation, they nevertheless show that people considered male clothing appropriate for stereotypical male activities, such as war and menial labor. Tang literary and visual depictions of cross-dressing women imply a more relaxed attitude toward gender difference than in subsequent eras, when the barriers separating women from men hardened.

The numerous shifts in stereotypical female image attest to the complexity, dynamism, and diversity of women's experiences in the Sui and Tang dynasties. In many respects, this was a transitional era that shows traces of the previous Six Dynasties culture, as well as characteristics associated with the later Song dynasty. Yet the high medieval era also had many distinct elements, and people thought about women in new and changing ways. The interaction of fluctuating ideals reveals the vitality of gender ideals, many of which had a lasting impact. Standard characteristics of the ideal woman that were common in later periods often date back to this critical phase in Chinese women's history. In many respects, the Tang dynasty remade womanhood, and aftershocks from this creative and dynamic era continued to reverberate down the centuries.

Glossary

An Lushan	安祿山
Bai Juyi	白居易
Ban Zhao	班昭
baoyang	褒揚
Beili	北里
biezhaifu	別宅婦
caizi jiaren	才子佳人
Chan (Zen)	禪
chang	娼
Chang E	嫦娥
Chang'an	長安
chanpo	禪婆
Chen Hong	陳鴻
Chu ci	楚辭
ci	詞
Cui (madam，Shandong family)	崔
cuju	蹴鞠
Daizong	代宗
danü	大女
Dao	道
Dazhang	大長

Deng	鄧
Dezong	德宗
Dizang	地藏
Dou (empress)	**竇**
Doumu	斗母
Dunhuang	敦煌
er	兒
Fale	法樂
Fazang	法藏
fengliu	風流
Fo shuo fumu enzhong jing	佛說父母恩重經
foxing	佛性
Gaozong	高宗
Gaozu	高祖
Goguryeo	고구려, 高句麗
gongnü	宮女
guaji	挂籍
Guandong	關東
Guanyin	觀音
Guanzhong	關中
guifei	貴妃
Hu Yin	胡憎
Hua Mulan	花木蘭
Huang Di	黃帝
huangdi	皇帝
Huayan	華嚴
hujue	戶絕
hunshu	婚書
ji	妓
Jiefu yin	節婦吟
jingbiao	旌表
Jinggan	靜感
Jinxian	金仙

Jiu Tangshu	舊唐書
Jiutian Xuannü	九天玄女
juntian	均田
Laozi	老子
Li (imperial clan)	李
li	里
Li Bai	李白
Li He	李賀
Li Jilan	李季蘭
Li She	李涉
Li Wa	李娃
Li Ye	李冶
Li Yuan	李淵
Lianhua jing	蓮華經
Lienü zhuan	列女傳
Liji	禮記
Liu (empress)	劉
Longmen	龍門
Longnü	龍女
Lu	盧
Lu Shinan	虞世南
Lunyu	論語
Luoyang	洛陽
ming	命
minghun	冥婚
Mulan	木蘭
Mulian	目連
mushi	姆師
Naitō Konan	内藤湖南
nü sishu	女四書
Nü Wa (Nü Gua)	女媧
Nü xiaojing	女孝經
nüguan	女冠，女官

Nüjie	女戒
nüshi (official)	女史
nüshi (Daoist nun)	女師
nüxia	女俠
Nüze	女則
Ouyang Tong	歐陽通
Ouyang Xun	歐陽詢
Pei	裴
Puxiang	普相
qi	氣
Qianjin	千金
Qiaoguo	譙國
qing	情
Qiu Hu	秋胡
Quan Tang shi	全唐詩
Ruizong	睿宗
Shandong	山東
Shangguan Waner	上官婉兒
Shanzi	睒子
shen	神
Shengmu	聖母
Shijing	詩經
shinü	仕女
shishifeng	食實封
shiyi	食邑
shuangju	孀居
sidu	私度
Sima Qian	司馬遷
Song Ruoxin	宋若莘
Song Ruozhao	宋若昭
Song Tai	宋態
sui	歲
Suishu	隋書

Taiping	太平
Taiping guangji	太平廣記
Taiyuan	太原
Taizong	太宗
Tang lü	唐律
tangyu	堂閾
tian	天
Tianlongshan	天龍山
tongjian	通姦
Tujue	突厥
Turpan	吐魯番
Wang	王
Wei (empress, Guanzhong family)	韋
Wei Huacun	魏華存
weiqi	圍棋
Wen (emperor)	文
Wenxian	文獻
Wu (empress)	武
Wu Zetian	武則天
Wu Zhao	武曌，武瞾
Xianbei	鮮卑
xiannü	仙女
Xianzong	憲宗
xiao	孝
Xiaojing	孝經
Xin Tangshu	新唐書
Xiwangmu	西王母
Xu (concubine)	徐
Xu Hui	徐惠
Xuanzong	玄宗
Xue Tao	薛濤
Yang (emperor)	煬
Yang Guang	楊廣

Yang Guifei	楊貴妃
Yang Guozhong	楊國忠
Yang Jian	楊堅
Yang Yong	楊勇
Yang Yuhuan	楊玉環
Yaoshifo	藥師佛
yi	義
yijue	義絕
yin	陰
Yingying	鶯鶯
yinlian	姻聯
yisi	邑司
Yongtai	永泰
youpoyi	優婆夷
Yu Nü	玉女
Yu Xuanji	魚玄機
Yunju	雲居
Yutai xinyong	玉臺新詠
Zhang (student)	張
Zhang Ji	張籍
Zhang Yaotiao	張窈窕
Zhangsun	長孫
Zhao Luanluan	趙鸞鸞
Zhao Wumeng	趙武孟
Zhao Yi	趙翼
Zheng (madam)	鄭
zhongmen	中門
Zhongzong	中宗
Zhou (Wu Zetian's dynasty)	周
zhuanlun wang	轉輪王
Zi Gu	紫姑

Notes

Epigraph: David Young and Jiann L. Lin, trans., *The Clouds Float North: The Complete Poems of Yu Xuanji, Bilingual Edition* (Middletown, CT: Wesleyan University Press, 1998), 56.

INTRODUCTION

1. For influential interpretations of the Tang, see C. P. Fitzgerald, "The Chinese Middle Ages in Communist Historiography," *China Quarterly* 23 (1965): 106–21; Tanigawa Michio, *Medieval Chinese Society and the Local "Community,"* trans. Joshua A. Fogel (Berkeley: University of California Press, 1985), xi–xxii; Dennis Grafflin, "The Great Family in Medieval South China," *Harvard Journal of Asiatic Studies* 41, no. 1 (1981): 65–74.

2. Arthur F. Wright, *The Sui Dynasty* (New York: Alfred A. Knopf, 1978).

3. For a concise overview of the dynasty, see Arthur F. Wright and Denis Twitchett, "Introduction," in *Perspectives on the T'ang* (New Haven: Yale University Press, 1973), 1–43.

4. Robert M. Somers, "Time, Space, and Structure in the Consolidation of the T'ang Dynasty (A.D. 617–700)," *Journal of Asian Studies* 45, no. 5 (1986): 988.

5. Thomas J. Barfield, *The Perilous Frontier: Nomadic Empires and China, 221 BC to AD 1757* (Cambridge, MA: Blackwell Publishers, 1989), 166.

6. Duan Tali, *Tangdai funü diwei yanjiu* (Beijing: Renmin, 2000), 151–52.

7. Mark Edward Lewis, *China's Cosmopolitan Empire: The Tang Dynasty* (Cambridge, MA: Belknap Press of Harvard University Press, 2009), 49. Nicolas Tackett, "Great Clansmen, Bureaucrats, and Local Magnates: The Structure and Circulation of the Elite in Late-Tang China," *Asia Major* 21, no. 2 (2008): 101–52 describes the Tang aristocracy.

8. Mao Hanguang, "Zhonggu Shandong dazu zhuofang zhi yanjiu—Tangdai jinhun jia yu xingzupu," *Zhongyang Yanjiuyuan Lishi Yuyan Yanjiusuo jikan* 54 (1993): 19.

9. Liu Xu et al., *Jiu Tangshu*, annotated by Liu Jie and Chen Naiqian (Beijing: Zhonghua, 1975), 55: 2247.

10. Denis Twitchett, "The Government of T'ang in the Eighth Century," *Bulletin of the School of Oriental and African Studies* 18, no. 2 (1956): 322–23.

11. Nicolas Tackett, *The Destruction of the Medieval Chinese Aristocracy* (Cambridge, MA: Harvard University Asia Center, 2014), 105, 196.

12. Richard von Glahn, *The Economic History of China: From Antiquity to the Nineteenth Century* (Cambridge: Cambridge University Press, 2016), 208–9, 216–19, 225.

13. Ni Wenjie et al., *Zuijia nüxing miaoxie cidian* (Beijing: Zhongguo guoji guangbo, 1990); Shiomi Kunihiko, *Tōdai kōgo no kenkyū* (Fukuoka: Chūgoku shoten, 1995), 114, 118–19 defines words traditionally used to describe women in this era.

14. Yi Jo-lan, "Social Status, Gender Division and Institutions: Sources Relating to Women in Chinese Standard Histories," in *Overt and Covert Treasures: Essays on the Sources for Chinese Women's History*, ed. Clara Wing-Chung Ho (Hong Kong: City University Press, 2012), 132–33 provides tables that give the locations of women's biographies in the standard histories.

15. Zhu Meilian, "Tangdai xiaoshuozhong de nüxing juese yanjiu" (MA thesis, National Chengchi University, 1989), 9.

16. Ping Yao, "Women's Epitaphs in Tang China (618–907)," in *Beyond Exemplar Tales: Women's Biography in Chinese History*, ed. Joan Judge and Hu Ying (Berkeley: University of California Press, 2011), 139, 141. Tackett, "Great Clansmen, Bureaucrats, and Local Magnates," 102–10 introduces the characteristics of Tang epitaphs. Zhou Xiaowei and Wang Qiyi, *Roushun zhi xiang: Suidai nüxing yu shehui* (Beijing: Zhongguo shehui kexue chubanshe, 2012), 3–26 discuss the epitaphs of 122 Sui dynasty women. Zhang Ping, "Tangdai kexie beizhi de fengqi," *Gugong wenwu yuekan* 15, no. 4 (1997): 84–91 introduces the study of Tang epitaphs. Zhou and Wang, *Roushun zhi xiang*, 119–54 define medieval terminology related to marriage and family life used in epitaphs, Dunhuang documents, and transmitted texts. Deng Xiaonan, "Women in Turfan during the Sixth to Eighth Centuries: A Look at Their Activities Outside the Home," *The Journal of Asian Studies* 58, no. 1 (1999): 85–59 discusses how early medieval epitaphs portrayed women and the ways that they differed from epitaphs of men.

17. Duan, *Tangdai funü diwei yanjiu*, 124–25.

18. Chen Liping, "*Zizhi tongjian* Tangdai houfei jishi xianyi," *Sui Tang Liao Song Jin Yuan shi luncong* 2 (2012): 179–86 discusses inconsistencies in statements about empresses and imperial concubines in *Zizhi tongjian* and the two *Tangshu*.

19. Jowen R. Tung, *Fables for the Patriarchs: Gender Politics in Tang Discourse* (Lanham, MD: Rowman & Littlefield, 2000), 19.

20. Tung, *Fables for the Patriarchs*, 6–7; Tang Ronglan, "Lun Tangdai funü shenghuo de bofan xianxiang," *Taizhou Xueyuan xuebao* 25, no. 5 (2003): 81.

21. Tung, *Fables for the Patriarchs*, 14.

22. The tomb of a titled lady reflects this wealth and luxury. Xi'an Shi Wenwu Baohu Kaogu Yanjiuyuan, "Xi'an nanjiao Tangdai Zhang Furen mu fajue jianbao," *Wenbo* 1 (2013): 11–16.

23. Kojiro Tomita, "Three Chinese Pottery Figurines of the T'ang Dynasty," *Bulletin of the Museum of Fine Arts* 42, no. 250 (1944): 66; Robert T. Paine Jr., "A Chinese Horse with a Female Rider," *Bulletin of the Museum of Fine Arts* 46, no. 265 (1948): 54–55; Duan, *Tangdai funü diwei yanjiu*, 118–23. A poem describes beautiful palace women taking riding lessons. Horseback riding added to their allure. Jeanne Larsen, trans., *Willow, Wine, Mirror, Moon: Women's Poems from Tang China* (Rochester, NY: BOA Editions, 2005), 50.

24. Fan Wenhui, "Tangdai huangjia nüzi cujudui," *Lantai shijie* 9 (2014): 117–18.

25. Sun Yurong, "Tangdai suishi jieri zhong de nüxing xiuxian huodong," *Hubei Ligong Xueyuan xuebao* 30, no. 2 (2013): 15–18, 60.

26. Li Mei, "Tangdai funü lüyou de fansheng chengyin ji zhuyao xingshi," *Lantai shijie* 4 (2015): 90–91.

27. Sanping Chen, "Succession Struggles and the Ethnic Identity of the Tang Imperial House," *Journal of the Royal Asiatic Society*, third series, 6, no. 3 (1996): 379–80.

28. Barfield, *The Perilous Frontier*, 25–26.

29. Sherry J. Mou, "Writing Virtues with Their Bodies: Rereading the Two Tang Histories' Biographies of Women," in *Presence and Presentation: Women in the Chinese Literati Tradition*, ed. Sherry J. Mou (New York: St. Martin's Press, 1999), 114–15.

30. Zhu, "Tangdai xiaoshuozhong de nüxing juese yanjiu," 46. In addition to these basic social roles, 4 percent of the women in these stories are concubines, 9 percent are slaves, and 5 percent are elderly.

31. Chen Ruoshui, *Tangdai de funü wenhua yu jiating shenghuo* (Taipei: Yunchen wenhua, 2007), 26–28; Yao, "Women's Epitaphs in Tang China," 144. Rosemary A. Joyce, "Girling the Girl and Boying the Boy: The Production of Adulthood in Ancient Mesoamerica," *World Archaeology* 31, no. 3 (2000): 473–74, 478, 480 provides a theoretical framework for interpreting the succession of gendered social roles in a person's life.

32. Mou, "Writing Virtues with Their Bodies," 130–33.

33. Yao, "Women's Epitaphs in Tang China," 140; Duan, *Tangdai funü diwei yanjiu*, 130, 152–56, 167–68.

34. Duan, *Tangdai funü diwei yanjiu*, 167–79.

CHAPTER 1: MARRIAGE

1. Liu, *Jiu Tangshu*, 27:1027, 67–68. Liu Yanli, "Cong falü mian kan Tangdai de fu yu diqi guanxi," in *Tangdai shenfen fazhi yanjiu—yi Tanglü minglilü wei zhongxin*, ed. Gao Mingshi (Taipei: Wunan tushu, 2003), 119; Liu Yurong, "Tangdai hunyin zhidu—yige *Tanglü* de guancha shijiao," *Changjiang luntan* 5 (2011): 67–68. Since antiquity, thinkers had often conceptualized marriage using metaphysical ideas. Jinhua Jia, "Gender and Early Chinese Cosmology Revisited," *Asian Philosophy* 26, no. 4 (2016): 281–93.

2. Suzanne Cahill, "Marriages Made in Heaven," *T'ang Studies* 10–11 (1992–1993): 111–22.

3. Larsen, *Willow, Wine, Mirror, Moon*, 63, 68, 71.

4. Liu, *Jiu Tangshu*, 55:2257.

5. Yang Xiangkui, *Tangdai muzhi yili yanjiu* (Changsha: Yuelu, 2013), 23–31.

6. Duan, *Tangdai funü diwei yanjiu*, 49–55; Guogang Zhang, "'Family Building in Inner Quarters': Conjugal Relationships in Tang Families," trans. Yipeng Lai, *Frontiers of History in China* 4, no. 1 (2009): 3–4.

7. Bannie Chow and Thomas Cleary, trans., *Autumn Willows: Poetry by Women of China's Golden Age* (Ashland, OR: Story Line Press, 2003), 37.

8. Duan, *Tangdai funü diwei yanjiu*, 216. In general, women were mourned more lightly than men. See pp. 218–22.

9. Wallace Johnson, *The T'ang Code, Volume I, General Principles* (Princeton: Princeton University Press, 1979), 33.

10. Ken Kumiko, "Yi 'nüxingxue' guandian shilun Li Bai Du Fu jinei yinei shi," in *Tangdai wenxue yanjiu 3*, ed. Fu Xuancong (Guilin: Guangxi Shifan Daxue chubanshe, 1992), 256, 260.

11. Sun-ming Wong, "Confucian Ideal and Reality: Transformation of the Institution of Marriage in T'ang China (A.D. 618–907)" (PhD diss., University of Washington, 1979), 71, 218, 228–31; Xiang Shuyun, *Tangdai hunyin fa yu hunyin shitai* (Taipei: Taiwan shangwu, 1991), 14–25; Liu Yutang, "Tangdai guanyu hunyin jinzhi tiaojian de falü guifan," *Jianghan luntan* 4 (2010): 90–95. A memorial reaffirmed the classical idea that ancient sage rulers set down the norms regulating relations between husband and wife. Liu, *Jiu Tangshu*, 119:3432.

12. Ouyang Xiu, *Xin Tangshu*, annotated by Song Qi, Dong Jiazun, et al. (Beijing: Zhonghua Shuju, 1975), 24:530.

13. Zhang Wenjing, "Tangdai de nüxing yu susong—yi panwen wei zhongxin," in *Xingbie, zongjiao, zhongzu, jieji yu Zhongguo chuantong sifa*, ed. Liu Liyan (Taipei: Zhongyang Yanjiuyuan Lishi Yuyan Yanjiusuo, 2013), 16–35.

14. Liu Yutang, "Tangdai dui guanli hunyin tequan de falü guifan," *Zhongguo wenhua yanjiu* 1 (2013): 82–85.

15. Duan, *Tangdai funü diwei yanjiu*, 259–63.

16. Zhang Guogang, *Jiating shihua* (Beijing: Shehui kexue wenxian, 2012), 57–58.

17. Ren Haiyan, "Lun Tangdai funü shengyu de yingxiang yinsu," *Shoudu Shifan Daxue xuebao* 1 (2009): 29–32.

18. Yue Qingping, *Handai jiating yu jiazu* (Zhengzhou: Daxiang chubanshe, 1997), 6–11.

19. Zhang, *Jiating shihua*, 56–57.

20. Ōzawa Masāki, "Tō Sō henkaku no kazoku kibo to kōsei—shōsetsu shiryō ni yoru bunseki, *Tōdaishi kenkyū* 6 (2003): 70; Ōzawa Masāki, *Tō Sō jidai no kazoku, konin, josei—tsuma wa tsuyoku* (Tokyo: Akashi, 2005), 155–67.

21. Keith N. Knapp, *Selfless Offspring: Filial Children and Social Order in Early Medieval China* (Honolulu: University of Hawaii Press, 2005), 16.

22. Ikeda On, "T'ang Household Registers and Related Documents," in *Perspectives on the T'ang*, ed. Arthur F. Wright and Denis Twitchett (New Haven: Yale University Press, 1973), 135–36; Knapp, *Selfless Offspring*, 16, 18.

23. Jennifer Holmgren, "Imperial Marriage in the Native Chinese and Non-Han State, Han to Ming," in *Marriage and Inequality in Chinese Society*, ed. Rubie S. Watson and Patricia Buckley Ebrey (Berkeley: University of California Press, 1991), 77.

24. Chen, *Tangdai de funü wenhua yu jiating shenghuo*, 74–94; Zhao Wenrun, "Chang'an huren yu Tangdai qianqi de hunwu wenhua," *Ganling wenhua yanjiu* 4 (2008): 31–32. Sororal polygyny is also called accompanying concubinage. For detailed descriptions of sororal polygyny in antiquity, see Marcel Granet, *La polygynie sororale et le sororat dans la Chine féodale* (Paris: Editions Ernest Leroux, 1920); Kurihara Keisuke, *Kodai Chūgoku koninsei no rei rinen to keitai* (Tokyo: Tōhō shoten, 1982), 301–81. For ancient levirate, see Xie Weiyang, *Zhoudai jiating xingtai* (Beijing: Zhongguo shehui kexue chubanshe, 1990), 72–74.

25. Jin Xia, "Qianlun Tangdai houqi hunyin de tedian," *Shandong Jiaoyu Xueyuan xuebao* 3 (2002): 46–48, 51; Zhao Mingyang, "Tangdai hunyin fengsu de qianhouqi chayi," *Anqing Shifan Xueyuan xuebao* 35, no. 2 (2016): 55–58, 63.

26. Denis Twitchett, "The Composition of the T'ang Ruling Class: New Evidence from Tunhuang," in *Perspectives on the T'ang*, ed. Arthur F. Wright and Denis Twitchett (New Haven: Yale University Press, 1973), 80–81; Xiang, *Tangdai hunyin fa yu hunyin shitai*, 26–27, 37–48.

27. Women from merchant families usually married merchants, minor clerks, physicians, and ruined literati. Merchants liked allying with ruined literati because they considered this kinship link prestigious. Xu Yanhua, "Shilun Tangdai de shangjia funü," *Shangye wenhua* 4 (2010): 79.

28. Zhang, "'Family Building in Inner Quarters,'" 4–5.

29. Tackett, *The Destruction of the Medieval Chinese Aristocracy*, 138.

30. Zhao Xiaofang and Lu Qingfu, "Shilun Tang Xizhou xiaceng nüxing de hunyin shenghuo," *Dunhuang yanjiu* 1 (2010): 74–75.

31. Tan Chanxue, *Dunhuang hunyin wenhua* (Lanzhou: Gansu renmin chubanshe, 1993), 85, 112–17, 122–25; Chen Li, "Tangdai Dunhuang funü hunyin shenghuo tanwei," *Dunhuang yanjiu* 5 (2004): 44; Niu Zhiping, *Tangdai hunsang* (Xi'an: Sanqin chubanshe, 2011), 107–21.

32. Tackett, *The Destruction of the Medieval Chinese Aristocracy*, 140–41.

33. Liu, *Jiu Tangshu*, 156:4130.

34. Xiang, *Tangdai hunyinfa yu yunyin shitai yanjiu*, 28–36 documents these marriage links in detail; Mao Hanguang, "Wan Tang wuxing zhuofang zhi hunyin guanxi," *Guoli Taiwan Daxue Lishi Xuexi xuebao* 15 (1990): 135–57 finds that intermarriage among the five surnames continued until the end of the Tang dynasty.

35. Maeda Aiko, "Tangdai Shandong wuxing hunyin yu qi zhengzhi yingxiangli—tongguo zhizuo Cui shi, Lu shi, Deng shi hunyinbiao kaocha," *Tangshi luncong* 1 (2012): 253.

36. Yao Ping, *Tangdai funü de shengming licheng* (Shanghai: Shanghai guji chubanshe, 2004), 43.

37. Lu Xuejun, "Jianxi Tangdai 'wuxing nü' de lifa chuancheng ji qi dui hunzu de yingxiang," *Tangdu xuekan* 28, no. 2 (2012): 33–38.

38. Ouyang, *Xin Tangshu*, 112:4172. For example, the elite in the capital intermarried, creating dense networks based on marriage ties. Tackett, *The Destruction of the Medieval Chinese Aristocracy*, 122–23, 126–28, 144.

39. Li Rui, "Tangdai Wei shi jiazu hunyin guanxi yanjiu," *Qianling wenhua yanjiu* (2007): 262–81. For another example, see Guo Feng, *Tangdai shizu gean yanjiu: yi Wu jun, Qinghe, Fanyang Dunhuang Zhang shi wei zhongxin* (Xiamen: Xiamen Daxue chubanshe, 1999), 129–44.

40. Qi Zhongming, "Tangdai dazu lianhun tanwei," *Xueshu jiaoliu* 9 (2011): 187–89.

41. Yao, *Tangdai funü de shengming licheng*, 76.

42. Jen-der Lee, "Women and Marriage in China During the Period of Disunion" (PhD diss., University of Washington, 1992), 54–58; Ping Yao, "Cousin Marriages in Tang China," *Chinese Historical Review* 18, no. 1 (2011): 25–55.

43. Yao, *Tangdai funü de shengming licheng*, 78, 83; Yao, "Women's Epitaphs in Tang China," 153–54.

44. Yao, "Cousin Marriages in Tang China," 49–50.

45. Zhang, *Jiating shihua*, 64; Song Junfeng, "Tangdai shangren hunyin fawei," *Tangdu xuekan* 6 (2006): 29–31.

46. Shiga Shūzō, *Chūgoku kazokuhō no genri* (Tokyo: Sōbunsha, 1967), 449–56; Sun Yurong and Xie Fang, "Lun Tangdai 'fu jian jiugu li' de bianqian," *Nanfang lunkan* 6 (2015): 98–100.

47. Luo Tonghua, *Tongju gongcai: Tangdai jiating yanjiu* (Taipei: Zhengda chubanshe, 2015), 354–60; Sun Yurong, "Lun Tangdai shehui biangeqi de nüxing jiaoyu," *Funü yanjiu luncong* 1 (2015): 44–46.

48. Liu, *Jiu Tangshu*, 62:2390 compares a virtuous woman who serves her elder brother's wife to the ancient paragon Mother Wen (Wen Mu 文母), consort of the revered King Wen of Zhou.

49. Chen Ruoshui, "Shitan Tangdai funü yu benjia de guanxi," *Zhongyang Yanjiuyuan Lishi Yuyan Yanjiusuo jikan* 3 (1997): 167–248; Li Zhende, "Nüren de Zhongguo zhonggushi—xingbie yu Han Tang zhijian de lilü yanjiu," in *Chūgoku no rekishi sekai—tōgō no shisutemu to takenteki hatsuten*, ed. Nihon Chūgokushi gakkai (Tokyo: Kyūko, 2002): 477–81. For overviews of the relations between women and their natal families, see Cen Jingwen, *Tangdai huanmen funü yanjiu* (Taipei: Wenjin, 2006), 162–85; Chen Ruoshui, *Yinbi de guangjing: Tangdai de funü wenhua yu jiating shenghuo* (Guangxi Shifan Daxue chubanshe, 2009), 3–164. Sun Yurong, "Tangdai benjia dui nüxing hunyin ganshequan de bianqian," *Zhonghua Nüzi Xueyuan xuebao* 3 (2015): 104 takes the contrarian position that the relationship between women and their natal kin weakened over the course of the Tang, making it a key period of transition in the history of Chinese kinship.

50. Duan, *Tangdai funü diwei yanjiu*, 263–77; Chen, *Tangdai de funü wenhua yu jiating shenghuo*, 106, 116–36; Li Runqiang, "Cong Dunhuang huji wenxian kaocha funü guizong dui Tangdai jiating de yingxiang," *Dunhuang yanji* 1 (2007): 68–72.

51. Duan, *Tangdai funü diwei yanjiu*, 45; Chen, *Tangdai de funü wenhua yu jiating shenghuo*, 113–15, 154–59, 170–87.

52. Hu Na, "Tangdai nüzi zhuban fumu sangzang xianxiang kaolue," *Guangdong Jishu Shifan Xueyuan xuebao* 9 (2014): 58–60.

53. Zheng Yaru, *Qin en nan bao: Tangdai shiren de xiaodao shijian ji qi tizhihua* (Taida chuban zhongxin, 2014), 121–23.

54. Wang Cui, "Cong muzhi kan Tangdai nüxing yu benjia de jingji guanxi—yi dahe wunian 'Lu fujun qi Qinghe Cui furen muzhiming' wei zhongxin," *Baise Xueyuan xuebao* 3 (2014): 122–25.

55. Yao, "Cousin Marriages in Tang China," 52–53; Tackett, *The Destruction of the Medieval Chinese Aristocracy*, 108–9, 136, 174.

56. Tackett, "Great Clansmen, Bureaucrats, and Local Magnates," 121–22.

57. Liu, *Jiu Tangshu*, 27:1019–22 describes mourning regulations for maternal kin. The proper length of time for mourning between brother-in-law and sister-in-law was a subject of debate. Some people feared that these two types of kin might become too close, so they argued that they should not mourn for one another to increase the distance between them. Li Xia, "Jianshu Tangdai jiating zhong de saoshu zhi li," *Shaanxi Shifan Daxue xuebao* 31 (2002): 152–53. For funerals, see Tackett, *The Destruction of the Medieval Chinese Aristocracy*, 76–77, 131.

58. Liang Ertao, "Lun Tangdai yinya shiqu ji qi wenxue yiyi," *Zhongzhou xuekan* 5 (2016): 139–44.

59. Wang Fu, *Tang huiyao* (Beijing: Zhonghua shuju, 1955), 83:1527–30; Liang Ruimin, "Tangdai funü de jiating diwei," *Hebei Shifan Daxue xuebao* 22, no. 3 (1999): 89; Xiang, *Tangdai hunyin fa yu hunyin shitai*, 55–57; Liu Yutang, "Lun Tangdai de hunling lifa," *Hubei Daxue xuebao* 32, no. 6 (2005): 725–26.

I give all ages in *sui* 歲, which differs somewhat from the Western method of reckoning age. Sanping Chen, "'Age Inflation and Deflation' in Medieval China," *Journal of the American Oriental Society* 133, no. 3 (2013): 527–33 discusses the ways used to calculate the year of birth. Sometimes a person's age differed from the number of years since birth. For another discussion of relevant terminology, see Yao, *Tangdai funü de shengming licheng*, 1–7.

60. Jin Mei, "Tangdai hunyin jiating jicheng falü zhidu chulun" (PhD diss., China University of Political Science and Law, 2000), 16–17.

61. Guo Haiwen, "Tangdai gongzhu jieli nianling kao—yi muzhi wei zhongxin," *Beilin jikan* 19 (2013): 198–200.

62. Liu, "Lun Tangdai de hunling lifa," 726–28 summarizes previous research regarding the average age of marriage. His own estimate is age thirteen to fourteen for women. Zhou and Wang, *Roushun zhi xiang*, 28–47 analyze Sui epitaphs. They conclude that these women most commonly wed at age fifteen.

Studies of Tang epitaphs give different average marriage ages:

Luo, *Tongju gongcai*, 301: 60 percent of women married by age seventeen and 89 percent married by age twenty.

Zhang, *Jiating shihua*, 60–61: age thirteen to twenty-two for women and seventeen to thirty for men.

Xiang, *Tangdai hunyin fa yu hunyin shitai*, 58–65: age thirteen to fifteen for women and fifteen to twenty for men.

Li Shutong, *Tangshi yanjiu* (Taipei: Zhonghua, 1979), 75: age fourteen to fifteen for women.

Wan Junjie, "Tangdai nüxing de chuhun nianling," *Huaxia kaogu* 2 (2014): 106–13: age fourteen to nineteen for women, with fifteen most common.

Zhang, *Tangdai jiating yu shehui*, 237–43: age fourteen to nineteen for women and seventeen to thirty for men.

Zhang Guogang and Jiang Aihua, "Tangdai nannü hunjia nianling kaolue," *Zhongguoshi yanjiu* 2 (2004): 68, 72: age fourteen to nineteen for women and seventeen to thirty for men.

Xiang, *Tangdai hunyin fa yu yunyin shitai yanjiu*, 66: age fifteen for women.

Chen, "Tangdai Dunhuang funnü hunyin shenghuo tangwei," 45: age seventeen for women.

Yao, *Tangdai funü de shengming licheng*, 10: age 17.6 for women.

63. Wan Junjie, *Tangdai nüxing de shengqian yu zuhou: weirao muzhi ziliao zhankai de ruogan tantao* (Tianjin: Tianjin guji, 2010), 14–15.

64. Weng Yuxuan, "Tangdai shiren de hunyin yu jiating—yi qiqie wenti wei zhongxin," in *Zhongguo zhonggu shehui yu guojia*, ed. Song Dexi (Banqiao: Daoxiang, 2009), 366.

65. Bao Ruchen, "Tangdai Taiyuan Wang shi nanxing hunling kaolue—yi 'Tangdai muzhi huibian' wei zhongxin," *Du tianxia* 15 (2016): 276–77.

66. Zhao and Lu, "Shilun Tang Xizhou xiaceng nüxing de hunyin shenghuo," 71–73.

67. Tan, *Dunhuang hunyin wenhua*, 95–99; Chen, "Tangdai Dunhuang funü hunyin shenghuo tanwei," 45–48.

68. Cui Guijin, "Tangdai pinnü nanjia xianxiang tanxi," *Ningbo Daxue xuebao* 27, no. 6 (2014): 63.

69. Cui, "Tangdai pinnü nanjia xianxiang tanxi," 65.

70. Wang Xiao, "Tangdai jiazhuang xiaofei kao," *Yibin Xueyuan xuebao* 14, no. 4 (2014): 56–59.

71. Zhang Yanyun, "Cong Dunhuang de hunshu chengshi kan Tangdai xuhun zhidu," *Dunhuang yanjiu* 6 (2002): 35–38; Qian Daqun, *Tang lü yanjiu* (Beijing: Falü, 2000), 302.

72. Chow and Cleary, *Autumn Willows*, 42.

73. Xiang, *Tangdai hunyin fa yu yunyin shitai yanjiu*, 82–86; Tan, *Dunhuang hunyin wenhua*, 27–33; Lai Liangjun, "Cong fangqishu kan Tangdai de heli," in *Tanglü yu chuantongfa wenhua*, ed. Huang Yuansheng (Taipei: Yuanzhao, 2011), 222 transcribe and analyze Dunhuang *hunshu*.

74. Li Shuyuan, "Huihun yu jiaqu zhi guanxi," *Tanglü yu guojia shehui yanjiu*, ed. Gao Mingshi (Taipei: Wunan tushu, 1999), 318–22.

75. Xiang, *Tangdai hunyin fa yu hunyin shitai*, 89–105; Tan, *Dunhuang hunyin wenhua*, 162–68; Jiang Lin, "*Taiping guangji* zhong suo jian Tangdai hunyin, hunsu luekao," *Hunan Daxue xuebao* 4 (2002): 20–22; Christian de Pee, *The Writing of Weddings in Middle-Period China: Text and Ritual Practice in the Eighth through Fourteenth Centuries* (Albany: State University of New York Press, 2007); Cai Weitang, "Guanyu Dunhuang bihua 'hunli tu' de jige wenti," *Dunhuang yanjiu* 1 (1990):

54–59; Fan Jinshi, *Dunhuang yu Sui Tang chengshi wenming* (Shanghai: Shanghai jiaoyu, 2010), 220–29. Weddings of princesses and the heir apparent were extremely lavish and featured elaborate rituals. Wei Zheng, *Suishu*, annotated by Linghu Defen and Wang Zhaoying (Beijing: Zhonghua Shuju, 1973), 9:178; Yue Lianjian and Ke Zhuoying, "Tang Huainan Dazhang Gongzhu muzhi suo fanying de Tangdai lishi wenti," *Huaxia kaogu* 2 (2008): 131–32; Guo Haiwen, "Tangdai gongzhu de hunyin liyi," *Shehui kexue pinglun* 3 (2009): 85–93.

76. Zhao, "Chang'an huren yu Tangdai qianqi de hunwu wenhua," 29–38; Sun Yurong, "Lun shaoshu minzu wenhua dui Tangdai hunsu de yingxiang," *Henan Keji Daxue xuebao* 33, no. 5 (2015): 21–25.

77. Duan, *Tangdai funü diwei yanjiu*, 223–27, 232; Chen, *Yinbi de guangjing*, 230–58; Chen Ruoshui, "Tangdai de yifuduoqi hezang yu fuqi guanxi—cong Jingyun ernian 'Yang Fu Jun furen Weishi muzhiming' tanqi," *Zhonghua wenshi luncong* 1 (2006): 173–202; Xing Xuemin, "Tangdai fuqi zangsu de wenhua kaocha—yi Xingyang Deng shi wei zhongxin," *Lishi jiaoxue* 4 (2008): 24–27.

78. Duan, *Tangdai funü diwei yanjiu*, 222.

79. For a detailed description of a representative intact grave of a high ranking Tang woman, see Sonja Filip and Alexandra Hilgner, eds., *The Lady with the Phoenix Crown: Tang-Period Grave Goods of the Noblewoman Li Chui (711–736)* (Regensburg and Mainz, Germany: Schnell and Steiner, 2014).

80. Lu Xuejun, "Ru Fo jian xiu yu Tangdai Shandong shiqu nüxing de jiafeng yanjin—yi Tangdai muzhi wei li," *Shoudu Shifan Daxue xuebao* 5 (2009): 30.

81. Xiang, *Tangdai hunyin fa yu hunyin shitai*, 105; Yao, *Tangdai funü de shengming licheng*, 173–75, 182–89, 191–97; Li Shiyu, "Tangdai minghun fengsu xinyi," *Ganling wenhua yanjiu* 4 (2008): 286–93; Xie Mingxun, "Tangdai 'minghun' shilun," in *2007 Dongya hanxue yu minsu wenhua guoji xueshu yantaohui*, ed. Wang Sanqing and Chen Yiyuan (Taipei: Lexue shuju, 2007), 139–66; Niu, *Tangdai hunsang*, 66–68; Tan, *Dunhuang hunyin wenhua*, 77–80, 127–30.

82. Zhang, "'Family Building in Inner Quarters,'" 28–35. Yang Jiping, "Dunhuang chutu de fangqi shu suoyi," *Ximen Daxue xuebao* 4 (1999): 34 defines the terminology used to discuss divorce. Chen Li and Kang Linyi, "Tangdai funü lihun gaijia shijian de chayixing fenxi," *Hebei Shifan Daxue xuebao* 2 (2007): 106 provides a table listing couples who divorced and the reason given for each divorce. The reasons included barrenness, mental problems, lack of affection, or a spouse being accused of a crime. Sometimes a man expelled his wife without giving an explicit reason.

83. Liu Yutang, "Tangdai 'heli' zhidu de falü toushi," *Jianghan luntan* 5 (2011): 95–100. Wang Yanhua, "Cong Dunhuang wenshu qianxi Tangdai heli zhidu," *Kexue zhi you* 12 (2008): 90–91 transcribes and discusses Dunhuang document S.0343, which records a consensual divorce.

84. Niu Zhigong, "Tangren de 'lihun' chuyi," *Xueshujie* 2 (1994): 25–26.

85. Liu Yutang, "Lun Tangdai de 'yijue' zhidu ji qi falü houguo," *Zhongguo Minzu Daxue xuebao* 6 (2005): 113–17.

86. Niu, "Tangren de 'lihun' chuyi," 24.

87. Liu, "Tangdai guanyu hunyin jinzhi tiaojian de falü guifan," 97.

88. Liu Yuhong, "Tangdai qifu shi pingxi," *Taiyuan Daxue xuebao* 3 (2003): 50–52; Yang Xiaomin, "Tangdai funü de 'jifu' shi," *Tianshui Shifan Xueyuan xuebao* 23, no. 3 (2003): 42.

89. Tan, *Dunhuang hunyin wenhua*, 72–76; Niu, "Tangren de 'lihun' chuyi," 27; Zhang Yanyun, "Cong Dunhuang 'fangqi shu' kan Tangdai hunyin zhong de heli zhidu," *Dunhuang yanjiu* 2 (1999): 73–75; Yang, "Dunhuang chutu de fangqi shu suoyi," 34–41; Wang, "Cong Dunhuang wenshu qianxi Tangdai heli zhidu," 90–91; Liu, "Tangdai 'heli' zhidu de falü toushi," 99–100; Lai, "Cong fangqishu kan Tangdai de heli," 225; Zhang, *Tangdai jiating yu shehui*, 145–48; Yue Hong, "Divorce Practice in Late Medieval Dunhuang: Reading 'Documents Setting the Wife Free,'" *Tang Studies* 34 (2016): 12–39. Norman P. Ho, "Law, Literature, and Gender in Tang China: An Exploration of Bai Juyi's Selected Panwen on Women," *Tsinghua China Law Review* 1 (2009): 78–91 discusses a specific case to show how divorce law was interpreted during the Tang.

90. Wan Junjie, "Tangdai 'qie' de sangzang wenti," *Wei Jin Nanbeichao Sui Tang shi ziliao* 25 (2009): 187.

91. Naomi Quinn, "Anthropological Studies on Women's Status," *Annual Review of Anthropology* 6 (1977): 211.

92. Yao, *Tangdai funü de shengming licheng*, 154–72; Zhang, *Tangdai jiating yu shehui*, 182–89; Zhang, "'Family Building in Inner Quarters,'" 12–26.

93. Jin, "Tangdai hunyin jiating jicheng falü zhidu chulun," 47–54. Nevertheless, some men still promoted a concubine to the status of wife. Liu, *Jiu Tangshu*, 147:3983.

94. Liao Yifang, *Tangdai de muzi guanxi* (Banqiao: Daoxiang, 2009), 155, 161–66.

95. Yao, "Women in Portraits," 174–76; Yu, "Tangdai nüxing shige yanjiu," 34–36.

96. Wan, "Tangdai 'qie' de sangzang wenti," 186–200.

97. Huang Zhengjian, "Tangdai 'biezhaofu' xianxiang xiaokao," in *Tang Song nüxing yu shehui*, ed. Deng Xiaonan (Shanghai: Shanghai cishu, 2003), 1:252–62.

CHAPTER 2: MOTHERS

1. Susan Carol Rogers, "Female Forms of Power and the Myth of Male Dominance: A Model of Female/Male Interaction in Peasant Society," *American Ethnologist* 2, no. 4 (1975): 728–30.

2. Elinor Ochs and Carolyn Taylor, "The 'Father Knows Best' Dynamic in Dinnertime Narratives," in *Linguistic Anthropology: A Reader*, second edition, ed. Alessandro Duranti (Chichester, UK: Wiley-Blackwell, 2009), 435–36.

3. Cai Hongsheng, *Tangdai jiuxing hu yu Tujue wenhua* (Beijing: Zhonghua, 1998), 19.

4. Martin King Whyte, *The Status of Women in Preindustrial Societies* (Princeton: Princeton University Press, 1978), 35; Rebecca L. Warner, Gary R. Lee, and Janet Lee, "Social Organization, Spousal Resources, and Marital Power: A Cross-Cultural Study," *Journal of Marriage and Family* 48, no. 1 (1986): 121–28.

5. Zhou and Wang, *Roushun zhi xiang*, 49.

6. Zhang Guogang, *Tangdai jiating yu shehui* (Beijing: Zhonghua, 2014), 2–5.

7. Yao, *Tangdai funü de shengming licheng*, 326–27, 336; Yao, "Women in Portraits," 167 calculates that the average woman documented in epitaphs had between 3.3 and 4.48 children. This number varies somewhat according to the statistical method used to analyze the data. Ping Yao, "Childbirth and Maternal Mortality in Tang China," *Chinese Historical Review* 12, no. 2 (2005): 263–86 estimates that women recorded in epitaphs likely had an average of 4.48 children, not counting those who did not survive infancy. Zhang, *Jiating shihua*, 70 concludes that the average household documented in epitaphs had 4.75 children. Guo Haiwen, Zhao Wenduo, and Jia Qiangqiang, "Tangdai gongzhu zinü kao," *Beilin jikan* 碑林集刊 20 (2014): 172 concludes that the average woman had 4.77 children. It was most common to have three or four children. This study posits a relatively balanced sex ratio among children.

8. Fei Sheng, *Tangdai renkou dili* (Xi'an: Xibei Daxue chubanshe, 1996), 79.

9. Liu, *Jiu Tangshu*, 20B:796.

10. Wei, *Suishu*, 1:1.

11. Liu, *Jiu Tangshu*, 143:3900.

12. Yao, *Tangdai funü de shengming licheng*, 292; Yao, "Childbirth and Maternal Mortality in Tang China," 275–77. Ouyang, *Xin Tangshu*, 111:4146 describes an incident in which more than ninety nursing women among a large group of captives were released as an act of benevolence. New mothers were seen as deserving special treatment.

13. Jen-der Lee, "Childbirth in Early Imperial China," *Nan Nü* 7, no. 2 (2005): 224–45.

14. Xu Zhiyin, "Tangdai nüxing songbie shi zonglun," *Henan shehui kexue* 16, no. 2 (2008): 56.

15. Qian, *Tang lü yanjiu*, 302–3.

16. Ikeda, "T'ang Household Registers and Related Documents," 135.

17. Liu, *Jiu Tangshu*, 62:2378.

18. Josephine Chiu-Duke, "Mothers and the Well-Being of the State in Tang China," *Nan Nü* 8, no. 1 (2006): 73, 112.

19. Liu, *Jiu Tangshu*, 92:2967.

20. Huang Meiyin, "Tangdai sanfu bamu de falü diwei," in *Tangdai shenfen fazhi yanjiu—yi Tanglü minglilü wei zhongxin*, ed. Gao Mingshi (Taipei: Wunan tushu, 2003), 89–117.

21. Hu Yunwei, "Tangdai de jimu zi guanxi—yi Wang Wan, Wei Chengqing wei zhongxin," *Zaoqi Zhongguo shi yanjiu* 6, no. 1 (2014): 85.

22. Liu, *Jiu Tangshu*, 193:5144.

23. Johnson, *The T'ang Code*, 74; Ho, "Law, Literature, and Gender," 78–84.

24. Liu, *Jiu Tangshu*, 48:2097, 97:3050, 98:3062; Ouyang, *Xin Tangshu*, 25:4405.

25. Liu, *Jiu Tangshu*, 188:4917. Niu Zhiping, *Tangdai shehui shenghuo conglun* (Taiyuan: Shuhai, 2001), 112–29.

26. Tackett, *The Destruction of the Medieval Chinese Aristocracy*, 131.

27. Liu, *Jiu Tangshu*, 94:2992, 149:4019, 159:4182, 188:4924, 188:4926.

28. Liu, *Jiu Tangshu*, 141:3842.

29. Liu, *Jiu Tangshu*, 56:2263.

30. Zhu Chun'e, Li Sifen, Yao Juan, and Long Juan, "Tangdai funü xiaoxing tezheng: nü zhi xiao zhongyu fu zhi xiao," *Hubei shehui kexue* 4 (2010): 112.

31. Hu Ji, "Tangdai jiali shulun," in *Diwujie Tangdai wenhua xueshu yantaohui lunwenji*, ed. Zhongguo Tangdai xuehui et al. (Kaohsiung: Liwen wenhua, 2001), 562–65.

32. Wang Chengju, "Tangdai *Xiaojing* wenxian kaoshu," *Changjiang Daxue xuebao* 36, no. 2 (2013): 179–80.

33. Qingping Liu, "Filiality versus Sociality and Individuality: On Confucianism and Consanguinitism," *Philosophy East and West* 53, no. 2 (2003): 234.

34. Ji Qingyang, "Shilun Tangdai de 'xiaozhi,'" *Ningxia Daxue xuebao* 1 (2009): 74–78.

35. Wright, *The Sui Dynasty*, 56.

36. Liu, *Jiu Tangshu*, 4:65.

37. Ochi Shigeaki, *Gi Shin nanchō no hito to shakai* (Tokyo: Kenbun shuppan, 1985), 41–46.

38. Liao, *Tangdai de muzi guanxi*, 125–32; Zhang, *Tangdai jiating yu shehui*, 250–52; Ping Yao, "Tang Women in the Transformation of Buddhist Filiality," in *Gendering Chinese Religion: Subject, Identity, and Body*, ed. Jinhua Jia et al. (Albany: State University of New York Press, 2014), 25–46.

39. Xie Shengbao, "Cong 'Shanzi bingbian' kan fojiao yishu zhong de xiaodao sixiang," *Dunhuang yanjiu* 2 (2001): 42–50; Cai Weitang, "Dunhuang bihua zhong de Shanzi bensheng gushi hua—cong E zang Mogao ku di 433 ku Shanzi bensheng gushi hua tanqi," *Dunhuang yanjiu* 5 (2004): 13–19.

40. Ogawa Kanichi, "Hubo onjū kei," in *Tonkō to Chūgoku bukkyō*, ed. Fukui Fumimasa (Tokyo: Daitō, 1984), 207–22; Li Chuanjun, "'Fumu enzhong jing' yu Tangdai xiao wenhua—jian tan fojiao Zhongguohua guocheng zhong de 'tong ru' yu 'ji su' xianxiang," *Kongzi yanjiu* 3 (2008): 90–96.

41. Alan Cole, *Mothers and Sons in Chinese Buddhism* (Stanford: Stanford University Press, 1998), 2–3, 42–46, 57–64, 159–91; Li Zhisheng and Wu Tingting, "Tangdai nüzi de fojiao xiaoqin huodong ji tedian—yi chujiafu wei zhu de kaocha," *Zhongyuan wenhua yanjiu* 6 (2015): 81–88.

42. Stephen F. Teiser, *The Ghost Festival in Medieval China* (Princeton: Princeton University Press, 1988).

43. Ma Jiyun, "Xiao de guannian yu Tangdai jiating," *Shandong Shifan Daxue xuebao* 48, no. 2 (2003): 112.

44. Qian, *Tang lü yanjiu*, 309–10; Ma, "Xiao de guannian yu Tangdai jiating," 112–13.

45. Liu, *Jiu Tangshu*, 185A:4797. Zhang, "Tangdai de nüxing yu susong," 36–39.

46. Keith N. Knapp, "Reverent Caring: The Parent-Son Relationship in Early Medieval Tales of Filial Offspring," in *Filial Piety in Chinese Thought and History*, ed. Alan K.L. Chan and Sor-hoon Tan (London: RoutledgeCurzon, 2004), 44–70.

47. Liu, *Jiu Tangshu*, 128:3583.

48. Mou, "Writing Virtues with their Bodies," 117–19.

49. Qian, *Tang lü yanjiu*, 309–10.

50. Chiu-Duke, "Mothers and the Well-Being of the State in Tang China," 61–62.

51. Luo, *Tongju gongcai*, 490–502; Zheng, *Qin en nan bao*, 26–30, 54–87.

52. Liu, *Jiu Tangshu*, 15:459.

53. Liu, *Jiu Tangshu*, 68:2501, 172:4460.

54. Wei, *Suishu*, 57:1400; Liu, *Jiu Tangshu*, 96:3022, 98:3067.

55. Ouyang, *Xin Tangshu*, 102:3974.

56. Ouyang, *Xin Tangshu*, 195:5579, 195:5583.

57. Ouyang, *Xin Tangshu*, 195:5580

58. Mou, "Writing Virtues with their Bodies," 117–19.

59. Liu, *Jiu Tangshu*, 149:4013–12 discusses disagreements over the proper way to mourn parents.

60. Ouyang, *Xin Tangshu*, 195:5583. Also 195:4491.

61. Qiu Zhonglin, "Bu xiao zhi xiao—Tang yilai gegu liaoqin xianxiang de shehuishi chutan," *Xin shixue* 6, no. 1 (1995): 49–92; Qiu Zhonglin, "Renyao yu xueqi—'gegu' liaoqin xianxiang zhong de yiliao gainian," *Xin shixue* 10, no. 4 (1999): 67–116; Key Ray Chong, *Cannibalism in China* (Wakefield, NH: Longwood Academic, 1990), ix.

62. James. A. Benn, *Burning for the Buddha: Self-Immolation in Chinese Buddhism* (Honolulu: University of Hawaii Press, 2007).

63. Keith N. Knapp, "Chinese Filial Cannibalism: A Silk Road Import?" in *China and Beyond in the Mediaeval Period: Cultural Crossings and Inter-Regional Connections*, ed. Dorothy C. Wong and Gustav Heldt (New Delhi: Manohar Publishers, 2014), 135–49.

64. Henry Rosemont Jr. and Roger T. Ames, *The Chinese Classic of Family Reverence: A Philosophical Translation of the* Xiaojing (Honolulu: University of Hawaii Press, 2009), 105. The *Xiaojing* prohibition of self-mutilation seems to be an extension of Mencian filial principles. Bryan W. Van Norden, trans., *Mengzi: With Selections from Traditional Commentaries* (Indianapolis: Hackett Publishing, 2008), 98.

CHAPTER 3: GOVERNMENT

1. Zhang Yanhui, "Tangdai waimingfu chaoye zhidu kao," *Leshan Shifan Xueyuan xuebao* 27, no. 1 (2012): 91–94. The six grades of titles were *fei* 妃, *guo furen* 國夫人, *jun furen* 郡夫人, *jun jun* 郡君, *xian jun* 縣君, and *xiang jun* 鄉君. The Tang custom of granting titles to women followed Han dynasty precedent. During the Han, the wives of *liehou* 列侯 received the title *furen* 夫人. Ban Gu, *Hanshu*, annotated by Yan Shigu (Beijing: Zhonghua, 1962), 4:122n1.

2. Liao, *Tangdai de muzi guanxi*, 39–62. Lin Kaixin, *Tangdai mingfu yanjiu* (MA thesis, Tunghai University, 2000) provides a detailed chart of these changes on pp. 46–55.

3. Liu, *Jiu Tangshu*, 193:5145–46.

4. Wright and Twitchett, "Introduction," 14; Chen Anli, *Gaogui de zangyi: Tangdai huangling yu huangqin guoqi mu* (Chengdu: Sichuan jiaoyu, 1998), 111–58;

Liu Xiangyang, *Tangdai diwang lingmu* (Xi'an: Sanqin, 2003). Liu, *Jiu Tangshu*, 126:3560 describes the system of granting posthumous names to deceased empresses. Also Zhao Yi, *Nianer shi zhaji* (Taipei: Shijie shuju, 1974), 19:252–53. Zhang Chen and Gou Lijun, "Tangdai zhuizun huanghou fumiao kao," *Qilu xuekan* 1 (2012): 54–58 describes the placement of memorial tablets of deceased empresses in the imperial ancestral temple. Also Liu, *Jiu Tangshu*, 25:965. Zhao, *Nianer shi zhaji*, 19:254–55 describes mourning for Tang empresses.

5. Holmgren, "Imperial Marriage in the Native Chinese and Non-Han State," 60. For example, Empress Changsun, wife of Tang Taizong, was the daughter of a Sui dynasty general. Her mother was the daughter of an official. Liu, *Jiu Tangshu*, 51:2164. Empress Wang, wife of Tang Gaozong, was the granddaughter of an empress and daughter of an official. Liu, *Jiu Tangshu*, 51:2169. Empress Zhao, wife of Tang Zhongzong, was the daughter of an official and a princess. Liu, *Jiu Tangshu*, 51:2171.

6. Liu, *Jiu Tangshu*, 21:817; Ouyang, *Xin Tangshu*, 76:3481.

7. For a detailed example, see Duan, *Tangdai funü diwei yanjiu*, 224–29.

8. Wei, *Suishu*, 12:250; Liu, *Jiu Tangshu*, 45:1933; Ouyang, *Xin Tangshu*, 24:512–13.

9. Wei, *Suishu*, 11:236, 247, 249; 12:260, 276–77.

10. For a cogent introduction to materialization theory, see Timothy Earle and Kristian Kristiansen, "Introduction: Theory and Practice in the Late Prehistory of Europe," in *Organizing Bronze Age Societies: The Mediterranean, Central Europe, and Scandinavia Compared*, ed. Timothy Earle and Kristian Kristiansen (Cambridge: Cambridge University Press, 2010), 8, 14.

11. Keith McMahon, "The Institution of Polygamy in the Chinese Imperial Palace," *Journal of Asian Studies* 72, no. 4 (2013): 917–19, 921 describes how people rationalized the system of imperial polygyny.

12. Ouyang, *Xin Tangshu*, 150:5856. Patricia Buckley Ebrey, "Rethinking the Imperial Harem: Why Were There So Many Palace Women?" in *Women and the Family in Chinese History*, ed. Patricia Buckley Ebrey (London: Routledge, 2003), 178.

13. Lin, *Tangdai mingfu yanjiu*, 22–30; Jiang Weigong and Jiang Weidong, "Tangdai gongnü shenghuo shulue," *Shehui kexue zhanxian* 3 (2010): 57–59.

14. Liu, *Jiu Tangshu*, 51:2161–62 notes that these ranks followed Sui precedents. Ouyang, *Xin Tangshu*, 47:1225, 76:3467. Lin, *Tangdai mingfu yanjiu*, 13–22; Paul W. Kroll, "The Life and Writings of Xu Hui (627–650), Worthy Consort at the Early Tang Court," *Asia Major*, third series, 22, no. 2 (2009): 38–39.

15. Wei, *Suishu*, 10:193; 11:237, 243, 248; 12:261–62, 277–78; Liu, *Jiu Tangshu*, 45:1935.

16. Lin, *Tangdai mingfu yanjiu*, 41–45.

17. Wan Junjie, "Tangdai gongren zhi mingyun tanxi," *Wuhan Daxue xuebao* 2 (2010): 147.

18. Zhou and Wang, *Roushun zhi xiang*, 155–57, 159–70.

19. Ouyang, *Xin Tangshu*, 47:1226–32; Pan Taiquan, "Tangdai de nüguan," in *Tangdai de lishi yu shehui* (Wuhan: Wuhan Daxue chubanshe, 1997), 558–61.

20. Yan Xiaomei, "Tangshi zhong suo fanying de Tangdai funü," *Zhejiang xuekan* 109 (1998): 103.

21. Kang-I Sun Chang and Haun Saussy, eds., *Women Writers of Traditional China: An Anthology of Poetry and Criticism* (Stanford: Stanford University Press, 1999), 52.

22. Hua Shikui and Luo Shijin, "Tangdai gongyuan shi fanrong yuanyin tanlun," *Shenzhen Daxue xuebao* 25, no. 6 (2008): 104–8.

23. Florence Hu-Sterk, "Les 'poèmes de lamentation du palais' sou les Tang: La vie recluse des dames de la Cour," *Études chinoises* 11, no. 2 (1992): 7–33.

24. Larsen, *Willow, Wine, Mirror, Moon*, 52.

25. Liu, *Jiu Tangshu*, 7:149.

26. Jiang and Jiang, "Tangdai gongnü shenghuo shulue," 60–61. Officials called for the expulsion of palace concubines as a way to reduce palace expenditures and symbolize a commitment to frugal government. Ouyang, *Xin Tangshu*, 107:4069.

27. Liu, *Jiu Tangshu*, 7:154.

28. Shang Minjie, "Tangdai gongren gongni mu xiangguan wenti tantao," *Tangshi luncong* 1 (2013): 211–33.

29. Wei, *Suishu*, 8:155.

30. Jiang and Jiang, "Tangdai gongnü shenghuo shulue," 60. Hu Yulan, "Tangdai wanggu gongnü muzhi mingwen de wenhua yiwen," *Haerbin Gongye Daxue xuebao* 5 (2006): 138.

31. Liu Qinli, "Lun Tangdai rumu," *Lanzhou xuekan* 11 (2009): 215–18.

32. Liu, *Jiu Tangshu*, 20B:799.

33. Rebecca Doran, "Royal Wet Nurses in Seventh- and Early Eighth-Century China: Historiographical Evaluation and Narrative Construction, *Nan Nü* 20 (2018): 205.

34. Doran, "Royal Wet Nurses," 201.

35. Princesses were *gongzhu* 公主. Daughters of the heir apparent were called *junzhu* 郡主. Daughters of princes had the title *xianzhu* 縣主.

36. Gao Shiyu, *Tangdai funü* (Xi'an: Sanqin, 1988), 31.

37. Ouyang, *Xin Tangshu*, chapter 83. Epitaphs of princesses provide additional information. Wang Qiwei and Zhou Xiaowei, "Tangdai gongzhu muzhi jilue," *Beilin jikan* (1995): 63–77. Zhuang Guorui, "Songdai gongzhu quanli pangluo yuanyin tanxi—yi Song Renzong nü Yanguo gongzhu wei li," *Henan Keji Daxue xuebao* 33, no. 5 (2015): 14–20 considers the Tang to have been the apex of princess power. During the Tang, princesses had unusually large incomes and high official status. There was also a government agency called *yisi* 邑司 that managed matters regarding princesses, giving them representatives in the bureaucracy. The Song abolished the *yisi* and gave princesses much lower status and smaller incomes.

38. Guo, "Tangdai gongzhu de jiating shenghuo," 71–72; Luo, *Tongju gongcai*, 365–71.

39. According to Tang law, the emperor's eldest daughter was to receive income from 600 households, and his younger daughters received tax income from 300 households. However, the actual amount varied. Sometimes an emperor granted a favored princess tax payments from 500, 800, 1,000, or 3,000 households. Xuanzong

revised this system. Henceforth sisters of the emperor were to receive income from 1,000 households, and his daughters received income from 500 households. Liu, *Jiu Tangshu*, 107:3266; Li Jingying, "Tangdai gongzhu yu shifeng zhidu," *Shoudu Shifan Daxue xuebao* 2 (2006): 25–28.

40. Guo, Zhao, and Jia, "Tangdai gongzhu zinü kao," 183–89 provides a long table with information about the offspring of Tang princesses.

41. Elinor Pearlstein, "Pictorial Stones from Chinese Tombs," *Bulletin of the Cleveland Museum of Art* 71, no. 9 (1984): 312, 316, 318; Ba Shanshan, Wang Xiaolin, and Sun Lili, "Tangdai peiling gongzhu kao," *Qianling wenhua yanjiu* 2 (2006): 75–90; Wu Yingying, "Tangdai gongzhu sangzang lisu yanjiu," *Beilin jikan* 19 (2013): 201–18.

42. Holmgren, "Imperial Marriage in the Native Chinese and Non-Han State," 61, 72.

43. Wei, *Suishu*, 54:1363; Liu, *Jiu Tangshu*, 5:97, 19A:664–65, 61:2362.

44. Howard J. Wechsler, "Factionalism in Early T'ang Government," in *Perspectives on the T'ang*, ed. Arthur F. Wright and Denis Twitchett (New Haven: Yale University Press, 1973), 108, 111.

45. Zhang Bangwei, *Hunyin yu shehui (Songdai)* (Chengdu: Sichuan renmin chubanshe, 1989), 106; Zhang Bangwei, *Songdai hunyin jiazu shilun* (Beijing: Renmin chubanshe, 2003), 44; Chen Han and Qu Min, "Luexi Tangdai gongzhu de hunyin jiating guanxi," *Zhanjiang Shifan Xueyuan xuebao* 2 (2006): 93–97; Sun Yu, "Luelun Tangdai gongzhu de zhengzhi hunyin," *Shanxi Datong Daxue xuebao* 23, no. 3 (2009): 16–19; Tackett, *The Destruction of the Medieval Chinese Aristocracy*, 169.

46. Guo Haiwen, "Lun Tangdai gongzhu de hunyin xingtai," *Xibei Shida xuebao* 49, no. 2 (2012): 92.

47. Mao Hanguang, "Guanzhong jun xing hunyin guanxi zhi yanjiu," in *Tangdai wenhua yanjiuhui lunwenji*, ed. Zhongguo Tangdai xuehui bianji weiyuanhui (Taipei: Wenshizhe, 1991), 130–32. For a detailed example, see Wang Wei, "Tangdai jingzhao Weishi yu huangshi hunyin guanxi ji qi yingxiang," *Beifang luncong* 1 (2012): 109–12.

48. Liu, *Jiu Tangshu*, 9:219.

49. Jennifer Holmgren, "A Question of Strength: Military Capacity and Princess Bestowal in Imperial China's Foreign Relations (Han to Ch'ing)," *Monumenta Serica* 39 (1990–1991): 36, 44, 47–48; Wang Tongling, "Han Tang zhi heqin zhengce," in *Zhongguo funüshi lunji sanji*, ed. Bao Jialin (Taipei: Daoxiang, 1993), 41–50; Michael R. Drompp, "From Qatar to Refugee: The Taiping Princess among the Uighurs," in *The Role of Women in the Altaic World*, ed. Veronica Veit (Wiesbaden: Harrrassowitz Verlag, 2007), 57–68.

50. Étienne de la Vaissière and Éric Trombert, "Des Chinois et des Hu: Migrations et Intégration des Iraniens Orientaux en Milieu Chinois durant le Haut Moyen Âge," *Annales: Histoire, Sciences Sociales* 59, nos. 5/6 (2004): 956.

51. Barfield, *The Perilous Frontier*, 152; Hirata Yoichiro, "Shū Zui kakumei to Tokketsu jōsei—Kita Shū Senkin kōshu no kōka o chūshin ni," *Tōdaishi kenkyū* 12 (2009): 27–56; Hayashi Kenichiro, "Nanshō ōken no kakuritsu, henshitsu to Tō,

Toban kankei—washin (kōshu kōka) no imi suru mono," *Tōdaishi kenkyū* 12 (2009): 57–87.

52. Michael R. Drompp, *Tang China and the Collapse of the Uighur Empire: A Documentary History* (Leiden: Brill, 2005), 22, 32.

53. *Jiaxia* 嫁下. Ouyang, *Xin Tangshu*, 104:4007.

54. Wei, *Suishu*, 4:86; Liu, *Jiu Tangshu*, 7:144, 149.

55. Ning Chia, "Women in China's Frontier Politics: *Heqin*," in *Presence and Presentation: Women in the Chinese Literati Tradition*, ed. Sherry J. Mou (New York: St. Martin's Press, 1999), 43, 45.

56. Holmgren, "Imperial Marriage in the Native Chinese and Non-Han State," 77.

57. David Curtis Wright, "A Chinese Princess Bride's Life and Activism among the Eastern Turks, 580–593 CE," *Journal of Asian History* 45, no. 1 (2011): 39–48.

58. Wu Liyu, *Tangli zheyi* (Beijing: Shangwu yinshuguan, 2002), 512–20. For a discussion of the nature of the kinship ties underpinning relations between emperors and their maternal uncles, see Bret Hinsch, "The Origins of Han-Dynasty Consort Kin Power," *East Asian History* 25/26 (2003): 1–24.

59. For biographies of important consort kin, see Ouyang, *Xin Tangshu*, ch. 206. Of course there were notable exceptions. A faction led by the family of Empress Wei unsuccessfully attempted to overthrow the imperial line during the reign of Emperor Xuanzong. Liu, *Jiu Tangshu*, 8:166–68.

60. Holmgren, "Imperial Marriage in the Native Chinese and Non-Han State," 58; Wang Shoudong, "Lun Tangdai gongfu shezheng," *Dezhou Xueyuan xuebao* 23, no. 3 (2007): 67; Chen, *Yinbi de guangjing*, 198. Duan Tali, "Beichao zhi Sui Tang shiqi nüxing canzheng xianxiang toushi," *Jianghai xuekan* 5 (2001): 111–16 notes that of the forty-two medieval women who participated in politics and whose background was recorded, 73.7 percent were of steppe extraction. Chen, "Succession Struggles and the Ethnic Identity of the Tang Imperial House," 395 holds that Wu Zetian's assumption of the role of emperor could only occur in a "Sarbo-Chinese dynasty with deeply-entrenched Turco-Mongol traditions."

61. Chen, *Yinbi de guangjing*, 198; Wang, "Lun Tangdai gongfu shezheng," 67.

62. Liu, *Jiu Tangshu*, 23:893.

63. Jennifer W. Jay, "Imagining Matriarchy: 'Kingdoms of Women' in Tang China," *Journal of the American Oriental Society* 116, no. 2 (1996): 220–29; Wright, *The Sui Dynasty*, 151–52.

64. Tung, *Fables for the Patriarchs*, 30–40.

65. Wang, "Lun Tangdai gongfu shezheng," 68; Ren Jia, "Lun Tangdai qianqi shangceng nüzi yu zhengzhi," *Daqing Shifan Xueyuan xuebao* 34, no. 5 (2014): 106–9.

66. Mary H. Fong, "Four Chinese Tombs of the Early Eighth Century," *Artibus Asiae* 35, no. 4 (1973): 307–8.

67. Liu, *Jiu Tangshu*, 7:150.

68. Wright, *The Sui Dynasty*, 71–73, 161–62; Keith McMahon, *Women Shall Not Rule: Imperial Wives and Concubines in China from Han to Liao* (Lanham, MD: Rowman & Littlefield, 2013), 182–83.

69. Zeng Xuanyan and Liu Chunxin, "Zhangsun huanghou yu 'zhenguan' shiqi de zhengzhi he shehui," *Wenshi bolan* 9 (2009): 13–15.

70. Yang Xiaomin, "Tangchu houfei jinjian yu zhengzhi qingming de guanxi," *Tianshui Shifan Xueyuan xuebao* 6 (2001): 43–46.

71. Liu, *Jiu Tangshu*, ch. 6; N. Harry Rothschild, *Wu Zhao: China's Only Woman Emperor* (New York: Pearson Longman, 2008).

72. Chang and Saussy, *Women Writers of Traditional China*, 47.

73. Some historians believe that Empress Wang and Wu Zetian represented two different factions, with the Guanglong faction supporting Wang and the Shandong faction supporting Wu. Wechsler, "Factionalism in Early T'ang Government," 89–90.

74. Historians traditionally view Gaozong as weak willed and easily manipulated. Andrew Eisenberg, "Emperor Gaozong, the Rise of Wu Zetian, and Factional Politics in the Early Tang," *Tang Studies* 30 (2012): 45–69 argues that Gaozong promoted Wu to weaken Empress Wang's kinsmen, who had alarmed him by gaining too much power. According to this interpretation, he considered Wu to be safeguarding his interests and saw Wang and her consort kinsmen as opponents.

75. Chen, "Succession Struggles and the Ethnic Identity of the Tang Imperial House," 394 notes that Tang emperors often had bad relationships with their sons. Because Empress Wu took on male roles, she and her sons ended up in with similar conflicts.

76. Chen, "Succession Struggle and the Ethnic Identity of the Tang Imperial House," 390; Sanping Chen, *Multicultural China in the Early Middle Ages* (Philadelphia: University of Pennsylvania Press, 2012), 19–20.

77. C. P. Fitzgerald, *The Empress Wu* (Melbourne: F. W. Cheshire for the Australian National University, 1968), 114–15; Twitchett, "The Composition of the T'ang Ruling Class," 64.

78. Richard W. Guisso, *Wu Tse-t'ien and the Politics of Legitimation in T'ang China* (Bellingham: Western Washington University Press, 1978), 53. For example, Wu took concrete steps to increase agricultural productivity. Yang Xiangchun, "Wu Zetian yu Tangdai nongye," *Ganling wenhua yanjiu* 4 (2008): 450–58.

79. Keith McMahon, "Women Rulers in Imperial China," *Nan Nü* 15, no. 2 (2013): 198–201.

80. Norman Harry Rothschild, "An Inquiry into Reign Era Changes Under Wu Zhao, China's Only Female Emperor," *Early Medieval China* 12 (2006): 123–47.

81. Norman Harry Rothschild, "Beyond Filial Piety: Biographies of Exemplary Women and Wu Zhao's New Paradigm of Political Authority," *T'ang Studies* 23/24 (2005–2006): 149–68.

82. Stephen R. Bokenkamp, "A Medieval Feminist Critique of the Chinese World Order: The Case of Wu Zhao (r. 690–705)," *Religion* 28, no. 4 (1998): 383–92.

83. Norman Harry Rothschild, "Wu Zhao and the Queen Mother of the West," *Journal of Daoist Studies* 3 (2010): 29–56; Harry N. Rothschild, "The Mother of Laozi and the Female Emperor Wu Zhao: From One Grand Dowager to Another," in *China and Beyond in the Mediaeval Period: Cultural Crossings and Inter-Regional Connections*, ed. Dorothy C. Wong and Gustav Heldt (Amherst, NY: Cambria Press,

2014), 219–42; Harry N. Rothschild, *Emperor Wu Zhao and Her Pantheon of Devis, Divinities, and Dynastic Mothers* (New York: Columbia University Press, 2015).

84. For example, a message written on a rock discovered in the Luo River, traditionally a source of mystical revelations, referred to her as "sacred mother" (*sheng mu* 聖母). Liu, *Jiu Tangshu*, 24:924. For a detailed discussions of omens during her reign, see Stephan N. Kory, "A Remarkably Resonant and Resilient Tang-Dynasty Augural Stone: Empress Wu's *Baotu*," *T'ang Studies* 26 (2008): 99–124; Bao Jiao, "Tangdai zhengzhi yu furui—yi Wu Zetian cheng di yu S. 6502 *Dayun jingshu* zhong de furui sixiang wei zhongxin," *Xibei Shida xuebao* 52, no. 6 (2015): 87–92.

85. Guisso, *Wu Tse-t'ien and the Politics of Legitimation in T'ang China*, 44; Patricia E. Karetzky, "Wu Zetian and Buddhist Art of the Tang Dynasty," *T'ang Studies* 20–21 (2002–2003): 113–50.

86. Timothy Barrett, *The Woman Who Discovered Printing* (New Haven: Yale University Press, 2008).

87. McMahon, "Women Rulers in Imperial China," 203.

88. Kitamura Takashi, *Tōdai kōtei misasagi no kenkyū* (Tokyo: Gakuseisha, 2001), 52–58 describes Wu's mausoleum. Pages 134–52 outline the basic principles for the burial of Tang imperial consorts and specific tomb configurations.

89. Lewis, *China's Cosmopolitan Empire*, 34, 38–40, 180.

90. Howard S. Levy, "The Selection of Yang Kuei-fei," *Oriens* 15 (1962): 411–24. Some historians suspect that the marriage was consummated then annulled.

91. Paul W. Kroll, "The Flight from the Capital and the Death of Precious Consort Yang," *T'ang Studies* 3 (1985): 25–53.

92. Y. W. Ma, "Fact and Fantasy in T'ang Tales," *Chinese Literature (CLEAR)* 2, no. 2 (1980): 167–69, 180. Stories about Yang Guifei conformed to a genre of Tang fiction describing events in the lives of historical beauties. However, writers had previously depicted female historical characters as harmless. Negative stories about Yang Guifei show a reinterpretation of the genre. Daniel Hsieh, *Love and Women in Early Chinese Fiction* (Hong Kong: Chinese University Press, 2008), 69.

93. Fan-Pen Chen, "Problems of Chinese Historiography as Seen in the Official Records on Yang Kuei-fei," *T'ang Studies* 8–9 (1990–1991): 83–96.

94. Mao Hanguang, "Tangdai houbanqi houfei zhi fenxi," *Guoli Taiwan Daxue wenshizhe xuebao* 37 (1989): 175, 183, 186, 189.

95. Jin, "Qianlun Tangdai houqi hunyin de tedian," 47.

96. Ouyang, *Xin Tangshu*, ch. 76.

97. Richard L. Davis, *From Warhorses to Ploughshares: The Later Tang Reign of Emperor Mingzong* (Hong Kong: Hong Kong University Press, 2014), 14–18, 39.

98. McMahon, "Women Rulers in Imperial China," 202; Keith McMahon, *Celestial Women: Imperial Wives and Concubines in China from Song to Qing* (Lanham, MD: Rowman & Littlefield, 2016), xvii.

99. Rebecca Doran, *Transgressive Typologies: Constructions of Gender and Power in Early Tang China* (Cambridge, MA: Harvard University Asia Center, 2016) explores the changing representations of female power during the Tang.

100. Shi Guanle, *Yang Taizhen waizhuan* (Beijing: Zhonghua, 1991).

101. Han Lin, "Wu Zetian gushi de wenben yanbian yu wenhua neihan" (PhD diss., Nankai University, 2012); Han Lin, "Ming Qing xushi wenxue zhong Wu Zetian de mingjun xingxiang yu nüxing xintai," *Wuyi Daxue xuebao* 17, no. 4 (2015): 32–35; Sun Shunhua, "Tangchao funüguan zhi shanbian yu shehui zhengzhi," *Wenshizhe* 2 (2000): 102–3.

102. Liu Yongcong, "Wei Jin yihuan shijia dui houfei zhuzheng zhi fumian pingjia," in *Zhongguo funüshi lunwenji sanji*, ed. Bao Jialin (Taipei: Sanlian, 1993), 30–31; Liu, *Jiu Tangshu*, 77:2683; Ouyang, *Xin Tangshu*, 76:3468, 119:4297. This discourse did not suddenly begin with the death of Yang Guifei. Throughout the Sui and early Tang there had been periodic critiques of female power. For example, *Suishu* takes a hard line against female power, not just casting women as a destabilizing influence for the state but also asserting that they are more likely to be cruel and immoral. Liu Jianming, "Suishu lienü zhuan de zhenlie guannian," *Tang yanjiu* 7 (Beijing: Beijing Daxue chubanshe, 2001), 249–62. Even during the Sui itself, some people had criticized female influence as licentious and debilitating. Wright, *The Sui Dynasty*, 141.

103. Liu, *Jiu Tangshu*, 51:2161. The eighth-century thinker Li Hua 李華 (714–778) argued that both the early Han and early Tang had faced the threat of destruction by overbearing empresses. However, the Han weathered this crisis better than the Tang because that dynasty had superior "substance" (*zhi* 質). David McMullen, "Historical and Literary Theory in the Mid-Eight Century," in *Perspectives on the T'ang*, ed. Arthur F. Wright and Denis Twitchett (New Haven: Yale University Press, 1973), 323.

104. Ning Qiang, "Imperial Portraiture as Symbol of Political Legitimacy: A New Study of the 'Portraits of Successive Emperors,'" *Ars Orientalis* 35 (2008): 96–128.

105. Ouyang, *Xin Tangshu*, 76:3468.

106. Chen, "Problems of Chinese Historiography," 84. Zhao, *Nianer shi zhaji*, 19:256 blames the catastrophes that occurred during the Tang on the sexual obsessions of the dynasty's emperors.

107. Bret Hinsch, "The Criticism of Powerful Women by Western Han Dynasty Portent Experts," *Journal of the Economic and Social History of the Orient* 49, no. 1 (2006): 96–121. Wei, *Suishu*, 22:622.

108. Li Jun, "Zaihai yinsu yu Tangdai chugong renkao," *Zhongguo lishi dili luncong* 1 (2007): 90–95, 105.

CHAPTER 4: WEALTH

1. H. J. Habakkuk, "Family Structure and Economic Change in Nineteenth Century Europe." *Journal of Economic History* 15, no. 1 (1955): 1–12 is an influential classic article on this idea.

2. Susan Carol Rogers and Sonya Salamon, "Inheritance and Social Organization among Family Farmers," *American Ethnologist* 10, no. 3 (1983): 539.

3. Wang Houxiang, "Tangdai jiating caichan he jicheng zhidu shulun," *Wenshi zazhi* 4 (2003): 67.

4. Wang, "Tangdai jiating caichan he jicheng zhidu shulun," 67.

5. Shiga, *Chūgoku kazokuhō no genri*, 50–58; Shūzō Shiga, "Family Property and the Law of Inheritance in Traditional China," in *Chinese Family Law and Social Change in Historical and Comparative Perspective*, ed. David C. Buxbaum (Seattle: University of Washington Press, 1978), 109–10; Kathryn Bernhardt, *Women and Property in China, 960–1949* (Stanford: Stanford University Press, 1999), 9–10; Li Shuyuan, *Zhengcai jingchan: Tang Song de jiachan yu falü* (Taipei: Wunan tushu, 2005), 10–11.

6. Xing Tie, *Tang Song fenjia zhidu* (Beijing: Shangwu, 2010), 82.

7. Jin, "Tangdai hunyin jiating jicheng falü zhidu chulun," 114–21; Wang, "Tangdai jiating caichan he jicheng zhidu shulun," 66.

8. Luo, *Tongju gongcai*, 32, 26, 42–49.

9. Duan Tali, "Tangdai nüxing jiating jiaose ji qi diwei," *Zhongguo wenhua yanjiu* (2002): 147; Zhang, "Tangdai de nüxing yu susong," 36–39.

10. Deng, "Women in Turfan during the Sixth to Eighth Centuries," 91–94.

11. Wang, "Tangdai jiating caichan he jicheng zhidu shulun," 66.

12. Cong Shuguang, "Tangdai hunyin leixing qianxi," *Shandong Shifan Daxue xuebao* 49, no. 4 (2004): 102; Cui, "Tangdai pinnü nanjia xianxiang tanxi," 61–66.

13. For examples of financial marriages in Dunhuang documents see Tan, *Dunhuang hunyin wenhua*, 87.

14. Patricia Buckley Ebrey, "Shifts in Marriage Finance from the Sixth to the Thirteenth Century," in *Women and the Family in Chinese History*, ed. Patricia Buckley Ebrey (London: Routledge, 2003), 66; Katsuyama Minoru, *Chūgoku Sō—Min dai ni okeru konin no gakusaiteki kenkyū* (Tokyo: Tōhoku Daigaku shuppankai, 2007), 136–38 provides examples of large bridewealth.

15. Liu, *Jiu Tangshu*, 65:2443; Ouyang, *Xin Tangshu*, 95:3841.

16. Ouyang, *Xin Tangshu*, 2:27.

17. Diane Owen Hughes, "From Brideprice to Dowry in Mediterranean Europe," *Journal of Family History* 3, no. 3 (1978): 290.

18. Li Zhende, "Han Tang zhijian nüxing caichanquan shitan," in *Zhongguo shi xinlun—xingbie shi fence*, ed. Li Zhende (Taipei: Zhongyang yanjiu yuan, 2009), 194–202 describes the early evolution of dowry customs as well as Tang dowries. Duan, *Tangdai funü diwei yanjiu*, 41; Cen, *Tangdai huanmen funü yanjiu*, 54–56; Wang, "Tangdai jiazhuang xiaofei kao," 56–61.

19. Zhang, *Tangdai jiating yu shehui*, 44–45.

20. Bettine Birge, "Inheritance and Property Law from Tang to Song: The Move away from Patrilineality," in *Tang Song nüxing yu shehui*, ed. Deng Xiaonan (Shanghai: Shanghai cishu, 2003), 2:852.

21. Poetry from the middle and late Tang attests to the difficulty of poor women getting married for lack of dowry. Sun Yurong and Hu Hui, "Tangdai 'pinnüshi' chengyin tanxi," *Lantai shijie* 12 (2012): 94.

22. Duan, *Tangdai funü diwei yanjiu*, 43; Wang, "Tangdai jiating caichan he jicheng zhidu shulun," 68.

23. Qi Shuzhen, "Tangdai guamu caichan chufenquan tanxi," *Cangsang* 3 (2013): 55.

24. Jin, "Tangdai hunyin jiating jicheng falü zhidu chulun," 44.

25. Wei, *Suishu*, 64:1509.

26. Bettine Birge, *Women, Property, and Confucian Reaction in Sung and Yüan China (960–1368)* (Cambridge: Cambridge University Press, 2002), 54–55 translates relevant sections of the Tang inheritance code.

27. Duan, *Tangdai funü diwei yanjiu*, 29.

28. Bernhardt, *Women and Property in China*, 2–3.

29. Birge, "Inheritance and Property Law from Tang to Song," 852–53; Bernhardt, *Women and Property in China*, 12–13.

30. Li Zhisheng, "Shixi jingji zhengce dui Zhongguo gudai funü zhenjie de yingxiang—jian tan Tang houqi funü zhenjie bianhua de yiyi," in *Tang Song nüxing yu shehui*, ed. Deng Xiaonan (Shanghai: Shanghai cishu, 2003), 2:890–93, 897.

31. Bettine Birge, "Women and Property in Sung Dynasty China (960–1279): Neo-Confucianism and Social Change in Chien-chou, Fukien" (PhD diss., Columbia University, 1992), 120–121.

32. Johnson, *The T'ang Code*, 33; Zhang, *Jiating shihua*, 78–79.

33. Jin, "Tangdai hunyin jiating jicheng falü zhidu chulun," 44–45, 154; Wang, "Tangdai jiating caichan he jicheng zhidu shulun," 68; Zhang, *Tangdai jiating yu shehui*, 45.

34. Deng, "Women in Turfan during the Sixth to Eighth Centuries," 93–99.

35. Liu, *Jiu Tangshu*, 170:5184; Liang, "Tangdai funü de jiating diwei," 86.

36. Zhang Jianguang and Zhang Jie, "Tangdai Chang'an nüxing xiaofei yanjiu," *Shilin* 5 (2008): 96–110.

37. Cui, "Tangdai pinnü nanjia xianxiang tanxi," 61–66; Yang Xiaomin, "Nüxing de beige—cong Tangshi kan Tangdai funü de mingyun," *Tianshui Shifan Xueyuan xuebao* 21, no. 3 (2001): 57–59; Hu, "Cong Tangshi kan Tangdai funü de hunyin zhuangkuang," 20–21; Xu Youfu, *Tangdai funü shenghuo yu shi* (Beijing: Zhonghua shuju, 2005), 211–17; Zhang Jing, "Lun Tangdai pinfu shi," *Nanjing Shifan Daxue Wenxueyuan xuebao* 3 (2006): 119–24; Zhang Jing, *Tangdai nüxing xingxiang shenghuo* (Lanzhou: Gansu renmin, 2007), 64–84; Sun and Hu, "Tangdai 'pinnüshi' chengyin tanxi," 94–95; Yu, "Tangdai nüxing shige yanjiu," 36–42.

38. Chang and Saussy, *Women Writers of Traditional China*, 80.

39. von Glahn, *The Economic History of China*, 173–78.

40. Liu Kairong, *Tangren shi zhong suojian dangshi funü shenghuo* (Chongqing: Shangwu yinshuguan, 1943), 18–28.

41. Qi Bin and Wang Rimei, "Tangdai juntian zhidu xia funü buzai shoutian de yuanyin tanxi," *Xuchang Xueyuan xuebao* 31, no. 1 (2012): 96–99; von Glahn, *The Economic History of China*, 183–86.

42. Duan Tali, "Cong fuqi guanxi kan Tangdai funü jiating diwei de bianhua," *Lanzhou Daxue xuebao* 29, no. 6 (2001): 56; Birge, "Inheritance and Property Law from Tang to Song," 850–51. Luo, *Tongju gongcai*, 523 provides a chart that shows how much land men and women of different ages were allocated during each era of the Tang. The amount of land received by women varied over the course of the dynasty.

43. Liu, *Tangren shi zhong suojian dangshi funü shenghuo*, 9–15; Hu, "Cong Tangshi kan Tangdai funü de hunyin zhuangkuang," 20; Yan, "Tangshi zhong suo fanying de Tangdai funü," 105; Sun Junhui, "Tangdai nüshangren luekao," *Lishi jiaoxue* 5 (2007): 21.

44. Wei, *Suishu*, 7:145.

45. Liu, *Jiu Tangshu*, 193:5140. For the origins of the association between textile manufacture and morality, see Bret Hinsch, "Textiles and Female Virtue in Early Imperial Chinese Historical Writing," *Nan Nü* 5, no. 12 (2003): 170–202. As before, some people criticized luxurious embroidery as immoral and harmful. Ouyang, *Xin Tangshu*, 105:4024.

46. T. H. Barrett, "Woodblock Dyeing and Printing Technology in China, c. 700 A.D.: The Innovations of Ms. Liu, and Other Evidence," *Bulletin of the School of Oriental and African Studies* 64, no. 2 (2001): 240–47.

47. Yan, "Tangshi zhong suo fanying de Tangdai funü," 104; Yang, "Nüxing de beige," 58; Yang, "Tangdai funü de 'jifu' shi," 42; Li Xiaoqi, "Tangdai shangfu shi chuyi," *Shaanxi Shifan Daxue jixu jiaoyu xuebao* 3 (2007): 61–64; Xu, "Shilun Tangdai de shangjia funü," 80; Cui Xiaoli, "Cong Tangdai wenxian kan Tangdai shangfu de shenghuo," *Anhui wenxue* 1 (2010): 144–45. For representative poems in this genre, see Larsen, *Willow, Wine, Mirror, Moon*, 90–91.

48. Liu, *Tangren shi zhong suojian dangshi funü shenghuo*, 15–17.

49. Ning Xin, "Tangdai funü de shehui jingji huodong—yi 'Taiping guangji' wei zhongxin," in *Tang Song nüxing yu shehui*, ed. Deng Xiaonan (Shanghai: Shanghai cishu, 2003), 1:236–46; Sun, "Tangdai nüshangren luekao," 21; Zhang and Zhang, "Tangdai Chang'an nüxing xiaofei yanjiu," 101–2.

50. Tian Feng, "Cong Tangshi kan Tangdai huji jiusi ji qi wenhua," *Qinghai Minzu Daxue xuebao* 37, no. 4 (2011): 129–34; Zou Shuqin, "Huji zhi 'hu'—Tangdai huji de zhongshu wenti suyuan," *Xibei minzu yanjiu* 4 (2012): 180–85.

51. Li Zhende, "Han Tang zhijian de nüxing yiliao zhaoguzhe," *Taida lishi xuebao* 23 (1999): 123–56; Li Zhende, "Han Tang zhijian jiating zhong de jiankang zhaogu yu xingbie," *Disanjie guoji hanxue huiyi lunwenji lishizu, xingbie yu yiliao* (Taipei: Institute of History and Philology, 2002), 3–6, 9–16.

52. Li Zhende, "Han Tang zhijian yifang zhong ji jian furen yu nüti wei yao," *Xin shixue* 13, no. 4 (2002): 6, 11, 15–19, 22–26; Jen-der Lee, "Gender and Medicine in Tang China," *Asia Major* 16, no. 2 (2003): 5, 13–14, 16, 21–23.

53. Zhou Jiren, "Lun Zhongguo gudai biaoyan yishu de shangpinhua wenti," *Zhongguoshi yanjiu* 15, no. 4 (1993): 44–57; Beverly Bossler, "Vocabularies of Pleasure: Categorizing Female Entertainers in the Late Tang Dynasty," *Harvard Journal of Asiatic Studies* 72, no. 1 (2012): 71–99.

54. Liao Meiyun, *Tang ji yanjiu* (Taipei: Xuesheng shuju, 1995); Xiao Guoliang, *Zhongguo changji shi* (Taipei: Wenjin chubanshe, 1996), 2–3, 60–81; Victor Xiong, "*Ji*-Entertainers in Tang Chang'an," in *Presence and Presentation: Women in the Chinese Literati Tradition*, ed. Sherry J. Mou (New York: St. Martin's Press, 1999), 149–50. The character *chang* 娼 does not appear in texts prior to the Tang. However, the related term *chang* 倡, meaning musician, dates back to antiquity. During the Han it was used to refer to musical performers. Song Dexi, "Tangdai de jinü," in *Zhongguo Funüshi lunji xuji*, ed. Bao Jialin (Taipei: Daoxiang chubanshe, 1991), 67–69.

55. Dunhuang Yanjiuyuan Wenxian Yanjiusuo, ed., *Dunhuang yueji* (Lanzhou: Ganxu renmin, 1995) reproduces excellent drawings of female musicians based on Dunhuang frescoes. For descriptions of the sophisticated culture of Tang music and dance, see Ouyang Yuqing, *Tangdai wudao* (Shanghai: Shanghai wenxue, 1980);

Shen Dong, *Tangdai yuewu xinlun* (Beijing: Beijing Daxue chubanshe, 2004); Jia Man, *Tangdai Chang'an yuewu yanjiu—yi Xi'an diqu chutu wenwu yuewu tuxiang wei zhongxin* (Beijing: Zhongguo shehui kexue, 2014); Han Lankui, ed., *Dunhuang yuewu yanjiu wenji* (Beijing: Wenhua yishu, 2014).

56. Xiong, "*Ji*-Entertainers in Tang Chang'an," 149–51; Yan Ming, *Zhongguo mingji yishu shi* (Taipei: Wenjin, 1992), 54, 57.

57. Some people considered entertainers a morally dubious sign of excessive luxury, and they were sometimes expelled from the palace. Liu, *Jiu Tangshu*, 15:468, 17A:523.

58. Wei, *Suishu*, 48:1291. During the Sui, the emperor would present a successful general with female musicians as a reward. Wei, *Suishu*, 52:1345, 56:1530.

59. Sing-chen Lydia Chiang, "Daoist Transcendence and Tang Literati Identities in 'Records of Mysterious Anomalies' by Niu Sengru (780–848)," *Chinese Literature (CLEAR)* 29 (2007): 9–11.

60. Qi Juan, "Li Bai jinü yu Tangdai yinyi wenxue," *Sichuan Wenli Xueyuan xuebao* 22, no. 4 (2012): 90–93.

61. Robert des Rotors, *Courtesanes Chinoises a la fin des T'ang entre circa 789 et le 8 Janvier 881, Pei-li Tche (Anecdotes du Quartier du Nord) par Souen K'i* (Paris: Presses Universitaires de France, 1968) describes and translates the main source describing the courtesan quarter of Chang'an.

62. Yao, *Tangdai funü de shengming licheng*, 199–26.

63. Song, "Tangdai de jinü," 72–73. Yu, "Tangdai nüxing shige yanjiu," 54–56.

64. Zheng Zhimin, "Tangdai shiren yu jinü guanxi de yanbian—yi *Quan Tangshi* wei zhongxin," *Zhongxing shixue* 12 (1994): 65–85.

65. Jing Wang, "From Immortality to Mortality: Images of Tang Courtesans in Verse, Painting, and Anecdote," *Frontiers of Literary Studies in China* 6, no. 2 (2012): 277–93.

66. Zheng Zhimin, *Xishuo Tang ji* (Taipei: Wenjin, 1997), 108–9, 112.

67. S.-C. Kevin Tsai, "Ritual and Gender in the 'Tale of Li Wa,'" *Chinese Literature (CLEAR)* 26 (2004): 99–127.

68. Anna M. Shields, "Remembering When: The Uses of Nostalgia in the Poetry of Bai Juyi and Yuan Zhen," *Harvard Journal of Asiatic Studies* 66, no. 2 (2006): 329–30.

69. Maureen Robertson, "Voicing the Feminine: Constructions of the Gendered Subject in Lyric Poetry by Women of Medieval and Late Imperial China," *Late Imperial China* 13, no. 1 (1992): 78.

70. Chang and Saussy, *Women Writers of Traditional China*, 76.

CHAPTER 5: RELIGION

1. Liu, *Jiu Tangshu*, 21:839, 23:891 describe the medieval versions of women featured in ancient myths. The Tang dynasty book Sun Wei, *Shennü zhuan* (Beijing: Zhonghua, 1991) describes how various goddesses were understood at the time.

2. Lu Ting, "Nü Wa shenhua de yiwei yu Tangdai shiwen zhong de Nü Wa xingxiang," *Tianshui Shifan Xueyuan xuebao* 34, no. 4 (2014): 6–9.

3. Suzanne E. Cahill, "The Moon Stopping in the Void: Daoism and the Literati Ideal in Mirrors of the Tang Dynasty," *Cleveland Studies in the History of Art* 9 (2005): 32–33; Eugene Y. Wang, "Mirror, Moon, and Memory in Eighth-Century China: From Dragon Pond to Lunar Palace," *Cleveland Studies in the History of Art* 9 (2005): 59. Li Li, *Shenhua shiyu xia de wenxue jiedu—yi Han Tang wenxue leixinghua yanbian wei zhongxin* (Beijing: Zhongguo shehui kexue, 2008), 52–89 describes the evolution of literature about Chang E.

4. Edward H. Schafer, *The Divine Woman: Dragon Ladies and Rain Maidens in T'ang Literature* (San Francisco: North Point Press, 1980).

5. Hao Chunwen, *Tang houqi wudai Song chu Dunhuang sengni de shehui shenghuo* (Beijing: Zhongguo shehui kexue, 1998), 59–61.

6. Monica Esposito, "Doumu: Mother of the Dipper," in *The Routledge Encyclopedia of Taoism, Volume I: A–L*, ed. Fabrizio Pregadio (London: Routledge, 2008), 382–83.

7. Hui-shu Lee, *Empresses, Art & Agency in Song Dynasty China* (Seattle: University of Washington Press, 2010), 23, 27–30.

8. Miyakawa Hisayuki, *Rikuchōshi kenkyū: shūkyō hen* (Tokyo: Heirakudera shoten, 1964), 342–55. Hao, *Tang houqi wudai Song chu Dunhuang sengni de shehui shenghuo*, 87–88.

9. Li, *Shenhua shiyu xia de wenxue jiedu*, 302–95.

10. Li, *Shenhua shiyu xia de wenxue jiedu*, 128–99.

11. Wei, *Suishu*, 28:776; Edward H. Schafer, "Ritual Exposure in Ancient China," *Harvard Journal of Asiatic Studies* 14, nos. 1/2 (1951): 157; Lin Xi, "Sui Tang Song jian wuxi zhengzhi diwei de yanbian," *Changchun Daxue xuebao* 26, no. 11 (2016): 92–93.

12. Liu, *Jiu Tangshu*, 130:3617; Ouyang, *Xin Tangshu*, 109:4108.

13. Gao Guofan, *Zhongguo gusu tanwei—Dunhuang wushu yu wushu liubian* (Nanjing: Hehai Daxue chubanshe, 1993), 172–90.

14. Stephan N. Kory, "Presence in Variety: De-Trivializing Female Diviners in Medieval China," *Nan Nü* 18, no. 1 (2016): 4, 19, 26–47.

15. Rebecca Doran, "The Cat Demon, Gender, and Religious Practice: Towards Reconstructing a Medieval Chinese Cultural Pattern," *Journal of the American Oriental Society* 135, no. 4 (2015): 689–707.

16. Stanley Weinstein, "Imperial Patronage in the Formation of T'ang Buddhism," in *Perspectives on the T'ang*, ed. Arthur F. Wright and Denis Twitchett (New Haven: Yale University Press, 1973), 265.

17. Arthur F. Wright, "T'ang T'ai-tsung and Buddhism," in *Perspectives on the T'ang*, ed. Arthur F. Wright and Denis Twitchett (New Haven: Yale University Press, 1973), 251, 257.

18. Roger T. Ames, "Taoism and the Androgynous Ideal," in *Women in China: Current Directions in Historical Scholarship*, ed. Richard W. Guisso and Stanley Johannesen (Youngstown, NY: Philo Press, 1981), 43; Zhao Shichuang, *Daojiao yu nüxing* (Shanghai: Shanghai guji chubanshe, 1990), 44–53.

19. Cahill, "The Moon Stopping in the Void," 33.

20. Suzanne E. Cahill, "Sublimation in Medieval China: The Case of the Mysterious Woman of the Nine Heavens," *Journal of Chinese Religions* 20 (1992): 91–102.

21. Suzanne Cahill, "Performers and Female Taoist Adepts: Hsi Wang Mu as the Patron Deity of Women in Medieval China," *Journal of the American Oriental Society* 106, no. 1 (1986): 155–68; Suzanne Cahill, *Transcendence and Divine Passion: The Queen Mother of the West in Medieval China* (Stanford: Stanford University Press, 1993). Paul R. Goldin, "On the Meaning of the Name Xi wangmu, Spirit-Mother of the West," *Journal of the American Oriental Society* 122, no. 1 (2002): 83–85 points out that the term *wang* as used here might be an honorific term for a deceased paternal grandmother that was also sometimes applied to spirits and deities. If so, a better translation would be "spirit-mother of the west."

22. Gao Qi'an and Zhao Hong, "Dunhuang 'yunü' kaoxie," *Dunhuang yanjiu* 2 (2005): 68–73.

23. Hu Jing and Di Xiaoping, "Tangdai nüshen nüxian xiaoshuo ji qi shisuhua qingxiang yanjiu," *Yindu xuekan* 2 (2008): 57–61.

24. Yan Jinxiong, *Tangdai youxian shi yanjiu* (Taipei: Wenjin, 1996), 339–54.

25. Jiao Jie, "Cong muzhi kan Tangdai funü chongdao de yuanyin," *Dongnan wenhua* 3 (2008): 41–45. Most information about individual Daoist believers comes from epitaphs. Zhao Juanning and Jiao Jie, "Cong muzhi kan Tangdai funü de daojiao xinyang," *Qianling wenhua yanjiu* 2 (2006): 190–94 discusses information from the epitaphs of thirty-three Tang dynasty Daoist women. Twelve percent are from early Tang, 24 percent from High Tang, and 64 percent from mid- and late Tang. These figures do not necessarily mean that Daoism became more popular over time. The custom of commissioning an epitaph for the deceased became increasingly popular in the later part of the dynasty, which might account for the surge in the number of epitaphs.

26. Nevertheless, poetry by Daoist nuns often fuses Confucianism and Daoism. Yu, "Tangdai nüxing shige yanjiu," 85.

27. For example Huang Lingwei 黃靈微 (or 黃令微) discovered two lost Daoist shrines. Russell Kirkland, "Huang Lingwei ca. 640–721; *hao* Huagu (Flowery Maiden)," in *The Routledge Encyclopedia of Taoism, Volume I: A–L*, ed. Fabrizio Pregadio (London: Routledge, 2008), 501–2.

28. Su Zhenfu, "*Taiping guangji* suo jian Tangdai minjian nüxing xiudao qingkuang yanjiu," *Mudanjiang Daxue xuebao* 23, no. 12 (2014): 56–59.

29. Edward H. Schafer, "The Jade Woman of Greatest Mystery," *History of Religions* 17, nos. 3–4 (1978): 390–91.

30. Suzanne E. Cahill, "Discipline and Transformation: Body and Practice in the Lives of Daoist Holy Women of Tang China," in *Women and Confucian Cultures of Premodern China, Korea, and Japan*, ed. Dorothy Ko, JaHyun Kim Habboush, and John R. Piggott (Berkeley: University of California Press, 2003), 251–78.

31. Russell Kirkland, "Fangzhong Shu: 'Arts of the Bedchamber'; Sexual Techniques," in *The Routledge Encyclopedia of Taoism, Volume I: A–L*, ed. Fabrizio Pregadio (London: Routledge, 2008), 409–11; Jinhua Jia, "The *Yaochi ji* and Three Daoist Priestesses," in *Gendering Chinese Religion: Subject, Identity, and Body*, ed.

Jinhua Jia et al. (Albany: State University of New York Press, 2014), 103–32. Daoist works about sex were part of the large genre of Tang sexual literature. Compared to later eras, educated members of Tang discussed sexuality very openly. Rudolph Pfister, "Gendering Sexual Pleasures in Early and Medieval China," *Asian Medicine* 7, no. 1 (2012): 34–64; Ping Yao, "Historicizing Great Bliss: Erotica in Tang China (618–907)," *Journal of the History of Sexuality* 22, no. 2 (2013): 207–29. Donald Harper, "La littérature sur la sexualité à Dunhuang," in *Médecine, religion, et société dans la Chine médiévale: Étude de manuscrits chinois de Dunhuang et de Turfan*, ed. Catherine Despeux (Paris: Collège de France, Institut des Hautes Études Chinoises, 2010), 2:871–98 describes Dunhuang texts related to sex. These are mostly recipes for male aphrodisiacs.

32. Suzanne Cahill, "Smell Good and Get a Job: How Daoist Women Saints Were Verified and Legitimized During the Tang Dynasty (618–907)," in *Presence and Presentation: Women in the Chinese Literati Tradition*, ed. Sherry J. Mou (New York: St. Martin's Press, 1999), 177–86. Li Pei, "Minjian yu guanfang, zhengzhi yu zongjiao: yi Tangdai nüzhen bairi shengxian xianxiang zhongxin de kaocha," *Sichuan Daxue xuebao* 4 (2011): 25–29 analyzes accounts of female Daoists who ascended to heaven in public. Li Xiaopei, *Tangdai rudao nüxing shijie zhong de xingbie yishi yu qingyu* (Taoyuan: Shanxi jiaoyu chubanshe, 2011), 34, 80–89 discusses nuns who became immortals. Yang Lirong and Wang Ting, "Ziran pi fa—Tangdai nüguan Xie Ziran chuanqi kaosuo," *Guizhou Daxue xuebao* 30, no. 2 (2012): 135–42 gives a detailed analysis of a literary account of a Daoist nun who ascended to heaven. Catherine Despeux and Livia Kohn, *Women in Daoism* (Cambridge, MA: Three Pines Press, 2003), 91–93 describes other magical transformations.

33. Sun Changwu, *Daojiao yu Tangdai wenxue* (Beijing: Renmin wenxue, 2001), 360–81; Despeux and Kohn, *Women in Daoism*, 113, 121; Livia Kohn, *Monastic Life in Medieval Daoism: A Cross Cultural Perspective* (Honolulu: University of Hawaii Press, 2003); Jinhua Jia, "Religious and Other Experiences of Daoist Priestesses in Tang China," *T'oung Pao* 102, no. 4 (2016): 321–57. Suzanne E. Cahill, *Divine Traces of the Daoist Sisterhood: "Records of the Assembled Transcendents of the Fortified Walled City" by Du Guangting (850–933)* (Magdalena, NM: Three Pines Press, 2006) translates biographies of prominent nuns. Stephen Bokenkamp, "Transmissions of a Female Daoist: Xie Ziran (767–795)," in *Affiliation and Transmission in Daoism: A Berlin Symposium*, ed. Florian C. Reiter (Wiesbden: Harrassowitz Verlag, 2012): 109–21 gives a detailed biography of an exceptional adept. Yao, *Tangdai funü de shengming licheng*, 247 gives information about the thirteen known epitaphs of Tang dynasty Daoist nuns. Most came from an aristocratic or palace background. One was a former courtesan. Qiu Meihua, "Tangdai nüxing rezhong rudao yuanyin chutan," *Anhui Daxue xuebao* 24, no. 3 (2000): 55 provides statistics regarding the number of female clerics.

34. Jiao Jie, "Tangdai daojiao nüxintu de zongjiao huodong ji qi shenghuo—yi muzhi cailiao wei zhongxin," *Shaanxi Shifan Daxue xuebao* 42, no. 2 (2013): 125; Li, *Tangdai rudao nüxing shijie zhong de xingbie yishi yu qingyu*, 19–22.

35. Catherine Despeux, "L'ordination des femmes Taoistes sous les T'ang," *Études chinoises* 5, no. 1 (1986): 55–61; Catherine Despeux, "Women in Taoism," in

The Routledge Encyclopedia of Taoism, Volume I: A–L, ed. Fabrizio Pregadio (London: Routledge, 2008), 171–73.

36. The sources offer conflicting numbers of princess nuns. Moreover, some princesses had the same name, and it is sometimes difficult to distinguish them. Jiao Jie, "Lun Tangdai gongzhu rudao yuanyin yu daoguan shenghuo," *Shijie zongjiao yanjiu* 2 (2013): 72–75, 77–78, 80 untangles contradictions among the sources and gives basic information for each woman. Jiao Jie and Sun Hua, "Tangdai Wenan Gongzhu zakao," *Pingdingshan Xueyuan xuebao* 31, no. 3 (2016): 75–77 describes the life of one princess nun in detail. Ping Yao, "Contested Virtue: The Daoist Investiture of Princesses Jinxian and Yuzhen and the Journey of Tang Imperial Daughters," *T'ang Studies* 22 (2004): 3, 6. Despeux, "L'ordination des femmes Taoistes sous les T'ang," 64–84 discusses two examples: Princesses Yuzhen and Jinxian. Yu-ping Luk, *The Empress and the Heavenly Masters: A Study of the Ordination Scroll of Empress Zhang (1493)* (Hong Kong: Chinese University Press, 2016), 15–18.

37. Edward Schafer, "The Princess Realized in Jade," *T'ang Studies* 3 (1985): 1–2; Jiao Jie and Zhang Lanhui, "Tangdai Chang'an gongzhu daoguan de kaifa yu liyong," *Tangdu xuekan* 28, no. 2 (2012): 25–30; Teng Yun, "Lun Tangdai gongzhu de daojiao qingyuan—jian lun Tangdai gongzhu zhuangyuan zhaidi shi de daojiao ziran shengtai yishi," *Guilin Shifan Gaodeng Zhuanke Xuexiao xuebao* 28, no. 4 (2014): 112–15.

38. Li Fengmao, "Tangdai gongzhu rudao yu song gongren rudao shi," in *Diyijie guoji Tangdai xueshu huiyi lunwenji*, ed. Diyijie guoji Tangdai xueshui huiyi lunwenji bianji weiyuanhui (Taipei: Xuesheng, 1989): 159–90.

39. Duan, *Tangdai funü diwei yanjiu*, 102–3; Chang Chun, "Tangdai nüguan, mingji shufa," *Zhongguo shuhuajia* 3 (2014): 110–12 describes the calligraphy of Tang Daoist nuns.

40. Jinhua Jia, "Longevity Technique and Medical Theory: The Legacy of the Tang Daoist Priestess-Physician Hu Yin," *Monumenta Serica* 63, no. 1 (2015): 1–31.

41. Jia, "Religious and Other Experiences," 348–51.

42. Jinhua Jia, "The Yaochi ji and Three Daoist Priestess-Poets in Tang China," *Nan Nü* 13, no. 2 (2011): 231–32.

43. Wendi Adamek, "The Literary Lives of Nuns: Poems Inscribed on a Memorial Niche for the Tang Nun Benxing," *T'ang Studies* 27 (2009): 40–65. There is only one example of a poem written by a Tang nun. Her name was Haiyin 海印 and she lived in the later part of the dynasty. Li Yuzhen, *Tangdai de biqiuni* (Taipei: Xuesheng shuju, 1989), 91.

44. Sun, *Daojiao yu Tangdai wenxue*, 381–90.

45. Gao Lihua, "Daojiao yu shijiao jiafeng zhong de qipa—lun Tangdai nüguan shifen," in *Tangdai wenxue yanjiu* 6, ed. Fu Xuancong (Guilin: Guangxi Shifan Daxue chubanshe, 1996), 75–79.

46. Liu Ning, "Tangdai nüxing shige chuangzuo de zhuti tedian—yi nüguan shi yu changji shi wei zhongxin," *Zhongguo nüxing de guoqu, xianzai yu weilai*, ed. Zheng Bijun and Tao Jie (Beijing: Beijing Daxue chubanshe, 2005), 25–26.

47. Jia, "The Yaochi ji and Three Daoist Priestess-Poets in Tang China," 230–33.

48. Chow and Cleary, *Autumn Willows*, 26.

49. Chow and Cleary, *Autumn Willows*, 33.

50. Jia, "The Yaochi ji and Three Daoist Priestess-Poets in Tang China," 220. For her love poetry see pp. 221–25.

51. Zhang Guogang, "Zhonggu Fojiao jielü yu jiating lunli," in *Jiating shi yanjiu de xin shiye*, ed. Zhang Guogang (Beijing: Sanlian shuju, 2004), 55–56.

52. Wright, *The Sui Dynasty*, 55, 89.

53. Sarah Milledge Nelson, "Ancient Queens: An Introduction," in *Ancient Queens: Archaeological Explorations*, ed. Sarah Milledge Nelson (Walnut Creek, CA: AltaMira Press, 2003), 7–8.

54. Stephanie Balkwill, "When Renunciation Is Good Politics: The Women of the Imperial Nunnery of the Northern Wei," *Nan Nü* 18, no. 2 (2016): 243.

55. Jinhua Chen, "More than a Philosopher: Fazang (643–712) as a Politician and Miracle Worker," *History of Religions* 42, no. 4 (2003): 322–38; Jinhua Chen, "Fazang (643–712) and Wuzhensi: With a Special Reference to His Daoist Ties," *Journal of the Royal Asiatic Society* (third series) 16, no. 2 (2006): 179, 196; Jinhua Chen, "Fazang (643–712) the Holy Man," *Journal of the International Association of Buddhist Studies* 28, no. 1 (2008): 11–16, 20–23, 30, 32.

56. Yue and Ke, "Tang Huainan Dazhang Gongzhu muzhi," 132–34.

57. Wright, *The Sui Dynasty*, 89, 132.

58. Amy McNair, "Early Tang Imperial Patronage at Longmen," *Ars Orientalis* 24 (1994): 65, 68–70.

59. Sherman E. Lee and Wai-Kam Ho, "A Colossal Eleven-Faced Kuan-yin of the T'ang Dynasty," *Bulletin of the Cleveland Museum of Art* 47, no. 1 (1960): 4.

60. Ning Qiang, "Gender Politics in Medieval Chinese Buddhist Art: Images of Empress Wu at Longmen and Dunhuang," *Oriental Art* 49, no. 2 (2003): 28–39; Karil Kucera, "Recontextualizing Kanjingsi: Finding Meaning in the Emptiness at Longmen," *Archives of Asian Art* 56 (2006): 61–80.

61. Antonino Forte, *Mingtang and Buddhist Utopias in the History of the Astronomical Clock: Statue and Armillary Sphere Constructed by Empress Wu* (Rome: Instituto Italiano per il Medio ed Estremo Oriente, 1988).

62. Jinhua Chen, "Śarīra and Scepter: Empress Wu's Political Use of Buddhist Relics," *Journal of the International Association of Buddhist Studies* 25, nos. 1–2 (2002): 36–37.

63. Jinhua Chen, "A Daoist Princess and a Buddhist Temple: A New Theory on the Causes of the Canon-Delivering Mission Originally Proposed by Princess Jinxian (689–732) in 730," *Bulletin of the School of Oriental and African Studies* 69, no. 2 (2006): 267, 271.

64. Marylin M. Rhie, "A T'ang Period Inscription and Cave XXI at T'ien-Lung Shan," *Archives of Asian Art* 28 (1974–1975): 6–9.

65. Henrik H. Sørensen, "The Buddhist Sculptures at Feixian Pavilion in Pujiang, Sichuan," *Artibus Asiae* 58, nos. 1–2 (1998): 39; Angela F. Howard, "Buddhist Sculpture of Pujiang, Sichuan: A Mirror of the Direct Link between Southwest China and India in the High Tang," *Archives of Asian Art* 42 (1989): 53.

66. Amy McNair, "On the Patronage by Tang-Dynasty Nuns at Wanfo Grotto, Longmen," *Artibus Asiae* 59, nos. 3/4 (2000): 161, 163, 165, 167, 172–73, 186.

67. Ping Yao, "Good Karmic Connections: Buddhist Mothers in Tang China," *Nan Nü* 10, no. 1 (2008): 61; Yao, "Women's Epitaphs in Tang China," 149.

68. Wu Minxia, "Cong Tang muzhi kan Tangdai nüxing fojiao xinyang ji qi tedian," *Fojiao yanjiu* (2002): 258; Zhang, "Zhonggu Fojiao jielü yu jiating lunli," 48–49, 51–54; Yao, *Tangdai funü de shengming licheng*, 278; Obara Hitoshi, *Chūsei kizoku shakai to bukkyō* (Tokyo: Yoshikawa kōbunkan, 2007), 8–11; Lu, "Ru Fo jian xiu," 25–31; Yao, "Women's Epitaphs in Tang China," 150.

69. Su Shimei, "Cong muzhi kan fojiao dui Tangdai funü shenghuo de yingxiang," *Shixue yuekan* 5 (2003): 84 concludes that 11.76 percent of epitaphs for both sexes mention that the deceased was a Buddhist devotee. Half of these Buddhists were women. Yan Yaozhong, "Muzhi jiwen zhong de Tangdai funü fojiao Xinyang," in *Tang Song nüxing yu shehui*, ed. Deng Xiaonan (Shanghai: Shanghai cishu, 2003), 2:472–73 notes that the percentage of female Buddhists mentioned in epitaphs varied for each era of the Tang, ranging from 3.13 percent to 8.47 percent. Yao, "Women's Epitaphs in Tang China," 149 asserts that about 10 percent of epitaphs identify the female deceased as a lay Buddhist, and an additional 5 percent are for nuns.

70. Li, *Tangdai de biqiuni*, 39.

71. Yang Xiaomin, "Tangdai funü yu fojiao," *Shenyang Shifan Daxue xuebao* 3 (2003): 20–21; Yan Huizhong, "Fojiao jielü yu Tangdai funü jiating shenghuo," *Xueshu yuekan* 8 (2004): 98–99; Jiao Jie, "Cong Tang muzhi kan Tangdai funü yu fojiao de guanxi," *Shaanxi Shifan Daxue xuebao* 29, no. 1 (2000): 96; Yao, "Good Karmic Connections," 57, 62, 75.

72. Wu, "Cong Tang muzhi kan Tangdai nüxing fojiao xinyang," 259–60.

73. Duan Tali, "Tangdai minjian fojiao shenqi xinyang zhong de nüxing juese yu diwei," *Shaanxi Shifan Daxue xuebao* 40, no. 4 (2011): 114–20.

74. Duan Tali, "Lun Tangdai fojiao de shisuhua ji dui nüxing hunyin jiatingguan de yingxiang," *Shaanxi Shifan Daxue xuebao* 1 (2010): 76–83.

75. Kenneth K. S. Chen, "The Role of Buddhist Monasteries in T'ang Society," *History of Religions* 15, no. 3 (1976): 224.

76. Wu, "Cong Tang muzhi kan Tangdai nüxing fojiao xinyang," 263–65; Yang, "Tangdai funü yu fojiao," 21–22; Liu Gaoyang, "Xi Tangdai Dunhuang bihua zhong nüxing gongyang ren xingxiang de shenmei tezheng," *Suzhou Xueyuan xuebao* 30, no. 9 (2015): 80–83.

77. Yan, "Muzhi jiwen zhong de Tangdai funü fojiao xinyang," 277–78; Yan, "Fojiao jielü yu Tangdai funü jiating shenghuo," 96–97; Yaozhong Yan, "Buddhist Discipline and the Family Life of Tang Women," trans. Jeffrey Keller, *Chinese Studies in History* 45, no. 4 (2012): 24–42.

78. Yan, "Buddhist Discipline and the Family Life of Tang Women," 28.

79. Jiao, "Cong Tang muzhi kan Tangdai funü yu fojiao de guanxi," 97; Yan, "Muzhi jiwen zhong de Tangdai funü fojiao xinyang," 479–81.

80. Ning Ke and Hao Chunwen, "Beichao zhi Sui Tang Wudai jian de nüren jieshe," *Beijing Shifan Xueyuan xuebao* 5 (1990): 16–19; Deng, "Women in Turfan during the Sixth to Eighth Centuries," 85–103; Lin Yanzhi, "Tang Wudai shiqi Dunhuang diqu de nüren jieshe," *Zhongguo wenhua yuekan* 6 (2000): 32–50; Hao

Chunwen, "Zai lun beichao zhi Sui Tang wudai Songchu de nüren jieshe," *Dunhuang yanjiu* 6 (2006): 103–8.

81. Yao, *Tangdai funü de shengming licheng*, 240–41; Jiao Jie, "Fojiao xinyang yu Tangdai nüxing shenghuo xingtai zaitan—yi Tangdai muzhi ziliao wei zhongxin," *Tangshi luncong* 20 (2015): 231.

82. Song Rentao, "Qianyi Wei Jin nanbeichao shiqi nüxing chujia de xianxiang," *Jiangnan Shehui Xueyuan xuebao* 4, no. 3 (2002): 54; Yang, "Tangdai funü yu fo-jiao," 22; Huang Jianqin, "Tangdai biqiuni chujia de jingji yuanyin tanxi," *Chifeng Xueyuan xuebao* 33, no. 6 (2012): 19–20.

83. Xie Chongguang and Bai Wengu, *Zhongguo sengguan zhidu shi* (Xining: Qin-ghai renmin chubanshe, 1990), 28–30.

84. Ikeda, "T'ang Household Registers and Related Documents," 123, 131–32. During the Tang, nuns were also sometimes called *heshang* 和尚. Only later did the term refer exclusively to men. Yao Yali, "'Huiyuan biqiuni zhiming' suo fanyingde Tangdai Xiaoshi jiazu chongfo wenti," *Chengdu Daxue xuebao* 4 (2016): 89.

85. Yao, *Tangdai funü de shengming licheng*, 227–29. Most nuns with epitaphs belonged to elite families. Yao, *Tangdai funü de shengming lichen*, 232–34. Shiying Pang, "Eminent Nuns and / or / as Virtuous Women: The Representation of Tang Female Renunciants in Tomb Inscriptions," *T'ang Studies* 28 (2010): 77–96 describes standard epitaphs for nuns and explains how to interpret them.

86. Hao, *Tang houqi wudai Song chu Dunhuang sengni*, 97.

87. Yao, *Tangdai funü de shengming licheng*, 239.

88. Yao, *Tangdai funü de shengming licheng*, 230.

89. Hao, *Tang houqi wudai Song chu Dunhuang sengni*, 76–88; Jiao Jie, "Tangdai biqiuni de zhonglei: shoujie xiye yi ji hongfa huodong," *Xiamen Daxue xuebao* 6 (2014): 145–48.

90. Lu Tongyan, "Cong 'chujia wujia' dao chujia er you 'jia'—Tangdai sengni xiaodao lunli xianxiang luexi," *Linyi Shifan Xueyuan xuebao* 30, no. 4 (2008): 77–78. Dunhuang document P.4660 praises a monk who cut ties with his family.

91. Yan Guoquan, Zhang Yishou, and Zhang Kexin, *Dunhuang zongjiao wenhua* (Beijing: Xinhua, 1994), 34.

92. Yang Mei, "Tangdai niseng yu shisu jiating de guanxi," *Shoudu Shifan Daxue xuebao* 5 (2004): 20–26.

93. Yan, "Buddhist Discipline and the Family Life of Tang Women," 35–38.

94. Chen Jinhua, "Family Ties and Buddhist Nuns in Tang China: Two Studies," *Asia Major* (third series), 15, no. 2 (2002): 82.

95. Pang, "Eminent Nuns and / or / as Virtuous Women," 77, 79, 82. Buddhist thinkers emphasized the importance of filial piety to the life of nuns and explored how a nun could best express filiality. Ann Hierman, "Buddhist Nuns Through the Eyes of Leading Early Tang Masters," *Chinese Historical Review* 22, no. 1 (2015): 44–49.

96. Yao, "'Huiyuan biqiuni zhiming,'" 90–91 uses inscriptional information to describe interaction between a nun named Huiyuan 惠源 and her family.

97. Jiao, "Cong Tang muzhi kan Tangdai funü yu fojiao de guanxi," 98.

98. Yang, "Tangdai niseng yu shisu jiating de guanxi," 21, 24–25; Lu, "Cong 'chujia wujia' dao chujia er you 'jia,'" 77–78; Liu Qinli, "Muzhi suo jian Tangdai biqiuni yu jiaren guanxi," *Huaxia kaogu* 2 (2010): 108–10.

99. Wendi Adamek, "Inscriptions for Nuns at Lingquan Temple, Bao Shan," in *Tang Song nüxing yu shehui*, ed. Deng Xiaonan (Shanghai: Shanghai cishu, 2003), 2:499.

100. Cai Hongsheng, *Nigu tan* (Guangzhou: Zhongshan Daxue chubanshe, 1996), 13–21 describes the general lifestyle of nuns. Lü Mingming, "Guizi nisi chutan," *Dunhuang yanjiu* 1 (2007): 55–60 uses archaeological and textual evidence to describe a nunnery at Kucha. Ran Wanli, "Luelun Tangdai sengni de zangzhi," *Ganling wenhua yanjiu* (2005): 80–93 explains the various modes of burial for Buddhist clerics, which differed from secular funerary customs. In addition to cremation, some were buried or exposed to the elements in a forest.

101. Valentina Georgieva, "Representation of Buddhist Nuns in Chinese Edifying Miracle Tales during the Six Dynasties and the Tang," *Journal of Chinese Religions* 24 (1996): 47–62.

102. Wendi Leigh Adamek, "A Niche of Their Own: The Power of Convention in Two Inscriptions for Medieval Chinese Buddhist Nuns," *History of Religions* 49, no. 1 (2009): 5.

103. Huang Cheng, "'Pozi shuochan' yu nüzi foxing yishi de juexing—cong chanzong luyu kan Tangdai nüxing 'cheng fo zuo zu' de zongjiao xingxiang ji qi lishi yihan," *Xuehai* 6 (2010): 121–25.

104. Adamek, "Inscriptions for Nuns at Lingquan Temple, Bao Shan," 503–6, 510.

105. Chen Dawei, "Dunhuang sengsi yu nisi zhi jiang de wanglai guanxi," *Dunhuang yanjiu* 3 (2010): 36–90.

106. Zhao Jibin, "*Fahua jing* yu liuchao zhi biqiuni guanxi luekao," *Zhonghua wenhua luntan* 2 (2014): 126–30.

107. Jiao, "Tangdai biqiuni de zhonglei," 152–53.

CHAPTER 6: LEARNING

1. Dell R. Hales, "Dreams and the Daemonic in Traditional Chinese Short Stories," in *Critical Essays on Chinese Literature*, ed. William H. Nienhauser et al. (Hong Kong: Chinese University of Hong Kong, 1976), 71–87; Sarah M. Allen, *Shifting Stories: History, Gossip, and Lore in Narratives from Tang Dynasty China* (Cambridge, MA: Harvard University Asia Center, 2014), 55–63.

2. Nicholas DiFonzo and Prashant Bordia, *Rumor Psychology: Social and Organizational Approaches* (Washington, DC: American Psychological Association, 2007), 19; Jack W. Chen, "Introduction," in *Idle Talk: Gossip and Anecdote in Traditional China*, ed. Jack. W. Chen and David Schaberg (Berkeley: Global, Area, and International Archive and University of California Press, 2014), 3.

3. Sun, "Lun Tangdai shehui biangeqi de nüxing jiaoyu," 42–44; Ye Zilong, "Tangdai shiren jiating nüzi jiaoyu yanjiu," *Ganling wenhua yanjiu* 8 (2014): 304–11.

4. Duan, *Tangdai funü diwei yanjiu*, 93; Yao, "Women's Epitaphs in Tang China," 151–52.

5. Cen, *Tangdai huanmen funü yanjiu*, 188–98; Liao, *Tangdai de muzi guanxi*, 317–46. For example Liu, *Jiu Tangshu*, 190A:4983.

6. Lan Sihua, "Qianyi Tangdai juzi beihou nüxing de mingyun," *Guangxi Zhiye Jishu Xueyuan xuebao* 8, no. 1 (2015): 66–69.

7. Tao Yi, "Tangdai xianmu de jiaozi gushi," *Wenshi tiandi* 3 (2016): 25–28.

8. Xu Yougen, "Tangdai 'guamu jiaozi' xianxiang chutan," *Neimenggu Shifan Daxue xuebao* 10 (2005): 59–62.

9. Zhou and Wang, *Roushun zhi xiang*, 55–96; Zhou Yuwen, "Tangdai funü yu jiating jiaoyu chutan," in *Zhongguo chuantong funü yu jiating jiaoyu*, ed. Zhou Yuwen and Hong Renjin (Taipei: Shida shuyuan, 2005), 9–36; Zhu Fengyu, "Dunhuang mengshuzhong de funü jiaoyu," in *Zhongguo chuantong funü yu jiating jiaoyu*, ed. Zhou Yuwen and Hong Renjin (Taipei: Shida shuyuan, 2005), 37–57. The female education text *Cuishi furen xunnnü wen* 崔氏夫人訓女文 survives in three Dunhuang copies: S.4129, S.5643, P.2633.

10. Song Ruozhao, *Niu Yingzhen zhuan* (Beijing: Zhonghua, 1985), a Tang dynasty work, describes this woman's educational achievements. She memorized one hundred fascicles of Buddhist texts as well as a hundred fascicles of the classics. She could recite the *Zuo zhuan* 左傳 in her dreams. Also see Liu, *Jiu Tangshu*, 146:3955, 193:5142; Josephine Chiu-Duke, "The Role of Confucian Revivalists in the Confucianization of Tang Women," *Asia Major* 8 (1995): 67.

11. For example, *Taigong jiajiao* taught the moral values underpinning family life. Wang Houxiang and Ji Guangyun, "Lun Tangdai jiating jiaoyu," *Linyi Shifan Daxue xuebao* 23, no. 2 (2001): 48.

12. Duan, *Tangdai funü diwei yanjiu*, 94.

13. Liu, *Jiu Tangshu*, 51:2164, 2166; Huang Yunzhu, "Tangdai nüxing yu wenxue de xiangguanxing yanjiu" (PhD diss., Shaanxi Normal University, 2003), 4, 9–26.

14. Denis Twitchett, "Chen gui and Other Works Attributed to Empress Wu Zetian," *Asia Major* (third series) 16, no. 1 (2003): 33–109.

15. Liu, *Jiu Tangshu*, 51:2167–69. Kroll, "The Life and Writings of Xu Hui," 35–64 describes her life and poetry.

16. Jie Wu, "Vitality and Cohesiveness in the Poetry of Shangguan Wan'er (664–710)," *Tang Studies* 34 (2016): 40–72.

17. Wong, "Confucian Ideal and Reality," 230–31.

18. Wang Limei, "Tangdai nüzi jiaoyu xintan," *Jiaoyu pinglun* 5 (2011): 138–39. This institution went through several name changes. At the beginning of the dynasty it was called *Nei wenxueguan* 內文學館. Wu Zetian changed the name to *Xiyiguan* 習藝館. Soon afterward it was changed again to *Hanlin nei jiaofang* 翰林內教坊.

19. Wei, *Suishu*, 58:1431.

20. Liu, *Jiu Tangshu*, 72:2566.

21. Ouyang, *Xin Tangshu*, 76:3470–71.

22. Guo Haiwen, Zhao Wenduo, and Jia Qiangqiang, "Tangdai gongzhu jiaoyu zinü wenti zhitan," *Ganling wenhua yanjiu* 9 (2015): 253–78. Pages 266–69 give a list of the sons of Tang princesses who served in office. This table shows that it was

common for their sons to become high officials. Chang Chun, "Tangdai gongzhu shufa yishu guankui," *Shaanxi Shifan Daxue xuebao* 42, no. 3 (2013): 91–96 describes surviving examples of calligraphy written by Tang princesses in detail. Duan, *Tangdai funü diwei yanjiu*, 163 claims that fewer palace ladies received a comprehensive education in the late Tang than in the earlier part of the dynasty.

23. Adamek, "A Niche of Their Own," 15.

24. The first collection of women's letters was *Chidu xinyu* 尺牘新語. Liu, "Wei Jin yihuan shijia," 31.

25. Zhao Heping, "Tangdai shuyi zhong suojian de furen shuzha," in *Tang Song nüxing yu shehui*, ed. Deng Xiaonan (Shanghai: Shanghai cishu, 2003), 1:209–14.

26. Yamazaki Junichi, "Guanyu Tangdai liangbu nüxunshu 'Nü lunyu' 'Nü xiaojing' de jichu yanjiu," in *Tang Song nüxing yu shehui*, ed. Deng Xiaonan (Shanghai: Shanghai cishu, 2003), 1:158.

27. Patricia Buckley Ebrey, "The Book of Filial Piety for Women Attributed to a Woman Née Zheng (ca. 730)," in *Under Confucian Eyes: Writings on Gender in Chinese History*, ed. Susan Mann and Yu-yin Cheng (Berkeley: University of California Press, 2001), 47–69; Yamazaki, "Guanyu Tangdai liangbu nüxunshu," 167–69.

28. Huang Yanli, "'Nü xiaojing' yu 'Nü lunyu,'" in *Tang Song nüxing yu shehui*, ed. Deng Xiaonan (Shanghai: Shanghai cishu, 2003), 1:188–89; Yang Xin, "Nü xiaojing zuozhe ji chansheng shidai kao," *Zhongguo suwenhua yanjiu* 6 (2010): 102, 103, 107.

29. Van Norden, *Mengzi*, 101; Liu, "Filiality versus Sociality and Individuality," 234.

30. Terry Tak-ling Woo, "Emotions and Self-Cultivation in Nü Lunyu 女論語 (Women's Analects)," *Journal of Chinese Philosophy* 36, no. 2 (2009): 334–47. For the English translation, see Robin R. Wong, ed., "The Analects for Women," in *Images of Women in Chinese Thought and Culture: Writings from the Pre-Qin Period through the Song Dynasty* (Indianapolis, IN: Hackett Publishing, 2003), 327–40.

31. Chang and Saussy, *Women Writers of Traditional China*, 671–72; Huang, "'Nü xiaojing' yu 'Nü lunyu,'" 188–89; Liu Yanfei and Wang Honghai, "Nü lunyu de zhushu yu chuanbo tedian," *Hebei xuekan* 3 (2008): 46; Liu Yanfei, "Song Ruoxin jiemei yu *Nü lunyu* yanjiu," *Hebei Daxue xuebao* 33, no. 2 (2008): 37–38; Guo Li, "Tangdai nüjiaoshu *Nü lunyu* xiangguan wenti kaolun," *Henan Shifan Daxue xuebao* 1 (2011): 149. The authorship of this work remains contested. Some authorities believe that the sisters wrote it together. Others hold that Song Ruoxin wrote the book and her sister annotated it. And a few scholars argue that someone else wrote *Analects for Women* and later readers misattributed it to these sisters because of their prominence in the palace education system at the time. Yamazaki Junichi, *Kyōiku kara mita Chūgoku joseishi shiryō no kenkyū—"josisho" to "shinhuhu" sanbusho* (Tokyo: Meiji, 1986), 109; Yamazaki Junichi, *Joshisho—shinhuhu sanbusho zenshaku* (Tokyo: Meiji shoten, 2002), 109 argues that this book was written by a Madame Wei 韋氏, wife of the poet Xue Meng 薛蒙.

32. Wang Xiang 王相 (d. 1524), a Ming dynasty official and editor, collated the "Four Books for Women" and provided basic annotation. Sun Xinmei, "*Nü sishu* de bianzuan yu liuchuan," *Lantai shijie* 11 (2013): 156–57; Ann A. Pang-White, "Con-

fucius and the Four Books for Women (Nü Sishu 女四書)," in *Feminist Encounters with Confucius*, ed. Mathew A. Foust and Sor-hoon Tan (Leiden: Brill, 2016), 17–39.

33. Guo, "Tangdai nüjiaoshu *Nü lunyu* xiangguan wenti kaolun," 148.

34. Jin, "Qianlun Tangdai houqi hunyin de tedian," 48. Gao Shiyu, "Songshi jie-mei yu 'Nü lunyu' lunxi—jian ji gudai nüjiao de pingminhua qushi," in *Tang Song nüxing yu shehui*, ed. Deng Xiaonan (Shanghai: Shanghai cishu, 2003), 1:148–50.

35. Cui Li, "Qianlun *Nü lunyu* zhong de fojiao secai," *Wutaishan yanjiu* 2 (2006): 12–17.

36. Gao, "Songshi jiemei yu 'Nü lunyu' lunxi," 146–48.

37. *Yaochi xinyong ji* 瑤池新詠記 (Collection of New Songs from Turquoise Pond). It is the earliest extant collection of a work containing only poems written by women. Jia, "The Yaochi ji and Three Daoist Priestess-Poets in Tang China," 205–7.

38. Xue Dan, "Zui shi yaorao qing hong yan—Tangdai tibishi zhong de nüzi," *Yuwen xuekan* 1 (2015): 68–69.

39. Ye, "Tangdai shiren jiating nüzi jiaoyu yanjiu," 305; Yu, "Tangdai nüxing shige yanjiu," 1. Zhang Xiurong, *Han Tang guizu yu cianü shige yanjiu* (Taipei: Wenshizhe chubanshe, 1985), 47–184 brings together many poems written by Tang women.

40. Su Zhecong, *Guiwei de tanshi—Tangdai nüshiren* (Changsha: Hunan wenyi, 1991) provides biographies and sample poetry of the major Tang female poets.

41. Zhang Yinan, "Wo jian you ling—Tangdai nüshiren de Qi Liang ti chuang-zuo," *Wenshi zhishi* 3 (2014): 112–17.

42. Suzanne Cahill, "Resenting the Silk Robes that Hide Their Poems: Female Voices in the Poetry of Tang Dynasty Nuns," in *Tang Song nüxing yu shehui*, ed. Deng Xiaonan (Shanghai: Shanghai cishu, 2003), 2:521.

43. Zhao Xiaohua, "Gonggongxing: Tangdai nüxing shige de bieyang shijiao," *Huanan Shifan Daxue xuebao* 4 (2016): 145–50.

44. Cahill, "Resenting the Silk Robes that Hide Their Poems," 539.

45. Cahill, "Resenting the Silk Robes that Hide Their Poems," 541.

46. Yu, "Tangdai nüxing shige yanjiu," 82–93 discusses poetry written by Daoist nuns.

47. For her biography, see Xu, *Tangdai funü shenghuo yu shi*, 222–30; Li, *Tang-dai rudao nüxing shijie*," 39–45, 60–66. David Young and Jiann L. Lin, trans., *The Clouds Float North: The Complete Poems of Yu Xuanji, Bilingual Edition* (Middle-town, CT: Wesleyan University Press, 1998) gives a short biography of Yu Xuanji, assesses her work, and translates all forty-nine of her surviving poems.

48. Huang, "Tangdai nüxing yu wenxue de xiangguanxing yanjiu," 80–94. Jiao Jie, "Tangdai nüguan shiren Li Ye yu Yu Xuanji bijiao yanjiu," *Guangdong Jishu Shifan Xueyuan xuebao* 10 (2014): 1–6 compares the lives and poetry of Li Ye and Yu Xuanji.

49. Jeanne Larsen, trans., *Brocade River Poems: Selected Works of the Tang Dynasty Courtesan Xue Tao* (Princeton: Princeton University Press, 1987), xi–xxiv.

50. T. H. Barrett, "The Woman Who Invented Notepaper: Towards a Compara-tive Historiography of Paper and Print," *Journal of the Royal Asiatic Society* 21, no. 2 (2011): 206.

51. Huang, "Tangdai nüxing yu wenxue de xiangguanxing yanjiu," 54–78.

52. Huang, "Tangdai nüxing yu wenxue de xiangguanxing yanjiu," 26–36; Guo Haiwen, "Tangdai gongting nüxing zhishifenzi qinghuai—Tang Taizong xianfei Xu Hui shiwen zhi fenxi," *Henan Shifan Daxue xuebao* 39, no. 4 (2012): 147–51.

53. Ying Kerong, "Tangdai nüxing shuxie de 'sinanhua' tezheng," *Xueshujie* 7 (2015): 124.

54. Graham Sanders, "I Read They Said He Sang What He Wrote: Orality, Writing, and Gossip in Tang Poetry Anecdotes," in *Idle Talk: Gossip and Anecdote in Traditional China*, ed. Jack W. Chen and David Schaberg (Berkeley: Global, Area, and International Archive and University of California Press, 2014), 93.

55. Chen Wu and Wang Wenhua, "Tangdai nüshiren Xue Tao shige zhong de 'nanxinghua' biaoxian," *Lantai shijie* 10 (2015): 122–23.

56. Chow and Cleary, *Autumn Willows*, 48.

57. Chow and Cleary, *Autumn Willows,* 83. Also Young and Lin, *The Clouds Float North*, 23; Cahill, "Resenting the Silk Robes that Hide Their Poems," 539.

CHAPTER 7: VIRTUE

1. Jin, "Qianlun Tangdai houqi hunyin de tedian," 47; Chiu-Duke, "The Role of Confucian Revivalists," 74–76.

2. Richard L. Davis, "Chaste and Filial Women in Chinese Historical Writings of the Eleventh Century," *Journal of the American Oriental Society* 121, no. 2 (2001): 213–17.

3. Paul R. Goldin, "Women and Moral Dilemmas in Early Chinese Narrative," in *The Bloomsbury Research Handbook of Chinese Philosophy and Gender*, ed. Ann A. Pang-White (New York: Bloomsbury Publishing, 2016), 25–35.

4. Wong, "Confucian Ideal and Reality," 270–71.

5. Jiao Jie and Hu Na, "Tangdai shidaifu zhi jia zaishinü de jiating diwei—yi Tangdai zaishinü muzhi wei zhongxin," *Hua'nan Shifan Daxue xuebao* 6 (2012): 97–98. Many poems about women mention values similar to those conveyed in textbooks written for women, such as maternal love, filial piety, the rites, and Confucian ethics. Yu, "Tangdai nüxing shige yanjiu," 31–34, 44–49.

6. Xia Shaoxian, "Cong muzhi kan Tangdai funü de zhenjieguan," *Chuxiong Shizhuan xuebao* 16, no. 2 (2001): 133–34. In contrast with most scholars, Xia provocatively asserts that the lower strata put the most stress on chastity and other Confucian virtues, as they were less influenced by nomadic culture. This assertion is questionable

7. Mo Xiaobin, "Qianlun Tangdai hunyin zhidu yu shehui xishang de maodun xianxiang," *Changsha Daxue xuebao* 14, no. 3 (2003): 59; Cui Dequan, "Tangdai funü dui rujia jiaoyi de rentong yu fanpan," *Qingnian zuojia* 12 (2010): 18–20.

8. Lu, "Ru Fo jian xiu," 25–28.

9. Mou, "Writing Virtues with their Bodies," 114, 116, 130.

10. Beverly J. Bossler, *Powerful Relations: Kinship, Status, & the State in Sung China (960–1279)* (Cambridge, MA: Council on East Asian Studies, Harvard University, 1998), 21, 24.

11. Liu, *Jiu Tangshu*, 149:3027.

12. Chen Lishan, "Ershiwushi lienüzhuan leishi," *Daren xuebao* 14 (1996): 135–54 gives an overview of women's didactic biographies in the standard histories.

13. Jennifer Holmgren, "Widow Chastity in the Northern Dynasties: The Liehnu Biographies in the Wei-shu," *Papers on Far Eastern History* 23 (1981): 185–86.

14. Sherry J. Mou, *Gentlemen's Prescriptions for Women's Lives: A Thousand Years of Biographies of Chinese Women* (Armonk, NY: M.E. Sharpe, 2004), 122.

15. Jiao Jie, "'Lienü zhuan' yu Zhou Qin Han Tang fude biaozhun," *Shaanxi Shifan Daxue xuebao* 32, no. 6 (2003): 96.

16. Jiao, "'Lienü zhuan' yu Zhou Qin Han Tang fude biaozhun," 97; Yu Ya'nan, "Cong liang *Tangshu Lienü zhuan* kan Tangdai nüxing de chuantong daodeguan," *Shoudu Shifan Daxue xuebao* (2010): 30–33. Mou, "Writing Virtues with Their Bodies," 135–37 provides a table that compares the contents of didactic biographies of women in the two Tang standard histories.

17. Liu, *Jiu Tangshu*, 193:5138; Mou, *Gentlemen's Prescriptions for Women's Lives*, 136–37.

18. Liu, *Jiu Tangshu*, 193:5141–42.

19. Roland Altenburger, *The Sword or the Needle: The Female Knight-errant (xia) in Traditional Chinese Narrative* (Bern: Peter Lang, 2009); Manling Luo, "Gender, Genre, and Discourse: The Woman Avenger in Medieval Chinese Texts," *Journal of the American Oriental Society* 134, no. 4 (2014): 579–99; Sheau-Shi Ngo, "Nuxia: Historical Depiction and Modern Visuality," *Asian Journal of Women's Studies* 20, no. 3 (2014): 10.

20. Gu Lihua, *Handai funü shenghuo qingkuang* (Beijing: Shehui kexue wenxian, 2012), 38–63.

21. Lou Jin, "Zhengsheng yuannian chi yu Nanbeichao zhi Tangdai de jingbiao xiaoyi zhi zhidu—jian lun S.1344 hao Lundun canjuan de dingming wenti," *Zhejiang xuekan* 1 (2014): 11, 13–17.

22. Zhang Weidong, "Tangdai cishi yu jingbiao zhidu," *Jiangxi shehui kexue* 7 (2009): 146–52.

23. Zhang Jing, "Shilun Tangdai nüde jingbiao zhidu de fazhan," *Jiangsu shehui kexue* 6 (2012): 237.

24. Niu Zhiping, "Tangdai de yinyuan tiandingshuo," in *Zhongguo funüshi lunji sanji*, ed. Bao Jialin (Taipei: Daoxiang, 1993), 51–59; Niu, *Tangdai shehui shenghuo conglun*, 45–53; Yao, *Tangdai funü de shengming licheng*, 22–26; Niu, *Tangdai hunsang*, 33–37.

25. Niu, "Tangdai de yinyuan tiandingshuo," 57–59; Yao, *Tangdai funü de shengming licheng*, 26.

26. Niu, "Tangdai de yinyuan tiandingshuo," 55.

27. Niu, "Tangdai de yinyuan tiandingshuo," 56; Niu Zhiping, "Tangdai hunyin de tianmingguan," *Hainan Shifan Xueyuan xuebao* 2 (1995): 59–61; Niu, *Tangdai hunsang*, 91–93.

28. Ouyang, *Xin Tangshu*, 122:4346.

29. Li Zhisheng, "Zhongmen he zhongtang: Tangdai zhuzhai jianzhu zhong de funü shenghuo kongjian," *Zhongguo shehui lishi pinglun* 14 (2013): 198–205.

30. Liu, *Jiu Tangshu*, 57:2286; Ouyang, *Xin Tangshu*, 103:3994, 109:4095.

31. Li Yanshou, *Beishi* (Beijing: Zhonghua shuju, 1974), 12:470.

32. Zhang, *Jiating shihua*, 67.

33. Young and Lin, *The Clouds Float North*, 15.

34. Duan, *Tangdai funü diwei yanjiu*, 19–22; Yue Chunzhi, "Lun Tangdai hunwai xingwei ji qi shehui kongzhi," *Qi Lu xuekan* 5 (2006): 47–48.

35. Chen Liping, "Tang Song shiqi Dunhuang diqi feizhengshi hunyin zinü xianxiang luekao," *Dunhuang yanjiu* 4 (2006): 54–55.

36. Li Li, "Dunhuang ben Qiu Hu gushi jieju tanxi," *Gansu Jiaoyu Xueyuan xuebao* 19, no. 4 (2003): 5–8.

37. Ping Yao, "Changing Views on Sexuality in Early and Medieval China," *Journal of Daoist Studies* 8 (2015): 53–69.

38. D. L. Davis and R. G. Whitten, "The Cross-Cultural Study of Human Sexuality," *Annual Review of Anthropology* 16 (1987): 75.

39. Alice Schlegel, "Status, Property, and the Value on Virginity," *American Ethnologist* 18, no. 4 (1991): 719, 724, 730 argues that the link between marriage strategy and virginity holds true for many societies. For example, Tongan chiefs would tie their daughters' legs together at night to prevent them from taking lovers, thus keeping them virginal so that they could be married off strategically to create useful marriage alliances. Kent Flannery and Joyce Marcus, *The Creation of Inequality: How Our Prehistoric Ancestors Set the Stage for Monarchy, Slavery, and Empire* (Cambridge, MA: Harvard University Press, 2012), 319.

40. Susan Mann, "Widows in the Kinship, Class, and Community Structures of Qing Dynasty China," *Journal of Asian Studies* 46, no. 1 (1987): 49.

41. Mou, *Gentlemen's Prescriptions for Women's Lives*, 139.

42. Michael Herzfeld, "Honour and Shame: Problems in the Comparative Analysis of Moral Systems," *Man* 15 (1980): 343.

43. Liu, *Jiu Tangshu*, 151:4061.

44. McMahon, *Women Shall Not Rule*, 182–83.

45. Mou, *Gentlemen's Prescriptions for Women's Lives*, 120–21, 132.

46. Zhou and Wang, *Roushun zhi xiang*, 97–118.

47. Li Wencai and Xie Dan, "*Taiping guangji* suo jian Tangdai funü de hunlian shenghuo," *Jiangsu Keji Daxue xuebao* 2 (2007): 69–74.

48. Chiu-Duke, "The Role of Confucian Revivalists," 54, 92–93.

49. Jin, "Qianlun Tangdai houqi hunyin de tedian," 46.

50. Yang, "Tangdai funü de 'jifu' shi," 41–44; Yang Xiaomin, "Cong zhanzheng shi kan Tangdai funü de beican mingyun," *Chuxiong Shifan Xueyuan xuebao* 18, no. 2 (2003): 13–15.

51. Liu, "Tangdai qifu shi pingxi," 50–52.

52. Chang and Saussy, *Women Writers of Traditional China*, 55.

53. Liu, *Jiu Tangshu*, 166:4334.

54. Hu, "Cong Tangshi kan Tangdai funü de hunyin zhuangkuang," 20–21.

55. Yao, "Women's Epitaphs in Tang China," 141–42 concludes 42.1. Zhang, *Jiating shihua*, 56 posits 64.2. For methods used at the time to calculate age see Chen, "'Age Inflation and Deflation' in Medieval China," 527–33.

56. Wan, *Tangdai nüxing de shengqian yu zuhou*, 95–96. Yao, "Women's Epitaphs in Tang China," 154–55 also notes that the average age of death for women declined considerably after the An Lushan Rebellion.

57. Ping Yao, "Women in Portraits: An Overview of Epitaphs from Early and Medieval China," in *Overt and Covert Treasures: Essays on the Sources for Chinese Women's History*, ed. Clara Wing-Chung Ho (Hong Kong: City University Press, 2012), 167–68.

58. Luo Tonghua, "Tangdai jishi hunyin yanjiu," in *Zhongyuan yu yuwai: Qingzhu Zhang Guangda jiaoshou bashi zhounian songshou yantaohui lunwenji*, ed. Lü Shaoli and Zhou Huimin (Taipei: Cheng Chi University, Department of History, 2011), 131.

59. Weng Yuxuan, "Tō Sō bushi kara mita jōsei no shusetsu to saika ni tsuite—mibōjin no sentaku to sono seikatsu," *Tōdaishi kenkyū* 6 (2003): 42. Zhang Guogang, "Tangdai guaju funü de shenghuo shijie," *Anhui Shifan Daxue xuebao* 3 (2007): 309 discusses specific cases of women widowed in their forties and fifties.

60. Wan, *Tangdai nüxing de shengqian yu zuhou*, 63, 70.

61. Liu Litang and Wan Junjie, "Tangdai de guafu zangfu yu qianzang fuzu," *Jianghan luntan* 7 (2011): 85–88.

62. Qi Shuzhen and Zou Dianwei, "Cong muzhi kan Tangdai de guamu fugu," *Cangsang* 2 (2008): 12–13.

63. Qi, "Tangdai guamu caichan chufenquan tanxi," 55–57.

64. Shiga, *Chūgoku kazokuhō no genri*, 415–36; Zhang, "Tangdai guaju funü de shenghuo shijie," 318, 321–22. Virtuous women were called *baoyang* 褒揚. This category included chaste widows. The specific term for chaste widows was *shuangju* 孀居.

65. Zhao and Lu, "Shilun Tang Xizhou xiaceng nüxing de hunyin shenghuo," 75–76.

66. Jennifer Holmgren, "The Economic Foundations of Virtue: Widow-Remarriage in Early and Modern China," *Australian Journal of Chinese Affairs* 13 (1985): 7.

67. Matthew H. Sommer, "The Uses of Chastity: Sex, Law, and the Property of Widows in Qing China," *Late Imperial China* 17, no. 2 (1996): 78; Duan, *Tangdai funü diwei yanjiu*, 59.

68. Ouyang, *Xin Tangshu*, 205:5822.

69. Scholars arguing that remarriage was common: Niu, *Tangdai shehui shenghuo conglun*, 17, 33, 66–76; Zhang, "Huzu hunsu yu Tangdai guafu zaijia," 79. Those who believe that remarriage was uncommon: Zhang, *Hunyin yu shehui*, 66; Mao Yangguang, "Tangdai funü de zhenjieguan," *Wenbo* 4 (2000): 33–38; Xia, "Cong muzhi kan Tangdai funü de zhenjieguan," 132; Xiang, *Tangdai hunyin fa yu hunyin shitai*, 204–6. Ōzawa, *Tō sō jidai no kazoku, konin, josei*, 54 takes the middle position, arguing that the ideology of chastity conflicted with actual behavior, which remained fairly unrestrained.

70. Wang Shounan, "Tangdai gongzhu zhi hunyin," *Diyijie lishi yu Zhongguo shehui bianqian (Zhongguo shehuishi) yantaohui* (Taipei: Zhongyanyuan Sanminzhuyi

Yanjiuyuan congkan, 1982), 1:151–60 provides a long table with information about every Tang princess.

71. Ouyang, *Xin Tangshu*, 83:3672.

72. Chen Dongyuan, *Zhongguo funü shenghuo shi* (Shanghai: Shangwu Yinshuguan, 1937), 118; Jin, "Qianlun Tangdai houqi hunyin de tedian," 46.

73. Chen, *Multicultural China in the Early Middle Ages*, 6–14.

74. Zhang, "Tangdai guaju funü de shenghuo shijie," 309; Liu and Wan, "Tangdai de guafu zangfu yu qianzang fuzu," 85; Chen and Kang, "Tangdai funü lihun gaijia shijian de chayixing fenxi," 107–8.

75. Mann, "Widows in the Kinship, Class, and Community Structures," 47–48.

76. Luo, *Tongju gongcai*, 303, 330–36.

77. Tan, *Dunhuang hunyin wenhua*, 117–22; Liang, "Tangdai funü de jiating diwei," 89; Zhang Jintong, "Huzu hunsu yu Tangdai guafu zaijia," *Gansu shehui kexue* 1 (2001): 78.

78. Liu, *Jiu Tangshu*, 193:5138–39.

79. Xia, "Cong muzhi kan Tangdai funü de zhenjieguan," 132.

80. Qian, *Tang lü yanjiu*, 303.

81. Liu, *Jiu Tangshu*, 193:5140.

82. Wei, *Suishu*, 2:41.

83. Shigeru Maruyama, *Tōdai no bunka to shijin no kokoro—hakurakuten o chūshin ni* (Tokyo: Kyuko shoin, 2010), 90–93.

84. Chiu-Duke, "The Role of Confucian Revivalists," 60–61.

85. Xia, "Cong muzhi kan Tangdai funü de zhenjieguan," 132.

86. Jin, "Qianlun Tangdai houqi hunyin de tedian," 46.

87. Zhang, "Huzu hunsu yu Tangdai guafu zaijia," 78.

88. Wei, *Suishu*, 4:93; Lee, "Women and Marriage in China," 204.

89. Xiang, *Tangdai hunyin fa yu hunyin shitai*, 190; Xia, "Cong muzhi kan Tangdai funü de zhenjieguan," 131; Sun, "Tangchao funüguan zhi shanbian yu shehui zhengzhi," 100.

90. Zhang, "Huzu hunsu yu Tangdai guafu zaijia," 79–80.

91. Li, "Shixi jingji zhengce dui Zhongguo gudai funü zhenjie," 890–93, 897.

92. Wan Junjie, "Tangdai gaijia zaijia nüxing sangzang wenti tantao," *Tianjin Shifan Daxue xuebao* 5 (2007): 59–62.

93. T. F. Mumford, "Death Do Us Unite: Xunzang and Joint Burial in Ancient China," *Papers on Far Eastern History* 27 (2008): 11–12; Wu Congxiang, *Handai nüxing lijiao yanjiu* (Jinan: Qilu, 2013), 51; Zhang Chengzong and Chen Qun, *Zhongguo funü tongshi: Wei Jin nanbei chao juan* (Hangzhou: Hangzhou chubanshe, 2010), 649–85.

94. Obara, *Chūsei kizoku shakai to bukkyō*, 11–14; Zhou and Wang, *Roushun zhi xiang*, 110–11; Lu, "Ru Fo jian xiu," 29–30; Yao, "Women's Epitaphs in Tang China," 150.

95. Qi Shuzhen, "Cong muzhi kan Tangdai guamu de fojiao xinyang," *Zhonggong Jinanshi Weidangxiao xuebao* 5 (2013): 103–5. Su, "Cong muzhi kan fojiao dui Tangdai funü shenghuo de yingxiang," 85 comes up with the alternate figure of seventy-one inscriptions for Buddhist widows, or 34.47 percent. Also Zhang, "Tang-

dai guaju funü de shenghuo shijie," 319–21; Yang, "Tangdai funü yu fojiao," 21; Jiao, "Cong Tang muzhi kan Tangdai funü yu fojiao de guanxi," 96. Yan, "Muzhi jiwen zhong de Tangdai funü fojiao xinyang," 46 notes that the high number of widows in inscriptions for Buddhist devotees might have simply reflected the advanced age of these women, which made them more likely to have been considered worthy of a funerary inscription. Alternatively, widows might simply have been more religious than married women.

96. Qiu, "Tangdai nüxing rezhong rudao yuanyin chutan," 55–58; Zhao and Jiao, "Cong muzhi kan Tangdai funü de daojiao xinyang," 192.

97. Li, *Tangdai de biqiuni*, 75–82; Yao, *Tangdai funü de shengming licheng*, 240–41; Jiao, "Cong Tang muzhi kan Tangdai funü yu fojiao de guanxi," 97.

98. For overviews of widow chastity see Shiga, *Chūgoku kazokuhō no genri*, 415–36; Zhang, *Tangdai jiating yu shehui*, 203–33. Numerous Dunhuang documents contain the names of widows. Tan, *Dunhuang hunyin wenhua*, 90–93.

99. Chen, *Tangdai de funü wenhua yu jiating shenghuo*, 126–36.

100. Tackett, *The Destruction of the Medieval Chinese Aristocracy*, 95.

101. Tackett, *The Destruction of the Medieval Chinese Aristocracy*, 130–31.

102. Sommer, "The Uses of Chastity," 77.

103. Mou, "Writing Virtues with their Bodies," 115, 123–28.

104. For example, Liu, *Jiu Tangshu*, 193:5147. Tackett, *The Destruction of the Medieval Chinese Aristocracy*, 196.

105. Mou, *Gentlemen's Prescriptions for Women's Lives*, 160–61.

106. Ouyang, *Xin Tangshu*, 205:5816.

107. Lu Jianrong, "Cong nanxing shuxie cailiao kan san zhi qi shiji nüxing de shehui xingxiang suzao," *Guoli Taiwan Shifan Daxue lishi xuebao* 26 (1998): 24–31, 36.

CHAPTER 8: LOVE

1. Seo Tatsuhiko, "'Caizi' yu 'jiaren'—jiu shiji Zhongguo xin de nannü renshi de xingcheng," in *Tang Song nüxing yu shehui*, ed. Deng Xiaonan (Shanghai: Shanghai cishu, 2003), 2:697–98; Xu, *Tangdai funü shenghuo yu shi*, 199.

2. Larsen, *Brocade River Poems*, 17.

3. Fusheng Wu, *The Poetics of Decadence: Chinese Poetry of the Southern Dynasties and Late Tang Periods* (Albany: State University of New York Press, 1998), 77–79, 81. The subsequent reputation of this sort of poetry has fluctuated considerably. See p. 116.

4. Larsen, *Willow, Wine, Mirror, Moon*, 32, 34, 92; Larsen, *Brocade River Poems*, 43, 44, 47.

5. Michael E. Workman, "The Bedchamber Topos in the Tz'u Songs of Three Medieval Chinese Poets: Wen T'ing-yun, Wei Chuang, and Li Yu," in *Critical Essays on Chinese Literature*, ed. William H. Nienhauser Jr. et al. (Hong Kong: Chinese University Press, 1976), 172, 175.

6. Chow and Cleary, *Autumn Willows*, 109.

7. Liu Yanping, *Zhongwan Tang yanti shige yanjiu* (Zhengzhou: Henan Daxue chubanshe, 2011), 35, 38–40.

8. Chow and Cleary, *Autumn Willows*, 36.

9. Stephen Owen, *Readings in Chinese Literary Thought* (Cambridge, MA: Council on East Asian Studies, Harvard University, 1992), 45–46.

10. Tung, *Fables for the Patriarchs*, 153; Xiaorong Li, *Women's Poetry of Late Imperial China* (Seattle: University of Washington Press, 2012), 48.

11. Young and Lin, *The Clouds Float North*, 13–14.

12. Yue Hong, "Romantic Identity in the Funerary Inscriptions (*muzhi*) of Tang China," *Asia Major* (third series) 25, no. 1 (2012): 33–62.

13. Chen Zhizhuo, "Bai Juyi lianai shiyi yu Tangdai hunyinzhi," *Nei Menggu Dianda xuebao* 4 (1994): 5–10, 25.

14. Luo Ping, "Cong Tang chuanqi kan Tangdai nüxing hunlianguan," *Sichuan Shifan Xueyuan xuebao* 1 (1999): 97–98.

15. Young and Lin, *The Clouds Float North*, 2.

16. Cahill, "Resenting the Silk Robes that Hide Their Poems," 550–52.

17. Zhang, *Tangdai jiating yu shehui*, 140; Luo, "Cong Tang chuanqi kan Tangdai nüxing hunlianguan," 98–99; Ma Zili, "Tangren biji xiaoshuo zhong de Tangdai nüxing—cong ziliao yu wenti chufa de chubu kaocha," *Wenyi yanjiu* 6 (2001): 105.

18. Ma, "Tangren biji xiaoshuo zhong de Tangdai nüxing," 104.

19. Timothy C. Wong, "Self and Society in Tang Dynasty Love Tales," *Journal of the American Oriental Society* 99, no. 1 (1979): 95–99.

20. Allen, *Shifting Stories*, 136.

21. Hsieh, *Love and Women in Early Chinese Fiction*, 168.

22. Lai Jiaqi, "Shixi 'Sanshui xiaodu' nüxing beiju renwu (shang)—yi Bu Feiyan, Lü Qiao, Yu Xuanji wei li," *Zhongguo yuwen* 6 (1998): 79–86.

23. Hsieh, *Love and Women in Early Chinese Fiction*, 155, 197.

24. Li, *Shenhua shiyu xia de wenxue jiedu*, 202–301.

25. Guan Siping, "Shihuan jiding yu qinggan zhuiqiu de maodun—Tangdai difei guanxi xiaoshuo de wenhua jiedu," *Shenyang Shifan Daxue xuebao* 3 (2010): 6.

26. Hsieh, *Love and Women in Early Chinese Fiction*, 69.

27. Allen, *Shifting Stories*, 35.

28. Allen, *Shifting Stories*, 121.

29. Allen, *Shifting Stories*, 139. The rising importance of animal spirits seems to have been due to influence from pastoral cultures. Zhang Meijuan and Zhang Meihua, "*Taiping guangji* zhong de Tangdai nüxing jingguai yu shaoshu minzu wenhua lunkao," *Heilongjiang minzu congkan* 1 (2007): 166–70.

30. Allen, *Shifting Stories*, 54, 156–57.

31. Hsieh, *Love and Women in Early Chinese Fiction*, 55.

32. Kuroda Mamiko, "Riku chō Tōdai ni okeru yūkontan no tōjō jinbutsu—kankontan to no hikaku," *Nihon Chūgoku gakukaihou* 48 (1996): 119–32; Han Yu, "Tangdai rengui xianglian gushi de jizhong moshi," *Hunan Nongye Daxue xuebao* 12, no. 2 (2011): 77–81; Guan Siping, "Tangdai rengui hunlian xiaoshuo xinlun," *Xueshu jiaoliu* 1 (2012): 149–56.

33. Curtis P. Adkins, "The Hero in T'ang *Ch'uan-ch'i* Tales," in *Critical Essays on Chinese Fiction*, ed. Winston L. Y. Yang and Curtis P. Adkins (Hong Kong: Chinese University Press, 1980), 28–29.

34. Jiao Jie, "Xiannü xiafan—jituo Tangdai nanzi lixiang de wenhua xianxiang," *Lishi yuekan* 4 (1999): 122–26; Seo, "'Caizi' yu 'jiaren,'" 697–98.

35. Tsai, "Ritual and Gender in the Tale of Li Wa," 99–127.

36. James R. Hightower, "Yüan Chen and 'The Story of Ying-Ying,'" *Harvard Journal of Asiatic Studies* 33 (1973): 90–123 translates the Yingying story and provides basic commentary. Also Lorraine Dong, "The Many Faces of Cui Yingying," in *Women in China: Current Directions in Historical Scholarship*, ed. Richard W. Guisso and Stanley Johannesen (Youngstown, NY: Philo Press, 1981), 75–98; Kominami Ichiro, *Tōdai tenki shōsetsu ron—kanashimi to akogare to* (Tokyo: Iwanami, 2014), 101–38.

37. Xu, *Tangdai funü shenghuo yu shi*, 206–11; Sun Yurong, "Lun Tangdai de 'fuqi zhi qing,'" *Linyi Daxue xuebao* 35, no. 4 (2013): 119–21.

38. Yao, *Tangdai funü de shengming licheng*, 108–22.

39. Yan, "Tangshi zhong suo fanying de Tangdai funü," 104.

40. Jin Jinnan, "Lun Dunhuang ci zhong Tangdai funü de aiqing hunyin," *Tiecheng Shizhuan xuebao* 2 (1995): 30–34.

41. Yang, "Tangdai funü de 'jifu' shi," 41. For example, Dunhuang documents P.3502 and S.5613 are letters between spouses expressing mutual affection.

42. Young and Lin, *The Clouds Float North*, 31.

43. Ozawa, *Tō sō jidai no kazoku, konin, josei*, 71.

44. Li and Xie, "*Taiping guangji* suo jian," 69–71.

45. Yao, *Tangdai funü de shengming licheng*, 118.

46. Yao, "Women in Portraits," 174; Yao, "Women's Epitaphs in Tang China," 146–47.

47. "Jiangxia hang." Zhang Jian, *Li Bai shixuan* (Taipei: Wunan, 1998), 15–16.

48. Cahill, "Resenting the Silk Robes that Hide Their Poems," 531.

49. Seo, "'Caizi' yu 'jiaren,'" 699.

50. Wang Zhidong, *Tangdai shehui shenghuo (xiajuan)* (Beijing: Guoji wenhua, 2001), 40; Li Dongmei, "Cong longnü xingxiang de suzao tan Tangdai hunlian guannian de shenghua," *Qinghai Shizhuan xuebao* 4 (2008): 40–42.

51. Jen-der Lee, "Querelle des femmes? Les femmes jalouses et leur contrôle au début de la Chine médiévale," in *Éducation et Instruction en Chine III. Aux Marges de l'orthodoxie*, ed. Christine Nguyen Tri and Catherine Despeux (Paris: Éditions Peeters, 2004), 67–97.

52. Ban, *Hanshu*, 22:1027; Ōzawa, *Tō sō jidai no kazoku, konin, josei*, 128; Niu Zhiping, "Tangdai dufu shulun," in *Zhongguo Funüshi lunji xuji*, ed. Bao Jialin (Taipei: Daoxiang chubanshe, 1991), 61; Niu, *Tangdai hunsang*, 100–101. For an overview of terminology and concepts regarding jealousy, see Li Zhende, "Cong 'dufu ji' tanqi," *Funü yu liangxing jikan* 3 (1994): 12–15.

53. McMahon, *Women Shall Not Rule*, 182–83.

54. Zhao, *Nianer shi zhaji*, 15:208–9.

55. Wright, "T'ang T'ai-tsung and Buddhism," 240.

56. Duan, *Tangdai funü diwei yanjiu*, 131–34; Niu, *Tangdai shehui shenghuo conglun*, 77–95; Cen, *Tangdai huanmen funü yanjiu*, 71–82.

57. Liu, *Jiu Tangshu*, 111:3325.

58. Gao Guofan, "Dunhuang ben Qin Hu gushi yanjiu," *Dunhua yanjiu* 1 (1986): 77–89 discusses a Dunhuang manuscript version of the Qiu Hu story, an old tale about male infidelity. For poetry about jealousy see *Tangdai huanmen funü yanjiu*, 73.

59. Niu, *Tangdai hunsang*, 95–100.

60. Niu Zhiping, "Shuo Tangdai junei zhi feng," *Shixue yuekan* 2 (1988): 38–41.

61. Niu, "Tangdai dufu shulun," 55–65.

CONCLUSION

1. Charlotte Furth, *A Flourishing Yin: Gender in China's Medical History, 960–1665* (Berkeley: University of California Press, 1999), 46; Robin D. S. Yates, "Medicine for Women in Early China: A Preliminary Survey," *Nan Nü* 7, no. 2 (2005): 141, 173–74. Tang literature includes many tales about sex changes and physical anomalies. For example Lu Xun, *Jiyi zhi* (Beijing: Zhonghua, 1985), 2, 4.

2. Kong Min, "Tangdai xiaoshuo nüxing xingxiang dui Ming Qing wenxue zhi yingxiang," *Mingzuo xinshang* 2 (2016): 130–33.

3. Rosemary A. Joyce, "Archaeology of the Body," *Annual Review of Anthropology* 34 (2005): 140, 142, 146.

4. Mary H. Fong, "Tang Tomb Murals Reviewed in the Light of Tang Texts on Painting," *Artibus Asiae* 45, no. 1 (1984): 54–56; Ruan Li, "Tangdai nüxing xingxiang de xin sikao—yi Tang mubihua zhong de nüxing xingxiang yanjiu wei li," *Rongbao zhai* 1 (2011): 72–79; Qi Dongfang, "Nongzhuang danmo zong xiang yi—Tang yong yu funü shenghuo," in *Tang Song nüxing yu shehui*, ed. Deng Xiaonan (Shanghai: Shanghai cishu, 2003), 1:324, 331.

5. Huang Jun, *Shinühua de yanjiu yu jifa* (Beijing: Beijing gongyi meishu, 1995), 2–29; Mary H. Fong, "Images of Women in Traditional Chinese Painting," *Women's Art Journal* 17, no. 1 (1996): 22–24; Huang Peijie, *Tangdai gongbi shinü yanjiu* (Tianjin: Renmin meshu, 2007), 21–27, 40–62, 83–113.

6. Yu Shifen, "Tangdai nüxing shige yanjiu" (PhD diss., Zhejiang University, 2005), 65–67, 70–71.

7. Hong Shuhua, "Lun Tangdai xiaoshuo zhong de ren hu hunlian yuhe ji qi xingcheng yinsu," in *Tangdai wenxue yanjiu* 15, ed. Zhongguo Tangdai wenxue xue-hui et al. (Guilin: Guangxi Shifan Daxue chubanshe, 2014), 281, 284.

8. Zhou and Wang, *Roushun zhi xiang*, 82–96.

9. Jing Jing, "Shijing zhong meiren guannian dui Zhongguo shinühua de yingxiang," *Yishu baijia* 7 (2011): 223–25.

10. Ellen Johnston Laing, "Chinese Palace-Style Poetry and the Depiction of a Palace Beauty," *Art Bulletin* 72, no. 2 (1990): 284–89.

11. Yang Ming, "Tangdai wudao shi zhong de wuji xingxiang tanxi—jian lun Tangren de nüxing shenmei quxiang," *Jiamusi Daxue shehui kexue xuebao* 33, no. 3 (2015): 109–12.

12. Cao Fangyu, "Qiantan Tangdai qingnian funü de zicheng daici—er," *Taiyuan Shifan Xueyuan xuebao* 6 (2006): 114–15.

13. Yang Jin, "Kaogu ziliao suo jian de Tangdai huren nüxing," *Wenbo* 3 (2010): 26–31; Yang Jin, "Cong chutu wenwu kan Tangdai de huren nüxing xingxiang," *Qianling wenhua yanjiu* 5 (2010): 125–28, 134.

14. Ruan Li, *Tang Dunhuang bihua nüxing xingxiang yanjiu* (Wuhan: Wuhan Daxue chubanshe, 2012), 7–12, 140–48.

15. Su Dan, "Yindu Yaocha nüxiang dui Tangdai Dunhuang shiku nüxing zaoxiang de yingxiang," *Yishu yanjiu* 11 (2014): 79–80.

16. Patricia E. Karetzky, "The Representation of Women in Medieval China: Recent Archaeological Evidence," *T'ang Studies* 17 (1999): 244.

17. Young and Lin, *The Clouds Float North*, 25.

18. Bourdieu referred to this as "body habitus." Pierre Bourdieu, *Outline of a Theory of Practice* (Cambridge: Cambridge University Press, 1977), 195. Habitus refers to collective habits adopted by individuals. For a cogent explanation of the concept of habitus, see Charles Lemert, *Social Things: An Introduction to the Sociological Life*, fourth edition (Lanham, MD: Rowman & Littlefield, 2008), 43, 45, 99.

19. Guo Li, "Tangdai 'yi pang wei mei' zhi nüxing shenmeiguan yanbian kaolun," *Leshan Shifan Xueyuan xuebao* 24, no. 10 (2009): 7–10; Deng Tiankai, "Bianxi Tangdai de 'yi pang wei mei'—Tangdai nüxing shenmei de yanbian ji qi yuanyin," *Xi'an shehui kexue* 28, no. 6 (2010): 94–95, 133.

20. Karetzky, "The Representation of Women in Medieval China," 230; Luo Shiping, "Tangdai shinü hua ji qi xiangguan wenti," in *Tang Song nüxing yu shehui*, ed. Deng Xiaonan (Shanghai: Shanghai cishu, 2003), 1:309–13; Kyo Cho, *The Search for Beautiful Women: A Cultural History of Japanese and Chinese Beauty*, trans. Kyoto Selden (Lanham, MD: Rowman & Littlefield, 2012), 28–38.

21. Sun Wei, "Feishou suiqing—Tangdai yu Qingdai shinühua huafeng bijiao," *Yishu baijia* 1 (2014): 176.

22. Dorothy Ko, "In Search of Footbinding's Origins," in *Tang Song nüxing yu shehui*, ed. Deng Xiaonan (Shanghai: Shanghai cishu, 2003), 1:401–2, 406–7; Dorothy Ko, *Cinderella's Sisters: A Revisionist History of Footbinding* (Berkeley: University of California Press, 2005), 109–44.

23. Li Ya, *Zhongguo lidai zhuangshi* (Beijing: Zhongguo fangzhi chubanshe, 2004), 73–105 gives an overview of the clothing and hairstyles of Sui and Tang women. Harada Yoshito, *Tōdai no fukushoku* (Tokyo: Tōyō bunko, 1970), 82–104 discusses the clothing of Tang commoners. Plates in the back of the book illustrate these garments. He Jianguo, Zhang Yanying, and Guo Youmin, *Tangdai funü faji* (Hong Kong: Hair & Beauty, 1987) shows recreations of Tang hairstyles. You Liyun, *Tangdai shinü zhuangrong wenhua tanwei* (New Taipei: Daoxiang, 2015) provides an incredibly detailed study of Tang cosmetics.

24. Yu, "Tangdai nüxing shige yanjiu," 64.

25. Larsen, *Brocade River Poems*, 40.

26. Roland Barthes, *The Language of Fashion*, trans. Andy Stafford, ed. Andy Stafford and Michael Carter (London: Bloomsbury, 2004), 40–41.

27. Michael Carter, *Fashion Classics: From Carlyle to Barthes* (Oxford: Berg, 2003), 2, 156.

28. Wei, *Suishu*, 11:236, 247, 249, 2:260, 12:276–77.

29. Wei, *Suishu*, 11:248, 12:261, 12:277–78.

30. Ouyang, *Xin Tangshu*, 24:516–18; Harada, *Tōdai no fukushoku*, 47–49, 51–53.

31. Thorstein Veblen originally made these observations about clothing. Carter, *Fashion Classics*, 46–47.

32. Georg Simmel promoted the "trickle down" theory of fashion. Carter, *Fashion Classics*, 69.

33. Karetzky, "The Representation of Women in Medieval China," 228. Qi, "Nongzhuang danmo zong xiang yi," 332.

34. Carter, *Fashion Classics*, 136.

35. Hu Rong, "Cong Tangshi kan Tangdai funü de hunyin zhuangkuang," *Xingtai Xueyuan xuebao* 18, no. 2 (2003): 19.

36. BuYun Chen, "Dressing for the Times: Fashion in Tang Dynasty China" (PhD diss., Columbia University, 2016).

37. Kate A. Lingley, "Naturalizing the Exotic: On the Changing Meanings of Ethnic Dress in Medieval China," *Ars Orientalis* 38 (2010): 50–80.

38. Suzanne E. Cahill, "'Our Women Are Acting like Foreigners' Wives!' Western Influences on Tang Dynasty Women's Fashion," in *China Chic: East Meets West*, ed. Valerie Steele and John S. Major (New Haven: Yale University Press, 1999), 103–17; Karetzky, "The Representation of Women in Medieval China," 227–28, 243; Rong Xinjiang, "Nü ban nan zhuang—Tangdai qianqi de xingbie yishi," in *Tang Song nüxing yu shehui*, ed. Deng Xiaonan (Shanghai: Shanghai cishu, 2003), 2:739, 743; Rong Xinjiang, *Sui Tang Chang'an: xingbie, jiyi ji qita* (Hong Kong: Sanlian shudian, 2009), 45–65; Zhang Shan, "Tangdainü zhuo nanzhuang zhi xianxiang chutan," *Meishi yu sheji* 2 (2015): 36–42.

39. Yu, "Tangdai nüxing shige yanjiu," 42–43.

Bibliography

Adamek, Wendi. "Inscriptions for Nuns at Lingquan Temple, Bao Shan." In *Tang Song nüxing yu shehui* 唐宋女性與社會, edited by Deng Xiaonan 鄧小南, 2:493–518. Shanghai: Shanghai cishu, 2003.

———. "The Literary Lives of Nuns: Poems Inscribed on a Memorial Niche for the Tang Nun Benxing." *T'ang Studies* 27 (2009): 40–65.

———. "A Niche of Their Own: The Power of Convention in Two Inscriptions for Medieval Chinese Buddhist Nuns." *History of Religions* 49, no. 1 (2009): 1–26.

Adkins, Curtis P. "The Hero in T'ang *Ch'uan-ch'i* Tales." In *Critical Essays on Chinese Fiction*, edited by Winston L. Y. Yang and Curtis P. Adkins, 17–46. Hong Kong: Chinese University Press, 1980.

Allen, Sarah M. *Shifting Stories: History, Gossip, and Lore in Narratives from Tang Dynasty China*. Cambridge, MA: Harvard University Asia Center, 2014.

Altenburger, Roland. *The Sword or the Needle: The Female Knight-errant (xia) in Traditional Chinese Narrative*. Bern: Peter Lang, 2009.

Ames, Roger T. "Taoism and the Androgynous Ideal." In *Women in China: Current Directions in Historical Scholarship*, edited by Richard W. Guisso and Stanley Johannesen, 21–45. Youngstown, NY: Philo Press, 1981.

Ba Shanshan 巴姍姍, Wang Xiaolin 王曉林, and Sun Lili 孫麗麗. "Tangdai peiling gongzhu kao" 唐代陪陵公主考. *Qianling wenhua yanjiu* 乾陵文化研究 2 (2006): 75–90.

Balkwill, Stephanie. "When Renunciation Is Good Politics: The Women of the Imperial Nunnery of the Northern Wei." *Nan Nü* 18, no. 2 (2016): 224–56.

Ban Gu 班固. *Hanshu*漢書. Annotated by Yan Shigu 顏師古. Beijing: Zhonghua, 1962.

Bao Jiao 鮑嬌. "Tangdai zhengzhi yu furui—yi Wu Zetian cheng di yu S. 6502 *Dayun jingshu* zhong de furui sixiang wei zhongxin" 唐代政治與符瑞—以武則天稱帝與 S. 6502 '大雲經疏' 中的符瑞思想為中心. *Xibei Shida xuebao* 西北師大學報 52, no. 6 (2015): 87–92.

Bao Ruchen 白如辰. "Tangdai Taiyuan Wang shi nanxing hunling kaolue—yi 'Tang-dai muzhi huibian' wei zhongxin" 唐代太原王氏男性婚齡考略—以 '唐代墓志匯編' 為中心. *Du tianxia* 讀天下 15 (2016): 276–77.

Baquedano-López, Patricia. "Creating Social Identities through *Doctrina* Narratives." In *Linguistic Anthropology: A Reader*, second edition, edited by Alessandro Duranti, 364–77. Chichester, UK: Wiley-Blackwell, 2009.

Barfield, Thomas J. *The Perilous Frontier: Nomadic Empires and China, 221 BC to AD 1757*. Cambridge, MA: Blackwell Publishers, 1989.

Barrett, Timothy. *The Woman Who Discovered Printing*. New Haven: Yale University Press, 2008.

———. "The Woman Who Invented Notepaper: Towards a Comparative Historiography of Paper and Print." *Journal of the Royal Asiatic Society* 21, no. 2 (2011): 199–210.

———. "Woodblock Dyeing and Printing Technology in China, c. 700 A.D.: The Innovations of Ms. Liu, and Other Evidence." *Bulletin of the School of Oriental and African Studies* 64, no. 2 (2001): 240–27.

Barthes, Roland. *The Language of Fashion*. Translated by Andy Stafford. Edited by Andy Stafford and Michael Carter. London: Bloomsbury, 2004.

Benn, James A. *Burning for the Buddha: Self-Immolation in Chinese Buddhism*. Honolulu: University of Hawaii Press, 2007.

Bernhardt, Kathryn. *Women and Property in China, 960–1949*. Stanford: Stanford University Press, 1999.

Birge, Bettine. "Inheritance and Property Law from Tang to Song: The Move Away from Patrilineality." In *Tang Song nüxing yu shehui* 唐宋女性與社會, edited by Deng Xiaonan 鄧小南, 2:849–66. Shanghai: Shanghai cishu, 2003.

———. "Women and Property in Sung Dynasty China (960–1279): Neo-Confucianism and Social Change in Chien-chou, Fukien." PhD diss., Columbia University, 1992.

———. *Women, Property, and Confucian Reaction in Sung and Yüan China (960–1368)*. Cambridge: Cambridge University Press, 2002.

Bokenkamp, Stephen R. "A Medieval Feminist Critique of the Chinese World Order: The Case of Wu Zhao (r. 690–705)." *Religion* 28, no. 4 (1998): 383–92.

———. "Transmissions of a Female Daoist: Xie Ziran (767–795). In *Affiliation and Transmission in Daoism: A Berlin Symposium*, edited by Florian C. Reiter, 109–21. Wiesbden: Harrassowitz Verlag, 2012.

Bossler, Beverly J. *Powerful Relations: Kinship, Status, & the State in Sung China (960–1279)*. Cambridge, MA: Council on East Asian Studies, Harvard University, 1998.

———. "Vocabularies of Pleasure: Categorizing Female Entertainers in the Late Tang Dynasty." *Harvard Journal of Asiatic Studies* 72, no. 1 (2012): 71–99.

Bourdieu, Pierre. *Outline of a Theory of Practice*. Cambridge: Cambridge University Press, 1977.

Cahill, Suzanne E. "Discipline and Transformation: Body and Practice in the Lives of Daoist Holy Women of Tang China." In *Women and Confucian Cultures of Premodern China, Korea, and Japan*, edited by Dorothy Ko, JaHyun Kim Habboush, and John R. Piggott, 251–78. Berkeley: University of California Press, 2003.

———. *Divine Traces of the Daoist Sisterhood: "Records of the Assembled Tran-scendents of the Fortified Walled City" by Du Guangting (850–933)*. Magdalena, NM: Three Pines Press, 2006.

———. "Marriages Made in Heaven." *T'ang Studies* 10–11 (1992–1993): 111–22.

———. "The Moon Stopping in the Void: Daoism and the Literati Ideal in Mirrors of the Tang Dynasty." *Cleveland Studies in the History of Art* 9 (2005): 24–41.

———. "'Our Women Are Acting like Foreigners' Wives!' Western Influences on Tang Dynasty Women's Fashion." In *China Chic: East Meets West*, edited by Valerie Steele and John S. Major, 103–17. New Haven: Yale University Press, 1999.

———. "Performers and Female Taoist Adepts: Hsi Wang Mu as the Patron Deity of Women in Medieval China." *Journal of the American Oriental Society* 106, no. 1 (1986): 155–68.

———. "Resenting the Silk Robes that Hide Their Poems: Female Voices in the Poetry of Tang Dynasty Nuns." In *Tang Song nüxing yu shehui* 唐宋女性與社會, edited by Deng Xiaonan 鄧小南, 2:519–66. Shanghai: Shanghai cishu, 2003.

———. "Smell Good and Get a Job: How Daoist Women Saints Were Verified and Legitimized During the Tang Dynasty (618–907)." In *Presence and Presentation: Women in the Chinese Literati Tradition*, edited by Sherry J. Mou, 177–86. New York: St. Martin's Press, 1999.

———. "Sublimation in Medieval China: The Case of the Mysterious Woman of the Nine Heavens." *Journal of Chinese Religions* 20 (1992): 91–102.

———. *Transcendence and Divine Passion: The Queen Mother of the West in Medieval China*. Stanford: Stanford University Press, 1993.

Cai Hongsheng 蔡鴻生. *Nigu tan* 尼姑譚. Guangzhou: Zhongshan Daxue chubanshe, 1996.

———. *Tangdai jiuxing hu yu Tujue wenhua* 唐代九姓胡與突厥文化. Beijing: Zhonghua, 1998.

Cai Weitang 蔡偉堂. "Dunhuang bihua zhong de Shanzi bensheng gushi hua—cong E zang Mogao ku di 433 ku Shanzi bensheng gushi hua tanqi" 敦煌壁畫中的睒子本生故事畫—從俄藏莫高窟第 433 窟睒子本生故事畫談起. *Dunhuang yanjiu* 敦煌研究 5 (2004): 13–19.

———. "Guanyu Dunhuang bihua 'hunli tu' de jige wenti" 關於敦煌壁畫 '婚禮圖' 的幾個問題. *Dunhuang yanjiu* 1 (1990): 54–59.

Cao Fangyu 曹芳宇. "Qiantan Tangdai qingnian funü de zicheng daici—er" 淺談唐代青年婦女的自稱代詞—兒. *Taiyuan Shifan Xueyuan xuebao* 太原師範學院學報 6 (2006): 114–15.

Carter, Michael. *Fashion Classics: From Carlyle to Barthes*. Oxford: Berg, 2003.

Cen Jingwen 岑靜雯. *Tangdai huanmen funü yanjiu* 唐代宦門婦女研究. Taipei: Wenjin, 2006.

Chang Chun 常春. "Tangdai gongzhu shufa yishu guankui" 唐代公主書法藝術管窺. *Shaanxi Shifan Daxue xuebao* 陝西師範大學學報 42, no. 3 (2013): 91–96.

———. "Tangdai nüguan, mingji shufa" 唐代女冠, 名妓書法. *Zhongguo shuhuajia* 中國書畫家 3 (2014): 110–12.

Chang, Kang-I Sun, and Haun Saussy, eds. *Women Writers of Traditional China: An Anthology of Poetry and Criticism*. Stanford: Stanford University Press, 1999.

Chen Anli 陳安利. *Gaogui de zangyi: Tangdai huangling yu huangqin guoqi mu* 高貴的葬儀: 唐代皇陵與皇親國戚墓. Chengdu: Sichuan jiaoyu, 1998.

Chen, BuYun. "Dressing for the Times: Fashion in Tang Dynasty China." Columbia University, PhD diss., 2016.

Chen Dawei 陳大為. "Dunhuang sengsi yu nisi zhi jiang de wanglai guanxi" 敦煌僧寺與尼寺之間的往來關係. *Dunhuang yanjiu* 敦煌研究 3 (2010): 36–90.

Chen Dongyuan 陳東原. *Zhongguo funü shenghuo shi* 中國婦女生活史. Shanghai: Shangwu Yinshuguan, 1937.

Chen, Fan-Pen. "Problems of Chinese Historiography as Seen in the Official Records on Yang Kuei-fei." *T'ang Studies* 8–9 (1990–1991): 83–96.

Chen Han 陳寒 and Qu Min 屈敏. "Luexi Tangdai gongzhu de hunyin jiating guanxi" 略析唐代公主的婚姻家庭關係. *Zhanjiang Shifan Xueyuan xuebao* 湛江師範學院學報 2 (2006): 93–97.

Chen, Jack W. "Introduction." In *Idle Talk: Gossip and Anecdote in Traditional China*, edited by Jack W. Chen and David Schaberg, 1–16. Berkeley: Global, Area, and International Archive and University of California Press, 2014.

Chen, Jinhua. "A Daoist Princess and a Buddhist Temple: A New Theory on the Causes of the Canon-Delivering Mission Originally Proposed by Princess Jinxian (689–732) in 730." *Bulletin of the School of Oriental and African Studies* 69, no. 2 (2006): 267–92.

———. "Family Ties and Buddhist Nuns in Tang China: Two Studies." *Asia Major* (third series) 15, no. 2 (2002): 51–85.

———. "Fazang (643–712) the Holy Man." *Journal of the International Association of Buddhist Studies* 28, no. 1 (2008): 11–84.

———. "Fazang (643–712) and Wuzhensi: With a Special Reference to His Daoist Ties." *Journal of the Royal Asiatic Society* (third series) 16, no. 2 (2006): 179–97.

———. "More than a Philosopher: Fazang (643–712) as a Politician and Miracle Worker." *History of Religions* 42, no. 4 (2003): 320–58.

———. "Śarīra and Scepter: Empress Wu's Political Use of Buddhist Relics." *Journal of the International Association of Buddhist Studies* 25, nos. 1–2 (2002): 33–150.

Chen, Kenneth K. S. "The Role of Buddhist Monasteries in T'ang Society." *History of Religions* 15, no. 3 (1976): 209–30.

Chen Li 陳麗. "Tangdai Dunhuang funü hunyin shenghuo tanwei" 唐代敦煌婦女婚姻生活探微. *Dunhuang yanjiu* 敦煌研究 5 (2004): 44–51.

Chen Li 陳麗 and Kang Linyi 康林益. "Tangdai funü lihun gaijia shijian de chayixing fenxi" 唐代婦女離婚改嫁實踐的差異性分析. *Hebei Shifan Daxue xuebao* 河北師範大學學報 2 (2007): 105–8.

Chen Liping 陳麗萍. "Tang Song shiqi Dunhuang diqi feizhengshi hunyin zinü xianxiang luekao" 唐宋時期敦煌地區非正式婚姻子女現象略考. *Dunhuang yanjiu* 敦煌研究 4 (2006): 54–61.

———. "*Zizhi tongjian* Tangdai houfei jishi xianyi" 資治通鑑唐代后妃記事獻疑." *Sui Tang Liao Song Jin Yuan shi luncong* 隋唐遼宋金元史論叢 2 (2012): 179–86.

Chen Lishan 陳麗珊. "Ershiwushi lienüzhuan leishi" 二十五史列女傳類釋. *Daren xuebao* 大仁學報 14 (1996): 135–54.

Chen Ruoshui 陳弱水. "Shitan Tangdai funü yu benjia de guanxi" 試探唐代婦女與本家的關係. *Zhongyang Yanjiuyuan Lishi Yuyan Yanjiusuo jikan* 中央研究院歷史語言研究所集刊 3 (1997): 167–248.

———. *Tangdai de funü wenhua yu jiating shenghuo* 唐代的婦女文化與家庭生活. Taipei: Yunchen wenhua, 2007.

———. "Tangdai de yifuduoqi hezang yu fuqi guanxi—cong Jingyun ernian 'Yang Fu Jun furen Weishi muzhiming' tanqi" 唐代的一夫多妻合葬與夫妻關係—從景雲二年 '楊府君夫人韋氏墓誌銘' 談起. *Zhonghua wenshi luncong* 中華文史論叢 1 (2006): 173–202.

———. *Yinbi de guangjing: Tangdai de funü wenhua yu jiating shenghuo* 隱蔽的光景: 唐代的婦女文化與家庭生活. Guangxi Shifan Daxue chubanshe, 2009.

Chen, Sanping. "'Age Inflation and Deflation' in Medieval China." *Journal of the American Oriental Society* 133, no. 3 (2013): 527–33.

———. *Multicultural China in the Early Middle Ages*. Philadelphia: University of Pennsylvania Press, 2012.

———. "Succession Struggles and the Ethnic Identity of the Tang Imperial House." *Journal of the Royal Asiatic Society*, third series, 6, no. 3 (1996): 379–405.

Chen Wu 陳武 and Wang Wenhua 王文化. "Tangdai nüshiren Xue Tao shige zhong de 'nanxinghua' biaoxian" 唐代女詩人薛濤詩歌中的 '男性化' 表現. *Lantai shijie* 蘭台世界 10 (2015): 122–23.

Chen Zhizhuo 陳之卓. "Bai Juyi lianai shiyi yu Tangdai hunyinzhi" 白居易戀愛事遺與唐代婚姻制. *Nei Menggu Dianda xuebao* 內蒙古電大學報 4 (1994): 5–10, 25.

Chia, Ning. "Women in China's Frontier Politics: *Heqin*." In *Presence and Presentation: Women in the Chinese Literati Tradition*, edited by Sherry J. Mou, 39–75. New York: St. Martin's Press, 1999.

Chiang, Sing-chen Lydia. "Daoist Transcendence and Tang Literati Identities in 'Records of Mysterious Anomalies' by Niu Sengru (780–848)." *Chinese Literature (CLEAR)* 29 (2007): 1–21.

Chiu-Duke, Josephine. "Mothers and the Well-Being of the State in Tang China." *Nan Nü* 8, no. 1 (2006): 55–114.

———. "The Role of Confucian Revivalists in the Confucianization of Tang Women." *Asia Major* 8 (1995): 51–93.

Cho, Kyo. *The Search for Beautiful Women: A Cultural History of Japanese and Chinese Beauty*. Translated by Kyoto Selden. Lanham, MD: Rowman & Littlefield, 2012.

Chong, Key Ray. *Cannibalism in China*. Wakefield, NH: Longwood Academic, 1990.

Chow, Bannie, and Thomas Cleary, trans. *Autumn Willows: Poetry by Women of China's Golden Age*. Ashland, OR: Story Line Press, 2003.

Cole, Alan. *Mothers and Sons in Chinese Buddhism*. Stanford: Stanford University Press, 1998.

Cong Shuguang 叢曙光. "Tangdai hunyin leixing qianxi" 唐代婚姻類型淺析. *Shandong Shifan Daxue xuebao* 山東師範大學學報 49, no. 4 (2004): 101–3.

Cui Dequan 崔德全. "Tangdai funü dui rujia jiaoyi de rentong yu fanpan" 唐代婦女對儒教教義的認同與反叛. *Qingnian zuojia* 青年作家 12 (2010): 18–20.

Cui Guijin 崔桂金. "Tangdai pinnü nanjia xianxiang tanxi" 唐代貧女難嫁現象探析. *Ningbo Daxue xuebao* 寧波大學學報 27, no. 6 (2014): 61–66.

Cui Li 崔麗. "Qianlun *Nü lunyu* zhong de fojiao secai" 淺論 '女論語' 中的佛教色彩. *Wutaishan yanjiu* 五台山研究 2 (2006): 12–17.

Cui Xiaoli 崔曉莉. "Cong Tangdai wenxian kan Tangdai shangfu de shenghuo" 從唐代文獻看唐代商婦的生活. *Anhui wenxue* 安徽文學 1 (2010): 144–45.

Davis, D. L., and R. G. Whitten. "The Cross-Cultural Study of Human Sexuality." *Annual Review of Anthropology* 16 (1987): 69–98.

Davis, Richard L. "Chaste and Filial Women in Chinese Historical Writings of the Eleventh Century." *Journal of the American Oriental Society* 121, no. 2 (2001): 204–18.

———. *From Warhorses to Ploughshares: The Later Tang Reign of Emperor Mingzong.* Hong Kong: Hong Kong University Press, 2014.

de la Vaissière, Étienne, and Éric Trombert. "Des Chinois et des Hu: Migrations et Intégration des Iraniens Orientaux en Milieu Chinois durant le Haut Moyen Âge." *Annales: Histoire, Sciences Sociales* 59, nos. 5/6 (2004): 931–69.

de Pee, Christian. *The Writing of Weddings in Middle-Period China: Text and Ritual Practice in the Eighth through Fourteenth Centuries.* Albany: State University of New York Press, 2007.

Deng Tiankai 鄧天開. "Bianxi Tangdai de 'yi pang wei mei'—Tangdai nüxing shenmei de yanbian ji qi yuanyin" 辨析唐代的 '以胖為美'—唐代女性審美的演變及其原因. *Xi'an shehui kexue* 西安社會科學 28, no. 6 (2010): 94–95, 133.

Deng Xiaonan. "Women in Turfan during the Sixth to Eighth Centuries: A Look at Their Activities Outside the Home." *Journal of Asian Studies* 58, no. 1 (1999): 85–103.

Denzin, Norman K. *Interpretive Biography.* London: Sage, 1989.

des Rotors, Robert. *Courtesanes Chinoises a la fin des T'ang entre circa 789 et le 8 Janvier 881, Pei-li Tche (Anecdotes du Quartier du Nord) par Souen K'i.* Paris: Presses Universitaires de France, 1968.

Despeux, Catherine. "L'ordination des femmes Taoistes sous les T'ang." *Études chinoises* 5, no. 1 (1986): 53–100.

———. "Women in Taoism." In *The Routledge Encyclopedia of Taoism, Volume I: A–L,* edited by Fabrizio Pregadio, 171–73. London: Routledge, 2008.

Despeux, Catherine, and Livia Kohn. *Women in Daoism.* Cambridge, MA: Three Pines Press, 2003.

DiFonzo, Nicholas, and Prashant Bordia. *Rumor Psychology: Social and Organizational Approaches.* Washington, DC: American Psychological Association, 2007.

Dong, Lorraine. "The Many Faces of Cui Yingying." In *Women in China: Current Directions in Historical Scholarship,* edited by Richard W. Guisso and Stanley Johannesen, 75–98. Youngstown, NY: Philo Press, 1981.

Doran, Rebecca. "The Cat Demon, Gender, and Religious Practice: Towards Reconstructing a Medieval Chinese Cultural Pattern." *Journal of the American Oriental Society* 135, no. 4 (2015): 689–707.

———. "Royal Wet Nurses in Seventh- and Early Eighth-Century China: Historiographical Evaluation and Narrative Construction." *Nan Nü* 20 (2018): 198–224.

———. *Transgressive Typologies: Constructions of Gender and Power in Early Tang China.* Cambridge, MA: Harvard University Asia Center, 2016.

Drompp, Michael R. "From Qatar to Refugee: The Taiping Princess among the Uighurs." In *The Role of Women in the Altaic World*, edited by Veronica Veit, 57–68. Wiesbaden: Harrassowitz Verlag, 2007.

———. *Tang China and the Collapse of the Uighur Empire: A Documentary History.* Leiden: Brill, 2005.

Duan Tali 段塔麗. "Beichao zhi Sui Tang shiqi nüxing canzheng xianxiang toushi" 北朝至隋唐時期女性參政現象透視. *Jianghai xuekan* 江海學刊 5 (2001): 111–16.

———. "Cong fuqi guanxi kan Tangdai funü jiating diwei de bianhua" 從夫妻關係看唐代婦女家庭地位的變化. *Lanzhou Daxue xuebao* 蘭州大學學報 29, no. 6 (2001): 53–58.

———. "Lun Tangdai fojiao de shisuhua ji dui nüxing hunyin jiatingguan de yingxiang" 論唐代佛教的世俗化及對女性婚姻家庭觀的影響. *Shaanxi Shifan Daxue xuebao* 陝西師範大學學報 1 (2010): 76–83.

———. *Tangdai funü diwei yanjiu* 唐代婦女地位研究. Beijing: Renmin, 2000.

———. "Tangdai minjian fojiao shenqi xinyang zhong de nüxing juese yu diwei." 唐代民間佛教神祇信仰中的女性角色與地位. *Shaanxi Shifan Daxue xuebao* 陝西師範大學學報 40, no. 4 (2011): 114–20.

———. "Tangdai nüxing jiating jiaose ji qi diwei" 唐代女性家庭角色及其地位. *Zhongguo wenhua yanjiu* 中國文化研究 (2002): 141–49.

Dunhuang Yanjiuyuan Wenxian Yanjiusuo 敦煌研究院文獻研究所, ed. *Dunhuang yueji* 敦煌樂伎. Lanzhou: Ganxu renmin, 1995.

Earle, Timothy, and Kristian Kristiansen. "Introduction: Theory and Practice in the Late Prehistory of Europe." In *Organizing Bronze Age Societies: The Mediterranean, Central Europe, and Scandinavia Compared*, edited by Timothy Earle and Kristian Kristiansen, 1–33. Cambridge: Cambridge University Press, 2010.

Ebrey, Patricia Buckley. "The Book of Filial Piety for Women Attributed to a Woman Née Zheng (ca. 730)." In *Under Confucian Eyes: Writings on Gender in Chinese History*, edited by Susan Mann and Yu-yin Cheng, 47–69. Berkeley: University of California Press, 2001.

———. "Rethinking the Imperial Harem: Why Were There So Many Palace Women?" In *Women and the Family in Chinese History*, edited by Patricia Buckley Ebrey, 177–93. London: Routledge, 2003.

———. "Shifts in Marriage Finance from the Sixth to the Thirteenth Century." In *Women and the Family in Chinese History*, edited by Patricia Buckley Ebrey, 97–132. London: Routledge, 2003.

Eisenberg, Andrew. "Emperor Gaozong, the Rise of Wu Zetian, and Factional Politics in the Early Tang." *Tang Studies* 30 (2012): 45–69.

Esposito, Monica. "Doumu: Mother of the Dipper." In *The Routledge Encyclopedia of Taoism, Volume I: A–L*, edited by Fabrizio Pregadio, 382–83. London: Routledge, 2008.

Fan Jinshi 樊錦詩. *Dunhuang yu Sui Tang chengshi wenming* 敦煌與隋唐城市文明. Shanghai: Shanghai jiaoyu, 2010.

Fan Wenhui 范文慧. "Tangdai huangjia nüzi cujudui" 唐代皇家女子蹴鞠隊. *Lantai shijie* 蘭台世界 9 (2014): 117–18.

Fei Sheng 費省. *Tangdai renkou dili* 唐代人口地理. Xi'an: Xibei Daxue chubanshe, 1996.

Filip, Sonja, and Alexandra Hilgner, eds. *The Lady with the Phoenix Crown: Tang-Period Grave Goods of the Noblewoman Li Chui (711–736)*. Regensburg and Mainz, Germany: Schnell and Steiner, 2014.

Fitzgerald, C. P. "The Chinese Middle Ages in Communist Historiography." *China Quarterly* 23 (1965): 106–21.

———. *The Empress Wu*. Melbourne: F. W. Cheshire for the Australian National University, 1968.

Flannery, Kent, and Joyce Marcus. *The Creation of Inequality: How Our Prehistoric Ancestors Set the Stage for Monarchy, Slavery, and Empire*. Cambridge, MA: Harvard University Press, 2012.

Fong, Mary H. "Four Chinese Tombs of the Early Eighth Century." *Artibus Asiae* 35, no. 4 (1973): 307–34.

———. "Images of Women in Traditional Chinese Painting." *Women's Art Journal* 7, no. 1 (1996): 22–27.

———. "Tang Tomb Murals Reviewed in the Light of Tang Texts on Painting." *Artibus Asiae* 45, no. 1 (1984): 35–72.

Forte, Antonino. *Mingtang and Buddhist Utopias in the History of the Astronomical Clock: Statue and Armillary Sphere Constructed by Empress Wu*. Rome: Instituto Italiano per il Medio ed Estremo Oriente, 1988.

Furth, Charlotte. *A Flourishing Yin: Gender in China's Medical History, 960–1665*. Berkeley: University of California Press, 1999.

Gao Guofan 高國藩. "Dunhuang ben Qin Hu gushi yanjiu" 敦煌本秋胡故事研究. *Dunhua yanjiu* 敦煌研究 1 (1986): 77–89.

———. *Zhongguo gusu tanwei—Dunhuang wushu yu wushu liubian* 中國民俗探微—敦煌巫術與巫術流變. Nanjing: Hehai Daxue chubanshe, 1993.

Gao Lihua 高利華. "Daojiao yu shijiao jiafeng zhong de qipa—lun Tangdai nüguan shifen" 道教與詩教夾縫中的奇葩—論唐代女冠詩人. In *Tangdai wenxue yanjiu* 6 唐代文學研究, edited by Fu Xuancong 傅璇琮, 75–87. Guilin: Guangxi Shifan Daxue chubanshe, 1996.

Gao Qi'an 高啟安 and Zhao Hong 趙紅. "Dunhuang 'yunü' kaoxie" 敦煌 '玉女' 考屑. *Dunhuang yanjiu* 敦煌研究 2 (2005): 68–73.

Gao Shiyu 高世瑜. "Songshi jiemei yu 'Nü lunyu' lunxi—jian ji gudai nüjiao de pingminhua qushi" 宋氏姐妹與 '女論語' 論析—兼及古代女教的平民化趨勢. In *Tang Song nüxing yu shehui* 唐宋女性與社會, edited by Deng Xiaonan 鄧小南, 1:127–57. Shanghai: Shanghai cishu, 2003.

———. *Tangdai funü* 唐代婦女. Xi'an: Sanqin, 1988.

Georgieva, Valentina. "Representation of Buddhist Nuns in Chinese Edifying Miracle Tales during the Six Dynasties and the Tang." *Journal of Chinese Religions* 24 (1996): 47–96.

Goldin, Paul R. "On the Meaning of the Name Xi wangmu, Spirit-Mother of the West." *Journal of the American Oriental Society* 122, no. 1 (2002): 83–85.

———. "Women and Moral Dilemmas in Early Chinese Narrative." In *The Bloomsbury Research Handbook of Chinese Philosophy and Gender*, edited by Ann A. Pang-White, 25–35. New York: Bloomsbury, 2016.

Grafflin, Dennis. "The Great Family in Medieval South China." *Harvard Journal of Asiatic Studies* 41, no. 1 (1981): 65–74.

Granet, Marcel. *La polygynie sororale et le sororat dans la Chine féodale*. Paris: Editions Ernest Leroux, 1920.

Gu Lihua 顧麗華. *Handai funü shenghuo qingkuang* 漢代婦女生活情況. Beijing: Shehui kexue wenxian, 2012.

Guan Siping 關四平. "Shihuan jiding yu qinggan zhuiqiu de maodun—Tangdai difei guanxi xiaoshuo de wenhua jiedu" 仕宦極頂與情感追求的矛盾—唐代帝妃關係小說的文化解讀. *Shenyang Shifan Daxue xuebao* 瀋陽師範大學學報 3 (2010): 6–10.

———. "Tangdai rengui hunlian xiaoshuo xinlun" 唐代人鬼婚戀小說新論. *Xueshu jiaoliu* 學術交流 1 (2012): 149–56.

Guisso, Richard W. *Wu Tse-t'ien and the Politics of Legitimation in T'ang China*. Bellingham: Western Washington University Press, 1978.

Guo Feng 郭鋒. *Tangdai shizu gean yanjiu: yi Wu jun, Qinghe, Fanyang Dunhuang Zhang shi wei zhongxin* 唐代士族個案研究: 以吳郡, 清河, 范陽, 敦煌張氏為中心. Xiamen: Xiamen Daxue chubanshe, 1999.

Guo Haiwen 郭海文. "Lun Tangdai gongzhu de hunyin xingtai" 論唐代公主的婚姻型態. *Xibei Shida xuebao* 西北師大學報 49, no. 2 (2012): 89–94.

———. "Tangdai gongting nüxing zhishifenzi qinghuai—Tang Taizong xianfei Xu Hui shiwen zhi fenxi" 唐代宮廷女性知識分子情懷—唐太宗賢妃徐惠詩文之分析. *Henan Shifan Daxue xuebao* 河南師範大學學報 39, no. 4 (2012): 147–51.

———. "Tangdai gongzhu de hunyin liyi" 唐代公主的婚姻禮儀. *Shehui kexue pinglun* 社會科學評論 3 (2009): 85–93.

———. "Tangdai gongzhu de jiating shenghuo" 唐代公主的家庭生活. *Shaanxi Shifan Daxue xuebao* 陝西師範大學學報 40, no. 2 (2011): 71–78.

———. "Tangdai gongzhu jieli nianling kao—yi muzhi wei zhongxin" 唐代公主結縭年齡考—以墓誌為中心. *Beilin jikan* 碑林集刊 19 (2013): 186–200.

Guo Haiwen 郭海文, Zhao Wenduo 趙文朵, and Jia Qiangqiang 賈強強. "Tangdai gongzhu jiaoyu zinü wenti zhitan" 唐代公主教育子女問題摭談. *Ganling wenhua yanjiu* 乾陵文化研究 9 (2015): 253–78.

———. "Tangdai gongzhu zinü kao" 唐代公主子女考. *Beilin jikan* 碑林集刊 20 (2014): 172–89.

Guo Li 郭麗. "Tangdai nüjiaoshu *Nü lunyu* xiangguan wenti kaolun" 唐代女教書'女論語' 相關問題考論. *Henan Shifan Daxue xuebao* 河南師範大學學報 1 (2011): 148–51.

———. "Tangdai 'yi pang wei mei' zhi nüxing shenmeiguan yanbian kaolun" 唐代'以胖為美' 之女性審美觀演變考論. *Leshan Shifan Xueyuan xuebao* 樂山師範學院學報 24, no. 10 (2009): 7–10.

Habakkuk, H. J. "Family Structure and Economic Change in Nineteenth Century Europe." *Journal of Economic History* 15, no. 1 (1955): 1–12.

Hales, Dell R. "Dreams and the Daemonic in Traditional Chinese Short Stories." In *Critical Essays on Chinese Literature*, edited by William H. Nienhauser et al., 71–87. Hong Kong: Chinese University of Hong Kong, 1976.

Han Lankui 韓蘭魁, ed. *Dunhuang yuewu yanjiu wenji* 敦煌樂舞研究文集. Beijing: Wenhua yishu, 2014.

Han Lin 韓林. "Ming Qing xushi wenxue zhong Wu Zetian de mingjun xingxiang yu nüxing xintai" 明清敘事文學中武則天的明君形象與女性心態. *Wuyi Daxue xuebao* 五邑大學學報 17, no. 4 (2015): 32–35.

———. "Wu Zetian gushi de wenben yanbian yu wenhua neihan" 武則天故事的文本演變與文化內涵. PhD diss., Nankai University, 2012.

Han Yu 韓瑜. "Tangdai rengui xianglian gushi de jizhong moshi" 唐代人鬼相戀故事的機種模式. *Hunan Nongye Daxue xuebao* 湖南農業大學學報 12, no. 2 (2011): 77–81.

Hao Chunwen 郝春文. *Tang houqi wudai Song chu Dunhuang sengni de shehui shenghuo* 唐後期五代宋初敦煌僧尼的社會生活. Beijing: Zhongguo shehui kexue, 1998.

———. "Zai lun beichao zhi Sui Tang wudai Songchu de nüren jieshe" 再論北朝至隋唐五代宋初的女人結社. *Dunhuang yanjiu* 敦煌研究 6 (2006): 103–8.

Harada Yoshito 原田淑人. *Tōdai no fukushoku* 唐代の服飾. Tokyo: Tōyō bunko, 1970.

Harper, Donald. "La littérature sur la sexualité à Dunhuang." In *Médecine, religion, et société dans la Chine médiévale: Étude de manuscrits chinois de Dunhuang et de Turfan*, edited by Catherine Despeux, 2:871–98. Paris: Collège de France, Institut des Hautes Études Chinoises, 2010.

Hayashi Kenichiro 林謙一郎. "Nanshō ōken no kakuritsu, henshitsu to Tō, Toban kankei—washin (kōshu kōka) no imi suru mono" 南詔王權の確立・變質と唐・吐蕃關係—和親 (公主降嫁) の意味するもの. *Tōdaishi kenkyū* 唐代史研究 12 (2009): 57–87.

He Jianguo 何建國, Zhang Yanying 張艷鶯, and Guo Youmin 郭佑民. *Tangdai funü faji* 唐代婦女髮髻. Hong Kong: Hair & Beauty, 1987.

Herzfeld, Michael. "Honour and Shame: Problems in the Comparative Analysis of Moral Systems." *Man* 15 (1980): 339–51.

Hierman, Ann. "Buddhist Nuns Through the Eyes of Leading Early Tang Masters." *Chinese Historical Review* 22, no. 1 (2015): 31–51.

Hightower, James R. "Yüan Chen and 'The Story of Ying-Ying." *Harvard Journal of Asiatic Studies* 33 (1973): 90–123.

Hinsch, Bret. "The Criticism of Powerful Women by Western Han Dynasty Portent Experts." *Journal of the Economic and Social History of the Orient* 49, no. 1 (2006): 96–121.

———. "The Origins of Han-Dynasty Consort Kin Power." *East Asian History* 25/26 (2003): 1–24.

———. "Textiles and Female Virtue in Early Imperial Chinese Historical Writing." *Nan Nü* 5, no. 12 (2003): 170–202.

Hirata Yoichiro 平田陽一郎. "Shū Zui kakumei to Tokketsu jōsei—Kita Shū Senkin kōshu no kōka o chūshin ni" 周隨革命と突厥情勢—北周·千金公主の降嫁を中心に. *Tōdaishi kenkyū* 唐代史研究 12 (2009): 27–56.

Ho, Norman P. "Law, Literature, and Gender in Tang China: An Exploration of Bai Juyi's Selected Panwen on Women." *Tsinghua China Law Review* 1 (2009): 62–91.

Holmgren, Jennifer. "A Question of Strength: Military Capacity and Princess Bestowal in Imperial China's Foreign Relations (Han to Ch'ing)." *Monumenta Serica* 39 (1990–1991): 31–85.

———. "The Economic Foundations of Virtue: Widow-Remarriage in Early and Modern China." *Australian Journal of Chinese Affairs* 13 (1985): 1–27.

———. "Imperial Marriage in the Native Chinese and Non-Han State, Han to Ming." In *Marriage and Inequality in Chinese Society*, edited by Rubie S. Watson and Patricia Buckley Ebrey, 58–96. Berkeley: University of California Press, 1991.

———. "Widow Chastity in the Northern Dynasties: The Lieh-nu Biographies in the Wei-shu." *Papers on Far Eastern History* 23 (1981): 165–86.

Hong Shuhua 洪樹華. "Lun Tangdai xiaoshuo zhong de ren hu hunlian yuhe ji qi xingcheng yinsu" 論唐代小說中的人狐婚戀遇合及其形成因素. In *Tangdai wenxue yanjiu 15* 唐代文學研究 15, edited by Zhongguo Tangdai wenxue xuehui 中國唐代文學學會 et al., 272–85. Guilin: Guangxi Shifan Daxue chubanshe, 2014.

Howard, Angela F. "Buddhist Sculpture of Pujiang, Sichuan: A Mirror of the Direct Link between Southwest China and India in the High Tang." *Archives of Asian Art* 42 (1989): 49–61.

Hsieh, Daniel. *Love and Women in Early Chinese Fiction*. Hong Kong: Chinese University Press, 2008.

Hu Ji 胡戟. "Tangdai jiali shulun" 唐代家禮述論. In *Diwujie Tangdai wenhua xueshu yantaohui lunwenji* 第五屆唐代文化學術研討會論文集, edited by Zhongguo Tangdai xuehui 中國唐代學會 et al., 561–73. Kaohsiung: Liwen wenhua, 2001.

Hu Jing 胡璟 and Di Xiaoping 邸小平. "Tangdai nüshen nüxian xiaoshuo ji qi shisuhua qingxiang yanjiu" 唐代女神女仙小說及其世俗化傾向研究. *Yindu xuekan* 殷都學刊 2 (2008): 57–61.

Hu Na 胡娜. "Tangdai nüzi zhuban fumu sangzang xianxiang kaolue" 唐代女子主辦父母喪葬現象考略. *Guangdong Jishu Shifan Xueyuan xuebao* 廣東技術師範學院學報 9 (2014): 58–64.

Hu Rong 胡蓉. "Cong Tangshi kan Tangdai funü de hunyin zhuangkuang" 從唐詩看唐代婦女的婚姻狀況. *Xingtai Xueyuan xuebao* 邢台學院學報 18, no. 2 (2003): 19–23.

Hu Yulan 胡玉蘭. "Tangdai wanggu gongnü muzhi mingwen de wenhua yiwen" 唐代亡故宮女墓誌銘文的文化意蘊. *Haerbin Gongye Daxue xuebao* 哈爾濱工業大學學報 5 (2006): 136–39.

Hu Yunwei 胡雲薇. "Tangdai de jimu zi guanxi—yi Wang Wan, Wei Chengqing wei zhongxin" 唐代的繼母子關係—以王婉, 韋承慶為中心. *Zaoqi Zhongguo shi yanjiu* 早期中國史研究 6, no. 1 (2014): 79–112.

Hu-Sterk, Florence. "Les 'poèmes de lamentation du palais' sou les Tang: La vie recluse des dames de la Cour." *Études chinoises* 11, no. 2 (1992): 7–33.

Hua Shikui 華士奎 and Luo Shijin 羅時進. "Tangdai gongyuan shi fanrong yuanyin tanlun" 唐代宮怨詩繁榮原因探論. *Shenzhen Daxue xuebao* 深圳大學學報 25, no. 6 (2008): 104–8.

Huang Cheng 黃誠. "'Pozi shuochan' yu nüzi foxing yishi de juexing—cong chanzong luyu kan Tangdai nüxing 'cheng fo zuo zu' de zongjiao xingxiang ji qi lishi yihan" '婆子說禪' 與女子佛性意識的覺醒—從禪宗語錄看唐代女性 '成佛作祖' 的宗教形象及其歷史意涵. *Xuehai* 學海 6 (2010): 121–25.

Huang Jianqin 黃健琴. "Tangdai biqiuni chujia de jingji yuanyin tanxi" 唐代比丘尼出家的經濟原因探析. *Chifeng Xueyuan xuebao* 赤峰學院學報 33, no. 6 (2012): 19–20.

Huang Jun 黃均. *Shinühua de yanjiu yu jifa* 仕女畫的研究與技法. Beijing: Beijing gongyi meishu, 1995.

Huang Meiyin 黃玫茵. "Tangdai sanfu bamu de falü diwei" 唐代三父八母的法律地位. In *Tangdai shenfen fazhi yanjiu—yi Tanglü minglilü wei zhongxin* 唐代身分法制研究—以唐律名例律為中心, edited by Gao Mingshi 高明士, 89–117. Taipei: Wunan tushu, 2003.

Huang Peijie 黃培杰. *Tangdai gongbi shinü yanjiu* 唐代工筆仕女畫研究. Tianjin: Renmin meishu, 2007.

Huang Yanli 黃嫣梨. "'Nü xiaojing' yu 'Nü lunyu'" 女孝經與女論語. In *Tang Song nüxing yu shehui* 唐宋女性與社會, edited by Deng Xiaonan 鄧小南, 1:188–208. Shanghai: Shanghai cishu, 2003.

Huang Yunzhu 黃芸珠. "Tangdai nüxing yu wenxue de xiangguanxing yanjiu" 唐代女性與文學的相關性研究. PhD diss., Shaanxi Normal University, 2003.

Huang Zhengjian 黃正建. "Tangdai 'biezhaofu' xianxiang xiaokao" 唐代 '別宅婦' 現象小考. In *Tang Song nüxing yu shehui* 唐宋女性與社會, edited by Deng Xiaonan 鄧小南, 1:252–62. Shanghai: Shanghai cishu, 2003.

Hughes, Diane Owen. "From Brideprice to Dowry in Mediterranean Europe." *Journal of Family History* 3, no. 3 (1978): 262–98.

Ikeda On. "T'ang Household Registers and Related Documents." In *Perspectives on the T'ang*, edited by Arthur F. Wright and Denis Twitchett, 121–50. New Haven: Yale University Press, 1973.

Irvine, Judith T., and Susan Gal. "Language Ideology and Linguistic Differentiation." In *Linguistic Anthropology: A Reader*, second edition, edited by Alessandro Duranti, 402–34. Chichester, UK: Wiley-Blackwell, 2009.

Jay, Jennifer W. "Imagining Matriarchy: 'Kingdoms of Women' in Tang China." *Journal of the American Oriental Society* 116, no. 2 (1996): 220–29.

Ji Qingyang 季慶陽. "Shilun Tangdai de 'xiaozhi'" 試論唐代的 "孝治." *Ningxia Daxue xuebao* 寧夏大學學報 1 (2009): 74–78.

Jia, Jinhua. "Gender and Early Chinese Cosmology Revisited." *Asian Philosophy* 26, no. 4 (2016): 281–93.

———. "Longevity Technique and Medical Theory: The Legacy of the Tang Daoist Priestess-Physician Hu Yin." *Monumenta Serica* 63, no. 1 (2015): 1–31.

———. "Religious and Other Experiences of Daoist Priestesses in Tang China." *T'oung Pao* 102, no. 4 (2016): 321–57.

———. "The *Yaochi ji* and Three Daoist Priestess-Poets in Tang China." *Nan Nü* 13, no. 2 (2011): 205–43.

———. "The *Yaochi ji* and Three Daoist Priestesses." In *Gendering Chinese Religion: Subject, Identity, and Body*, edited by Jinhua Jia et al., 103–32. Albany: State University of New York Press, 2014.

Jia Man 賈嫚. *Tangdai Chang'an yuewu yanjiu—yi Xi'an diqu chutu wenwu yuewu tuxiang wei zhongxin* 唐代長安樂舞研究—以西安地區出土文物樂舞圖像為中心. Beijing: Zhongguo shehui kexue, 2014.

Jiang Lin 江林. "*Taiping guangji* zhong suo jian Tangdai hunyin, hunsu luekao" 太平廣記中所見唐代婚禮, 婚俗略考. *Hunan Daxue xuebao* 湖南大學學報 4 (2002): 20–22.

Jiang Weigong 姜維公 and Jiang Weidong 姜維東. "Tangdai gongnü shenghuo shulue" 唐代宮女生活述略. *Shehui kexue zhanxian* 社會科學戰線 3 (2010): 57–63.

Jiao Jie 焦杰. "Cong muzhi kan Tangdai funü chongdao de yuanyin" 從墓志看唐代婦女崇道的原因. *Dongnan wenhua* 東南文化 3 (2008): 41–45.

———. "Cong Tang muzhi kan Tangdai funü yu fojiao de guanxi" 從唐墓誌看唐代婦女與佛教的關係. *Shaanxi Shifan Daxue xuebao* 陝西師範大學學報 29, no. 1 (2000): 95–99.

———. "Fojiao xinyang yu Tangdai nüxing shenghuo xingtai zaitan—yi Tangdai muzhi ziliao wei zhongxin" 佛教信仰與唐代女性生活型態再探—以唐代墓誌資料為中心. *Tangshi luncong* 唐史論叢 20 (2015): 218–32.

———. "'Lienü zhuan' yu Zhou Qin Han Tang fude biaozhun" 列女傳與周秦漢唐婦德標準. *Shaanxi Shifan Daxue xuebao* 陝西師範大學學報 32, no. 6 (2003): 92–98.

———. "Lun Tangdai gongzhu rudao yuanyin yu daoguan shenghuo" 論唐代公主入道原因與道觀生活. *Shijie zongjiao yanjiu* 世界宗教研究 2 (2013): 72–81.

———. "Tangdai biqiuni de zhonglei: shoujie xiye yi ji hongfa huodong" 唐代比丘尼的種類: 受戒習業以及弘法活動. *Xiamen Daxue xuebao* 廈門大學學報 6 (2014): 145–56.

———. "Tangdai daojiao nüxintu de zongjiao huodong ji qi shenghuo—yi muzhi cailiao wei zhongxin" 唐代道教女信徒的宗教活動及其生活—以墓誌材料為中心. *Shaanxi Shifan Daxue xuebao* 陝西師範大學學報 42, no. 2 (2013): 124–29.

———. "Tangdai nüguan shiren Li Ye yu Yu Xuanji bijiao yanjiu" 唐代女冠詩人李冶與魚玄機比較研究. *Guangdong Jishu Shifan Xueyuan xuebao* 廣東技術師範學院學報 10 (2014): 1–6.

———. "Xiannü xiafan—jituo Tangdai nanzi lixiang de wenhua xianxiang" 仙女下凡—寄託唐代男子理想的文化現象. *Lishi yuekan* 歷史月刊 4 (1999): 122–26.

Jiao Jie 焦杰 and Hu Na 胡娜. "Tangdai shidaifu zhi jia zaishinü de jiating diwei—yi Tangdai zaishinü muzhi wei zhongxin" 唐代士大夫之家在室女的家庭地位—以唐代在室女墓誌為中心. *Hua'nan Shifan Daxue xuebao* 華南師範大學學報 6 (2012): 95–101.

Jiao Jie 焦杰 and Sun Hua 孫華. "Tangdai Wenan Gongzhu zakao" 唐代文安公主雜考. *Pingdingshan Xueyuan xuebao* 平頂山學院學報 31, no. 3 (2016): 75–77.

Jiao Jie 焦杰 and Zhang Lanhui 張蘭惠. "Tangdai Chang'an gongzhu daoguan de kaifa yu liyong" 唐代長安公主道觀的開發與利用. *Tangdu xuekan* 唐都學刊 28, no. 2 (2012): 25–30.

Jin Jinnan 金金南. "Lun Dunhuang ci zhong Tangdai funü de aiqing hunyin" 論敦煌詞中唐代婦女的愛情婚姻. *Tiecheng Shizhuan xuebao* 鐵城師專學報 2 (1995): 30–34.

Jin Mei 金眉. "Tangdai hunyin jiating jicheng falü zhidu chulun" 唐代婚姻家庭繼承法律制度初論. PhD diss., China University of Political Science and Law, 2000.

Jin Xia 金霞. "Qianlun Tangdai houqi hunyin de tedian" 淺論唐代後期婚姻的特點. *Shandong Jiaoyu Xueyuan xuebao* 山東教育學院學報 3 (2002): 46–48, 51.

Jing Jing 井精. "Shijing zhong meiren guannian dui Zhongguo shinühua de yingxiang" 詩經中美人觀念對中國仕女畫的影響. *Yishu baijia* 藝術百家 7 (2011): 223–25.

Johnson, Wallace. *The T'ang Code, Volume I, General Principles*. Princeton: Princeton University Press, 1979.

Joyce, Rosemary A. "Archaeology of the Body." *Annual Review of Anthropology* 34 (2005): 139–58.

———. "Girling the Girl and Boying the Boy: The Production of Adulthood in Ancient Mesoamerica." *World Archaeology* 31, no. 3 (2000): 473–83.

Kansteiner, Wulf. "Hayden White's Critique of the Writing of History." *History and Theory* 32, no. 3 (1993): 273–95.

Karetzky, Patricia E. "The Representation of Women in Medieval China: Recent Archaeological Evidence." *T'ang Studies* 17 (1999): 213–71.

———. "Wu Zetian and Buddhist Art of the Tang Dynasty." *T'ang Studies* 20–21 (2002–2003): 113–50.

Katsuyama Minoru 騰山稔. *Chūgoku Sō—Min dai ni okeru konin no gakusaiteki kenkyū* 中國宋—明代における婚姻の學際的研究. Tokyo: Tōhoku Daigaku shuppankai, 2007.

Ken Kumiko 筧久美子. "Yi 'nüxingxue' guandian shilun Li Bai Du Fu jinei yinei shi" 以 '女性學' 觀點試論李白杜甫寄內憶內詩. In *Tangdai wenxue yanjiu 3* 唐代文學研究 3, edited by Fu Xuancong 傅璇琮, 254–61. Guilin: Guangxi Shifan Daxue chubanshe, 1992.

Kinney, Anne Behnke. "The Theme of the Precocious Child in Early Chinese Literature." *T'oung Pao* 81 (1995): 1–24.

Kirkland, Russell. "Fangzhong Shu: 'Arts of the Bedchamber'; Sexual Techniques." In *The Routledge Encyclopedia of Taoism, Volume I: A–L*, edited by Fabrizio Pregadio, 409–11. London: Routledge, 2008.

———. "Huang Lingwei ca. 640–721; *hao* Huagu (Flowery Maiden)." In *The Routledge Encyclopedia of Taoism, Volume I: A–L*, edited by Fabrizio Pregadio, 501–2. London: Routledge, 2008.

Kitamura Takashi 來村多加史. *Tōdai kōtei misasagi no kenkyū* 唐代皇帝陵の研究. Tokyo: Gakuseisha, 2001.

Knapp, Keith N. "Chinese Filial Cannibalism: A Silk Road Import?" In *China and Beyond in the Mediaeval Period: Cultural Crossings and Inter-Regional Connec-*

tions, edited by Dorothy C. Wong and Gustav Heldt, 135–49. New Delhi: Manohar Publishers, 2014.

———. "Reverent Caring: The Parent-Son Relationship in Early Medieval Tales of Filial Offspring." In *Filial Piety in Chinese Thought and History*, edited by Alan K. L. Chan and Sor-hoon Tan, 44–70. London: RoutledgeCurzon, 2004.

———. *Selfless Offspring: Filial Children and Social Order in Early Medieval China*. Honolulu: University of Hawaii Press, 2005.

Ko, Dorothy. *Cinderella's Sisters: A Revisionist History of Footbinding*. Berkeley: University of California Press, 2005.

———. "In Search of Footbinding's Origins." In *Tang Song nüxing yu shehui* 唐宋女性與社會, edited by Deng Xiaonan 鄧小南, 1:375–414. Shanghai: Shanghai cishu, 2003.

Kohn, Livia. *Monastic Life in Medieval Daoism: A Cross Cultural Perspective*. Honolulu: University of Hawaii Press, 2003.

Kominami Ichiro 小南一郎. *Tōdai tenki shōsetsu ron—kanashimi to akogare to* 唐代傳奇小說論—悲しみと憧れと. Tokyo: Iwanami, 2014.

Kong Min 孔敏. "Tangdai xiaoshuo nüxing xingxiang dui Ming Qing wenxue zhi yingxiang" 唐代小說女性形象對明清文學之影響. *Mingzuo xinshang* 名作欣賞 2 (2016): 130–33.

Kory, Stephan N. "Presence in Variety: De-Trivializing Female Diviners in Medieval China." *Nan Nü* 18, no. 1 (2016): 3–48.

———. "A Remarkably Resonant and Resilient Tang-Dynasty Augural Stone: Empress Wu's *Baotu*." *T'ang Studies* 26 (2008): 99–124.

Kroll, Paul W. "The Flight from the Capital and the Death of Precious Consort Yang." *T'ang Studies* 3 (1985): 25–53.

———. "The Life and Writings of Xu Hui (627–650), Worthy Consort at the Early Tang Court." *Asia Major*, third series, 22, no. 2 (2009): 35–64.

Kucera, Karil. "Recontextualizing Kanjingsi: Finding Meaning in the Emptiness at Longmen." *Archives of Asian Art* 56 (2006): 61–80.

Kurihara Keisuke 栗原圭介. *Kodai Chūgoku koninsei no rei rinen to keitai* 古代中國婚姻制の禮理念と形態. Tokyo: Tōhō shoten, 1982.

Kuroda Mamiko 黒田真美子. "Riku chō Tōdai ni okeru yūkontan no tōjō jinbutsu—kankontan to no hikaku" 六朝唐代における幽婚譚の登場人物—神婚譚との比較. *Nihon Chūgoku gakukaihou* 日本中国学会報 48 (1996): 119–32.

Lai Jiaqi 賴嘉麒. "Shixi 'Sanshui xiaodu' nüxing beiju renwu (shang)—yi Bu Fei-yan, Lü Qiao, Yu Xuanji wei li" 試析三水小牘女性悲劇人物 (上)—以步飛煙，綠翹，魚玄機為例. *Zhongguo yuwen* 中國語文 6 (1998): 79–86.

Lai Liangjun 賴亮郡. "Cong fangqishu kan Tangdai de heli" 從放妻書看唐代的和離. In *Tanglü yu chuantongfa wenhua* 唐律與傳統法文化, edited by Huang Yuansheng 黃源盛, 221–60. Taipei: Yuanzhao, 2011.

Laing, Ellen Johnston. "Chinese Palace-Style Poetry and the Depiction of a Palace Beauty." *Art Bulletin* 72, no. 2 (1990): 284–95.

Lan Sihua 藍思華. "Qianyi Tangdai juzi beihou nüxing de mingyun" 淺議唐代舉子背后女性的命運. *Guangxi Zhiye Jishu Xueyuan xuebao* 廣西職業技術學院學報 8, no. 1 (2015): 66–69.

Larsen, Jeanne, trans. *Brocade River Poems: Selected Works of the Tang Dynasty Courtesan Xue Tao*. Princeton: Princeton University Press, 1987.

———. *Willow, Wine, Mirror, Moon: Women's Poems from Tang China*. Rochester, NY: BOA Editions, 2005.

Lee, Hui-shu. *Empresses, Art & Agency in Song Dynasty China*. Seattle: University of Washington Press, 2010.

Lee, Jen-der. "Childbirth in Early Imperial China." *Nan Nü* 7, no. 2 (2005): 216–86.

———. "Gender and Medicine in Tang China." *Asia Major* 16, no. 2 (2003): 1–32.

———. "Querelle des femmes? Les femmes jalouses et leur contrôle au début de la Chine médiévale." In *Éducation et Instruction en Chine III. Aux Marges de l'orthodoxie*, edited by Christine Nguyen Tri and Catherine Despeux, 67–97. Paris: Éditions Peeters, 2004.

———. "Women and Marriage in China During the Period of Disunion." PhD diss., University of Washington, 1992.

Lee, Sherman E., and Wai-Kam Ho. "A Colossal Eleven-Faced Kuan-yin of the T'ang Dynasty." *Bulletin of the Cleveland Museum of Art* 47, no. 1 (1960): 3–6.

Lemert, Charles. *Social Things: An Introduction to the Sociological Life*, fourth edition. Lanham, MD: Rowman & Littlefield, 2008.

Levy, Howard S. "The Selection of Yang Kuei-fei." *Oriens* 15 (1962): 411–24.

Lewis, Mark Edward. *China's Cosmopolitan Empire: The Tang Dynasty*. Cambridge, MA: Belknap Press of Harvard University Press, 2009.

Li Chuanjun 李傳軍. "'Fumu enzhong jing' yu Tangdai xiao wenhua—jian tan fojiao Zhongguohua guocheng zhong de 'tong ru' yu 'ji su' xianxiang' 父母恩重經' 與唐代孝文化—兼談佛教中國化過程中的 '通儒' 與 ' 濟俗' 現象. *Kongzi yanjiu* 孔子研究 3 (2008): 90–96.

Li Dongmei 李冬梅. "Cong longnü xingxiang de suzao tan Tangdai hunlian guannian de shenghua" 從龍女形象的塑造談唐代婚戀觀念的昇華. *Qinghai Shizhuan xuebao* 青海師專學報 4 (2008): 40–42.

Li Fengmao 李豐楙. "Tangdai gongzhu rudao yu song gongren rudao shi" 唐代公主入道與送宮人入道詩. In *Diyijie guoji Tangdai xueshu huiyi lunwenji* 第一屆國際唐代學術會議論文集, edited by Diyijie guoji Tangdai xueshui huiyi lunwenji bianji weiyuanhui, 159–90. Taipei: Xuesheng, 1989.

Li Jingying 李晶瑩. "Tangdai gongzhu yu shifeng zhidu" 唐代公主與食封制度. *Shoudu Shifan Daxue xuebao* 首都師範大學學報 2 (2006): 25–28.

Li Jun 李軍. "Zaihai yinsu yu Tangdai chugong renkao" 災害因素與唐代出宮人考. *Zhongguo lishi dili luncong* 中國歷史地理論叢 1 (2007): 90–95, 105.

Li Li 李莉, "Dunhuang ben Qiu Hu gushi jieju tanxi" 敦煌本秋胡故事結局探析. *Gansu Jiaoyu Xueyuan xuebao* 甘肅教育學院學報 19, no. 4 (2003): 5–8.

———. *Shenhua shiyu xia de wenxue jiedu—yi Han Tang wenxue leixinghua yanbian wei zhongxin* 神話視閾下的文學解讀—以漢唐文學類型化演變為中心. Beijing: Zhongguo shehui kexue, 2008.

Li Mei 李玫. "Tangdai funü lüyou de fansheng chengyin ji zhuyao xingshi" 唐代婦女旅遊的繁盛成因及主要形式. *Lantai shijie* 蘭台世界 4 (2015): 90–91.

Li Pei 李裴. "Minjian yu guanfang, zhengzhi yu zongjiao: yi Tangdai nüzhen bairi shengxian xianxiang zhongxin de kaocha" 民間與官方, 政治與宗教: 以唐代女真白日升仙現象中心的考察. *Sichuan Daxue xuebao* 四川大學學報 4 (2011): 25–29.

Li Rui 李睿. "Tangdai Wei shi jiazu hunyin guanxi yanjiu" 唐代韋氏家族婚姻關係研究. *Qianling wenhua yanjiu* 乾陵文化研究 (2007): 262–81.

Li Runqiang 李潤強. "Cong Dunhuang huji wenxian kaocha funü guizong dui Tangdai jiating de yingxiang" 從敦煌戶籍文獻考察婦女歸宗對唐代家庭的影響. *Dunhuang yanjiu* 敦煌研究 1 (2007): 68–72.

Li Shiyu 李詩語. "Tangdai minghun fengsu xinyi" 唐代冥婚風俗新議. *Ganling wenhua yanjiu* 4 乾陵文化研究 (2008): 286–93.

Li Shutong 李樹桐. *Tangshi yanjiu* 唐史研究. Taipei: Zhonghua, 1979.

Li Shuyuan 李淑媛. "Huihun yu jiaqu zhi guanxi" 悔婚與嫁娶之關係. In *Tanglü yu guojia shehui yanjiu* 唐律與國家社會研究, edited by Gao Mingshi 高明士, 317–59. Taipei: Wunan tushu, 1999.

———. *Zhengcai jingchan: Tang Song de jiachan yu falü* 爭財競產: 唐宋的家產與法律. Taipei: Wunan tushu, 2005.

Li Wencai 李文才 and Xie Dan 謝丹. "*Taiping guangji* suo jian Tangdai funü de hunlian shenghuo" 太平廣記所見唐代婦女的婚戀生活. *Jiangsu Keji Daxue xuebao* 江蘇科技大學學報 2 (2007): 69–74.

Li Xia 李霞. "Jianshu Tangdai jiating zhong de saoshu zhi li" 簡述唐代家庭中的嫂叔之禮. *Shaanxi Shifan Daxue xuebao* 陝西師範大學學報 31 (2002): 152–53.

Li Xiaopei 李曉培. *Tangdai rudao nüxing shijie zhong de xingbie yishi yu qingyu* 唐代入道女性世界中的性別意識與情慾. Taoyuan: Shanxi jiaoyu chubanshe, 2011.

Li Xiaoqi 李小奇. "Tangdai shangfu shi chuyi" 唐代商婦詩芻議. *Shaanxi Shifan Daxue jixu jiaoyu xuebao* 陝西師範大學繼續教育學報 3 (2007): 61–64.

Li, Xiaorong. *Women's Poetry of Late Imperial China.* Seattle: University of Washington Press, 2012.

Li Ya 李芽. *Zhongguo lidai zhuangshi* 中國歷代妝飾. Beijing: Zhongguo fangzhi chubanshe, 2004.

Li Yanshou 李延壽. *Beishi* 北史. Beijing: Zhonghua shuju, 1974.

Li Yuzhen 李玉珍. *Tangdai de biqiuni* 唐代的比丘尼. Taipei: Xuesheng shuju, 1989.

Li Zhende 李貞德. "Cong 'dufu ji' tanqi" 從 '妒婦記' 談起. *Funü yu liangxing jikan* 婦女與兩性季刊 3 (1994): 12–15.

———. "Han Tang zhijian de nüxing yiliao zhaoguzhe" 漢唐之間的女性醫療照顧者. *Taida lishi xuebao* 台大歷史學報 23 (1999): 123–56.

———. "Han Tang zhijian jiating zhong de jiankang zhaogu yu xingbie" 漢唐之間家庭中的健康照顧與性別. *Disanjie guoji hanxue huiyi lunwenji lishizu, xingbie yu yiliao* 第三屆國際漢學會議論文集歷史組, 性別與醫療. Taipei: Institute of History and Philology, 2002, 1–49.

———. "Han Tang zhijian nüxing caichanquan shitan" 漢唐之間女性財產權試探. In *Zhongguo shi xinlun—xingbie shi fence* 中國史新論—性別史分冊, edited by Li Zhende 李貞德, 191–237. Taipei: Zhongyang yanjiu yuan, 2009.

———. "Han Tang zhijian yifang zhong ji jian furen yu nüti wei yao" 漢唐之間醫方中德忌見婦人與女體為藥. *Xin shixue* 新史學 13, no. 4 (2002): 1–35.

———. "Nüren de Zhongguo zhonggushi—xingbie yu Han Tang zhijian de lilü yanjiu" 女人的中國中古史—性別與漢唐之間的禮律研究. In *Chūgoku no rekishi sekai—tōgō no shisutemu to takenteki hatsuten* 中國の歴史世界—統合のシステムと多元的發展, edited by Nihon Chūgokushi gakkai 日本中國史學會, 469–92. Tokyo: Kyūko, 2002.

Li Zhisheng 李志生. "Shixi jingji zhengce dui Zhongguo gudai funü zhenjie de yingxiang—jian tan Tang houqi funü zhenjie bianhua de yiyi" 試析經濟政策對中國古代婦女貞節的影響—兼談唐後期婦女貞節變化的意義. In *Tang Song nüxing yu shehui* 唐宋女性與社會, edited by Deng Xiaonan 鄧小南, 2:884–904. Shanghai: Shanghai cishu, 2003.

———. "Zhongmen he zhongtang: Tangdai zhuzhai jianzhu zhong de funü shenghuo kongjian" 中門和中堂: 唐代住宅建築中的婦女生活空間. *Zhongguo shehui lishi pinglun* 中國社會歷史評論 14 (2013): 198–223.

Li Zhisheng 李志生 and Wu Tingting 伍婷婷. "Tangdai nüzi de fojiao xiaoqin huodong ji tedian—yi chujiafu wei zhu de kaocha" 唐代女子的佛教孝親活動及特點—以出嫁婦為主的考察. *Zhongyuan wenhua yanjiu* 中原文化研究 6 (2015): 81–88.

Liang Ertao 梁爾淘. "Lun Tangdai yinya shiqu ji qi wenxue yiyi" 論唐代姻婭詩群及其文學意義. *Zhongzhou xuekan* 中州學刊 5 (2016): 139–44.

Liang Ruimin 梁瑞敏. "Tangdai funü de jiating diwei," 唐代婦女的家庭地位. *Hebei Shifan Daxue xuebao* 河北師範大學學報 22, no. 3 (1999): 89–92.

Liao Meiyun 廖美雲. *Tang ji yanjiu* 唐伎研究. Taipei: Xuesheng shuju, 1995.

Liao Yifang 廖宜方. *Tangdai de muzi guanxi* 唐代的母子關係. Banqiao: Daoxiang, 2009.

Lin Kaixin 林凱欣. *Tangdai mingfu yanjiu* 唐代命婦研究. MA thesis, Tunghai University, 2000.

Lin Xi 林希. "Sui Tang Song jian wuxi zhengzhi diwei de yanbian" 隋唐宋間巫覡政治地位的演變. *Changchun Daxue xuebao* 長春大學學報 26, no. 11 (2016): 91–95.

Lin Yanzhi 林艷枝. "Tang Wudai shiqi Dunhuang diqu de nüren jieshe" 唐五代時期敦煌地區的女人結社. *Zhongguo wenhua yuekan* 中國文化月刊 6 (2000): 32–50.

Lingley, Kate A. "Naturalizing the Exotic: On the Changing Meanings of Ethnic Dress in Medieval China." *Ars Orientalis* 38 (2010): 50–80.

Liu Gaoyang 劉高陽. "Xi Tangdai Dunhuang bihua zhong nüxing gongyang ren xingxiang de shenmei tezheng" 析唐代敦煌壁畫中女性供養人形象的審美特徵. *Suzhou Xueyuan xuebao* 宿州學院學報 30, no. 9 (2015): 80–83.

Liu Jianming 劉建明. "Suishu lienü zhuan de zhenlie guannian" 隋書列女傳的貞烈觀念. *Tang yanjiu* 唐研究 7. Beijing: Beijing Daxue chubanshe, 2001, 249–62.

Liu Kairong 劉開榮. *Tangren shi zhong suojian dangshi funü shenghuo* 唐人詩中所見當時婦女生活. Chongqing: Shangwu yinshuguan, 1943.

Liu Litang 劉禮堂 and Wan Junjie 萬軍杰. "Tangdai de guafu zangfu yu qianzang fuzu" 唐代的寡婦葬夫與遷葬夫族. *Jianghan luntan* 江漢論壇 7 (2011): 85–88.

Liu Ning 劉寧. "Tangdai nüxing shige chuangzuo de zhuti tedian—yi nüguan shi yu changji shi wei zhongxin" 唐代女性詩歌創作的主題特點—以女冠詩與娼妓詩為中心. *Zhongguo nüxing de guoqu, xianzai yu weilai* 中國女性的過去, 現在與未來, edited by Zheng Bijun 鄭必俊 and Tao Jie 陶潔, 14–31. Beijing: Beijing Daxue chubanshe, 2005.

Liu, Qingping. "Filiality versus Sociality and Individuality: On Confucianism and Consanguinitism." *Philosophy East and West* 53, no. 2 (2003): 234–50.

Liu Qinli 劉琴麗. "Lun Tangdai rumu" 論唐代乳母角色地位的新發展. *Lanzhou xuekan* 蘭州學刊 11 (2009): 215–18.

———. "Muzhi suo jian Tangdai biqiuni yu jiaren guanxi" 墓誌所見唐代比丘尼與家人關係. *Huaxia kaogu* 華夏考古 2 (2010): 108–11.

Liu Xiangyang 劉向陽. *Tangdai diwang lingmu* 唐代帝王陵墓. Xi'an: Sanqin, 2003.

Liu Xu 劉昫 et al. *Jiu Tangshu* 舊唐書. Annotated by Liu Jie 劉節 and Chen Naiqian 陳乃乾. Beijing: Zhonghua, 1975.

Liu Yanfei 劉燕飛. "Song Ruoxin jiemei yu *Nü lunyu* yanjiu" 宋若莘姐妹與女論語研究. *Hebei Daxue xuebao* 河北大學學報 33, no. 2 (2008): 37–41.

Liu Yanfei 劉燕飛 and Wang Honghai 王宏海. "Nü lunyu de zhushu yu chuanbo tedian" 女論語的著述與傳播特點. *Hebei xuekan* 河北學刊 3 (2008): 46–49.

Liu Yanli 劉燕儷. "Cong falü mian kan Tangdai de fu yu diqi guanxi" 從法律面看唐代的夫與嫡妻關係. In *Tangdai shenfen fazhi yanjiu—yi Tanglü minglilü wei zhongxin* 唐代身分法制研究—以唐律名例律為中心, edited by Gao Mingshi 高明士, 119–47. Taipei: Wunan tushu, 2003.

Liu Yanping 劉艷萍. *Zhongwan Tang yanti shige yanjiu* 中晚唐艷體詩歌研究. Zhengzhou: Henan Daxue chubanshe, 2011.

Liu Yongcong 劉詠聰. "Wei Jin yihuan shijia dui houfei zhuzheng zhi fumian pingjia 魏晉以還史家對后妃主政之負面評價. In *Zhongguo funüshi lunwenji sanji* 中國婦女史論文集三集, edited by Bao Jialin 鮑家麟, 29–40. Taipei: Sanlian, 1993.

Liu Yuhong 劉育紅. "Tangdai qifu shi pingxi" 唐代棄婦詩評析. *Taiyuan Daxue xuebao* 太原大學學報 3 (2003): 50–52.

Liu Yurong 劉宇蓉. "Tangdai hunyin zhidu—yige *Tanglü* de guancha shijiao." 唐代婚姻制度—一個 '唐律' 的觀察視角. *Changjiang luntan* 長江論壇 5 (2011): 67–72.

Liu Yutang 劉玉堂. "Lun Tangdai de hunling lifa" 論唐代的婚齡立法. *Hubei Daxue xuebao* 湖北大學學報 32, no. 6 (2005): 725–29.

———. "Lun Tangdai de 'yijue' zhidu ji qi falü houguo" 論唐代的 '義絕' 制度及其法律後果. *Zhongguo Minzu Daxue xuebao* 中國民族大學學報 6 (2005): 113–17.

———. "Tangdai dui guanli hunyin tequan de falü guifan" 唐代對官吏婚姻特權的法律規範. *Zhongguo wenhua yanjiu* 中國文化研究 1 (2013): 82–85.

———. "Tangdai guanyu hunyin jinzhi tiaojian de falü guifan" 唐代關於結婚禁止條件的法律規範. *Jianghan luntan* 江漢論壇 4 (2010): 90–97.

———. "Tangdai 'heli' zhidu de falü toushi" 唐代和離制度的法律透視. *Jianghan luntan* 江漢論壇 5 (2011): 95–100.

Lou Jin 樓勁. "Zhengsheng yuannian chi yu Nanbeichao zhi Tangdai de jingbiao xiaoyi zhi zhidu—jian lun S.1344 hao Lundun canjuan de dingming wenti" 證聖

元年敕與南北朝至唐代的旌表孝義之制度—兼論 S.1344 號倫敦殘卷的定名問題. *Zhejiang xuekan* 浙江學刊 1 (2014): 11–29.

Lu Jianrong 盧建榮. "Cong nanxing shuxie cailiao kan san zhi qi shiji nüxing de shehui xingxiang suzao" 從男性書寫材料看三至七世紀女性的社會形象塑造. *Guoli Taiwan Shifan Daxue lishi xuebao* 國立台灣師範大學歷史學報 26 (1998): 1–42.

Lü Mingming 呂明明. "Guizi nisi chutan" 龜茲尼寺初探. *Dunhuang yanjiu* 敦煌研究 1 (2007): 55–60.

Lu Ting 盧婷. "Nü Wa shenhua de yiwei yu Tangdai shiwen zhong de Nü Wa xingxiang" 女娲神話的移位與唐代詩文中的女娲形象. *Tianshui Shifan Xueyuan xuebao* 天水師範學院學報 34, no. 4 (2014): 6–9.

Lu Tongyan 魯統彥. "Cong 'chujia wujia' dao chujia er you 'jia'—Tangdai sengni xiaodao lunli xianxiang luexi" 從 '出家無家' 到出家而有 '家'—唐代僧尼孝道倫理現象略析. *Linyi Shifan Xueyuan xuebao* 臨沂師範學院學報 30, no. 4 (2008): 77–81.

Lu Xuejun 路學軍. "Jianxi Tangdai 'wuxing nü' de lifa chuancheng ji qi dui hunzu de yingxiang" 簡析唐代 '五姓女' 的禮法傳承及其對婚族的影響. *Tangdu xuekan* 唐都學刊 28, no. 2 (2012): 33–38.

———. "Ru Fo jian xiu yu Tangdai Shandong shiqu nüxing de jiafeng yanjin—yi Tangdai muzhi wei li" 儒佛兼修與唐代山東士族女性的家風演進—以唐代墓誌為例. *Shoudu Shifan Daxue xuebao* 首都師範大學學報 5 (2009): 25–31.

Lu Xun 陸勳. *Jiyi zhi* 集異志. Beijing: Zhonghua, 1985.

Luk, Yu-ping. *The Empress and the Heavenly Masters: A Study of the Ordination Scroll of Empress Zhang (1493)*. Hong Kong: Chinese University Press, 2016.

Luo, Manling. "Gender, Genre, and Discourse: The Woman Avenger in Medieval Chinese Texts." *Journal of the American Oriental Society* 134, no. 4 (2014): 579–99.

———. "The Seduction of Authenticity: 'The Story of Yingying.'" *Nan Nü* 7, no. 1 (2005): 40–70.

Luo Ping 羅萍. "Cong Tang chuanqi kan Tangdai nüxing hunlianguan" 從唐傳奇看唐代女性婚戀觀. *Sichuan Shifan Xueyuan xuebao* 四川師範學院學報 1 (1999): 96–99.

Luo Shiping 羅世平. "Tangdai shinü hua ji qi xiangguan wenti" 唐代侍女畫及其相關問題. In *Tang Song nüxing yu shehui* 唐宋女性與社會, edited by Deng Xiaonan 鄧小南, 1:301–21. Shanghai: Shanghai cishu, 2003.

Luo Tonghua 羅彤華. "Tangdai jishi hunyin yanjiu" 唐代繼室婚姻研究. In *Zhongyuan yu yuwai: Qingzhu Zhang Guangda jiaoshou bashi zhounian songshou yantaohui lunwenji* 中原與域外: 慶祝張廣達教授八十週年嵩壽研討會論文集, edited by Lü Shaoli 呂紹理 and Zhou Huimin 周惠民, 113–70. Taipei: Cheng Chi University, Department of History, 2011.

———. *Tongju gongcai: Tangdai jiating yanjiu* 同居共財: 唐代家庭研究. Taipei: Zhengda chubanshe, 2015.

Ma Jiyun 馬繼雲. "Xiao de guannian yu Tangdai jiating" 孝的觀念與唐代家庭. *Shandong Shifan Daxue xuebao* 山東師範大學學報 48, no. 2 (2003): 112–14.

Ma, Y. W. "Fact and Fantasy in T'ang Tales." *Chinese Literature (CLEAR)* 2, no. 2 (1980): 167–81.

Ma Zili 馬自力. "Tangren biji xiaoshuo zhong de Tangdai nüxing—cong ziliao yu wenti chufa de chubu kaocha" 唐人筆記小說中的唐代女性—從資料與問題出發的初步考察. *Wenyi yanjiu* 文藝研究 6 (2001): 102–6.

Maeda Aiko 前田愛子. "Tangdai Shandong wuxing hunyin yu qi zhengzhi yingxiangli—tongguo zhizuo Cui shi, Lu shi, Deng shi hunyinbiao kaocha" 唐代山東五姓婚姻與其政治影響力—通過制作崔氏, 盧氏, 鄧氏婚姻 表考察. *Tangshi luncong* 唐史論叢 1 (2012): 247–71.

Mann, Susan. "Widows in the Kinship, Class, and Community Structures of Qing Dynasty China." *Journal of Asian Studies* 46, no. 1 (1987): 37–56.

Mao Hanguang 毛漢光. "Guanzhong jun xing hunyin guanxi zhi yanjiu" 關中郡姓婚姻關係之研究. In *Tangdai wenhua yanjiuhui lunwenji* 唐代文化研討會論文集, edited by Zhongguo Tangdai xuehui bianji weiyuanhui 中國唐代學會編輯委員會, 87–140. Taipei: Wenshizhe, 1991.

———. "Tangdai houbanqi houfei zhi fenxi" 唐代後半期后妃之分析. *Guoli Taiwan Daxue wenshizhe xuebao* 國立臺灣大學文史哲學報 37 (1989): 175–95.

———. "Wan Tang wuxing zhuofang zhi hunyin guanxi" 晚唐五姓著房之婚姻關係. *Guoli Taiwan Daxue Lishi Xuexi xuebao* 國立臺灣大學歷史學系學報 15 (1990): 135–57.

———. "Zhonggu Shandong dazu zhuofang zhi yanjiu—Tangdai jinhun jia yu xingzupu" 中古山東大族著房之研究—唐代禁婚家與姓族. *Zhongyang Yanjiuyuan Lishi Yuyan Yanjiusuo jikan* 中央研究院歷史語言研究所集刊 54 (1993): 19–61.

Mao Yangguang, 毛陽光. "Tangdai funü de zhenjieguan" 唐代婦女的貞節觀. *Wenbo* 文博 4 (2000): 33–38, 43.

Martin, Michael. *The Uses of Understanding in Social Science: Verstehen*. New Brunswick, NJ: Transaction Publishers, 2000.

McMahon, Keith. *Celestial Women: Imperial Wives and Concubines in China from Song to Qing*. Lanham, MD: Rowman & Littlefield, 2016.

———. "The Institution of Polygamy in the Chinese Imperial Palace." *Journal of Asian Studies* 72, no. 4 (2013): 917–36.

———. "Women Rulers in Imperial China." *Nan Nü* 15, no. 2 (2013): 179–218.

———. *Women Shall Not Rule: Imperial Wives and Concubines in China from Han to Liao*. Lanham, MD: Rowman & Littlefield, 2013.

McMullen, David. "Historical and Literary Theory in the Mid-Eighth Century." In *Perspectives on the T'ang*, edited by Arthur F. Wright and Denis Twitchett, 307–42. New Haven: Yale University Press, 1973.

McNair, Amy. "Early Tang Imperial Patronage at Longmen." *Ars Orientalis* 24 (1994): 65–81.

———. "On the Patronage by Tang-Dynasty Nuns at Wanfo Grotto, Longmen." *Artibus Asiae* 59, nos. 3/4 (2000): 161–88.

Miyakawa Hisayuki 宮川尚志. *Rikuchōshi kenkyū: shūkyō hen* 六朝史研究: 宗教篇. Tokyo: Heirakudera shoten, 1964.

Mo Xiaobin 莫曉斌. "Qianlun Tangdai hunyin zhidu yu shehui xishang de maodun xianxiang" 淺論唐代婚姻制度與社會習尚的矛盾現象. *Changsha Daxue xuebao* 長沙大學學報 14, no. 3 (2003): 58–60.

Mou, Sherry J. *Gentlemen's Prescriptions for Women's Lives: A Thousand Years of Biographies of Chinese Women.* Armonk, NY: M. E. Sharpe, 2004.

———. "Writing Virtues with Their Bodies: Rereading the Two Tang Histories' Biographies of Women." In *Presence and Presention: Women in the Chinese Literati Tradition*, edited by Sherry J. Mou, 109–47. New York: St. Martin's Press, 1999.

Mumford, T. F. "Death Do Us Unite: Xunzang and Joint Burial in Ancient China." *Papers on Far Eastern History* 27 (2008): 1–19.

Nadel, Ira Bruce. *Biography: Fiction, Fact, and Form.* London: Macmillan, 1984.

Neinhauser Jr., William H. "Some Preliminary Remarks on Fiction, The Classical Tradition and Society in Late Ninth-Century China." In *Critical Essays on Chinese Fiction*, edited by Winston L. Y. Yang and Curtis P. Adkins, 1–16. Hong Kong: Chinese University Press, 1980.

Nelson, Sarah Milledge. "Ancient Queens: An Introduction." In *Ancient Queens: Archaeological Explorations*, edited by Sarah Milledge Nelson, 1–18. Walnut Creek, CA: AltaMira Press, 2003.

Ngo, Sheau-Shi. "Nuxia: Historical Depiction and Modern Visuality." *Asian Journal of Women's Studies* 20, no. 3 (2014): 7–26.

Ni Wenjie 倪文杰 et al. *Zuijia nüxing miaoxie cidian* 最佳女性描寫辭典. Beijing: Zhongguo guoji guangbo, 1990.

Ning Ke 寧可 and Hao Chunwen 郝春文. "Beichao zhi Sui Tang Wudai jian de nüren jieshe" 北朝至隋唐五代間的女人結社. *Beijing Shifan Xueyuan xuebao* 北京師範學院學報 5 (1990): 16–19.

Ning Qiang. "Gender Politics in Medieval Chinese Buddhist Art: Images of Empress Wu at Longmen and Dunhuang." *Oriental Art* 49, no. 2 (2003): 28–39.

———. "Imperial Portraiture as Symbol of Political Legitimacy: A New Study of the 'Portraits of Successive Emperors.'" *Ars Orientalis* 35 (2008): 96–128.

Ning Xin 寧欣. "Tangdai funü de shehui jingji huodong—yi 'Taiping guangji' wei zhongxin" 唐代婦女的社會經濟活動—以 '太平廣記' 為中心. In *Tang Song nüxing yu shehui* 唐宋女性與社會, edited by Deng Xiaonan 鄧小南, 1:235–51. Shanghai: Shanghai cishu, 2003.

Niu Zhigong 牛致功. "Tangren de 'lihun' chuyi" 唐人的 '離婚' 芻議. *Xueshujie* 學術界 2 (1994): 24–27.

Niu Zhiping 牛志平. "Shuo Tangdai junei zhi feng" 說唐代懼內之風. *Shixue yuekan* 史學月刊 2 (1988): 38–41.

———. "Tangdai de yinyuan tiandingshuo" 唐代的姻緣天定說. In *Zhongguo funüshi lunji sanji* 中國婦女史論集三集, edited by Bao Jialin 鮑家麟, 51–59. Taipei: Daoxiang, 1993.

———. "Tangdai dufu shulun" 唐代妒婦述論. In *Zhongguo Funüshi lunji xuji* 中國婦女史論集續集, edited by Bao Jialin 鮑家麟, 55–65. Taipei: Daoxiang chubanshe, 1991.

———. *Tangdai hunsang* 唐代婚喪. Xi'an: Sanqin chubanshe, 2011.

———. "Tangdai hunyin de tianmingguan." *Hainan Shifan Xueyuan xuebao* 海南師院學報 2 (1995): 59–61.

———. *Tangdai shehui shenghuo conglun* 唐代社會生活叢論. Taiyuan: Shuhai, 2001.

Obara Hitoshi 小源仁. *Chūsei kizoku shakai to bukkyō* 中世貴族社會と佛教. Tokyo: Yoshikawa kōbunkan, 2007.

Ochi Shigeaki 越智重明. *Gi Shin nanchō no hito to shakai* 魏晉南朝の人と社會. Tokyo: Kenbun shuppan, 1985.

Ochs, Elinor, and Carolyn Taylor. "The 'Father Knows Best' Dynamic in Dinnertime Narratives." In *Linguistic Anthropology: A Reader* (second edition), edited by Alessandro Duranti, 435–51. Chichester, UK: Wiley-Blackwell, 2009.

Ogawa Kanichi 小川貫弌. "Hubo onjū kei" 父母恩重經. In *Tonkō to Chūgoku bukkyō* 敦煌と中國佛教, edited by Fukui Fumimasa 福井文雅, 207–22. Tokyo: Daitō, 1984.

Oppenheim, A. Leo. *Ancient Mesopotamia: Portrait of a Dead Civilization.* Revised edition completed by Erica Reiner. Chicago: University of Chicago Press, 1964.

Ouyang Xiu 歐陽修. *Xin Tangshu* 新唐書, annotated by Song Qi 宋祁, Dong Jiazun 董家遵, et al. Beijing: Zhonghua Shuju, 1975.

Ouyang Yuqing 歐陽予倩. *Tangdai wudao* 唐代舞蹈. Shanghai: Shanghai wenxue, 1980.

Owen, Stephen. *Readings in Chinese Literary Thought.* Cambridge, MA: Council on East Asian Studies, Harvard University, 1992.

Ōzawa Masāki 大澤正昭. "Tō Sō henkaku no kazoku kibo to kōsei—shōsetsu shiryō ni yoru bunseki 唐宋變革期の家族規模と構成—小說史料による分析. *Tōdaishi kenkyū* 唐代史研究 6 (2003): 59–90.

———. *Tō sō jidai no kazoku, konin, josei—tsuma wa tsuyoku* 唐宋時代の家族, 婚姻, 女性－婦は強く. Tokyo: Akashi, 2005.

Paine Jr., Robert T. "A Chinese Horse with a Female Rider." *Bulletin of the Museum of Fine Arts* 46, no. 265 (1948): 54–55.

Pan Taiquan 潘泰泉. "Tangdai de nuguan" 唐代的女官. In *Tangdai de lishi yu shehui* 唐代的歷史與社會, 557–67. Wuhan: Wuhan Daxue chubanshe, 1997.

Pang, Shiying. "Eminent Nuns and / or / as Virtuous Women: The Representation of Tang Female Renunciants in Tomb Inscriptions." *T'ang Studies* 28 (2010): 77–96.

Pang-White, Ann A. "Confucius and the Four Books for Women (Nü Sishu 女四書)." In *Feminist Encounters with Confucius*, edited by Mathew A. Foust and Sor-hoon Tan, 17–39. Leiden: Brill, 2016.

Pearlstein, Elinor. "Pictorial Stones from Chinese Tombs." *Bulletin of the Cleveland Museum of Art* 71, no. 9 (1984): 302–31.

Pfister, Rudolph. "Gendering Sexual Pleasures in Early and Medieval China." *Asian Medicine* 7, no. 1 (2012): 34–64.

Qi Bin 齊斌 and Wang Rimei 王日美. "Tangdai juntian zhidu xia funü buzai shoutian de yuanyin tanxi" 唐代均田制度下婦女不再受田的原因探析. *Xuchang Xueyuan xuebao* 許昌學院學報 31, no. 1 (2012): 96–99.

Qi Dongfang 齊東方. "Nongzhuang danmo zong xiang yi—Tang yong yu funü shenghuo" 濃妝淡抹總相宜—唐俑與婦女生活. In *Tang Song nüxing yu shehui*

唐宋女性與社會, edited by Deng Xiaonan 鄧小南, 1:322–37. Shanghai: Shanghai cishu, 2003.

Qi Juan 漆娟. "Li Bai jinü yu Tangdai yinyi wenxue" 李白妓女與唐代隱逸文學. *Sichuan Wenli Xueyuan xuebao* 四川文理學院學報 22, no. 4 (2012): 90–93.

Qi Shuzhen 齊淑珍. "Cong muzhi kan Tangdai guamu de fojiao xinyang" 從墓志看唐代寡母的佛教信仰. *Zhonggong Jinanshi Weidangxiao xuebao* 中共濟南市委黨校學報 5 (2013): 103–5.

———. "Tangdai guamu caichan chufenquan tanxi" 唐代寡母財產處分權探析. *Cangsang* 滄桑 3 (2013): 55–57.

Qi Shuzhen 齊淑珍 and Zou Dianwei 鄒殿偉. "Cong muzhi kan Tangdai de guamu fugu" 從墓誌看唐代的寡母撫孤. *Cangsang* 滄桑 2 (2008): 12–13.

Qi Zhongming 綦中明. "Tangdai dazu lianhun tanwei" 唐代大族聯婚探微. *Xueshu jiaoliu* 學術交流 9 (2011): 187–89.

Qian Daqun 錢大群. *Tang lü yanjiu* 唐律研究. Beijing: Falü, 2000.

Qiu Meihua 邱瑰華. "Tangdai nüxing rezhong rudao yuanyin chutan" 唐代女性熱衷入道原因初探. *Anhui Daxue xuebao* 安徽大學學報 24, no. 3 (2000): 55–58.

Qiu Zhonglin 邱仲麟. "Bu xiao zhi xiao—Tang yilai gegu liaoqin xianxiang de shehuishi chutan" 不孝之孝—唐以來割股療親現象的社會史初探. *Xin shixue* 新史學 6, no. 1 (1995): 49–92.

———. "Renyao yu xueqi—'gegu' liaoqin xianxiang zhong de yiliao gainian" 人藥與血氣—'割股' 療親現象中的醫療概念. *Xin shixue* 新史學 10, no. 4 (1999): 67–116.

Quinn, Naomi. "Anthropological Studies on Women's Status." *Annual Review of Anthropology* 6 (1977): 181–225.

Ran Wanli 冉萬里. "Luelun Tangdai sengni de zangzhi" 略論唐代僧尼的葬制. *Ganling wenhua yanjiu* 乾陵文化研究 (2005): 80–93.

Ren Haiyan 任海燕. "Lun Tangdai funü shengyu de yingxiang yinsu" 論唐代婦女生育的影響因素. *Shoudu Shifan Daxue xuebao* 首都師範大學學報 1 (2009): 29–32.

Ren Jia 仁佳. "Lun Tangdai qianqi shangceng nüzi yu zhengzhi" 論唐代前期上層女子與政治. *Daqing Shifan Xueyuan xuebao* 大慶師範學院學報 34, no. 5 (2014): 106–9.

Rhie, Marylin M. "A T'ang Period Inscription and Cave XXI at T'ien-Lung Shan." *Archives of Asian Art* 28 (1974–1975): 6–33.

Ricoeur, Paul. "Narrative Identity." *Philosophy Today* 35, no. 1 (1991): 73–81.

Robertson, Maureen. "Voicing the Feminine: Constructions of the Gendered Subject in Lyric Poetry by Women of Medieval and Late Imperial China." *Late Imperial China* 13, no. 1 (1992): 63–110.

Rodgers, Susan Carol. "Female Forms of Power and the Myth of Male Dominance: A Model of Female/Male Interaction in Peasant Society." *American Ethnologist* 2, no. 4 (1975): 727–56.

Rogers, Susan Carol, and Sonya Salamon. "Inheritance and Social Organization among Family Farmers." *American Ethnologist* 10, no. 3 (1983): 529–50.

Rong Xinjiang 榮新江. "Nü ban nan zhuang—Tangdai qianqi de xingbie yishi" 女扮男裝—唐代前期婦女的性別意識. In *Tang Song nüxing yu shehui* 唐宋女性與社會, edited by Deng Xiaonan 鄧小南, 2:723–50. Shanghai: Shanghai cishu, 2003.

———. *Sui Tang Chang'an: xingbie, jiyi ji qita* 隋唐長安 性別 記憶及其他. Hong Kong: Sanlian shudian, 2009.

Rosemont, Jr., Henry, and Roger T. Ames. *The Chinese Classic of Family Reverence: A Philosophical Translation of the* Xiaojing. Honolulu: University of Hawaii Press, 2009.

Rothschild, Norman Harry. "Beyond Filial Piety: Biographies of Exemplary Women and Wu Zhao's New Paradigm of Political Authority." *T'ang Studies* 23/24 (2005–2006): 149–68.

———. *Emperor Wu Zhao and Her Pantheon of Devis, Divinities, and Dynastic Mothers*. New York: Columbia University Press, 2015.

———. "An Inquiry into Reign Era Changes Under Wu Zhao, China's Only Female Emperor." *Early Medieval China* 12 (2006): 123–47.

———. "The Mother of Laozi and the Female Emperor Wu Zhao: From One Grand Dowager to Another." In *China and Beyond in the Mediaeval Period: Cultural Crossings and Inter-Regional Connections*, edited by Dorothy C. Wong and Gustav Heldt, 219–42. Amherst, NY: Cambria Press, 2014.

———. *Wu Zhao: China's Only Woman Emperor*. New York: Pearson Longman, 2008.

———. "Wu Zhao and the Queen Mother of the West." *Journal of Daoist Studies* 3 (2010): 29–56.

Ruan Li 阮立. *Tang Dunhuang bihua nüxing xingxiang yanjiu* 唐敦煌壁畫女性形象研究. Wuhan: Wuhan Daxue chubanshe, 2012.

———. "Tangdai nüxing xingxiang de xin sikao—yi Tang mubihua zhong de nüxing xingxiang yanjiu wei li" 唐代女性形象的新思考—以唐墓壁畫中的女性形象研究為例. *Rongbao zhai* 榮寶齋 1 (2011): 72–79.

Sanders, Graham. "I Read They Said He Sang What He Wrote: Orality, Writing, and Gossip in Tang Poetry Anecdotes." In *Idle Talk: Gossip and Anecdote in Traditional China*, edited by Jack W. Chen and David Schaberg, 88–106. Berkeley: Global, Area, and International Archive and University of California Press, 2014.

Schafer, Edward H. *The Divine Woman: Dragon Ladies and Rain Maidens in T'ang Literature*. San Francisco: North Point Press, 1980.

———. "The Jade Woman of Greatest Mystery." *History of Religions* 17, nos. 3–4 (1978): 387–98.

———. "The Princess Realized in Jade." *T'ang Studies* 3 (1985): 1–23.

———. "Ritual Exposure in Ancient China." *Harvard Journal of Asiatic Studies* 14, nos. 1/2 (1951): 130–84.

Schlegel, Alice. "Status, Property, and the Value on Virginity." *American Ethnologist* 18, no. 4 (1991): 719–34.

Seo Tatsuhiko 妹尾達彦. "'Caizi' yu 'jiaren'—jiu shiji Zhongguo xin de nannü renshi de xingcheng" '才子' 與 '佳人'—九世紀中國新的男女認識的形成. In *Tang Song nüxing yu shehui* 唐宋女性與社會, edited by Deng Xiaonan 鄧小南, 2:695–722. Shanghai: Shanghai cishu, 2003.

Shang Minjie 尚民杰. "Tangdai gongren gongni mu xiangguan wenti tantao" 唐代宮人宮尼墓相關問題探討. *Tangshi luncong* 唐史論叢 1 (2013): 211–33.

Shen Dong 沈冬. *Tangdai yuewu xinlun* 唐代樂舞新論. Beijing: Beijing Daxue chubanshe, 2004.

Shi Guanle 史官樂. *Yang Taizhen waizhuan* 楊太真外傳. Beijing: Zhonghua, 1991.

Shields, Anna M. "Remembering When: The Uses of Nostalgia in the Poetry of Bai Juyi and Yuan Zhen." *Harvard Journal of Asiatic Studies* 66, no. 2 (2006): 321–61.

Shiga Shūzō 滋賀秀三. *Chūgoku kazokuhō no genri* 中國家族法の原理. Tokyo: Sōbunsha, 1967.

———. "Family Property and the Law of Inheritance in Traditional China." In *Chinese Family Law and Social Change in Historical and Comparative Perspective*, edited by David C. Buxbaum, 109–50. Seattle: University of Washington Press, 1978.

Shigeru Maruyama 丸山茂. *Tōdai no bunka to shijin no kokoro—hakurakuten o chūshin ni* 唐代の文化と詩人の心—白樂天を中心に. Tokyo: Kyuko shoin, 2010.

Shiomi Kunihiko 塩見邦彦. *Tōdai kōgo no kenkyū* 唐詩口語の研究. Fukuoka: Chūgoku shoten, 1995.

Siebenschuh, William R. *Fictional Techniques and Factual Works*. Athens: University of Georgia Press, 1983.

Smith, Sidonie. *Subjectivity, Identity, and the Body: Women's Autobiographical Practices in the Twentieth Century*. Bloomington: Indiana University Press, 1993.

Somers, Robert M. "Time, Space, and Structure in the Consolidation of the T'ang Dynasty (A.D. 617–700)." *Journal of Asian Studies* 45, no. 5 (1986): 971–94.

Sommer, Matthew H. "The Uses of Chastity: Sex, Law, and the Property of Widows in Qing China." *Late Imperial China* 17, no. 2 (1996): 77–130.

Song Dexi 宋德熹. "Tangdai de jinü" 唐代的妓女. In *Zhongguo Funüshi lunji xuji* 中國婦女史論集續集, edited by Bao Jialin 鮑家麟, 67–121. Taipei: Daoxiang chubanshe, 1991.

Song Junfeng 宋軍風. "Tangdai shangren hunyin fawei" 唐代商人婚姻發微. *Tangdu xuekan* 唐都學刊 6 (2006): 29–33.

Song Rentao 宋仁桃. "Qianyi Wei Jin nanbeichao shiqi nüxing chujia de xianxiang" 淺議魏晉南北朝時期女性出嫁的現象. *Jiangnan Shehui Xueyuan xuebao* 江南社會學院學報 4, no. 3 (2002): 51–54.

Song Ruozhao 宋若昭. *Niu Yingzhen zhuan* 牛應貞傳. Beijing: Zhonghua, 1985.

Sørensen, Henrik H. "The Buddhist Sculptures at Feixian Pavilion in Pujiang, Sichuan." *Artibus Asiae* 58, nos. 1–2 (1998): 33–67.

Spitulnik, Debra. "The Social Circulation of Media Discourse and the Mediation of Communities." In *Linguistic Anthropology: A Reader* (second edition), ed. Alessandro Durant, 93–113. Chinchester, UK: Wiley-Blackwell, 2009.

Su Dan 蘇丹. "Yindu Yaocha nüxiang dui Tangdai Dunhuang shiku nüxing zaoxiang de yingxiang" 印度藥叉女像對唐代敦煌石窟女性造像的影響. *Yishu yanjiu* 藝術研究 11 (2014): 79–80.

Su Shimei 蘇士梅. "Cong muzhi kan fojiao dui Tangdai funü shenghuo de yingxiang" 從墓誌看佛教對唐代婦女生活的影響. *Shixue yuekan* 史學月刊 5 (2003): 84–88.

Su Zhecong 蘇者聰. *Guiwei de tanshi—Tangdai nüshiren* 閨幃的探視—唐代女詩人. Changsha: Hunan wenyi, 1991.

Su Zhenfu 蘇振富. "*Taiping guangji* suo jian Tangdai minjian nüxing xiudao qingkuang yanjiu" '太平廣記' 所見唐代民間女性修道情況研究. *Mudanjiang Daxue xuebao* 牡丹江大學學報 23, no. 12 (2014): 56–59.

Sun Changwu 孫昌武. *Daojiao yu Tangdai wenxue* 道教與唐代文學. Beijing: Renmin wenxue, 2001.

Sun Junhui 孫軍輝. "Tangdai nüshangren luekao" 唐代女商人略考. *Lishi jiaoxue* 歷史教學 5 (2007): 21–23.

Sun Shunhua 孫順華. "Tangchao funüguan zhi shanbian yu shehui zhengzhi" 唐朝婦女觀之嬗變與社會政治. *Wenshizhe* 文史哲 2 (2000): 100–105.

Sun Wei 孫煒. "Feishou suiqing—Tangdai yu Qingdai shinühua huafeng bijiao" 肥瘦雖情—唐代與清代仕女畫畫風比較. *Yishu baijia* 藝術百家 1 (2014): 176–78.

Sun Wei 孫頠. *Shennü zhuan* 神女傳. Beijing: Zhonghua, 1991.

Sun Xinmei 孫新梅. "*Nü sishu* de bianzuan yu liuchuan" 女四書的編纂與流傳. *Lantai shijie* 蘭台世界 11 (2013): 156–57.

Sun Yu 孫瑜. "Luelun Tangdai gongzhu de zhengzhi hunyin" 略論唐代公主的政治婚姻. *Shanxi Datong Daxue xuebao* 山西大同大學學報 23, no. 3 (2009): 16–19.

Sun Yurong 孫玉榮. "Lun shaoshu minzu wenhua dui Tangdai hunsu de yingxiang" 論少數民族文化對唐代婚俗的影響. *Henan Keji Daxue xuebao* 河南科技大學學報 33, no. 5 (2015): 21–25.

———. "Lun Tangdai de 'fuqi zhi qing'" 論唐代的 '夫妻之情.' *Linyi Daxue xuebao* 臨沂大學學報 35, no. 4 (2013): 119–21.

———. "Lun Tangdai shehui biangeqi de nüxing jiaoyu" 論唐代社會變革期的女性教育. *Funü yanjiu luncong* 婦女研究論叢 1 (2015): 41–47.

———. "Tangdai benjia dui nüxing hunyin ganshequan de bianqian" 唐代本家對女性婚姻干涉權的變遷. *Zhonghua Nüzi Xueyuan xuebao* 中華女子學院學報 3 (2015): 104–7.

———. "Tangdai suishi jieri zhong de nüxing xiuxian huodong" 唐代歲時節日中的女性休閒活動. *Hubei Ligong Xueyuan xuebao* 湖北理工學院學報 30, no. 2 (2013): 15–18, 60.

Sun Yurong 孫玉榮 and Hu Hui 胡輝. "Tangdai 'pinnüshi' chengyin tanxi" 唐代 '貧女詩' 成因探析. *Lantai shijie* 蘭台世界 12 (2012): 94–95.

Sun Yurong 孫玉榮 and Xie Fang 謝芳. "Lun Tangdai 'fu jian jiugu li' de bianqian" 論唐代 '婦見舅姑禮' 的變遷. *Nanfang lunkan* 南方論刊 6 (2015): 98–100.

Tackett, Nicolas. *The Destruction of the Medieval Chinese Aristocracy.* Cambridge, MA: Harvard University Asia Center, 2014.

———. "Great Clansmen, Bureaucrats, and Local Magnates: The Structure and Circulation of the Elite in Late-Tang China." *Asia Major* 21, no. 2 (2008): 101–52.

Tan Chanxue 談蟬雪. *Dunhuang hunyin wenhua* 敦煌婚姻文化. Lanzhou: Gansu renmin chubanshe, 1993.

Tang Ronglan 湯蓉嵐. "Lun Tangdai funü shenghuo de bofan xianxiang" 論唐代婦女生活的悖反現象. *Taizhou Xueyuan xuebao* 台州學院學報 25, no. 5 (2003): 79–82.

Tanigawa Michio. *Medieval Chinese Society and the Local "Community."* Translated by Joshua A. Fogel. Berkeley: University of California Press, 1985.

Tao Yi 陶易. "Tangdai xianmu de jiaozi gushi" 唐代賢母的教子故事. *Wenshi tiandi* 文史天地 3 (2016): 25–28.

Teiser, Stephen F. *The Ghost Festival in Medieval China.* Princeton: Princeton University Press, 1988.

Teng Yun 藤雲. "Lun Tangdai gongzhu de daojiao qingyuan—jian lun Tangdai gongzhu zhuangyuan zhaidi shi de daojiao ziran shengtai yishi" 論唐代公主的道教情緣—兼論唐代公主莊園宅第詩的道教自然生態意識. *Guilin Shifan Gaodeng Zhuanke Xuexiao xuebao* 桂林師範高等專科學校學報 28, no. 4 (2014): 112–15.

Tian Feng 田峰. "Cong Tangshi kan Tangdai huji jiusi ji qi wenhua" 從唐詩看唐代胡妓酒肆及其文化. *Qinghai Minzu Daxue xuebao* 青海民族大學學報 37, no. 4 (2011): 129–34.

Tomita, Kojiro. "Three Chinese Pottery Figurines of the T'ang Dynasty." *Bulletin of the Museum of Fine Arts* 42, no. 250 (1944): 64–67.

Tsai, S.-C. Kevin. "Ritual and Gender in the 'Tale of Li Wa.'" *Chinese Literature (CLEAR)* 26 (2004): 99–127.

Tung, Jowen R. *Fables for the Patriarchs: Gender Politics in Tang Discourse.* Lanham, MD: Rowman & Littlefield, 2000.

Twitchett, Denis. "Chen gui and Other Works Attributed to Empress Wu Zetian." *Asia Major* (third series) 16, no. 1 (2003): 33–109.

———. "The Composition of the T'ang Ruling Class: New Evidence from Tunhuang." In *Perspectives on the T'ang*, edited by Arthur F. Wright and Denis Twitchett, 47–85. New Haven: Yale University Press, 1973.

———. "The Government of T'ang in the Eighth Century." *Bulletin of the School of Oriental and African Studies* 18, no. 2 (1956): 322–30.

Van Norden, Bryan W., trans. *Mengzi: With Selections from Traditional Commentaries.* Indianapolis: Hackett Publishing, 2008.

von Glahn, Richard. *The Economic History of China: From Antiquity to the Nineteenth Century.* Cambridge: Cambridge University Press, 2016.

Wan Junjie 萬軍杰. "Tangdai gaijia zaijia nüxing sangzang wenti tantao" 唐代改嫁再嫁女性喪葬問題探討. *Tianjin Shifan Daxue xuebao* 天津師範大學學報 5 (2007): 59–62.

———. "Tangdai gongren zhi mingyun tanxi" 唐代宮人之命運探析. *Wuhan Daxue xuebao* 武漢大學學報 2 (2010): 145–51.

———. "Tangdai nüxing de chuhun nianling" 唐代女性的初婚年齡. *Huaxia kaogu* 華夏考古 2 (2014): 106–13.

———. *Tangdai nüxing de shengqian yu zuhou: weirao muzhi ziliao zhankai de ruogan tantao* 唐代女性的生前與卒後: 圍繞墓誌資料展開的若干探討. Tianjin: Tianjin guji, 2010.

———. "Tangdai 'qie' de sangzang wenti" 唐代 '妾' 的喪葬問題. *Wei Jin Nan-beichao Sui Tang shi ziliao* 魏晉南北朝隋唐史資料 25 (2009): 186–200.

Wang Chengju 王承舉. "Tangdai *Xiaojing* wenxian kaoshu" 唐代孝經文獻考述. *Changjiang Daxue xuebao* 長江大學學報 36, no. 2 (2013): 179–80.

Wang Cui 王翠. "Cong muzhi kan Tangdai nüxing yu benjia de jingji guanxi—yi dahe wunian 'Lu fujun qi Qinghe Cui furen muzhiming' wei zhongxin" 從墓志看唐代女性與本家的經濟關係—以大和五年 '盧府君妻清河崔夫人墓誌銘' 為中心. *Baise Xueyuan xuebao* 百色學院學報 3 (2014): 122–25.

Wang, Eugene Y. "Mirror, Moon, and Memory in Eighth-Century China: From Dragon Pond to Lunar Palace." *Cleveland Studies in the History of Art* 9 (2005): 42–67.

Wang Fu 王溥. *Tang huiyao* 唐會要. Beijing: Zhonghua shuju, 1955.

Wang Houxiang 王厚香. "Tangdai jiating caichan he jicheng zhidu shulun" 唐代家庭財產和繼承制度述論. *Wenshi zazhi* 文史雜誌 4 (2003): 66–68.

Wang Houxiang 王厚香 and Ji Guangyun 汲廣運. "Lun Tangdai jiating jiaoyu" 論唐代家庭教育. *Linyi Shifan Daxue xuebao* 臨沂師範大學學報 23, no. 2 (2001): 48–51.

Wang, Jing. "From Immortality to Mortality: Images of Tang Courtesans in Verse, Painting, and Anecdote." *Frontiers of Literary Studies in China* 6, no. 2 (2012): 277–93.

Wang Limei 王麗梅. "Tangdai nüzi jiaoyu xintan" 唐代女子教育新探. *Jiaoyu pinglun* 教育評論 5 (2011): 138–40.

Wang Qiwei 王其禕 and Zhou Xiaowei 周曉薇. "Tangdai gongzhu muzhi jilue" 唐代公主墓誌輯略. *Beilin jikan* 碑林集刊 (1995): 63–77.

Wang Shoudong 王守棟. "Lun Tangdai gongfu shezheng" 論唐代宮婦涉政. *Dezhou Xueyuan xuebao* 德州學院學報 23, no. 3 (2007): 67–70.

Wang Shounan 王壽南. "Tangdai gongzhu zhi hunyin" 唐代公主之婚姻. In *Diyijie lishi yu Zhongguo shehui bianqian (Zhongguo shehuishi) yantaohui* 第一屆歷史與中國社會變遷 (中國社會史) 研討會, 1:151–91. Taipei: Zhongyanyuan San-minzhuyi Yanjiuyuan congkan, 1982.

Wang Tongling 王桐齡. "Han Tang zhi heqin zhengce" 漢唐之和親政策. In *Zhongguo funüshi lunji sanji* 中國婦女史論集三集, edited by Bao Jialin 鮑家麟, 41–50. Taipei: Daoxiang, 1993.

Wang Wei 王偉. "Tangdai jingzhao Weishi yu huangshi hunyin guanxi ji qi yingxiang" 唐代京兆韋氏與皇室婚姻關係及其影響. *Beifang luncong* 北方論叢 1 (2012): 109–12.

Wang Xiao 王曉. "Tangdai jiazhuang xiaofei kao" 唐代嫁妝消費考. *Yibin Xueyuan xuebao* 宜賓學院學報 14, no. 4 (2014): 56–61.

Wang Yanhua 王岩華. "Cong Dunhuang wenshu qianxi Tangdai heli zhidu" 從敦煌文書淺析唐代和離制度. *Kexue zhi you* 科學之友 12 (2008): 90–91.

Wang Zhidong 王志東. *Tangdai shehui shenghuo (xiajuan)* 唐代社會生活 (下卷). Beijing: Guoji wenhua, 2001.

Warner, Rebecca L., Gary R. Lee, and Janet Lee. "Social Organization, Spousal Resources, and Marital Power: A Cross-Cultural Study." *Journal of Marriage and Family* 48, no. 1 (1986): 121–28.

Wechsler, Howard J. "Factionalism in Early T'ang Government." In *Perspectives on the T'ang*, edited by Arthur F. Wright and Denis Twitchett, 87–120. New Haven: Yale University Press, 1973.

Wei Zheng 魏徵. *Suishu* 隋書, annotated by Linghu Defen 令狐德棻 and Wang Zhaoying 汪紹楹. Beijing: Zhonghua Shuju, 1973.

Weinstein, Stanley. "Imperial Patronage in the Formation of T'ang Buddhism." In *Perspectives on the T'ang*, edited by Arthur F. Wright and Denis Twitchett, 265–306. New Haven: Yale University Press, 1973.

Weng Yuxuan 翁育瑄. "Tangdai shiren de hunyin yu jiating—yi qiqie wenti wei zhongxin" 唐代士人的婚姻與家庭—以妻妾問題為中心. In *Zhongguo zhonggu shehui yu guojia* 中國中古社會與國家, edited by Song Dexi 宋德熹, 355–76. Banqiao: Daoxiang, 2009.

———. "Tō Sō bushi kara mita jōsei no shusetsu to saika ni tsuite—mibōjin no sentaku to sono seikatsu" 唐宋墓誌から見た女性の守節と再嫁について—未亡人の選擇とその生活. *Tōdaishi kenkyū* 唐代史研究 6 (2003): 41–58.

Whyte, Martin King. *The Status of Women in Preindustrial Societies*. Princeton: Princeton University Press, 1978.

Wong, Robin R., ed. *Images of Women in Chinese Thought and Culture: Writings from the Pre-Qin Period through the Song Dynasty*. Indianapolis, IN: Hackett Publishing, 2003.

Wong, Sun-ming. "Confucian Ideal and Reality: Transformation of the Institution of Marriage in T'ang China (A.D. 618–907)." PhD diss., University of Washington, 1979.

Wong, Timothy C. "Self and Society in Tang Dynasty Love Tales." *Journal of the American Oriental Society* 99, no. 1 (1979): 95–100.

Woo, Terry Tak-ling. "Emotions and Self-Cultivation in Nü Lunyu 女論語 (Women's Analects)." *Journal of Chinese Philosophy* 36, no. 2 (2009): 334–47.

Workman, Michael E. "The Bedchamber Topos in the Tz'u Songs of Three Medieval Chinese Poets: Wen T'ing-yun, Wei Chuang, and Li Yu." In *Critical Essays on Chinese Literature*, edited by William H. Nienhauser Jr. et al., 167–86. Hong Kong: Chinese University Press, 1976.

Wright, Arthur F. *The Sui Dynasty*. New York: Alfred A. Knopf, 1978.

———. "T'ang T'ai-tsung and Buddhism." In *Perspectives on the T'ang*, edited by Arthur F. Wright and Denis Twitchett, 239–63. New Haven: Yale University Press, 1973.

Wright, Arthur F., and Denis Twitchett. "Introduction." *Perspectives on the T'ang*. New Haven: Yale University Press, 1973.

Wright, David Curtis. "A Chinese Princess Bride's Life and Activism among the Eastern Turks, 580–593 CE." *Journal of Asian History* 45, no. 1 (2011): 39–48.

Wu Congxiang 吳從祥. *Handai nüxing lijiao yanjiu* 漢代女性禮教研究. Jinan: Qilu, 2013.

Wu, Fusheng. *The Poetics of Decadence: Chinese Poetry of the Southern Dynasties and Late Tang Periods*. Albany: State University of New York Press, 1998.

Wu, Jie. "Vitality and Cohesiveness in the Poetry of Shangguan Wan'er (664–710)." *Tang Studies* 34 (2016): 40–72.

Wu Liyu 吳麗娛. *Tangli zheyi* 唐禮遮遺. Beijing: Shangwu yinshuguan, 2002.

Wu Minxia 吳敏霞. "Cong Tang muzhi kan Tangdai nüxing fojiao xinyang ji qi te-dian" 從唐墓誌看唐代女性佛教信仰及其特點. *Fojiao yanjiu* 佛教研究 (2002): 256–67.

Wu Yingying 武瑩瑩. "Tangdai gongzhu sangzang lisu yanjiu" 唐代公主喪葬禮俗研究. *Beilin jikan* 碑林集刊 19 (2013): 201–18.

Xia Shaoxian 夏紹先. "Cong muzhi kan Tangdai funü de zhenjieguan" 從墓誌看唐代婦女的貞節觀. *Chuxiong Shizhuan xuebao* 楚雄師專學報 16, no. 2 (2001): 131–34.

Xi'an Shi Wenwu Baohu Kaogu Yanjiuyuan 西安市文物保護考古研究院. "Xi'an nanjiao Tangdai Zhang Furen mu fajue jianbao" 西安南郊唐代張夫人墓發掘簡報. *Wenbo* 文博 1 (2013): 11–16.

Xiang Shuyun 向淑雲. *Tangdai hunyin fa yu hunyin shitai* 唐代婚姻法與婚姻實態. Taipei: Taiwan shangwu, 1991.

Xiao Guoliang 蕭國亮. *Zhongguo changji shi* 中國娼妓史. Taipei: Wenjin chubanshe, 1996.

Xie Chongguang 謝重光 and Bai Wengu 白文固. *Zhongguo sengguan zhidu shi* 中國僧官制度史. Xining: Qinghai renmin chubanshe, 1990.

Xie Mingxun 謝明勳. "Tangdai 'minghun' shilun" 唐代 '冥婚' 試論. In *2007 Dongya hanxue yu minsu wenhua guoji xueshu yantaohui* 2007 東亞漢學與民俗文化國際學術研討會, edited by Wang Sanqing 王三慶 and Chen Yiyuan 陳益源, 139–66. Taipei: Lexue shuju, 2007.

Xie Shengbao 謝生保. "Cong 'Shanzi bingbian' kan fojiao yishu zhong de xiaodao sixiang" 從 '睒子經變' 看佛教藝術中的孝道思想. *Dunhuang yanjiu* 敦煌研究 2 (2001): 42–50.

Xie Weiyang 謝維揚. *Zhoudai jiating xingtai* 周代家庭形態. Beijing: Zhongguo shehui kexue chubanshe, 1990.

Xing Tie 邢鐵. *Tang Song fenjia zhidu* 唐宋分家制度. Beijing: Shangwu, 2010.

Xing Xuemin 邢學敏. "Tangdai fuqi zangsu de wenhua kaocha—yi Xingyang Deng shi wei zhongxin" 唐代夫妻葬俗的文化考察—以滎陽鄧氏為中心. *Lishi jiaoxue* 歷史教學 4 (2008): 24–27.

Xiong, Victor. "*Ji*-Entertainers in Tang Chang'an." In *Presence and Presentation: Women in the Chinese Literati Tradition*, edited by Sherry J. Mou, 149–69. New York: St. Martin's Press, 1999.

Xu Yanhua 徐嚴華. "Shilun Tangdai de shangjia funü" 試論唐代的商賈婦女. *Shangye wenhua* 商業文化 4 (2010): 79–81.

Xu Youfu 徐有富. *Tangdai funü shenghuo yu shi* 唐代婦女生活與詩. Beijing: Zhonghua shuju, 2005.

Xu Yougen 許友根. "Tangdai 'guamu jiaozi' xianxiang chutan" 唐代寡母教子現象初探. *Neimenggu Shifan Daxue xuebao* 內蒙古師範大學學報 10 (2005): 59–62.

Xu Zhiyin 許智銀. "Tangdai nüxing songbie shi zonglun" 唐代女性送別詩綜論. *Henan shehui kexue* 河南社會科學 16, no. 2 (2008): 53–56.

Xue Dan 薛丹. "Zui shi yaorao qing hong yan—Tangdai tibishi zhong de nüzi" 最是妖嬈傾紅顏—唐代題壁詩中的女子. *Yuwen xuekan* 語文學刊 1 (2015): 68–69.

Yamazaki Junichi 山崎純一. "Guanyu Tangdai liangbu nüxunshu 'Nü lunyu' 'Nü xiaojing' de jichu yanjiu" 關於唐代兩部女訓書 '女論語' '女孝經' 的基礎研究. In *Tang Song nüxing yu shehui* 唐宋女性與社會, edited by Deng Xiaonan 鄧小南, 1:158–87. Shanghai: Shanghai cishu, 2003.

———. *Joshisho—shinhuhu sanbusho zenshaku* 女四書—新婦譜三部書全釈. Tokyo: Meiji shoten, 2002.

———. *Kyōiku kara mita Chūgoku joseishi shiryō no kenkyū—"josisho" to "shin-huhu" sanbusho* 教育からみた中国女性史資料の研究—'女四書' と '新婦譜' 三部書. Tokyo: Meiji, 1986.

Yan Guoquan 閆國權, Zhang Yishou 張益壽, and Zhang Kexin 張克炘. *Dunhuang zongjiao wenhua* 敦煌宗教文化. Beijing: Xinhua, 1994.

Yan Huizhong 嚴輝中. "Fojiao jielü yu Tangdai funü jiating shenghuo" 佛教戒律與唐代婦女家庭生活. *Xueshu yuekan* 學術月刊 8 (2004): 95–101.

Yan Jinxiong 顏進雄. *Tangdai youxian shi yanjiu* 唐代遊仙詩研究. Taipei: Wenjin, 1996.

Yan Ming 嚴明. *Zhongguo mingji yishu shi* 中國名妓藝術史. Taipei: Wenjin, 1992.

Yan Xiaomei 晏筱梅. "Tangshi zhong suo fanying de Tangdai funü" 唐詩中所反映的唐代婦女. *Zhejiang xuekan* 浙江學刊 109 (1998): 103–7.

Yan, Yaozhong. "Buddhist Discipline and the Family Life of Tang Women." Translated by Jeffrey Keller. *Chinese Studies in History* 45, no. 4 (2012): 24–42.

Yan Yaozhong 嚴耀中. "Muzhi jiwen zhong de Tangdai funü fojiao xinyang" 墓誌祭文中的唐代婦女佛教信仰. In *Tang Song nüxing yu shehui* 唐宋女性與社會, edited by Deng Xiaonan 鄧小南, 2:467–92. Shanghai: Shanghai cishu, 2003.

Yang Jin 楊瑾. "Cong chutu wenwu kan Tangdai de huren nüxing xingxiang" 從出土文物看唐代的胡人女性形象. *Qianling wenhua yanjiu* 乾陵文化研究 5 (2010): 125–37.

———. "Kaogu ziliao suo jian de Tangdai huren nüxing" 考古資料所見的唐代胡人女性. *Wenbo* 文博 3 (2010): 26–31.

Yang Jiping 楊祭平. "Dunhuang chutu de fangqi shu suoyi" 敦煌出土的放妻書瑣議. *Ximen Daxue xuebao* 西門大學學報 4 (1999): 34–41.

Yang Lirong 楊麗容 and Wang Ting 王頲. "Ziran pi fa—Tangdai nüguan Xie Ziran chuanqi kaosuo" 自然披髮—唐代女冠謝自然傳奇考索. *Guizhou Daxue xuebao* 貴州大學學報 30, no. 2 (2012): 135–42.

Yang Mei 楊梅. "Tangdai niseng yu shisu jiating de guanxi" 唐代尼僧與世俗家庭的關係. *Shoudu Shifan Daxue xuebao* 首都師範大學學報 5 (2004): 20–26.

Yang Ming 楊名. "Tangdai wudao shi zhong de wuji xingxiang tanxi—jian lun Tangren de nüxing shenmei quxiang" 唐代舞蹈詩中的舞妓形象探析—兼論唐人的女性審美取向. *Jiamusi Daxue shehui kexue xuebao* 佳木斯大學社會科學學報 33, no. 3 (2015): 109–12.

Yang Xiangchun 楊向春. "Wu Zetian yu Tangdai nongye" 武則天與唐代農業. *Ganling wenhua yanjiu* 乾陵文化研究 4 (2008): 450–58.

Yang Xiangkui 楊向奎. *Tangdai muzhi yili yanjiu* 唐代墓誌義例研究. Changsha: Yuelu, 2013.

Yang Xiaomin 楊小敏. "Cong zhanzheng shi kan Tangdai funü de beican mingyun" 從戰爭詩看唐代婦女的悲慘命運. *Chuxiong Shifan Xueyuan xuebao* 楚雄師範學院學報 18, no. 2 (2003): 13–15.

———. "Nüxing de beige—cong Tangshi kan Tangdai funü de mingyun" 女性的悲歌—從唐詩看唐代婦女的命運. *Tianshui Shifan Xueyuan xuebao* 天水師範學院學報 21, no. 3 (2001): 57–60.

———. "Tangchu houfei jinjian yu zhengzhi qingming de guanxi" 唐初后妃進諫與政治清明的關係. *Tianshui Shifan Xueyuan xuebao* 天水師範學院學報 6 (2001): 43–46.

———. "Tangdai funü de 'jifu' shi" 唐代婦女的 '寄夫' 詩. *Tianshui Shifan Xueyuan xuebao* 天水師範學院學報 23, no. 3 (2003): 41–44.

———. "Tangdai funü yu fojiao" 唐代婦女與佛教. *Shenyang Shifan Daxue xuebao* 瀋陽師範大學學報 3 (2003): 20–23.

Yang Xin 楊欣. "Nü xiaojing zuozhe ji chansheng shidai kao" 女孝經作者及產生時代考. *Zhongguo suwenhua yanjiu* 中國俗文化研究 6 (2010): 102–9.

Yao Ping 姚平. *Tangdai funü de shengming licheng* 唐代婦女的生命歷程. Shanghai: Shanghai guji chubanshe, 2004.

Yao, Ping. "Changing Views on Sexuality in Early and Medieval China." *Journal of Daoist Studies* 8 (2015): 53–69.

———. "Childbirth and Maternal Mortality in Tang China." *Chinese Historical Review* 12, no. 2 (2005): 263–86.

———. "Contested Virtue: The Daoist Investiture of Princesses Jinxian and Yuzhen and the Journey of Tang Imperial Daughters." *T'ang Studies* 22 (2004): 3, 6.

———. "Cousin Marriages in Tang China." *Chinese Historical Review* 18, no. 1 (2011): 25–55.

———. "Good Karmic Connections: Buddhist Mothers in Tang China." *Nan Nü* 10, no. 1 (2008): 57–85.

———. "Historicizing Great Bliss: Erotica in Tang China (618–907)." *Journal of the History of Sexuality* 22, no. 2 (2013): 207–29.

———. "Tang Women In the Transformation of Buddhist Filiality." In *Gendering Chinese Religion: Subject, Identity, and Body*, edited by Jinhua Jia et al., 25–46. Albany: State University of New York Press, 2014.

———. "Women in Portraits: An Overview of Epitaphs from Early and Medieval China." In *Overt and Covert Treasures: Essays on the Sources for Chinese Women's History*, edited by Clara Wing-Chung Ho, 157–83. Hong Kong: City University Press, 2012.

———. "Women's Epitaphs in Tang China (618–907)." In *Beyond Exemplar Tales: Women's Biography in Chinese History*, edited by Joan Judge and Hu Ying, 139–57. Berkeley: University of California Press, 2011.

Yao Yali 姚亞麗. "'Huiyuan biqiuni zhiming' suo fanyingde Tangdai Xiaoshi jiazu chongfo wenti" 惠源比丘尼志銘所反映的唐代蕭氏家族崇佛問題. *Chengdu Daxue xuebao* 成都大學學報 4 (2016): 88–93.

Yates, Robin D. S. "Medicine for Women in Early China: A Preliminary Survey." *Nan Nü* 7, no. 2 (2005): 127–81.

Ye Zilong 葉子龍. "Tangdai shiren jiating nüzi jiaoyu yanjiu" 唐代士人家庭女子教育研究. *Ganling wenhua yanjiu* 乾陵文化研究 8 (2014): 304–11.

Yi Jo-lan. "Social Status, Gender Division and Institutions: Sources Relating to Women in Chinese Standard Histories." In *Overt and Covert Treasures: Essays on the Sources for Chinese Women's History*, edited by Clara Wing-Chung Ho, 131–55. Hong Kong: City University Press, 2012.

Ying Kerong 應克榮. "Tangdai nüxing shuxie de 'sinanhua' tezheng" 唐代女性書寫的 '似男化' 特徵. *Xueshujie* 學術界 7 (2015): 123–32.

You Liyun 游麗雲. *Tangdai shinü zhuangrong wenhua tanwei* 唐代仕女妝容文化探微. New Taipei: Daoxiang, 2015.

Young, David, and Jiann L. Lin, trans. *The Clouds Float North: The Complete Poems of Yu Xuanji, Bilingual Edition*. Middletown, CT: Wesleyan University Press, 1998.

Yu Shifen 俞世芬. "Tangdai nüxing shige yanjiu" 唐代女性詩歌研究. PhD diss., Zhejiang University, 2005.

Yu Ya'nan 于亞男. "Cong liang *Tangshu Lienü zhuan* kan Tangdai nüxing de chuantong daodeguan" 從兩 '唐書·列女傳' 看唐代女性的傳統道德觀. *Shoudu Shifan Daxue xuebao* 首都師範大學學報 S1 (2010): 30–33.

Yue Chunzhi 岳純之. "Lun Tangdai hunwai xingwei ji qi shehui kongzhi" 論唐代婚外性行為及其社會控制. *Qi Lu xuekan* 齊魯學刊 5 (2006): 47–51.

Yue Hong. "Divorce Practice in Late Medieval Dunhuang: Reading 'Documents Setting the Wife Free.'" *Tang Studies* 34 (2016): 12–39.

———. "Romantic Identity in the Funerary Inscriptions (*muzhi*) of Tang China." *Asia Major* (third series) 25, no. 1 (2012): 33–62.

Yue Lianjian 岳連建 and Ke Zhuoying 柯桌英. "Tang Huainan Dazhang Gongzhu muzhi suo fanying de Tangdai lishi wenti" 唐淮南大長公主墓誌所反應的唐代歷史問題. *Huaxia kaogu* 華夏考古 2 (2008): 130–36.

Yue Qingping 岳慶平. *Handai jiating yu jiazu* 漢代家庭與家族. Zhengzhou: Daxiang chubanshe, 1997.

Zeng Xuanyan 曾絢艷 and Liu Chunxin 柳春新. "Zhangsun huanghou yu 'zhenguan' shiqi de zhengzhi he shehui" 長孫皇后與 '貞觀' 時期的政治和社會. *Wenshi bolan* 文史博覽 9 (2009): 13–15.

Zhang Bangwei 張邦煒. *Hunyin yu shehui (Songdai)* 婚姻與社會 (宋代). Chengdu: Sichuan renmin chubanshe, 1989.

———. *Songdai hunyin jiazu shilun* 宋代婚姻家族史論. Beijing: Renmin chubanshe, 2003.

Zhang Chen 張琛 and Gou Lijun 勾利軍. "Tangdai zhuizun huanghou fumiao kao" 唐代追尊皇后祔廟考. *Qilu xuekan* 齊魯學刊 1 (2012): 54–58.

Zhang Chengzong 張承宗 and Chen Qun 陳群. *Zhongguo funü tongshi: Wei Jin nanbei chao juan* 中國婦女通史: 魏晉南北朝卷. Hangzhou: Hangzhou chubanshe, 2010.

Zhang Guogang 張國剛. "'Family Building in Inner Quarters': Conjugal Relationships in Tang Families." Translated by Yipeng Lai. *Frontiers of History in China* 4, no. 1 (2009): 1–38.

———. *Jiating shihua* 家庭史話. Beijing: Shehui kexue wenxian, 2012.

———. "Tangdai guaju funü de shenghuo shijie" 唐代寡居婦女的生活世界. *Anhui Shifan Daxue xuebao* 安徽師範大學學報 3 (2007): 307–24.

———. *Tangdai jiating yu shehui* 唐代家庭與社會. Beijing: Zhonghua, 2014.

———. "Zhonggu Fojiao jielü yu jiating lunli" 中古佛教戒律與家庭倫理. In *Jiating shi yanjiu de xin shiye* 家庭史研究的新視野, edited by Zhang Guogang 張國剛, 48–70. Beijing: Sanlian shuju, 2004.

Zhang Guogang 張國剛 and Jiang Aihua 蔣愛花. "Tangdai nannü hunjia nianling kaolue" 唐代男女婚嫁年齡靠略. *Zhongguoshi yanjiu* 中國史研究 2 (2004): 65–75.

Zhang Jian 張健. *Li Bai shixuan* 李白詩選. Taipei: Wunan, 1998.

Zhang Jianguang 張劍光 and Zhang Jie 張潔. "Tangdai Chang'an nüxing xiaofei yanjiu" 唐代長安女性消費研究. *Shilin* 史林 5 (2008): 96–110.

Zhang Jing 張菁. "Lun Tangdai pinfu shi" 論唐代貧婦詩. *Nanjing Shifan Daxue Wenxueyuan xuebao* 南京師範大學文學院學報 3 (2006): 119–24.

———. "Shilun Tangdai nüde jingbiao zhidu de fazhan" 試論唐代女德旌表制度的發展. *Jiangsu shehui kexue* 江蘇社會科學 6 (2012): 232–38.

———. *Tangdai nüxing xingxiang shenghuo* 唐代女性形象生活. Lanzhou: Gansu renmin, 2007.

Zhang Jintong 張金同. "Huzu hunsu yu Tangdai guafu zaijia" 胡族婚俗與唐代寡婦再嫁. *Gansu shehui kexue* 甘肅社會科學 1 (2001): 77–80.

Zhang Meijuan 張美娟 and Zhang Meihua 張美華. "*Taiping guangji* zhong de Tangdai nüxing jingguai yu shaoshu minzu wenhua lunkao" 太平廣記中的唐代女性精怪與少數民族文化論考. *Heilongjiang minzu congkan* 黑龍江民族叢刊 1 (2007): 166–70.

Zhang Ping 張萍. "Tangdai kexie beizhi de fengqi" 唐代刻寫碑誌的風氣. *Gugong wenwu yuekan* 故宮文物月刊 15, no. 4 (1997): 84–91.

Zhang Shan 張珊. "Tangdainü zhuo nanzhuang zhi xianxiang chutan" 唐代女着男裝之現象初探. *Meishi yu sheji* 美術與設計 2 (2015): 36–42.

Zhang Weidong 張衛東. "Tangdai cishi yu jingbiao zhidu" 唐代刺史與旌表制度. *Jiangxi shehui kexue* 江西社會科學 7 (2009): 146–52.

Zhang Wenjing 張文晶. "Tangdai de nüxing yu susong—yi panwen wei zhongxin" 唐代的女性與訴訟—以判文為中心. In *Xingbie, zongjiao, zhongzu, jieji yu Zhongguo chuantong sifa* 性別, 宗教, 種族, 階級與中國傳統司法, edited by Liu Liyan 柳立言, 1–46. Taipei: Zhongyang Yanjiuyuan Lishi Yuyan Yanjiusuo, 2013.

Zhang Xiurong 張修蓉. *Han Tang guizu yu cianü shige yanjiu* 漢唐貴族與才女詩歌研究. Taipei: Wenshizhe chubanshe, 1985.

Zhang Yanhui 張艷輝. "Tangdai waimingfu chaoye zhidu kao" 唐代外命婦朝謁制度考. *Leshan Shifan Xueyuan xuebao* 樂山師範學院學報 27, no. 1 (2012): 91–94.

Zhang Yanyun 張艷雲. "Cong Dunhuang de hunshu chengshi kan Tangdai xuhun zhidu" 從敦煌的婚書程式看唐代許婚制度. *Dunhuang yanjiu* 敦煌研究 6 (2002): 35–38.

———. "Cong Dunhuang 'fangqi shu' kan Tangdai hunyin zhong de heli zhidu" 從敦煌 '放妻書' 看唐代婚姻中的合離制度. *Dunhuang yanjiu* 敦煌研究 2 (1999): 72–76.

Zhang Yinan 張一南. "Wo jian you ling—Tangdai nüshiren de Qi Liang ti chuang-zuo" 我見猶怜—唐代女詩人的齊梁體創作. *Wenshi zhishi* 文史知識 3 (2014): 112–17.

Zhao Heping 趙和平. "Tangdai shuyi zhong suojian de furen shuzha" 唐代書儀中所見的婦人書札. In *Tang Song nüxing yu shehui* 唐宋女性與社會, edited by Deng Xiaonan 鄧小南, 1:209–22. Shanghai: Shanghai cishu, 2003.

Zhao Jibin 趙紀彬. "*Fahua jing* yu liuchao zhi biqiuni guanxi luekao" 法華經與六朝之比丘尼關係考略. *Zhonghua wenhua luntan* 中華文化論壇 2 (2014): 126–30.

Zhao Juanning 趙娟寧 and Jiao Jie 焦杰. "Cong muzhi kan Tangdai funü de daojiao xinyang" 從墓誌看唐代婦女的道教信仰. *Qianling wenhua yanjiu* 乾陵文化研究 2 (2006): 190–94.

Zhao Mingyang 趙明暘. "Tangdai hunyin fengsu de qianhouqi chayi" 唐代婚姻風俗的前後期差異. *Anqing Shifan Xueyuan xuebao* 安慶師範學院學報 35, no. 2 (2016): 55–58, 63.

Zhao Shichuang 詹石窗. *Daojiao yu nüxing* 道教與女性. Shanghai: Shanghai guji chubanshe, 1990.

Zhao Wenrun 趙文潤. "Chang'an huren yu Tangdai qianqi de hunwu wenhua" 長安胡人與唐代前期的婚俗文化. *Ganling wenhua yanjiu* 乾陵文化研究 4 (2008): 29–38.

Zhao Xiaofang 趙曉芳 and Lu Qingfu 陸慶夫. "Shilun Tang Xizhou xiaceng nüxing de hunyin shenghuo" 試論唐西州下層女性的婚姻生活. *Dunhuang yanjiu* 敦煌研究 1 (2010): 70–78.

Zhao Xiaohua 趙小華. "Gonggongxing: Tangdai nüxing shige de bieyang shijiao" 公共性: 唐代女性詩歌的別樣視角. *Huanan Shifan Daxue xuebao* 華南師範大學學報 4 (2016): 145–50.

Zhao Yi 趙翼. *Nianer shi zhaji* 廿二史箚記. Taipei: Shijie shuju, 1974.

Zheng Yaru 鄭邪如. *Qin en nan bao: Tangdai shiren de xiaodao shijian ji qi tizhihua* 親恩難報: 唐代士人的孝道實踐及其體制化. Taipei: Taida chuban zhongxin, 2014.

Zheng Zhimin 鄭志敏. "Tangdai shiren yu jinü guanxi de yanbian—yi *Quan Tang-shi* wei zhongxin" 唐代士人與妓女關係的演變—以全唐詩為中心. *Zhongxing shixue* 中興史學 12 (1994): 65–85.

———. *Xishuo Tang ji* 細說唐妓. Taipei: Wenjin, 1997.

Zhou Jiren 周繼仁. "Lun Zhongguo gudai biaoyan yishu de shangpinhua wenti" 論中國古代表演藝術的商品化問題. *Zhongguoshi yanjiu* 中國史研究, 15, no. 4 (1993): 44–57.

Zhou Xiaowei 周曉薇 and Wang Qiyi 王其禕. *Roushun zhi xiang: Suidai nüxing yu shehui* 柔順之象: 隋代女性與社會. Beijing: Zhongguo shehui kexue chubanshe, 2012.

Zhou Yuwen 周愚文. "Tangdai funü yu jiating jiaoyu chutan" 唐代婦女與家庭教育初探. In *Zhongguo chuantong funü yu jiating jiaoyu* 中國傳統婦女與家庭教育, edited by Zhou Yuwen and Hong Renjin 洪仁進, 9–36. Taipei: Shida shuyuan, 2005.

Zhu Chun'e 祝春娥, Li Sifen 李四芬, Yao Juan 姚娟, and Long Juan 龍娟. "Tangdai funü xiaoxing tezheng: nü zhi xiao zhongyu fu zhi xiao" 唐代婦女孝行特徵: 女之孝重於婦之孝. *Hubei shehui kexue* 湖北社會科學 4 (2010): 112–14.

Zhu Fengyu 朱鳳玉. "Dunhuang mengshuzhong de funü jiaoyu" 敦煌蒙書中的婦女教育. In *Zhongguo chuantong funü yu jiating jiaoyu* 中國傳統婦女與家庭教育, edited by Zhou Yuwen 周愚文 and Hong Renjin 洪仁進, 37–57. Taipei: Shida shuyuan, 2005.

Zhu Meilian 朱美璉. "Tangdai xiaoshuozhong de nüxing juese yanjiu" 唐代小說中的女性角色研究. MA thesis, National Chengchi University, 1989.

Zhuang Guorui 庄國瑞. "Songdai gongzhu quanli pangluo yuanyin tanxi—yi Song Renzong nü Yanguo gongzhu wei li" 宋代公主權利旁落原因探析—以宋仁宗女兗國公主為例. *Henan Keji Daxue xuebao* 河南科技大學學報 33, no. 5 (2015): 14–20.

Zou Shuqin 鄒淑琴. "Huji zhi 'hu'—Tangdai huji de zhongshu wenti suyuan" 胡妓之 '胡'—唐代胡妓的種屬問題溯源. *Xibei minzu yanjiu* 西北民族研究 4 (2012): 180–85.

Index

ASIAN VOICES
An Asia/Pacific/Perspectives Series
Series Editor: Mark Selden

A Thousand Miles of Dreams: The Journeys of Two Chinese Sisters
    by Sasha Su-Ling Welland
Dancing in Shadows: Sihanouk, the Khmer Rouge, and the United Nations in Cambodia
    by Benny Widyono
Voices Carry: Behind Bars and Backstage during China's Revolution and Reform
    by Ying Ruocheng and Claire Conceison